THE WOMAN'S BIBLE

THE WOMAN'S BIBLE

ELIZABETH CADY STANTON

GREAT MINDS SERIES

 **Prometheus Books**

59 John Glenn Drive
Amherst, New York 14228-2197

Published 1999 by Prometheus Books

59 John Glenn Drive, Amherst, New York 14228–2197,
716–691–0133, ext. 207. FAX: 716–564–2711.
WWW.PROMETHEUSBOOKS.COM

Library of Congress Cataloging-in-Publication Data

Stanton, Elizabeth Cady, 1815–1902.
   The woman's Bible / Elizabeth Cady Stanton.
      p.   cm. — (Great minds series)
   Originally published: New York : European Publishing
Company, 1898.
   ISBN 1–57392–696–5 (pbk. : alk. paper)
   1. Women in the Bible. 2. Bible—Feminist criticism.
I. Title. II. Series.
B3575.S68   1999
220.8′3058—dc21   98–56038
                                                 CIP

Printed in the United States of America on acid-free paper.

Great Minds Paperback Series
(Religion/Freethought)

❑ Desiderius Erasmus—*The Praise of Folly*
❑ Thomas Henry Huxley—*Agnosticism and Christianity and Other Essays*
❑ Ernest Renan—*The Life of Jesus*
❑ Upton Sinclair—*The Profits of Religion*
❑ Elizabeth Cady Stanton—*The Woman's Bible*
❑ Voltaire—*A Treatise on Toleration and Other Essays*
❑ Andrew D. White—*A History of the Warfare of Science
with Theology in Christendom*

See the back of this volume for a complete list of titles in
Prometheus's Great Books in Philosophy and Great Minds series.

ELIZABETH CADY STANTON, American reformer and feminist, was born in Johnstown, New York, on November 12, 1815. Though few institutions in the early nineteenth century offered more than rudimentary education for women, Stanton's father, a judge, arranged to have her attend the all-male Johnstown Academy, where she won second prize in Greek; later she studied at Emma Willard's Academy in Troy, New York, and read law with her father. Stanton became outraged at the legal strictures against women, which prevented them from owning property or assuming control of their lives.

Denied access to a legal career, Stanton became active in the abolitionist and temperance movements. In 1840 she married Henry Brewster Stanton, an abolitionist lawyer, and accompanied him to London to a world conference against slavery. The only other American woman attending was Lucretia Mott, with whom, in 1848, Stanton organized the first U.S. women's rights convention in Seneca Falls, New York. There Stanton read her famous Declaration of Sentiments that had been modeled on the Declaration of Independence. Three years later she met Susan B. Anthony, a Unitarian social activist. They were joined by fellow Unitarians Lucy Stone and Ralph Waldo Emerson, among others. Although met with ridicule and even violence, Stanton never ceased speaking out and writing in behalf of equality for women.

Raised in a conventionally pious household, Stanton nevertheless considered organized religion a major obstacle to equality of the sexes. As she wrote in *Free Thought* magazine in 1896: "The history of mankind is a history of repeated injuries and usurpations on the part of man toward woman, having as its direct object the establishment of an absolute tyranny over her." This male dominance being biblically based and therefore publicly sanctioned, Stanton challenged it with *The Woman's Bible* (1895), a compilation of commentaries and essays by women on the biblical passages which deal with women and the sections from which they are glaringly excluded. *The Woman's Bible* demonstrates, among other things, that Jesus was truly a feminist who believed in equal rights. Such a feminist rereading of scripture also underscores the ignorance, arrogance, and hypocrisy of the male-dominated church hierarchy who, ignoring Christ's teachings, have denied women their equality, slaughtering them as witches and treating them as slaves.

Stanton worked tirelessly as a champion of equal rights and as an opponent of religious orthodoxy. She founded and served as president (1869–90) of the National Woman Suffrage Association and edited (1868–70) *Revolution*, a militant women's rights magazine. She also compiled, with Susan B. Anthony and Matilda Gage, the *History of Woman Suffrage* (1881–86). Elizabeth Cady Stanton died in New York on October 26, 1902, eighteen years before ratification of the Nineteenth Amendment, which at last allowed women to vote.

Contents

THE WOMAN'S BIBLE.

PART I.

Comments on Genesis, Exodus, Leviticus, Numbers and Deuteronomy.

"In every soul there is bound up some truth and some error, and each gives to the world of thought what no other one possesses."—*Cousin.*

Revising Committee.

COMMENTS

ON

Genesis, Exodus, Leviticus, Numbers and Deuteronomy,

BY

ELIZABETH CADY STANTON,
LILLIE DEVEREUX BLAKE,
REV. PHEBE HANAFORD,
CLARA BEWICK COLBY,

ELLEN BATTELLE DIETRICK,
URSULA N. GESTEFELD,
MRS. LOUISA SOUTHWORTH,
FRANCES ELLEN BURR.

PREFACE.

SO many letters are daily received asking questions about the Woman's Bible,—as to the extent of the revision, and the standpoint from which it will be conducted—that it seems best, though every detail is not as yet matured, to state the plan, as concisely as possible, upon which those who have been in consultation during the summer, propose to do the work.

I. The object is to revise only those texts and chapters directly referring to women, and those also in which women are made prominent by exclusion. As all such passages combined form but one-tenth of the Scriptures, the undertaking will not be so laborious as, at the first thought, one would imagine. These texts, with the commentaries, can easily be compressed into a duodecimo volume of about four hundred pages.

II. The commentaries will be of a threefold character, the writers in the different branches being selected according to their special aptitude for the work:

1. Two or three Greek and Hebrew scholars will devote themselves to the translation and the meaning of particular words and texts in the original.

2. Others will devote themselves to Biblical history, old manuscripts, to the new version, and to the latest theories as to the occult meaning of certain texts and parables.

3. For the commentaries on the plain English version a committee of some thirty members has been formed. These are women of earnestness and liberal ideas, quick to see the real purport of the Bible as regards their sex. Among them the various books of the Old and New Testament will be distributed for comment.

III. There will be two or more editors to bring the work of the various committees into one consistent whole.

IV. The completed work will be submitted to an advisory committee assembled at some central point, as London, New York, or Chicago, to sit in final judgment on " The Woman's Bible."

As to the manner of doing the practical work:

Those who have been engaged this summer have adopted the following plan, which may be suggestive to new members of the committee. Each person purchased two Bibles, ran through them from Genesis to Revelations, marking all the texts that concerned women. The passages were cut out, and pasted in a blank book, and the commentaries then written underneath.

Those not having time to read all the books can confine their labors to the particular ones they propose to review.

It is thought best to publish the different parts as soon as prepared so that the Committee may have all in print in a compact form before the final revision.

E. C. S.

AUGUST 1ST, 1895.

INTRODUCTION.

F ROM the inauguration of the movement for woman's emancipation the Bible has been used to hold her in the
"divinely ordained sphere," prescribed in the Old and New
Testaments.

The canon and civil law; church and state; priests and
legislators; all political parties and religious denominations
have alike taught that woman was made after man, of man, and
for man, an inferior being, subject to man. Creeds, codes,
Scriptures and statutes, are all based on this idea. The fashions,
forms, ceremonies and customs of society, church ordinances
and discipline all grow out of this idea.

Of the old English common law, responsible for woman's
civil and political status, Lord Brougham said, "it is a disgrace
to the civilization and Christianity of the Nineteenth Century."
Of the canon law, which is responsible for woman's status in the
church, Charles Kingsley said, "this will never be a good world
for women until the last remnant of the canon law is swept from
the face of the earth."

The Bible teaches that woman brought sin and death into
the world, that she precipitated the fall of the race, that she
was arraigned before the judgment seat of Heaven, tried, condemned and sentenced. Marriage for her was to be a condition
of bondage, maternity a period of suffering and anguish, and in
silence and subjection, she was to play the role of a dependent
on man's bounty for all her material wants, and for all the
information she might desire on the vital questions of the hour,
she was commanded to ask her husband at home. Here is the
Bible position of woman briefly summed up.

Those who have the divine insight to translate, transpose and
transfigure this mournful object of pity into an exalted, dignified

personage, worthy our worship as the mother of the race, are
to be congratulated as having a share of the occult mystic
power of the eastern Mahatmas.

The plain English to the ordinary mind admits of no such
liberal interpretation. The unvarnished texts speak for themselves. The canon law, church ordinances and Scriptures, are
homogeneous, and all reflect the same spirit and sentiments.

These familiar texts are quoted by clergymen in their
pulpits, by statesmen in the halls of legislation, by lawyers in
the courts, and are echoed by the press of all civilized nations,
and accepted by woman herself as "The Word of God." So
perverted is the religious element in her nature, that with faith
and works she is the chief support of the church and clergy ; the
very powers that make her emancipation impossible. When, in
the early part of the Nineteenth Century, women began to protest against their civil and political degradation, they were
referred to the Bible for an answer. When they protested
against their unequal position in the church, they were referred
to the Bible for an answer.

This led to a general and critical study of the Scriptures.
Some, having made a fetish of these books and believing them to
be the veritable "Word of God," with liberal translations, interpretations, allegories and symbols, glossed over the most objectionable features of the various books and clung to them as
divinely inspired. Others, seeing the family resemblance between
the Mosaic code, the canon law, and the old English common law,
came to the conclusion that all alike emanated from the same
source ; wholly human in their origin and inspired by the
natural love of domination in the historians. Others, bewildered
with their doubts and fears, came to no conclusion. While
their clergymen told them on the one hand, that they
owed all the blessings and freedom they enjoyed to the Bible,
on the other, they said it clearly marked out their circumscribed
sphere of action : that the demands for political and civil rights
were irreligious, dangerous to the stability of the home, the
state and the church. Clerical appeals were circulated from

time to time conjuring members of their churches to take no part in the anti-slavery or woman suffrage movements, as they were infidel in their tendencies, undermining the very foundations of society. No wonder the majority of women stood still, and with bowed heads, accepted the situation.

Listening to the varied opinions of women, I have long thought it would be interesting and profitable to get them clearly stated in book form. To this end six years ago I proposed to a committee of women to issue a Woman's Bible, that we might have women's commentaries on women's position in the Old and New Testaments. It was agreed on by several leading women in England and America and the work was begun, but from various causes it has been delayed, until now the idea is received with renewed enthusiasm, and a large committee has been formed, and we hope to complete the work within a year.

Those who have undertaken the labor are desirous to have some Hebrew and Greek scholars, versed in Biblical criticism, to gild our pages with their learning. Several distinguished women have been urged to do so, but they are afraid that their high reputation and scholarly attainments might be compromised by taking part in an enterprise that for a time may prove very unpopular. Hence we may not be able to get help from that class.

Others fear that they might compromise their evangelical faith by affiliating with those of more liberal views, who do not regard the Bible as the "Word of God," but like any other book, to be judged by its merits. If the Bible teaches the equality of Woman, why does the church refuse to ordain women to preach the gospel, to fill the offices of deacons and elders, and to administer the Sacraments, or to admit them as delegates to the Synods, General Assemblies and Conferences of the different denominations? They have never yet invited a woman to join one of their Revising Committees, nor tried to mitigate the sentence pronounced on her by changing one count in the indictment served on her in Paradise.

The large number of letters received, highly appreciative of the undertaking, is very encouraging to those who have inaugurated the movement, and indicate a growing self-respect and self-assertion in the women of this generation.   But we have the usual array of objectors to meet and answer.   One correspondent conjures us to suspend the work, as it is "ridiculous" for "women to attempt the revision of the Scriptures."   I wonder if any man wrote to the late revising committee of Divines to stop their work on the ground that it was ridiculous for men to revise the Bible.   Why is it more ridiculous for women to protest against her present status in the Old and New Testament, in the ordinances and discipline of the church, than in the statutes and constitution of the state ?   Why is it more ridiculous to arraign ecclesiastics for their false teaching and acts of injustice to women, than members of Congress and the House of Commons ?   Why is it more audacious to review Moses than Blackstone, the Jewish code of laws, than the English system of jurisprudence ?   Women have compelled their legislators in every state in this Union to so modify their statutes for women that the old common law is now almost a dead letter.   Why not compel Bishops and Revising Committees to modify their creeds and dogmas ?   Forty years ago it seemed as ridiculous to timid, time-serving and retrograde folk for women to demand an expurgated edition of the laws, as it now does to demand an expurgated edition of the Liturgies and the Scriptures.   Come, come, my conservative friend, wipe the dew off your spectacles, and see that the world is moving.   Whatever your views may be as to the importance of the proposed work, your political and social degradation are but an outgrowth of your status in the Bible.   When you express your aversion, based on a blind feeling of reverence in which reason has no control, to the revision of the Scriptures, you do but echo Cowper, who, when asked to read Paine's " Rights of Man," exclaimed, "No man shall convince me that I am improperly governed while I *feel* the contrary."

Others say it is not *politic* to rouse religious opposition.

This much-lauded policy is but another word for *cowardice*. How can woman's position be changed from that of a subordinate to an equal, without opposition, without the broadest discussion of all the questions involved in her present degradation? For so far-reaching and momentous a reform as her complete independence, an entire revolution in all existing institutions is inevitable.

Let us remember that all reforms are interdependent, and that whatever is done to establish one principle on a solid basis, strengthens all. Reformers who are always compromising, have not yet grasped the idea that truth is the only safe ground to stand upon. The object of an individual life is not to carry one fragmentary measure in human progress, but to utter the highest truth clearly seen in all directions, and thus to round out and perfect a well balanced character. Was not the sum of influence exerted by John Stuart Mill on political, religious and social questions far greater than that of any statesman or reformer who has sedulously limited his sympathies and activities to carrying one specific measure? We have many women abundantly endowed with capabilities to understand and revise what men have thus far written. But they are all suffering from inherited ideas of their inferiority; they do not perceive it, yet such is the true explanation of their solicitude, lest they should seem to be too self-asserting.

Again there are some who write us that our work is a useless expenditure of force over a book that has lost its hold on the human mind. Most intelligent women, they say, regard it simply as the history of a rude people in a barbarous age, and have no more reverence for the Scriptures than any other work. So long as tens of thousands of Bibles are printed every year, and circulated over the whole habitable globe, and the masses in all English-speaking nations revere it as the word of God, it is vain to belittle its influence. The sentimental feelings we all have for those things we were educated to believe sacred, do not readily yield to pure reason. I distinctly remember the shudder that passed over me on seeing a mother take our family Bible to make a high seat for her child at table. It seemed such a desecration. I was tempted to protest against its use for such a purpose, and this, too, long after my reason had repudiated its divine authority.

To women still believing in the plenary inspiration of the Scriptures, we say give us by all means your exegesis in the light of the higher criticism learned men are now making, and illumine the Woman's Bible, with your inspiration.

Bible historians claim special inspiration for the Old and New Testaments containing most contradictory records of the same events, of miracles opposed to all known laws, of customs that degrade the female sex of all human and animal life, stated in most questionable language that could not be read in a promiscuous assembly, and call all this " The Word of God."

The only points in which I differ from all ecclesiastical teaching is that I do not believe that any man ever saw or talked with God, I do not believe that God inspired the Mosaic code, or told the historians what they say he did about woman, for all the religions on the face of the earth degrade her, and so long as woman accepts the position that they assign her, her emancipation is impossible. Whatever the Bible may be made to do in Hebrew or Greek, in plain English it does not exalt and dignify woman. My standpoint for criticism is the revised edition of 1888. I will so far honor the revising committee of wise men who have given us the best exegesis they can according to their ability, although Disraeli said the last one before he died, contained 150,000 blunders in the Hebrew, and 7,000 in the Greek.

But the verbal criticism in regard to woman's position amounts to little. The spirit is the same in all periods and languages, hostile to her as an equal.

There are some general principles in the holy books of all religions that teach love, charity, liberty, justice and equality for all the human family, there are many grand and beautiful passages, the golden rule has been echoed and re-echoed around the world. There are lofty examples of good and true men and women, all worthy our acceptance and imitation whose lustre cannot be dimmed by the false sentiments and vicious characters bound up in the same volume. The Bible cannot be accepted or rejected as a whole, its teachings are varied and its lessons differ widely from each other. In criticising the peccadilloes of Sarah, Rebecca and Rachel, we would not shadow the virtues of Deborah, Huldah and Vashti. In criticising the Mosaic code we would not question the wisdom of the golden rule and the fifth Commandment Again the church claims special consecration for its cathedrals and priesthood, parts of these aristocratic churches are too holy for women to enter, boys were early introduced into the choirs for this reason, woman singing in an obscure corner closely veiled. A few of the more democratic denominations accord women some privileges, but invidious discriminations of sex are found in all religious organizations, and the most bitter outspoken enemies of woman are found among clergymen and bishops of the Protestant religion.※

The canon law, the Scriptures, the creeds and codes and church discipline of the leading religions bear the impress of fallible man, and not of our ideal great first cause, "the Spirit of all Good," that set the universe of matter and mind in motion, and by immutable law holds the land, the sea, the planets, revolving round the great centre of light and heat, each in its own elliptic, with millions of stars in harmony all singing together, the glory of creation forever and ever.

ELIZABETH CADY STANTON.

※ See the address of Bishop Doane, June 7th, 1895, in the closing exercises of St. Agnes School, Albany

THE BOOK OF GENESIS.

CHAPTER I.

Genesis i: 26, 27, 28.

26 ¶ And God said, Let us make man in our image, after our likeness: and let them have dominion over the fish of the sea, and over the fowl of the air, and over the cattle, and over all the earth, and over every creeping thing that creepeth upon the earth.

27 So God created man in his *own* image, in the image of God created he him; male and female created he them.

28 And God blessed them, and God said unto them, Be fruitful, and multiply, and replenish the earth, and subdue it; and have dominion over the fish of the sea, and over the fowl of the air, and over every living thing that moveth upon the earth.

———

HERE is the sacred historian's first account of the advent of woman; a simultaneous creation of both sexes, in the image of God. It is evident from the language that there was consultation in the Godhead, and that the masculine and feminine elements were equally represented. Scott in his commentaries says, " this consultation of the Gods is the origin of the doctrine of the trinity." But instead of three male personages, as generally represented, a Heavenly Father, Mother, and Son would seem more rational.

The first step in the elevation of woman to her true position, as an equal factor in human progress, is the cultivation of the religious sentiment in regard to her dignity and equality, the recognition by the rising generation of an ideal Heavenly Mother, to whom their prayers should be addressed, as well as to a Father.

If language has any meaning, we have in these texts a plain declaration of the existence of the feminine element in the Godhead, equal in power and glory with the masculine. The Heavenly Mother and Father ! God created man in his *own*

14

image, male and female. Thus Scripture, as well as science and philosophy, declares the eternity and equality of sex—the philosophical fact, without which there could have been no perpetuation of creation, no growth or development in the animal, vegetable, or mineral kingdoms, no awakening nor progressing in the world of thought. The masculine and feminine elements, exactly equal and balancing each other, are as essential to the maintenance of the equilibrium of the universe as positive and negative electricity, the centripetal and centrifugal forces, the laws of attraction which bind together all we know of this planet whereon we dwell and of the system in which we revolve.

In the great work of creation the crowning glory was realized, when man and woman were evolved on the sixth day, the masculine and feminine forces in the image of God, that must have existed eternally, in all forms of matter and mind. All the persons in the Godhead are represented in the Elohim the divine plurality taking counsel in regard to this last and highest form of life. Who were the members of this high council, and were they a duality or a trinity? Verse 27 declares the image of God male and female. How then is it possible to make woman an afterthought? We find in verses 5-16 the pronoun "he" used. Should it not in harmony with verse 26 be "they," a dual pronoun? We may attribute this to the same cause as the use of "his" in verse 11 instead of "it." The fruit tree yielding fruit after "his" kind instead of after "its" kind. The paucity of a language may give rise to many misunderstandings.

The above texts plainly show the simultaneous creation of man and woman, and their equal importance in the development of the race. All those theories based on the assumption that man was prior in the creation, have no foundation in Scripture.

As to woman's subjection, on which both the canon and the civil law delight to dwell, it is important to note that equal dominion is given to woman over every living thing, but not one word is said giving man dominion over woman.

Here is the first title deed to this green earth giving alike
to the sons and daughters of God. No lesson of woman's subjection can be fairly drawn from the first chapter of the Old
Testament.   E. C. S.

———

The most important thing for a woman to note, in reading
Genesis, is that that portion which is now divided into "the
first three chapters" (there was no such division until about
five centuries ago), contains two entirely separate, and very
contradictory, stories of creation, written by two different,
but equally anonymous, authors. No Christian theologian of
to-day, with any pretensions to scholarship, claims that Genesis
was written by Moses. As was long ago pointed out, the Bible
itself declares that all the books the Jews originally possessed
were burned in the destruction of Jerusalem, about 588 B. C., at
the time the people were taken to Babylonia as slaves to the
Assyrians, (see II Esdras, ch. xiv, v. 21, Apocrypha). Not
until about 247 B. C. (some theologians say 226 and others 169
B. C.) is there any record of a collection of literature in the
re-built Jerusalem, and, then, the anonymous writer of
II Maccabees briefly mentions that some Nehemiah "gathered
together the acts of the kings and the prophets and those of
David" when "founding a library" for use in Jerusalem. But
the earliest mention anywhere in the Bible of a book that might
have corresponded to Genesis is made by an apocryphal writer,
who says that *Ezra* wrote "all that hath been done in the world
since the beginning," after the Jews returned from Babylon,
under his leadership, about 450 B. C. (see II Esdras, ch. xiv, v.
22, of the Apocrypha).

When it is remembered that the Jewish books were written
on rolls of leather, without much attention to vowel points and
with no division into verses or chapters, by uncritical copyists,
who altered passages greatly, and did not always even pretend
to understand what they were copying, then the reader of
Genesis begins to put herself in position to understand how it

can be contradictory. Great as were the liberties which the Jews took with Genesis, those of the English translators, however, greatly surpassed them.

The first chapter of Genesis, for instance, in Hebrew, tells us, in verses one and two, "As to origin, created the gods (Elohim) these skies (or air or clouds) and this earth. . . And a wind moved upon the face of the waters." Here we have the opening of a polytheistic fable of creation, but, so strongly convinced were the English translators that the ancient Hebrews must have been originally monotheistic that they rendered the above, as follows: "In the beginning God created the heaven and the earth. . . . And the spirit of God (!) moved upon the face of the waters."

It is now generally conceded that some one (nobody pretends to know who) at some time (nobody pretends to know exactly when), copied two creation myths on the same leather roll, one immediately following the other. About one hundred years ago, it was discovered by Dr. Astruc, of France, that from Genesis ch. i, v. 1 to Genesis ch. ii, v. 4, is given one complete account of creation, by an author who always used the term "the gods" (*Elohim*), in speaking of the fashioning of the universe, mentioning it altogether thirty-four times, while, in Genesis ch. ii, v. 4, to the end of chapter iii, we have a totally different narrative, by an author of unmistakably different style, who uses the term "Iahveh of the gods" twenty times, but "Elohim" only three times. The first author, evidently, attributes creation to a council of gods, acting in concert, and seems never to have heard of Iahveh. The second attributes creation to Iahveh, a tribal god of ancient Israel, but represents Iahveh as one of two or more gods, conferring with them (in Genesis ch. xiii, v. 22) as to the danger of man's acquiring immortality.

Modern theologians have, for convenience sake, entitled these two fables, respectively, the Elohistic and the Iahoistic stories. They differ, not only in the point I have mentioned above, but in the order of the "creative acts;" in regard to the mutual attitude of man and woman, and in regard to human freedom from prohibitions imposed by deity.   In order to exhibit their striking contradictions, I will place them in parallel columns:

ELOHISTIC.	IAHOISTIC.
Order of Creation :	Order of Creation :
First—Water.	First—Land.
Second—Land.	Second—Water.
Third—Vegetation.	Third—Male Man, only.
Fourth—Animals.	Fourth—Vegetation.
Fifth—Mankind ; male and female.	Fifth—Animals.
	Sixth—Woman.

* * * *

In this story male and female man are created simultaneously, both alike, in the image of the gods, *after* all animals have been called into existence.

* * * *

Here, joint dominion over the earth is given to woman and man, without limit or prohibition.

* * * *

Everything, without exception, is pronounced "very good."

* * * *

Man and woman are told that "every plant bearing seed upon the face of the earth and *every tree.* . . "To you it shall be for meat." They are thus given perfect freedom.

* * * *

Man and woman are given special dominion over all the animals—"every creeping thing that creepeth upon the earth."

* * * *

In this story male man is sculptured out of clay, *before* any animals are created, and *before* female man has been constructed.

* * * *

Here, woman is punished with subjection to man for breaking a prohibitory law.

* * * *

There is a tree of evil, whose fruit, is said by Iahveh to cause sudden death, but which does not do so, as Adam lived 930 years after eating it.

* * * *

Man is told there is *one tree* of which he must not eat, "for in the day thou eatest thereof, thou shalt surely die."

* * * *

An animal, a "creeping thing," is given dominion over man and woman, and proves himself more truthful than Iahveh Elohim. (Compare Genesis chapter ii, verse 17, with chapter iii, verses 4 and 22.)

* * * *

Now as it is manifest that both of these stories cannot be true; intelligent women, who feel bound to give the preference to either, may decide according to their own judgment of which is more worthy of an intelligent woman's acceptance.   Paul's rule is a good one in this dilemma, "Prove all things: hold fast to that which is good."   My own opinion is that the second story was manipulated by some Jew, in an endeavor to give "heavenly authority" for requiring a woman to obey the man she married.   In a work which I am now completing, I give some facts concerning ancient Israelitish history, which will be of peculiar interest to those who wish to understand the origin of woman's subjection.   E. B. D.

Many orientalists and students of theology have maintained that the consultation of the Gods here described is proof that the Hebrews were in early days polytheists—Scott's supposition that this is the origin of the Trinity has no foundation in fact, as the beginning of that conception is to be found in the earliest of all known religious nature worship. The acknowledgment of the dual principal, masculine and feminine, is much more probably the explanation of the expressions here used.

In the detailed description of creation we find a gradually ascending series. Creep·ng things, "great sea monsters," (chap. I, v. 21, literal translation). "Every bird of wing," cattle and living things of the earth, the fish of the sea and the "birds of the heavens," then man, and last and crowning glory of the whole, woman.

It cannot be maintained that woman was inferior to man even if, as asserted in chapter ii, she was created after him without at once admitting that man is inferior to the creeping things, because created after them.   L. D. B.

Chapter II.

Genesis ii: 21-25.

21 And the Lord God caused a deep sleep to fall upon Adam, and he slept; and he took one of his ribs, and closed up the flesh thereof.

22 And the rib which the Lord God had taken from man, made he a woman, and brought her unto the man.

23 And Adam said, This *is* now bone of my bone, and flesh of my flesh: she shall be called' Woman, because she was taken out of man.

24 Therefore shall a man leave his father and his mother, and shall cleave unto his wife; and they shall be one flesh.

25 And they were both naked, the man and his wife, and were not ashamed.

A S the account of the creation in the first chapter is in harmony with science, common sense, and the experience of mankind in natural laws, the inquiry naturally arises, why should there be two contradictory accounts in the same book, of the same event? It is fair to infer that the second version, which is found in some form in the different religions of all nations, is a mere allegory, symbolizing some mysterious conception of a highly imaginative editor.

The first account dignifies woman as an important factor in the creation, equal in power and glory with man. The second makes her a mere afterthought. The world in good running order without her. The only reason for her advent being the solitude of man.

There is something sublime in bringing order out of chaos; light out of darkness; giving each planet its place in the solar system; oceans and lands their limits; wholly inconsistent with a petty surgical operation, to find material for the mother of the race. It is on this allegory that all the enemies of women rest their battering rams, to prove her inferiority. Accepting the view that man was prior in the creation, some Scriptural writers say that as the woman was of the man, therefore, her position should be one of subjection. Grant it, then as the historical fact is reversed in our day, and the man is now of the woman, shall his place be one of subjection?

The equal position declared in the first account must prove more satisfactory to both sexes; created alike in the image of God—The Heavenly Mother and Father.

Thus, the Old Testament, "in the beginning," proclaims the simultaneous creation of man and woman, the eternity and equality of sex; and the New Testament echoes back through the centuries the individual sovereignty of woman growing out of this natural fact. Paul, in speaking of equality as the very soul and essence of Christianity, said, "There is neither Jew nor Greek, there is neither bond nor free, there is neither male nor female; for ye are all one in Christ Jesus." With this recognition of the feminine element in the Godhead in the Old Testament, and this declaration of the equality of the sexes in the New, we may well wonder at the contemptible status woman occupies in the Christian Church of to-day.

All the commentators and publicists writing on woman's position, go through an immense amount of fine-spun metaphysical speculations, to prove her subordination in harmony with the Creator's original design.

It is evident that some wily writer, seeing the perfect equality of man and woman in the first chapter, felt it important for the dignity and dominion of man to effect woman's subordination in some way. To do this a spirit of evil must be introduced, which at once proved itself stronger than the spirit of good, and man's supremacy was based on the downfall of all that had just been pronounced very good. This spirit of evil evidently existed before the supposed fall of man, hence woman was not the origin of sin as so often asserted.   E. C. S.

———

In v. 23 Adam proclaims the eternal oneness of the happy pair, "This is now bone of my bone and flesh of my flesh," no hint of her subordination. How could men, admitting these words to be divine revelation, ever have preached the subjection of woman!

Next comes the naming of the mother of the race. "She

shall be called Woman," in the ancient form of the word Womb-man. She was man and more than man because of her maternity.

The assertion of the supremacy of the woman in the marriage relation is contained in v. 24: "Therefore shall a man leave his father and his mother and cleave unto his wife." Nothing is said of the headship of man, but he is commanded to make her the head of the household, the home, a rule followed for centuries under the Matriarchate   L. D. B.

CHAPTER III.

Genesis iii: 1-24.

1 Now the serpent was more subtle than any beast of the field which the Lord God had made. And he said unto the woman, Yea, hath God said, Ye shall not eat of every tree of the garden?

2 And the woman said unto the serpent, We may eat of the fruit of the trees of the garden:

3 But of the fruit of the tree which *is* in the midst of the garden, God hath said Ye shall not eat of it, neither shall ye touch it, lest ye die.

4 And the serpent said unto the woman, Ye shall not surely die:

5 For God doth know that in the day ye eat thereof then your eyes shall be opened, and ye shall be as gods, knowing good and evil.

6 And when the woman saw that the tree *was* good for food, and that it *was* pleasant to the eyes, and a tree to be desired to make *one* wise, she took of the fruit thereof, and did eat and gave also unto her husband with her ; and he did eat.

7 And the eyes of them both were opened, and they knew that they *were* naked ; and they sewed fig leaves together, and made themselves aprons.

8 And they heard the voice of the Lord God walking in the garden in the cool of the day ; and Adam and his wife hid themselves from the presence of the Lord God amongst the trees in the garden.

9 And the Lord God called unto Adam, and said unto him, Where *art* thou?

10 And he said, I heard thy voice in the garden, and I was afraid, because I *was* naked ; and I hid myself.

11 And he said, Who told thee that thou *wast* naked? Hast thou eaten of the tree, whereof I commanded thee that thou shouldst not eat?

12 And the man said, The woman whom thou gavest *to be* with me, she gave me of the tree, and I did eat.

13 And the Lord God said unto the woman, What *is* this *that* thou hast done? And the woman said, The serpent beguiled me, and I did eat.

14 And the Lord God said unto the serpent, Because thou hast done this, thou *art* cursed above all cattle, and above every beast of the field ; upon thy belly shalt thou go, and dust shalt thou eat all the days of thy life :

15 And I will put enmity between thee and the woman, and between thy seed and her seed ; it shall bruise thy head and thou shalt bruise his heel.

16 Unto the woman he said, I will greatly multiply thy sorrow and thy conception ; in sorrow thou shalt bring forth children ; and thy desire *shall be* to thy husband, and he shall rule over thee.

17 And unto Adam he said, Because thou hast hearkened unto the voice of thy wife, and hast eaten of the tree, of which I commanded thee, saying, Thou shalt not eat of it : cursed *is* the ground for thy sake ; in sorrow shalt thou eat *of* it all the days of thy life ;

18 Thorns also and thistles shall it bring forth to thee ; and thou shalt eat the herb of the field ;

19 In the sweat of thy face shalt thou eat bread till thou return unto the ground ; for out of it wast thou taken ; for dust thou *art*, and unto dust shalt thou return.

20 And Adam called his wife's name Eve : because she was the mother of all living.

21 Unto Adam also and to his wife did the Lord God make coats of skins, and clothed them.

22 ¶ And the Lord God said, Behold the man is become as one of us, to know good and evil : and now, lest he put forth his hand, and take also of the tree of life, and eat, and live for ever :

23 Therefore the Lord God sent him forth from the garden of Eden, to till the ground from whence he was taken.

24 So he drove out the man : and he placed at the east of the garden of Eden cherubim, and a flaming sword which turned every way, to keep the way of the tree of life.

ADAM CLARKE, in his commentaries, asks the question, "is this an allegory?" He finds it beset with so many difficulties as an historical fact, that he inclines at first to regard it as a fable, a mere symbol, of some hidden truth. His mind seems more troubled about the serpent than any other personage in the drama. As snakes cannot walk upright, and have never been known to speak, he thinks this beguiling creature must have been an ourang-outang, or some species of ape. However, after expressing all his doubts, he rests in the assumption that it must be taken literally, and that with higher knowledge of the possibilities of all living things, many seeming improbabilities will be fully realized.

A learned professor in Yale College,* before a large class of students, expressed serious doubts as to the forbidden fruit being an apple, as none grew in that latitude. He said it must have been a quince. If the serpent and the apple are to be withdrawn thus recklessly from the tableaux, it is feared that with advancing civilization the whole drama may fall into discredit. Scientists tells us that "the missing link" between the ape and man, has recently been discovered, so that we can now trace back an unbroken line of ancestors to the dawn of creation.

As out of this allegory grows the doctrines of original sin, the fall of man, and woman the author of all our woes, and the curses on the serpent, the woman, and the man; the Darwinian theory of the gradual growth of the race from a lower to a higher type of animal life, is more hopeful and encouraging. However, as our chief interest is in woman's part in the drama, we are equally pleased with her attitude, whether as a myth in an allegory, or as the heroine of an historical occurrence.

In this prolonged interview, the unprejudiced reader must be impressed with the courage, the dignity, and the lofty ambition of the woman. The tempter evidently had a profound knowledge of human nature, and saw at a glance the high character of the person he met by chance in his walks in the garden. He did not try to tempt her from the path of duty by brilliant jewels, rich dresses, worldly luxuries or pleasures, but with the promise of knowledge, with the wisdom of the Gods.

---

* Daniel Cady Eaton, Professor of Botany.

Like Socrates or Plato, his powers of conversation and asking puzzling questions, were no doubt marvellous, and he roused in the woman that intense thirst for knowledge, that the simple pleasures of picking flowers and talking with Adam did not satisfy. Compared with Adam she appears to great advantage through the entire drama.

The curse pronounced on woman is inserted in an unfriendly spirit to justify her degradation and subjection to man. With obedience to the laws of health, diet, dress, and exercise, the period of maternity should be one of added vigor in both body and mind, a perfectly natural operation should not be attended with suffering. By the observance of physical and psychical laws the supposed curse can be easily transformed into a blessing. Some churchmen speak of maternity as a disability, and then chant the Magnificat in all their cathedrals round the globe. Through all life's shifting scenes, the mother of the race has been the greatest factor in civilization.

We hear the opinion often expressed, that woman always has, and always will be in subjection. Neither assertion is true. She enjoyed unlimited individual freedom for many centuries, and the events of the present day all point to her speedy emancipation. Scientists now give 85,000 years for the growth of the race. They assign 60,000 to savagism, 20,000 to barbarism, and 5,000 to civilization. Recent historians tell us that for centuries woman reigned supreme. That period was called the Matriarchate. Then man seized the reins of government, and we are now under the Patriarchate. But we see on all sides new forces gathering, and woman is already abreast with man in art, science, literature, and government. The next dynasty, in which both will reign as equals, will be the Amphiarchate, which is close at hand.

Psychologists tell us of a sixth sense now in process of development, by which we can read each other's mind and communicate without speech. The Tempter might have had that sense, as he evidently read the minds of both the creature and

the Creator, if we are to take this account as literally true, as
Adam Clarke advises.　　　　　　　　　　　　　　E. C. S.

Note the significant fact that we always hear of the "fall of
man," not the fall of woman, showing that the consensus of
human thought has been more unerring than masculine interpretation. Reading this narrative carefully, it is amazing that
any set of men ever claimed that the dogma of the inferiority
of woman is here set forth. The conduct of Eve from the beginning to the end is so superior to that of Adam. The command not to eat of the fruit of the tree of Knowledge was given
to the man alone before woman was formed. Genesis ii, 17.
Therefore the injunction was not brought to Eve with the impressive solemnity of a Divine Voice, but whispered to her by
her husband and equal. It was a serpent supernaturally endowed, a seraphim as Scott and other commentators have
claimed, who talked with Eve, and whose words might reason-
ably seem superior to the second-hand story of her companion—
nor does the woman yield at once. She quotes the command
not to eat of the fruit to which the serpent replies "Dying ye
shall not die," v. 4, literal translation. In other words telling
her that if the mortal body does perish, the immortal part shall
live forever, and offering as the reward of her act the attainment of Knowledge.

Then the woman fearless of death if she can gain wisdom
takes of the fruit ; and all this time Adam standing beside her
interposes no word of objection. "Her husband with her" are
the words of v. 6. Had he been the representative of the
divinely appointed head in married life, he assuredly would have
taken upon himself the burden of the discussion with the serpent,
but no, he is silent in this crisis of their fate. Having had the
command from God himself he interposes no word of warning
or remonstrance, but takes the fruit from the hand of his wife
without a protest. It takes six verses to describe the "fall" of

woman, the fall of man is contemptuously dismissed in a line and a half.

The subsequent conduct of Adam was to the last degree dastardly. When the awful time of reckoning comes, and the Jehovah God appears to demand why his command has been disobeyed, Adam endeavors to shield himself behind the gentle being he has declared to be so dear. "The woman thou gavest to be with me, she gave me and I did eat," he whines—trying to shield himself at his wife's expense! Again we are amazed that upon such a story men have built up a theory of their superiority!

Then follows what has been called the curse. Is it not rather a prediction? First is the future fate of the serpent described, the enmity of the whole human race—"it shall lie in wait for thee as to the head" (v. 15, literal translation). Next the subjection of the woman is foretold, thy husband "shall rule over thee," v. 16. Lastly the long struggle of man with the forces of nature is portrayed. "In the sweat of thy face thou shalt eat food until thy turning back to the earth" (v. 19, literal translation). With the evolution of humanity an ever increasing number of men have ceased to toil for their bread with their hands, and with the introduction of improved machinery, and the uplifting of the race there will come a time when there shall be no severities of labor, and when women shall be freed from all oppressions.

"And Adam called his wife's name Life for she was the mother of all living" (v. 20, literal translation).

It is a pity that all versions of the Bible do not give this word instead of the Hebrew Eve. She was Life, the eternal mother, the first representative of the more valuable and important half of the human race.   L. D. B.

CHAPTER IV.

Genesis iv: 1–12, 19, 23.

1 And Adam knew Eve his wife; and she con-ceived, and bare Cain, and said, I have gotten a man from the Lord.

2 And she again bare his brother Abel. And Abel was a keeper of sheep, but Cain was a tiller of the ground.

3 And in process of time it came to pass, that Cain brought of the fruit of the ground an offering unto the Lord.

4 And Abel, he also brought of the firstlings of his flock and of the fat thereof. And the Lord had respect unto Abel and to his offering.

5 But unto Cain and to his offering he had not respect. And Cain was very wroth, and his coun-tenance fell.

6 And the Lord said unto Cain, Why art thou wroth? and why is thy countenance fallen?

7 If thou doest well, shalt thou not be accepted: and if thou doest not well, sin lieth at the door: and unto thee *shall be* his desire, and thou shalt rule over him.

8 And Cain talked with Abel his brother: and it came to pass, when they were in the field, that Cain rose up against Abel his brother, and slew him.

9 ¶ And the Lord said unto Cain, where *is* Abel thy brother? And he said, I know not: *Am* I my brother's keeper?

10 And he said, What hast thou done? the voice of thy brother's blood crieth unto me from the ground.

11 And now *art* thou cursed from the earth which hath opened her mouth to receive thy brother's blood from thy hand.

12 When thou tillest the ground, it shall not henceforth yield unto thee her strength; a fugitive and a vagabond shalt thou be in the earth.

19 ¶ And Lamech took unto him two wives: the name of the one *was* Adah, and the name of the other Zillah.

23 And Lamech said unto his wives, Adah and Zillah, hear my voice; ye wives of Lamech, hearken unto my speech.

ONE would naturally suppose that Cain's offering of fruit indicated a more refined and spiritual idea of the fitness of things than Abel's of animal food. Why Cain's offering was rejected as unworthy does not appear.

There is something pathetic in Eve's joy and faith at the advent of her first-born: "Lo I have a man child from the Lord." She evidently thought that Cain was to be to her a great blessing. Some expositors say that Eve thought that Cain was the promised seed that was to bruise the serpent's head; but Adam Clarke, in estimating woman's reasoning powers, says, "it was too metaphysical an idea for that period." But as that is just what the Lord said to Eve, she must have had the capacity to understand it. But all speculations as to what Eve thought in that eventful hour are vain. Clarke asserts that Cain and Abel were twins. Eve must have been too much occupied with her vacillating joys and sorrows to have indulged in any connected train of thought. Her grief in the fratricidal tragedy that followed can be more easily understood. The dreary environments of the mother, and the hopeless prophesies of her future struggling life, banished to a dreary, desolate region, beyond the love and care of her Creator, is revenged on her children. If Adam and Eve merited the severe punishment inflicted on them, they should have had some advice from the Heavenly Mother and Father as to the sin of propagating such an unworthy stock. No good avails in increasing and multiplying evil propensities and deformities that produce only crime and misery from generation to generation. During the ante-natal period the mother should be held sacred, and surrounded with all the sweetest influences that Heaven and earth can give, loving companionship, beautiful scenery, music and flowers, and all the pleasures that art in its highest form can produce.

As the women at this period seem to be myths, no one takes the trouble to tell from whence they came. It is sufficient that their husbands know, and it is not necessary that the casual reader should. The question is often asked, whom did Cain marry? Some expositors say that Adam and Eve had other sons and daughters living in different parts of the planet, and that they married each other.

There seems to have been no scarcity of women, for Lamech, Cain's great grandson, took unto himself two wives. Thus early in the history of the race polygamic relations were recognized. The phraseology announcing the marriage of Lamech is very significant.

In the case of Adam and Eve the ceremony was more imposing and dignified. It was declared an equal relation. But with the announcement of Lamech's, he simply took two wives, Adah and Zillah. Whether the women were willingly captured will ever remain an open question. The manner in which he is accustomed to issue his orders does not indicate a tender relation between the parties.

" Hear my voice : ye wives of Lamech, and hearken unto my speech ! "

As the wives made no reply, it shows that they had already learned that discreet silence is the only security for domestic happiness.

Naamah the sister of Tubal Cain was supposed to be the wife of Noah. Her name in Hebrew signifies the beautiful or the gracious. Jewish doctors say her name is recorded here because she was an upright, chaste woman, but others affirm the contrary because "the whole world wandered after her." But the fact that Naamah's beauty attracted the multitude, does not prove that she either courted or accepted their attentions.

The manner in which the writer of these chapters presents the women so in conflict with Chapters i and v, which immediately precede and follow, inclines the unprejudiced mind to relegate the ii, iii and iv chapters to the realm of fancy as no part of the real history of creation's dawn.

The curse pronounced on Cain is similar to that inflicted on Adam, both were to till the ground, which was to bring forth weeds abundantly. Hale's statistics of weeds show their rapid and widespread power of propagation. " A progeny," he says, "more than sufficient in a few years to stock every planet of the solar system." In the face of such discouraging facts, Hale coolly remarks. " Such provisions has the just God made to fulfil the curse which he promised on man."

It seems far more rational to believe that the curses on both woman and man were but figments of the human brain, and that by the observance of natural laws, both labor and maternity may prove great blessings.

With all the modern appliances of steam and electricity, and the new inventions in machinery, the cultivation of the soil is fast coming to be a recreation and amusement. The farmer now sits at ease on his plough, while his steed turns up the furrows at his will. With machinery the sons of Adam now sow and reap their harvests, keep the wheels of their great manufactories in motion, and with daily increasing speed carry on the commerce of the world. The time is at hand when the heavy burdens of the laborer will all be shifted on the shoulders of these tireless machines. And when the woman, too, learns and obeys the laws of life, these supposed curses will be but idle dreams of the past. The curse falls lightly even now on women who live in natural conditions, and with anæsthetics is essentially mitigated in all cases.

When these remedial agents were first discovered, some women refused to avail themselves of their blessings, and some orthodox physicians refused to administer them, lest they should interfere with the wise provisions of Providence in making maternity a curse. E. C. S.

MYTHS OF CREATION.

Nothing would be more interesting in connection with the "Woman's Bible" than a comparative study of the accounts of the creation held by people of different races and faiths. Our Norse ancestors, whose myths were of a very exalted nature, recorded in their Bible, the Edda, that one day the sons of Bor (a frost giant), Odin, Hoener, and Loder, found two trees on the sea beach, and from them created the first human pair, man and woman. Odin gave them life and spirit, Hoener endowed them with reason and motion, and Loder gave them the senses and physical characteristics. The man they called Ask, and the woman Embla. Prof. Anderson finds in the brothers the three-fold Trinity of the Bible. It is easy to fancy that there is some philological connection between the names of the first pair in the Bible and in the Edda. Perhaps the formation of the first pair out of trees had a deep connection with the tree of life, Ygdrasil, which extended, according to Norse mythology throughout the universe, furnishing bodies for mankind from its branches. It had three great roots, one extending to the nebulous world, and this was constantly gnawed by the serpent Nidhug. There was nothing in the Norse mythology that taught the degradation of woman, and the lay of Sigdrifa, in the Edda, is one of the noblest conceptions of the character of woman in all literature.

North American Indian mythology has the human race
born of the earth, but the writer cannot learn that women held
an inferior place. Among the Quiches the mothers and fathers
of old slept in the waters, covered with green, under a limpid
twilight, from which the earth and they were called out by a
mighty wind. The Algonkins believed the human family were
the children of Michabo, the spirit of the dawn, and their
supreme deity. In their language the words earth, mother and
father were from the same root. Many tribes claim descent
from a raven, symbolizing the clouds; others from a dog, which
is the symbol of the water goddess.

Dr. and Madame Le Plongeon relate that in their discoveries
among the buried remains of the Mayas in Yucatan, everything
marks a very high state of civilization. In one of the exhumed
temples they found pictures on the walls, which seem to be a
combination of the stories of the Garden of Eden and Cain and
Abel. The Serpent was always the royal emblem, because the
shape of Yucatan is that of a serpent ready to spring. It was
the custom among the Mayas for the oldest son of the king to
be a priest, and the second son to marry the oldest daughter.
The pictures represent that the oldest son in this particular case
was dissatisfied with this arrangement, and wanted to marry the
sister himself. To tempt her he sends a basket of apples by a
messenger. He stands watching the way in which the present
is received, and the serpent in the picture (indicating the royal
family), makes it curiously suggestive of the temptation of Eve.
The sister, however, rejects the present, and this so enrages the
elder brother that he kills the younger, who accordingly is
deified by the Mayas. The image of Chacmohl was discovered
by the Le Plongeons, and is now in the possession of the
Mexican Government. Perhaps these brothers were twins, as
the commentator says Cain and Abel were, and that gave rise
to the jealousy.

Nothing can surpass in grandeur the account in the first
chapter of Genesis of the creation of the race, and it satisfies
the highest aspirations and the deepest longings of the human

soul. No matter of what material formed, or through how many ages the formative period ran, or is to run, the image of God is the birthright of man, male and female. Whatever the second chapter may mean, it cannot set aside the first. It probably has a deep spiritual significance which mankind will appreciate when cavilling about the letter ceases. To the writer's mind its meaning is best expressed in the words of Goethe: "The eternal womanly leads us on."   C. B. C.

CHAPTER V.

Genesis v: 1, 2.

1 This is the book of the generations of Adam. In the day that God created man, in the likeness of God made he him.

2 Male and female created he them ; and blessed them, and called their name Adam, in the day when they were created.

H ERE we have the first account of the dual creation verified. Man and woman a simultaneous creation, alike in the image of God.

The dual relation, both in the Godhead and humanity, is here again declared, though contradicted in the intervening chapters. In this and the following chapters we have a prolix statement of the births, deaths, and ages in the male line. They all take wives, beget sons, but nothing is said of the origin or destiny of the wives and daughters ; they are incidentally mentioned merely as necessary factors in the propagation of the male line.

The men of this period seem to have lived to a ripe old age, but nothing is said of the age of the women ; it is probable as child-bearing was their chief ambition, that men had a succession of wives, all gathered to their fathers in the prime of life. Although Eve and her daughters devoted their energies to this occupation, yet the entire credit for the growth of the race is given to Adam and his male descendants. In all this chapter the begetting of the oldest son is made prominent, his name only is given, and the begetting of more "sons and daughters" is cursorily mentioned. Here is the first suggestion of the law of primogeniture responsible for so many of the evils that perplexed our Saxon fathers.   E. C. S.

Genesis vi: 1–8, 14–22.

1 And it came to pass, when men began to multiply on the face of the earth, and daughters were born unto them,

2 That the sons of God saw the daughters of men that they *were* fair ; and they took them wives of all which they chose.

3 And the Lord said, My spirit shall not always strive with man, for that he also *is* flesh : yet his days shall be a hundred and twenty years.

4 There were giants in the earth in those days ; and also after that, when the sons of God came in unto the daughters of men, and they bare *children* to them, the same *became* mighty men which *were* of old, men of renown.

5 ¶ And God saw that the wickedness of man *was* great in the earth, and *that* every imagination of the thoughts of his heart was only evil continually.

6 And it repented the Lord that he had made man on the earth, and it grieved him at his heart.

7 And the Lord said, I will destroy man whom I have created from the face of the earth ; both man and beast, and the creeping thing, and the fowls of the air ; for it repenteth me that I have made them.

8 But Noah found grace in the eyes of the Lord.

13 And God said unto Noah,

14 ¶ Make thee an ark of gopher wood ; rooms shalt thou make in the ark, and shalt pitch it within and without with pitch.

15 And this *is the fashion* which thou shalt make it *of* ; The *length* of the ark *shall* be three hundred cubits, the breadth of it fifty cubits and the height of it thirty cubits.

16 A window shalt thou make to the ark, and in a cubit shalt thou finish it above ; and the door of the ark shalt thou set in the side thereof ; *with* lower, second, and third *stories* shalt thou make it.

17 And, behold, I, even I, do bring a flood of waters upon the earth, to destroy all flesh, wherein *is* the breath of life, from under heaven ; *and* everything that *is* in the earth shall die.

18 But with thee will I establish my covenant ; and thou shalt come into the ark, thou, and thy sons, and thy wife, and thy sons' wives with thee.

19 And of every living thing of all flesh, two of every *sort* shalt thou bring into the ark, to keep *them* alive with thee ; they shall be male and female.

20 Of fowls after their kind, and of cattle after their kind, of every creeping thing of the earth, after his kind ; two of every *sort* shall come unto thee, to keep *them* alive.

21 And take thou unto thee of all food that is eaten, and thou shalt gather *it* to thee ; and it shall be for food for thee, and for them.

22 Thus did Noah ; according to all that God commanded him, so did he.

The Jews evidently believed the males the superior sex. Men are called "the sons of God," women "the daughters of men." From the text it would seem that the influence of the wives was not elevating and inspiring, and that the sin and misery resulting from their marriages, all attributed to the women. This condition of things so discouraged the Creator that he determined to blot out both man and beast, the fowls of the air and the creeping things on the earth. How very human this sounds. It shows what a low ideal the Jews had of the great first cause, from which the moral and material world of thought and action were evolved.

It was in mature life, when chastened by the experiences and trials of her early day, that Seth was born to Eve. It was among the descendants of Seth that purer morals and religion were cultivated. Intermarriage with the descendants of Cain had corrupted the progeny, perplexed the Creator, and precipitated the flood.

The female of each species of animal was preserved; males and females all walked into the ark two by two, and out again in equal and loving companionship. It has been a question with critics whether the ark was large enough for all it was supposed to contain. Commentators seem to agree as to its capacity to accommodate men, women, children, animals, and the food necessary for their preservation. Adam Clarke tells us that Noah and his family and the birds occupied the third story, so they had the benefit of the one window it contained.

The paucity of light and air in this ancient vessel shows that woman had no part in its architecture, or a series of port holes would have been deemed indispensable. Commentators relegate all difficulties to the direct intervention of Providence. The ark, made by unseen hands, like a palace of india rubber, was capable of expanding indefinitely; the spirit of all good, caused the lion and lamb to lie down peaceably together. To attribute all the myths, allegories, and parables to the interposition of Providence, ever working outside of his own inexorable laws, is to confuse and set at defiance human reason, and prevent all stimulus to investigation.

In several following chapters we have the history of Abram and Sarah, their wanderings from the land of their nativity to Canaan, their blunders on the journey, their grief at having no children, except one son by Hagar, his concubine, who was afterwards driven from their door, into the wilderness. However, Sarah in her old age was blessed with a son of her own, which event gave them great joy and satisfaction. As Sarah did not possess any of the heroic virtues, worthy our imitation, we need not linger either to praise or blame her characteristics. Neither she nor Abraham deemed it important to speak the truth when any form of tergiversation might serve them. In fact the wives of the patriarchs, all untruthful, and one a kleptomaniac, but illustrate the law, that the cardinal virtues are seldom found in oppressed classes.   E. C. S.

Hagar & Ishmael

A careful study of the Bible would alter the views of many as to what it teaches about the position of women. The trouble is too often instead of searching the Bible to see what is right, we form our belief, and then search for Bible texts to sustain us, and are satisfied with isolated texts without regard to context, and ask no questions as to the circumstances that may have existed then but do not now. We forget that portions of the Bible are only histories of events given as a chain of evidence to sustain the fact that the real revelations of the Godhead, be it in any form, are true. Second, that our translators were not inspired, and that we have strong presumptive proof that prejudice of education was in some instances stronger than the grammatical context, in translating these contested points. For instance, the word translated *obey* between husband and wife, is in but one instance in the New Testament the word used between master and servant, parent and child, but is the word that in other places is translated *defer*. The one instance states Sarah obeyed Abram. Read that history and you will find that in both instances in which she obeyed, God had to interfere with a miracle to save them from the result of that obedience, and both Abram and Sarah were reproved. While twice, once by direct command of God, Abram obeyed Sarah. You cannot find a direct command of God or Christ for the wife to obey the husband.

It was Eve's curse that her desire should be to her husband, and he should rule over her. Have you not seen her clinging to a drunken or brutal husband, and read in letters of fire upon her forehead her curse? But God did not say the curse was good, nor bid Adam enforce it. Nor did he say, all men shall rule over thee. For Adam, not Eve, the earth was to bring forth the thorn and the thistle, and he was to eat his bread by the sweat of his brow. Yet I never heard a sermon on the sin of uprooting weeds, or letting Eve, as she does, help him to bear his burden. It is when she tries to lighten her load that the world is afraid of sacrilege and the overthrow of nature.   C. B. C.

In the story "of the sons of God, and the daughters of men"—we find a myth like those of Greek, Roman and Scandinavian fable, demi-gods love mortal maidens and their offspring are giants. Then follows the traditional account of some great cataclysm of the last glacial epoch. According to the latest geological students, Wright, McGee and others; the records of Niagara, the falls of St. Anthony and other glacial chasms, indicate that the great ice caps receded for the last time about seven thousand years ago; the latest archeological discoveries carry our historical knowledge of mankind back nearly four thousand years B. C., so that some record of the mighty floods which must have followed the breaking of great glacial dams might well survive in the stories of the nations.

Abram who came from Ur of the Chaldees brought with him the Chaldean story of the flood. (At that time Ur, now a town fifty miles inland, was a great seaport of the Persian gulf,) Their story of the flood is that of a maritime people; in it the ark is a well built ship, Hasisadra, the Chaldean Noah takes on board not only his own family, but his neighbors and friends; a pilot is employed to guide the course, and proper provision is made for the voyage. A raven and a dove are sent out as in the biblical account, and a fortunate landing effected.

L. D. B.

CHAPTER VI.

Genesis xxi.

1 And the Lord visited Sarah as he had said.

2 For Sarah bare Abraham a son in his old age.

3 And Abraham called the name of his son whom Sarah bare to him, Isaac.

5 And Abraham was a hundred years old, when his son Isaac was born unto him.

6 ¶ And Sarah said, God hath made me to laugh, *so that* all that hear will laugh with me.

9 ¶ And Sarah saw the son of Hagar the Egyptian, which she had borne unto Abraham, mocking.

10 Wherefore she said unto Abraham, Cast out this bondwoman and her son; for the son of this bondwoman shall not be heir with my son, even with Isaac.

11 And the thing was very grievous in Abraham's sight.

12 ¶ And God said unto Abraham, Let it not be grievous in thy sight; in all that Sarah hath said unto thee, hearken unto her voice; for in Isaac shall thy seed be called.

13 And also of the son of the bondwoman will I make a nation, because he *is* thy seed.

14 And Abraham rose up early in the morning, and took bread, and a bottle of water, and gave *it* unto Hagar, putting it on her shoulder, and the child, and sent her away; and she departed, and wandered in the wilderness of Beer-sheba.

15 And the water was spent in the bottle, and she cast the child under one of the shrubs.

17 And she went, and sat her down over against *him* a good way off : for she said, Let me not see the death of the child. And she lifted up her voice, and wept.

17 And God heard the voice of the lad ; and the angel of God called to Hagar out of heaven, and said unto her, What aileth thee, Hagar ? fear not, for God hath heard the voice of the lad where he *is*.

18 Arise, lift up the lad, and hold him in thine hand: for I will make him a great nation.

19 And God opened her eyes, and she saw a well of water : and she went, and filled the bottle with water, and gave the lad drink.

20 And God was with the lad ; and he grew, and dwelt in the wilderness, and became an archer.

21 And he dwelt in the wilderness of Paran ; and his mother took him a wife out of the land of Egypt

---

THE great event of Isaac's birth having taken place, Sarah is represented through several chapters as laughing, even in the presence of angels, not only in the anticipation of motherhood, but in its realization. She evidently forgot that maternity was intended as a curse on all Eve's daughters, for the sin of the first woman, and all merry-making on such occasions was unpardonable. Some philosophers consider the most exalted of all forms of love to be that of a mother for her children. But this divine awakening of a new affection does not seem to have softened Sarah's heart towards her unfortunate slave Hagar. And so far from Sarah's desire being to her husband, and Abraham dominating her, he seemed to be under her control, as the Lord told him " to hearken to her voice, and to obey her command." In so doing he drives Hagar out of his house.

In this scene Abraham does not appear in a very attractive light, rising early in the morning, and sending his child and its mother forth into the wilderness, with a breakfast of bread and water, to care for themselves. Why did he not provide them with a servant, an ass laden with provisions, and a tent to shelter them from the elements, or better still, some abiding, resting place. Common humanity demanded this much attention to his own son and tne woman who bore him. But the worst feature in this drama is that it seems to have been done with Jehovah's approval.

Does any one seriously believe that the great spirit of all good talked with these Jews, and really said the extraordinary things they report? It was, however, a very cunning way for the Patriarchs to enforce their own authority, to do whatever they desired, and say the Lord commanded them to do and say thus and so. Many pulpits even in our day enforce their lessons of subjection for woman with the same authority, "Thus saith the Lord," "Thou shalt," and "Thou shall not." E. C. S.

Genesis xxiii.

1 And Sarah was a hundred and seven and twenty years old.

2 And Sarah died in Kirjath-arba; the same *is* Hebron in the land of Canaan: and Abraham came to mourn for Sarah, and to weep for her.

3 ¶ And Abraham stood up from before his dead, and spake unto the sons of Heth, saying,

4 I *am* a stranger and a sojourner with you: give me a possession of a buryingplace with you, that I may bury my dead out of my sight.

5 And the children of Heth answered Abraham, saying unto him.

6 Hear us, my lord: thou *art* a mighty prince among us: in the choice of our sepulchres bury thy dead; none of us shall withhold from thee his sepulchre.

7 And Abraham stood up, and bowed himself to the people of the land.

8 And he communed with them, saying, If it be your mind that I should bury my dead out of my

sight, hear me, and entreat Ephron the son of Zohar.

9 That he may give me the cave of Machpelah, which he hath, which *is* in the end of his field; for as much money as it is worth.

14 And Ephron answered Abraham, saying unto him.

15 My lord, hearken unto me: the land *is worth* four hundred shekels of silver; what *is* that betwixt me and thee? bury therefore thy dead.

16 And Abraham hearkened unto Ephron; and Abraham weighed to Ephron the silver, which he had named in the audience of the sons of Heth, four hundred shekels of silver, current *money* with the merchant.

19 And after this, Abraham buried Sarah his wife in the cave of the field of Machpelah before Mamre.

20 And the field, and the cave that *is* therein, were made sure unto Abraham for a buryingplace by the sons of Heth.

It is seldom that the age and death of any woman, are recorded by the sacred historian, but Sarah seems to have been specially honored, not only in the mention of her demise and ripe years, but in the tender manifestations of grief by Abraham, and his painstaking selection of her burial place. That Abraham paid for all this in silver, "current money with the merchant," might suggest to the financiers of our day that our commercial relations might be adjusted with the same coin, especially as we have plenty of it.

If our bimetallists in the halls of legislation were conversant with sacred history, they might get fresh inspiration from the views of the Patriarchs on good money.

Some critics tell us that there was no coined money at that time ; the Israelites had no written language, no commerce with neighboring tribes, and that they could neither read nor write.

Whilst we drop a tear at the tomb of Sarah, we cannot recommend her as an example to the young women of our day, as she lacked several of the cardinal virtues. She was undignified, untruthful, and unkind to Hagar. But our moral standard differs from that of the period in which she lived, as our ideas of right and wrong are not innate, but depend on education. Sarah probably lived up to the light that was in her.   E. C. S.

The cruelty and injustice of Abraham and Sarah, as commented on by Mrs. Stanton, doubtless stand out much more prominently in this condensed account than their proper proportions to the motives which actuated the figures in the drama. If we take any part of the story we must take it all, and remember that it had been promised to Abraham that of Ishmael a great nation should be born. Whether this was an actual revelation from God, or a prophetic vision that Abraham had, or is interpolated by the historian to correspond with the actual facts that transpired, in either case the firm belief that no harm could come to Ishmael, must be taken into account when estimating the motives which led Abraham and Sarah, for doubtless Abraham told Sarah of his vision, to send Hagar and her son off into the wilderness ; just as much as the firm belief that the promise of God with regard to his seed would be fulfilled made Abraham, a little afterward, prepare to offer up his son Isaac.

Abraham loved and honored his wife very greatly, probably admiring equally her beauty and strength of character. Abraham was ten years older than Sarah and we read that he was seventy-five years old when he started from Haran for the land of Canaan. Some time after this driven, by famine, he went down into Egypt, and here when she must have been at least seventy years of age the Egyptians saw that she was very fair, and the princes of Pharaoh so praised her beauty to their royal master that he sent and took her for his wife. The same thing happened when she was ninety years old, when she was seized by Abimelech, king of Gerar. In both cases they told, not a lie, but a half truth, for Sarah was Abraham's half sister. it being then the custom for children of the same father by different mothers to marry. Abraham's deceit was brought about by cowardice, while Sarah connived at the fraud for love of her husband, being besought to do so to save his life. Perhaps, too, she might have been amenable to the gracious tribute to her beauty that Abraham gave in making the request.

Sarah's strength of character is shown all through her history. Wherever she is mentioned the reader is made to feel that she is an important part of the narrative, and not merely a connecting link between two generations. In this story she carries her point, and Abraham follows her instructions implicitly, nay, is even commanded by God to do so.

Notwithstanding that Abraham mourned Sarah so sincerely, within three years after she died, and when at the ripe age of a hundred and forty years, he married again and the six children he begat by Keturah he took quite as a matter of course, although half a century before, when told that a son should be born to him, he laughed incredulously. Abraham had his failings, some of which are shared by the moderns, yet doubtless he was a moral giant compared with other men of the land from which he came and of the nations around him. As such he was chosen as the founder of a race whose history should promulgate the idea of the one true God. Certainly the descendants from this remarkable trio have retained their own peculiar characteristics and have ever been worshippers at the shrine of Jehovah.

A singular fact may be mentioned here that Mrs. Souvielle in her book "The Sequel to the Parliament of Religions," has shown that from Midian, one of the sons of Keturah, came Jethro or Zoroaster.

Western thinkers are so matter-of-fact in their speech and thought that it might not have occurred to them that the true value of this story of Sarah and Hagar, like that of all else, not only in our own Bible but in the scriptures of other faiths, lies in the esoteric meaning, had it not been for Paul, that prince of occult philosophers, who distinctly says, according to the old version, that it is an allegory; according to the revised, that it contains an allegory: "for these women are two covenants," one bearing children unto bondage, the other unto freedom. It is our privilege, Paul goes on to teach, to be children of the free woman, but although we are this by birthright, yet there has to be a personal appreciation of that fact, and an effort to maintain our liberty. The mystical significance of this allegory has never been elucidated in reference to the position of woman, but it may well be considered as establishing her claim, not only for personal freedom, but for the integrity of the home. Acting according to the customs of the day, Sarah connived at her own degradation. Later, when her womanly dignity was developed by reason of her motherhood, she saw what should be her true position in her home, and she made her rightful demand for unrivalled supremacy in that home and in her husband's affections. She was blessed of God in taking that attitude, and was held up to the elect descendants of Abraham nearly 1660 years later by the Apostle Peter as an example to be imitated. And these later women are to be Sarah's daughters, we are told, if like her, they "are not afraid with any amazement," or as the new version hath it, if they "are not put in fear by any terror."

Even as mere history the life and character of Sarah certainly do not intimate that it was the Divine plan that woman was to be a subordinate, either in person or in her home. Taken esoterically, as all ancient Oriental writings must be to get their full significance, it is an inspiration to woman to-day to stand for her liberty. The bondwoman must be cast out. All that makes for industrial bondage, for sex slavery and humiliation, for the dwarfing of individuality, and for the thralldom of the soul, must be cast out from our home, from society, and from our lives. The woman who does not claim her birthright of freedom will remain in the wilderness with the children that she has borne in degradation, heart starvation, and anguish of spirit, only to find that they are Ishmaels, with their hand against every man. They will be the subjects of Divine care and protection until their destiny is worked out. But she who is to be the mother of kings must herself be free, and have surroundings conducive to maintaining her own purity and dignity. After long ages of freedom shall have eradicated from woman's mind and heart the thought habits of the slave, then will she be a true daughter of Sarah, the Princess.

C. B. C.

Abraham has been held up as one of the model men of sacred history. One credit he doubtless deserves, he was a monotheist, in the midst of the degraded and cruel forms of religion then prevalent in all the oriental world ; this man and his wife saw enough of the light to worship a God of Spirit. Yet we find his conduct to the last degree reprehensible. While in Egypt in order to gain wealth he voluntarily surrenders his wife to Pharaoh. Sarah having been trained in subjection to her husband had no choice but to obey his will. When she left the king, Abraham complacently took her back without objection, which was no more than he should do seeing that her sacrifice had brought him wealth and honor. Like many a modern millionaire he was not a self-made but a wife-made man. When Pharaoh sent him away with his dangerously beautiful wife he is described as, " being rich in cattle, in silver and in gold," but it is a little curious that the man who thus gained wealth as the price of his wife's dishonor should have been held up as a model of all the patriarchal virtues.

L. D. B.

CHAPTER VII.

Genesis xxiv.

37 And my master made me swear, saying, Thou shall not take a wife to my son of the daughters of the Canaanites in whose land I dwell.

38 But thou shalt go unto my fathers house, and to my kindred, and take a wife unto my son.

39 And I said unto my master, Peradventure the woman will not follow me.

40 And he said unto me, The Lord, before whom I walk, will send his angel with thee, and prosper thy way ; and thou shalt take a wife for my son of my kindred, and of my father's house:

42 And I came this day unto the well, and said, O Lord God of my master Abraham, if now thou do prosper my way which I go:

43 Behold, I stand by the well of water; and it shall come to pass, that when the virgin cometh to draw *water*, and I say to her, Give me, I pray thee, a little water of thy pitcher to drink:

44 And she say to me, Both drink thou, and *I* will also draw for thy camels: *let* the same *be* the woman whom the Lord hath appointed out for my master's son.

45 And before I had done speaking in mine heart behold Rebekah came forth with her pitcher on her shoulder; and she went down unto the well, and drew *water*: and I said unto her; Let me drink, I pray thee.

46 And she made haste, and let down her pitcher from her *shoulder*, and said, Drink, and I will give thy camels drink also: so I drank, and she made the camels drink also.

47 And I asked her, and said, Whose daughter *art* thou ? And she said, The daughter of Bethuel Nahor's son, whom Malcah bare unto him : and I put the earring upon her face, and the bracelets upon her hands.

49 And now, if ye will deal kindly and truly with my master, tell me: and if not, tell me; that I may turn to the right hand, or to the left.

50 Then Laban and Bethuel answered and said. The thing proceedeth from the Lord: we cannot speak unto thee bad or good.

51 Behold, Rebekah *is* before thee; take *her*, and go, and let her be thy master's son's wife, as the Lord hath spoken.

53 And the servant brought forth jewels of silver, and jewels of gold, and raiment, and gave *them* to Rebekah; he gave also to her brother and to her mother precious things.

56 And he said unto them, Hinder me not, seeing the Lord hath prospered my way; send me away that I may go to my master.

57 And they said, we will call the damsel and inquire at her mouth.

58 And they called Rebekah, and said unto her, Wilt thou go with this man ? And she said, I will go.

59 And they sent away Rebekah their sister. and her nurse and Abraham's servant, and his men.

61 ¶ And Rebekah arose, and her damsels, and they rode upon the camels, and followed the man: and the servant took Rebekah and went his way.

63 And Isaac went out to meditate in the field at the eventide : and he lifted up his eyes, and saw, and behold, the camels *were* coming.

64 And Rebekah lifted up her eyes, and when she saw Isaac she lighted off the camel.

65 For she *had* said unto the servant, What man *is* this that walketh in the field to meet us ? And the servant *had* said, It *is* my master: therefore she took a vail, and covered herself.

66 And the servant told Isaac all things that he had done.

67 And Isaac brought her into his mother Sarah's tent, and took Rebekah, and she became his wife : and he loved her: and Isaac was comforted after his mother's *death*.

HERE is the first account we have of a Jewish courtship. The women seem quite as resigned to the custom of " being taken " as the men " to take." Outside parties could no doubt in most cases make more judicious selections of partners, than young folks themselves under the glamour of their ideals. Altogether the marriage of Isaac, though rather prosaic, has a touch of the romantic.

It has furnished the subject for some charming pictures, that decorate the galleries in the old world and the new. "Rebekah at the' well," has been immortalized both on canvas and in marble. Women as milk-maids and drawers of water, with pails and pitchers on their heads, are always artistic, and far more attractive to men than those with votes in their hands at the polling booths, or as queens, ruling over the destinies of nations.

In fact, as soon as man left Paradise, he began by degrees to roll off of his own shoulders all he could of his curse, and place it on woman. Why did not Laban and Bethuel draw the water for the household and the cattle. Scott says that Eliezer had attendants with him who might have saved Rebekah the labor of drawing water for ten camels, but he would not interfere, as he wished to see whether she possessed the virtues of industry, affability and cheerfulness in being serviceable and hospitable.

It was certainly a good test of her patience and humility to draw water for an hour, with a dozen men looking on at their ease, and none offering help. The Rebekahs of 1895 would have promptly summoned the spectators to share their labors, even at the risk of sacrificing a desirable matrimonial alliance. The virtue of self-sacrifice has its wise limitations. Though it is most commendable to serve our fellow-beings, yet woman's first duty is to herself, to develop all her own powers and possibilities, that she may better guide and serve the next generation.

It is refreshing to find in the fifty-eighth verse that Rebekah was really supposed to have some personal interest and rights in the betrothal.

The meeting of Isaac and Rebekah in the field at eventide is charming. That sweet restful hour after the sun had gone down, at the end of a long journey from a far-off country. Rebekah must have been in just the mood to appreciate a strong right arm on which to rest, a loving heart to trust, on the threshold of her conjugal life. To see her future lord for the first time, must have been very embarrassing to Rebekah. She no doubt concealed her blushes behind her veil, which Isaac probably raised at the first opportunity, to behold the charms of the bride whom the Lord had chosen for him. As Isaac was forty years old at this time, he probably made a most judicious and affectionate husband.

The 67th verse would be more appropriate to the occasion if the words "took Rebekah" had been omitted, leaving the text to read thus : " And Isaac brought her into his mother's tent, and she became his wife, and he loved her." This verse is remarkable as the first announcement of love on the part of a husband at first sight. We may indulge the hope that he confessed his love to Rebekah, and thus placed their conjugal relations on a more spiritual plane than was usual in those days. The Revising Committees by the infusion of a little sentiment into these ancient manuscripts, might have improved the moral tone of our ancestors' domestic relations, without falsifying the important facts of history. Many ancient writings in both sacred and profane history might be translated into more choice language, to the advantage of the rising generation. What we glean in regard to Rebekah's character in the following chapter shows, she, too, is lacking in a nice sense of honor.

With our ideal of the great first cause, a God of justice, wisdom and truth, the Jewish Lord, guiding and directing that people in all their devious ways, and sanctioning their petty immoralities seems strangely out of place; a very contradictory character, unworthy our love and admiration. The ancient Jewish ideal of Jehovah was not an exalted one.

E. C. S.

———

This romantic pastoral is most instructive as to the high position which women really held among the people whose religious history is the foundation of our own, and still further substanti-

ates our claim that the Bible does not teach woman's subordination.   The fact that Rebekah was drawing water for family use
does not indicate lack of dignity in her position, any more than
the household tasks performed by Sarah.   The wives and
daughters of patriarchal families had their maid-servants just as
the men of the family had their man-servants, and their position indicates only a division of responsibility.   At this period,
although queens and princesses were cooks and waiters, kings
and princes did not hesitate to reap their own fields and slay
their own cattle.   We are told that Abraham rushed out to his
herd and caught a calf to make a meal for the strangers, and
that while he asked Sarah to make the cakes, he turned over
the calf to a man servant to prepare for the table.   Thus the
labor of securing the food fell upon the male sex, while the
labor of preparing it was divided between both.

The one supreme virtue among the patriarchs was hospitality, and no matter how many servants a person had it must be
the royal service of his own hands that he performed for a
guest.   In harmony with this spirit Rebekah volunteered to
water the thirsty camels of the tired and way-worn travellers.
It is not at all likely that, as Mr. Scott suggests, Eliezer waited
simply to test Rebekah's amiability.   The test which he had
asked for was sufficiently answered by her offering the service
in the first place, and doubtless it would have been a churlish
and ungracious breach of courtesy to have refused the proffered
kindness.

That the Jewish women were treated with greater politeness
than the daughters of neighboring peoples we may learn from the
incident narrated of the daughters of Jethro who, even though
their father was high priest of the country were driven away by
the shepherds from the wells where they came to water their
flocks.   Of all outdoor occupations that of watering thirsty
animals is, perhaps, the most fascinating, and if the work was
harder for Rebekah than for our country maidens who water
their animals from the trough well filled by the windmill she
had the strength and the will for it, else she would have en-

trusted the task to some of the damsels of whom we read as her especial servants and who, as such, accompanied her to the land of Canaan.

The whole narrative shows Rebekah's personal freedom and dignity. She was alone at some distance from her family. She was not afraid of the strangers, but greeted them with the self-possession of a queen. The decision whether she should go or stay, was left wholly with herself, and her nurse and servants accompanied her. With grace and modesty she relieved the embarrassment of the situation by getting down from the altitude of the camel when Isaac came to meet her, and by enshrouding herself in a veil she very tactfully gave him an opportunity to do his courting in his own proper person, if he should be pleased to do so after hearing the servant's report.

It has been the judgment of masculine commentators that the veil was a sign of woman's subject condition, but even this may be disputed now that women are looking into history for themselves. The fashion of veiling a prospective bride was common to many nations, but to none where there were brutal ceremonies. The custom was sometimes carried to the extent, as in some parts of Turkey, of keeping the woman wholly covered for eight days previous to marriage, sometimes, as among the Russians, by not only veiling the bride, but putting a curtain between her and the groom at the bridal feast. In all cases the veil seems to have been worn to protect a woman from premature or unwelcome intrusion, and not to indicate her humiliated position. The veil is rather a reflection upon the habits and thoughts of men than a badge of inferiority for women.

How serenely beautiful and chaste appear the marriage customs of the Bible as compared with some that are wholly of man's invention. The Kamchatkan had to find his future wife alone and then fight with her and her female friends until every particle of clothing had been stripped from her and then the ceremony was complete. This may be called the other extreme from the veil. Something akin to this appears among our own kith and kin, so to speak, in modern times. Many instances of marriage *en chemise* are on record in England of quite recent dates, the notion being that if a man married a woman in this garment only he was not liable for any debts which she might previously have contracted. At Whitehaven, England, 1766, a woman stripped herself to her chemise in the church and in that condition stood at the altar and was married.

There is nothing so degrading to the wife in all Oriental customs as our modern common law ruling that the husband owns the wife's clothing. This has been so held times innumerable, and in Connecticut quite recently a husband did not like the gowns his wife bought so he burned them. He was arrested for destruction of property, but his claim was sustained that they were his own so he could not be punished.

As long as woman's condition, outside of the Bible, has been as described by Macaulay when he said: " If there be a word of truth in history, women have been always, and still are over the greater part of the globe, humble companions, playthings, captives, menials, and beasts of burden," it is a comfort to reflect that among the Hebrews, whose records are relied on by the enemies of woman's freedom to teach her subjection, we find women holding the dignified position in the family that was held by Sarah and Rebekah.   C. B. C.

CHAPTER VIII.

Genesis x.xv.

1 Then again Abraham took a wife, and her name was Keturah.

2 And she bare him Zimran and Jokshan, and Medan, and Midian, and Ishbak, and Shuah.

5 ¶ And Abraham gave all that he had unto Isaac.

6 But unto the sons of the concubines, which Abraham had, Abraham gave gifts, and sent them away from Isaac his son, while he yet lived, unto the east country.

7 And these are the days of the years of Abraham's life which he lived, a hundred and three score and fifteen years.

8 Then Abraham gave up the ghost.

9 And his sons Isaac and Ishmael buried him in the grave of Machpelah.

10 The field which Abraham purchased of the sons of Heth; there was Abraham buried, and Sarah his wife.

21 And Isaac entreated the Lord for his wife, and Rebekah his wife conceived.

24 ¶ And when her days to be delivered were fulfilled she bore twins.

27 And the boys grew; and Esau was a cunning hunter, a man of the field; and Jacob *was* a plain man, dwelling in tents.

28 And Isaac loved Esau, because he did eat of *his* venison; but Rebekah loved Jacob.

29 ¶ And Jacob sod pottage: and Esau came from the field, and he *was* faint.

30 And Esau said to Jacob, Feed me, I pray thee, with that same red *pottage*: for I am faint; therefore was his name called Edom.

31 And Jacob said, Sell me this day thy birthright.

32 And Esau said, Behold, I *am* at the point to die; and what profit shall this birthright do to me?

33 And Jacob said, Swear to me this day; and he sware unto him; and he sold his birthright unto Jacob.

34 Then Jacob gave Esau bread and pottage of lentiles; and he did eat and drink, and rose up, and went his way. Thus Esau despised his birthright.

IN these verses we have the account of Abraham's second marriage, and the birth of several sons. It does not seem clear from the text whether Keturah was a legal wife, or one of the Patriarch's numerous concubines. Clarke inclines to the latter idea, on account of Abraham's age, and then he gave all that he had to Isaac, and left Keturah's sons to share with those of other concubines, to whom he gave gifts and sent them away from his son Isaac to an eastern country. Abraham evidently thought that the descendants of Isaac might be superior in moral probity to those of his other sons, hence he desired to keep Isaac as exclusive as possible. But Jacob and Esau did not fulfill the Patriarch's expectations. Esau in selling his birthright for a mess of pottage, and Jacob taking advantage of his brother in a weak moment, and overreaching him in a bargain, alike illustrate the hereditary qualities of their ancestors.

Genesis xxvi.

6 ¶ And Isaac dwelt in Gerar.

7 And the men of the place asked him of his wife; and he said, She *is* my sister; for he feared to say, *She is* my wife; lest, *said he,* the men of the place should kill me for Rebekah; because she was fair to look upon.

9 And Abimelech called Isaac, and said Behold, of a surety she *is* thy wife; and how saidst thou, She *is* my sister? And Isaac said unto him, Because I said, Lest I die for her.

11 And Abimelech charged all *his* people, saying, He that toucheth this man or his wife shall surely be put to death.

34 ¶ And Esau was forty years old when he took to wife Judith the daughter of Beeri the Hittite, and Bashemath the daughter of Elon the Hittite;

35 Which were a grief of mind unto Isaac and to Rebekah.

The account of the private family affairs of Isaac and Rebekah; their partiality to different sons; Jacob, aided and abetted by his mother, robbing his elder brother of both his birthright and his father's blessing; the parents on one of their eventful journeys representing themselves as brother and sister, instead of husband and wife, for fear that some potentate might kill Isaac, in order to possess his beautiful wife; all these petty deceptions handed down from generation to generation, show that the law of heredity asserted itself even at that early day.

Abraham through fear denied that Sarah was his wife, and Isaac does the same thing. The grief of Isaac and Rebekah over Esau, was not that he took two wives, but that they were Hittites. Chapter xxvii gives the details of the manner that Jacob and his mother betrayed Isaac into giving the blessing to Jacob intended for Esau. One must read the whole story in order to appreciate the blind confidence Isaac placed in Rebekah's integrity; the pathos of his situation; the bitter disappointment of Esau; Jacob's temptation, and the supreme wickedness of Rebekah in deceiving Isaac, defrauding Esau, and undermining the moral sense of the son she loved.

Having entirely undermined his moral sense, Rebekah **fears** the influence of Jacob's marriage with a daughter of the Hittites, and she sends him to her own people, to find a wife in the household of her uncle Laban. This is indeed a sad record of the cruel deception that Jacob and his mother palmed off on Isaac and Esau. Both verbal and practical lying were necessary to defraud the elder son, and Rebekah was equal to the occasion. Neither she nor Jacob faltered in the hour of peril. Altogether it is a pitiful tale of greed and deception. Alas! where can a child look for lessons in truth, honor, and gener-osity, when the mother they naturally trust, sets at defiance every principle of justice and mercy to secure some worldly advantage. Rebekah in her beautiful girlhood at the well drawing water for man and beast, so full of compassion, does not exemplify the virtues we looked for, in her mature womanhood. The con-jugal and maternal relations so far from expanding her most tender sentiments, making the heart from love to one grow bountiful to all, seem rather to have narrowed hers into the extreme of individual selfishness. In obedience to his mother's commands, Jacob starts on his journey to find a fitting wife. If Sarah and Rebekah are the types of womanhood the Patri-archs admired, Jacob need not have gone far to find their equal.

In woman's struggle for freedom during the last half century, men have been continually pointing her to the women of the Bible for examples worthy imitation, but we fail to see the merits of their character, their position, the laws and sentiments concerning them. The only significance of dwelling on these women and this period of woman's history, is to show the absurd-ity of pointing the women of the nineteenth century to these as examples of virtue.   E. C. S.

————

Keturah is spoken of as a concubine in I Chronicles i, 32. As such she held a recognized legal position which implied no disgrace in those days of polygamy, only the children of these secondary wives were not equal in inheritance. For this reason the sons of Keturah had to be satisfied with gifts while Isaac received the patrimony. Notice the charge of Abimelech to his people showing the high sense of honor in this Philistine. He seems also in the 10th verse to have realized the terrible guilt that it would have been if one of them had taken Rebekah, not knowing she was Isaac's wife. With all Rebekah's faults she seems to have had things her own way and therefore she did not set any marked example of wifely submission for women of to-day to follow. Her great error was deceiving her husband to carry her point and this is always the result where woman is deprived in any degree of personal freedom unless she has attained high moral development. **C. B. C.**

CHAPTER IX.

Genesis xxix.

1 Then Jacob went on his journey, and came into the land of the people of the east.

2 And he looked, and behold a well in the field, and lo, there *were* three flocks of sheep lying by it; for out of that well they watered the flocks; and a great stone *was* upon the well's mouth.

3 And thither were all the flocks gathered, and they rolled the stone from the well's mouth, and watered the sheep, and put the stone again upon the well's mouth in his place.

4 And Jacob said unto them, My brethren, whence be ye? And they said, Of Haran *are* we.

5 And he said unto them, Know ye Laban the son of Nahor? And they said, we know *him*.

6 And he said unto them, *Is* he well? And they said, *He is* well: and behold Rachel his daughter cometh with the sheep.

9 ¶ And while he yet spake with them, Rachel came with her father's sheep: for she kept them.

10 And it came to pass, when Jacob saw Rachel the daughter of Laban his mother's brother, and the sheep of Laban, his mother's brother, and Jacob went near, and rolled the stone from the well's mouth, and watered the flock of Laban his mother's brother.

11 And Jacob kissed Rachel, and lifted up his voice and wept.

12 And Jacob told Rachel that he *was* her father's brother, and that he was Rebekah's son: and she ran and told her father:

13 And it came to pass, when Laban heard the tidings of Jacob his sister's son, that he ran to meet him, and embraced him, and kissed him, and brought him to his house. And he told Laban all these things.

14 And Laban said to him, Surely thou *art* my bone and my flesh. And he abode with him the space of a month.

15 ¶ And Laban said unto Jacob, Because thou *art* my brother, shouldst thou therefore serve me for nought? tell me, what shall thy wages *be*?

18 And Jacob loved Rachel: and said, I will serve thee seven years for Rachel thy younger daughter.

19 And Laban said, *It is* better that I give her to thee, than that I should give her to another man: abide with me.

20 And Jacob served seven years for Rachel, and they seemed unto him but a few days, for the love he had to her.

21 ¶ And Jacob said unto Laban, Give *me* my wife, for my days are fulfilled.

JACOB'S journey to the land of Canaan in search of a wife, and the details of his courtship, have a passing interest with the ordinary reader, interested in his happiness and success. The classic ground for the cultivation of the tender emotions in these early days, seems to have been near a well, where the daughters of those who were rich in flocks and herds found opportunities to exhibit their fine points in drawing water for men and cattle. From the records of these interesting events, the girls seemed ready to accept the slightest advances from passing strangers, and to give their hands and hearts as readily as they gave a drink of water to the thirsty. Marriage was as simple a contract as the purchase of a lamb, the lamb and the woman having about an equal voice in the purchase, though the lamb was not quite as ready to leave his accustomed grazing ground.   Jacob loved Rachel at first sight, and agreed to serve Laban seven years, but when the time expired Laban did not keep his agreement, but insisted on Jacob taking the other sister, and serving seven years more for Rachel.   Jacob submitted, but by the knowledge of a physiological law of which Laban was ignorant, he revenged himself, and obtained all the strongest and best of the flocks and herds.   Thus in their business relations as well as in family matters, the Patriarchs seem to have played as sharp games in overreaching each other as the sons of our Pilgrim Fathers do to-day.   In getting all they could out of Laban, Jacob and Rachel seem to have been of one mind.

A critical study of the Pentateuch is just now agitating the learned classes in Germany.   Bonn is an ancient stronghold of theological learning, and two of the professors of its famous university have recently exhibited a courage in Biblical criticism and interpretation which has further extended the celebrity of the school, if it has not added to its repute for orthodoxy.   In a course of lectures held during the university holidays, addressed to and largely attended by pastors, they declared the Old Testament history to "be a series of legends, and Abraham, Isaac and Jacob mythical persons."   Israel, they declared, was an idolatrous people, Jehovah being nothing more than a "God of the Jewish Nation."   This radical outbreak of criticism and interpretation has aroused considerable attention throughout Germany, and a declaration against it and other teachings of the kind has been signed by some hundreds of pastors and some thousands of laymen, but so far it has produced no effect whatever on the professors of Bonn, and there is no prospect of its doing so. It is fortunate for the faith thus assailed that the critical and rhetorical style of the ordinary German professor is too heavy for export or general circulation.   So that the theories of Messrs. Graef and Meinhold are not likely to do the faith of the Fatherland any particular harm.   That country has always been divided into two classes, one of which believes nothing and the other everything, the latter numerically preponderant, but the former exceeding in erudition and dialectic—a condition of things quite certain to continue and on which a few essays more or less in destructive criticism can produce little effect.

E. C. S.

———

Mrs. Stanton's statements concerning the undeveloped religious sentiment of the early Hebrews cannot be criticized from the orthodox standpoint as in this account, where the God of Abraham is represented as taking an active personal interest in the affairs of the chosen people, they did not trust wholly to Him, but kept images of the gods of the neighboring tribes in their houses, Laban feeling sorry enough over their loss to go seven days' journey to recover them while his daughter felt she could not leave her father's house without taking the images with her as a protection.

The faults of Laban, of Jacob and of most of his sons are brought out without any reserve by the historian who follows the custom of early writers in stating things exactly as they were. There was no secrecy and little delicacy in connection with sexual matters. It may, however, be noticed that while this people had the same crude notions about these things that were common to other nations, yet every infraction of the Divine law of monogamy, symbolized in the account of the creation of woman in the second chapter of Genesis, brings its own punishment whether in or out of the marriage relation. When one or another people sinned against a Jewish woman the men of the family were the avengers, as when the sons of Jacob slew a whole city to avenge an outrage committed against their sister. Polygamy and concubinage wove a thread of disaster and complications throughout the whole lives of families and its dire effects are directly traceable in the feuds and degeneration of their descendants. The chief lesson taught by history is danger of violating, physically, mentally, or spiritually the personal integrity of woman. Customs of the

country and the cupidity of Laban, forced polygamy on Jacob,
and all the shadows in his life, and he had no end of trouble in
after years, are due to this. Perhaps nothing but telling their
stories in this brutally frank way would make the lesson so
plain.

If we search this narrative ever so closely it gives us no
hint of Divinely intended subordination of woman. Jacob had
to buy his wives with service which indicates that a high value
was placed upon them. Now-a-days in high life men demand
instead of give. The degradation of woman involved in being
sold to a husband, to put it in the most humiliating way, is not
comparable to the degradation of having to buy a husband.
Euripides made Medea say : "We women are the most unfor·
tunate of all creatures since we have to buy our masters at so
dear a price," and the degradation of Grecian women is
repeated—all flower-garlanded and disguised by show—in the
marriage sentiments of our own civilization. Jacob was dominated by his wives as Abraham and Isaac had been and there
is no hint of their subjection. Rachel's refusal to move when
the gods were being searched for, showed that her will was
supreme, nobody tried to force her to rise against her own
desire.

The love which Jacob bore for Rachel has been through all
time the symbol of constancy. Seven years he served for her,
and so great was his love, so pure his delight in her presence
that the time seemed but as a day. Had this simple, absorbing
affection not been interfered with by Laban, how different
would have been the tranquil life of Jacob and Rachel, developing undisturbed by the inevitable jealousies and vexations connected with the double marriage. Still this love was the solace
of Jacob's troubled life and remained unabated until Rachel
died and then found expression in tenderness for Benjamin,
"the son of my right hand." It was no accident, but has a
great significance, that this most ardent and faithful of Jewish
lovers should have deeper spiritual experiences than any of his
predecessors.   C. B. C.

CHAPTER X.

Genesis, xxix, xxxi.

18 And Jacob loved Rachel; and said I will serve thee seven years for Rachel thy younger daughter.

19 And Laban said, *It is* better that I give her to thee, than that I should give her to another man; abide with me.

20 And Jacob served seven years for Rachel; and they seemed unto him *but* a few days, for the love he had to her.

21 ¶ And Jacob said unto Laban, Give *me* my wife, for my days are fulfilled.

22 And Laban gathered together all the men of the place and made a feast.

23 And it came to pass in the evening that he took Leah his daughter, and brought her to him.

26 And Laban said, It must not be so done in our country, to give the younger before the first-born.

27 We will give thee Rachel also thou shalt serve with me yet seven other years.

28 And Jacob did so, and he gave him Rachel his daughter to wife also.

25 ¶ And it came to pass, when Rachel had borne Joseph, that Jacob said unto Laban, Send me away, that I may go unto my mine own place, and to my country.

26 Give *me* my wives and my children, for whom I have served thee, and let me go; for thou knowest my service which I have done thee.

17 ¶ Then Jacob rose up, and set his sons and his wives upon camels;

18 And he carried away all his cattle, and all his goods which he had gotten, the cattle of his getting, which he had gotten in Padan-aram, for to go to Isaac his father in the land of Canaan.

19 And Laban went to shear his sheep; and Rachel had stolen the images that *were* her father's

20 And Jacob stole away unawares to Laban the Syrian, in that he told him not that he fled;

22 And it was told Laban on the third day, that Jacob was fled.

23 And he took his brethren with him, and pursued after him seven days' journey; and they overtook him in the mount Gilead.

WHILE Laban played his petty deceptions on Jacob, the latter proved himself in fraud and overreaching fully his match. In being compelled to labor fourteen years for Rachel instead of seven, as agreed upon, he amply revenged himself in getting possession of all Laban's best cattle, availing himself of a physiological law in breeding of which Laban was profoundly ignorant.

The parting of Jacob and Laban was not amicable, although they did not come to an open rupture. Rachel's character for theft and deception is still further illustrated. Having stolen her father's images and hidden them under the camel's saddles and furniture, and sat thereon, when her father came to search for the images, which he valued highly, she said she was too ill to rise, so she calmly kept her seat, while the tent was searched and nothing found, thus by act as well as word, deceiving her father.

Jacob and his wives alike seemed to think Laban fair game for fraud and deception. As Laban knew his images were gone, he was left to suspect that Jacob knew where they were, so little regard had Rachel for the reputation of her husband. In making a God after their own image, who approved of whatever they did, the Jews did not differ much from ourselves ; the men of our day talk too as if they reflected the opinions of Jehovah on the vital questions of the hour. In our late civil war both armies carried the Bible in their knapsacks, and both alike prayed to the same God for victory, as if he could be in favor of slavery and against it at the same time.

Like the women, too, who are working and praying for woman suffrage, both in the state legislature and in their closets, and others against it, to the same God and legislative assembly. One must accept the conclusion that their acquaintance with the Lord was quite as limited as our own in this century, and that they were governed by their own desires and judgment, whether for good or evil, just as we are; their plans by day and their dreams by night having no deeper significance than our own. Some writers say that the constant interposition of God in their behalf was because they needed his special care and attention. But the irregularity and ignorance of their lives show clearly that their guiding hand was of human origin. If the Jewish account is true, then the God of the Hebrews falls far short of the Christian ideal of a good, true manhood, and the Christian ideal as set forth in the New Testament falls short of our ideal of the Heavenly Father to-day. We have no fault to find with the Bible as a mere history of an ignorant, undeveloped people, but when special inspiration is claimed for the historian, we must judge of its merits by the moral standard of to-day, and the refinement of the writer by the questionable language in which he clothes his descriptions.

We have often wondered that the revising committees that have gone over these documents so often, should have adhered so closely to such gross translations. Surely a fact related to us in coarse language, is not less a fact when repeated in choice words. We need an expurgated edition of most of the books called holy before they are fit to place in the hands of the rising generation.

Some members of the Revising Committee write me that the tone of some of my comments should be more reverent in criticising the "Word of God." Does any one at this stage of civilization think the Bible was written by the finger of God, that the Old and New Testaments emanated from the highest divine thought in the universe? Do they think that all the men who wrote the different books were specially inspired, and that all the various revising committees that have translated, interpolated, rejected some books and accepted others, who have dug round the roots of the Greek and Hebrew to find out the true meaning, have one and all been watched and guided in their literary labors by the great spirit of the universe, who by immutable law holds the solar system in place, every planet steadily moving in its own elliptic, worlds upon worlds revolving in order and harmony?

These great object-lessons in nature and the efforts of the soul to fathom the incomprehensible, are more inspiring than any written page. To this "Word of God" I bow with reverence, and I can find no language too exalted to express my love, my faith, my admiration.

To criticise the peccadilloes of Sarah, Rebekah and Rachel does not shadow the virtues of Deborah, Huldah and Vashti; to condemn the laws and customs of the Jews as recorded in the book of Genesis, does not destroy the force of the golden rule and the ten commandments. Parts of the Bible are so true, so grand, so beautiful, that it is a pity it should have been bound in the same volume with sentiments and descriptions so gross and immoral.   E. C. S.

CHAPTER XI.

Genesis xxxv.

8 But Deborah Rebekah's nurse died, and she was buried beneath Beth-el under an oak: and the name of it was called Allonbachuth.

9 ¶ And God appeared unto Jacob again, when he came out of Padan-aram, and blessed him.

10 And God said unto him, Thy name is Jacob: Thy name shall not be called any more Jacob, but Israel shall be thy name: and he called his name Israel.

16 ¶ And they journeyed from Beth-el; and there was but a little way to come to Ephrath: and Rachel travailed, and she had hard labor.

17 The midwife said unto her, Fear not; thou shalt have this son also.

18 And it came to pass as her soul was in departing (for she died), that she called his name Ben-oni; but his father called him Benjamin.

19 And Rachel died, and was buried in the way to Ephrath, which is Beth-lehem.

20 And Jacob set a pillar upon her grave: that is the pillar of Rachel's grave unto this day.

WHY Deborah, Rebekah's nurse, should be interjected here does not appear. However, if all Isaac's and Jacob's children had been intrusted to her care through the perils of infancy, it was fitting that the younger generation with their father should pause in their journey and drop a tear to her memory, and cultivate a tender sentiment for the old oak tree at Bethel.

There is no manifestation of gratitude more beautiful in family life than kindness and respect to servants for long years of faithful service, especially for those who have watched the children night and day, tender in sickness, and patient with all their mischief in health. In dealing with children one needs to exercise all the cardinal virtues, more tact, diplomacy, more honor and honesty than even an ambassador to the Court of St. James. Children readily see whom they can trust, on whose word they can rely.

In Rachel's hour of peril the midwife whispers sweet words of consolation. She tells her to fear not, that she will have a son, and he will be born alive. Whether she died herself is of small importance so that the boy lived. Scott points a moral on the death of Rachel. He thinks she was unduly anxious to have sons, and so the Lord granted her prayers to her own destruction. If she had accepted with pious resignation what-ever weal or woe naturally fell to her lot, she might have lived to a good old age, and been buried by Jacob's side at last, and not left alone in Bethlehem. People who obstinately seek what they deem their highest good, ofttimes perish in the attainment of their ambition. (Thus Scott philosophizes.)

Jacob was evidently a man of but little sentiment. The dying wife gasps a name for her son, but the father pays no heed to her request, and chooses one to suit himself. Though we must admit that Benjamin is more dignified than Ben-oni; the former more suited to a public officer, the latter to a household pet. And now Rachel is gone, and her race with Leah for children is ended. The latter with her maids is the victor, for she can reckon eight sons, while Rachel with hers can muster only four. One may smile at this ambition of the women for children, but a man's wealth was estimated at that time by the number of his children and cattle ; women who had no children were objects of pity and dislike among the Jewish tribes. The Jews of to-day have much of the same feel-ing. They believe in the home sphere for all women, that wife-hood and motherhood are the most exalted offices. If they are really so considered, why does every Jew on each returning Holy Day say in reading the service, "I thank thee, oh Lord! that I was not born a woman!"? And if Gentiles are of the same opinion, why do they consider the education of boys more important than that of girls ? Surely those who are to fill the most responsible offices should have the most thorough and liberal education.

The home sphere has so many attractions that most women prefer it to all others. A strong right arm on which to lean, a safe harbor where adverse winds never blow, nor rough seas roll, makes a most inviting picture. But alas ! even good husbands sometime die, and the family drifts out on the great ocean of life, without chart or compass, or the least knowledge of the science of navigation. In such emergencies the woman trained to self-protection, self-independence, and self-support holds the vantage ground against all theories on the home sphere.

The first mention we have of an aristocratic class of Kings and Dukes, is in the line of Cain's descendants.

Genesis xxxvi.

18 And these are the sons of Aholibamah, Esau's wife: duke Jeush, duke Jaalam, duke Korah: these *were* the dukes *that came* of Aholibamah the daughter of Anah Esau's wife.

The name Aholibamah has a suggestion of high descent, but the historian tells us nothing of the virtues or idiosyncrasies of character,   such a high-sounding name suggests, but simply that she was the daughter of Anah, and the wife of Esau, and that she was blessed with children, all interesting facts, which might have been intensified with a knowledge of some of her characteristics, what she thought, said and did, her theories of life in general.   One longs all through Genesis to know what the women thought of a strictly masculine dynasty.

Some writers claim that these gross records of primitive races, have a deep spiritual meaning, that they are symbolical of the struggles of an individual soul from animalism to the highest, purest development of all the Godlike in man.

Some on the Revising Committee take this view, and will give us from time to time more exalted interpretations than the account in plain English conveys to the ordinary mind.

In my exegesis thus far, not being versed in scriptural metaphors and symbols, I have attempted no scientific interpretation of the simple narration, merely commenting on the supposed facts as stated.   As the Bible is placed in the hands of children and uneducated men and women to point them the way of salvation, the letter should have no doubtful meaning.   What should we think of guide posts on our highways, if we needed a symbolical interpreter at every point to tell us which way to go ? the significance of the letters ? and the point of compass indicated by the digital finger ?   Learned men have revised the Scriptures times without number, and I do not propose to go back of the latest Revision.   E. C. S.

CHAPTER XII.

Genesis xxxix.

1 And Joseph was brought down to Egypt; and Potiphar an officer of Pharaoh, captain of the guard, an Egyptian, bought him of the Ishmaelites, which had brought him down thither.

2 And the Lord was with Joseph, and he was a prosperous man ; and he was in the house of his master, the Egyptian.

4 And Joseph found grace in his sight, and he served him: and he made him overseer over his house and all that he had he put into his hand.

7 ¶ And it came to pass after these things, that his master's wife cast her eyes upon Joseph; and she solicited him.

8 But he refused, and said unto his master's wife, Behold, my master wotteth not what *is* with me in the house, and he hath committed all that he hath to my hand.

9 How then can I do this great wickedness and sin against God ?

10 And it came to pass, as she spake to Joseph day by day, that he hearkened not unto her, and she caught him by his garment, and he left his garment in her hand and fled.

13 And it came to pass, when she saw that he had left his garment in her hand and was fled forth,

14 That she called unto the men of her house, and spake unto them, saying, See, he hath brought in a Hebrew unto us to mock us; he came in unto me, and I cried with a loud voice:

15 And it came to pass, when he heard that I lifted up my voice and cried, that he left his garment with me, and fled.

16 And she laid up his garment by her, until his lord came home.

17 And she spake unto him according to these words, saying, The Hebrew servant which thou hast brought unto us, came in unto me to mock me:

18 And it came to pass, as I lifted up my voice and cried, that he left his garment with me, and fled out.

19 And it came to pass, when his master heard the words of his wife, that his wrath was kindled.

20 And Joseph's master took him; and put him into the prison, a place where the king's prisoners *were* bound : and he was there in the prison.

21 ¶ But the Lord was with Joseph, and shewed him mercy, and gave him favour in the sight of the keeper of the prison.

22 And the keeper of the prison committed to Joseph's hand all the prisoners that *were* in the prison; and whatever they did there, he was the doer *of it.*

POTIPHAR'S wife surpasses all the women yet mentioned in perfidy and dishonor.

Joseph's virtues, his dignity, his honor, go far to redeem the reputation of his ancestors, and the customs of his times. It would have been generous, at least, if the editor of these pages could have given us one woman the counterpart of Joseph, a noble, high-minded, virtuous type. Thus far those of all the different nationalities have been of an ordinary low type. Historians usually dwell on the virtues of the people, the heroism of their deeds, the wisdom of their words, but the sacred fabulist dwells on the most questionable behavior of the Jewish race.

and much in character and language that we can neither print nor answer.

Indeed the Pentateuch is a long painful record of war, corruption, rapine, and lust. Why Christians who wished to convert the heathen to our religion should send them these books, passes all understanding. It is most demoralizing reading for children and the unthinking masses, giving all alike the lowest possible idea of womanhood, having no hope nor ambition beyond conjugal unions with men they scarcely knew, for whom they could not have had the slighest sentiment of friendship, to say nothing of affection. There is no mention of women except when the advent of sons is announced. When the Children of Israel go down into Egypt we are told that the wives of Jacob's sons were taken too, but we hear nothing of Jacob's wives or concubines, until the death and burial of Leah is incidentally mentioned. Throughout the book of Genesis the leading men declare from time to that the Lord comes to them and promises great fruitfulness. A strange promise in that it could only be fulfilled in questionable relations. To begin with Abraham, and go through to Joseph, leaving out all conjugal irregularities, we find Abraham and Sarah had Isaac, Isaac and Rebekah had Jacob and Esau. Jacob and Rachel (for she alone was his true wife), had Joseph and Benjamin. Joseph and Asenath had Manassah and Ephraim. Thus giving the Patriarchs just seven legitimate descendants in the first generation. If it had not been for polygamy and concubinage, the great harvest so recklessly promised would have been meagre indeed.

Genesis xli.

45 ¶ And Pharaoh called Joseph's name Zaphnathpaaneah; and he gave him to wife Asenath the daughter of Potar-pherah priest of On. And Joseph went out over all the land of Egypt.

46 ¶ And Joseph was thirty years old when he stood before Pharaoh king of Egypt.

50 And unto Joseph were born two sons, before the years of the famine came: which Asenath the daughter of Poti-pherah priest of On bare unto him.

51 And Joseph called the name of the first-born Manassah: For God, *said he*, hath made me forget all my toil, and all my father's house.

52 And the name of the second called he Ephraim: For God hath caused me to be fruitful in the land of my affliction.

This is all we ever hear of Asenath, that she was a good woman, probably worthy of Joseph, it is fair to infer, for had she been otherwise her evil deeds would have been recorded. A few passing remarks where ever we find the mention of woman is about all we can vouchsafe. The writer probably took the same view of the virtuous woman as the great Roman General who said "the highest praise for Cæsar's wife is that she should never be mentioned at all."

The texts on Lot's daughters and Tamar we omit altogether, as unworthy a place in the "Woman's Bible." In the remaining chapters of Genesis, the brethren of Joseph take leave of each other ; the fathers bless their sons and grandsons, and also take leave of each other, some to go to remote parts of the country, some to die at a ripe old age. As nothing is said of their wives and daughters, the historian probably knew nothing of their occupations nor environments. Joseph was a hundred and ten years old when he died. They embalmed him according to the custom in Egypt, and put him in a coffin, and buried him in the land of his fathers, where his brethren had promised to take his bones after death to rest with his kindred at last.

E. C. S.

The literal translation of the first verse of chapter xxxix of Genesis is as follows :

"And Joseph was brought down to Egypt, and Potiphar, Pharaoh's eunuch, chief of the cooks, an Egyptian bought him of the Ishmaelites who brought him down."

These facts which are given in Julia Smith's translation of the Bible throw a new light on the story of Joseph and the woman who was Potiphar's wife only in name. L. D. B.

THE BOOK OF EXODUS.

CHAPTER I.

Exodus i.

1 Now these are the names of the children of Israel, which came into Egypt : every man and his household came with Jacob.

2 Reuben, Simeon, Levi, and Judah,

3 Issachar, Zebulun, and Benjamin,

4 Dan, and Naphtali, Gad and Asher.

5 And all the souls that came out of the loins of Jacob were seventy souls : for Joseph was in Egypt *already*.

15 ¶ And the king of Egypt spake to the Hebrew midwives, of which the name of the one *was* Shiphrah and the name of the other Puah :

16 And he said, When ye do the office of a midwife to the Hebrew women, and they bare a son, then ye shall kill him ; but if it *be* a daughter, then she shall live.

17 But the midwives feared God, and did not as the king of Egypt commanded them, but saved the men children alive.

18 And the king of Egypt called for the midwives, and said unto them, Why have ye done this thing and have saved the men children alive ?

19 And the midwives said unto Pharaoh, Because the Hebrew women are delivered ere the midwives come in unto them:

20 Therefore God dealt well with the midwives : and the people multiplied, and waxed very mighty.

21 And it came to pass, because the midwives feared God, that he made them houses.

22 And Pharaoh charged all his people, saying, Every son that is born ye shall cast into the river, and every daughter ye shall save alive.

THE Book of Exodus or the Departure, so called because of the escape of the children of Israel from the land of Egypt, and their wanderings in the wilderness for forty years, are herein recalled.

The unparalleled multiplication of the children of Israel renewed Pharaoh's anxiety especially as the Israelites were very large and strong as compared with the Egyptians, and their numbers were computed to double every fourteen years. Hence their multitude and power grew more formidable day by day in the eyes of the Egyptians, though they feared their presence, yet as their labors added greatly to the wealth of the nation, they were unwilling to let them go. Pharaoh hoped by making their daily tasks much harder and killing all the male children at birth, they would be so crippled and dispirited that there would be no danger of rebellion against his government.

68

For a list of the seventy souls, turn to Genesis, chapter xlvi, where Dinah, Jacob's daughter, and Sarah, Asher's daughter, are mentioned among the seventy souls. It is certainly curious that there should have been only two daughters to sixty-eight sons. But perhaps the seventy souls refer only to sons, and the daughters are merely persons, not souls. It is not an uncommon idea with many nations that women have no souls. A missionary to China tells of a native who asked him why he preached the Gospel to women. "To save their souls, to be sure." "Why," said he, "women have no souls." "Yes they have," said the missionary. When the thought dawned on the Chinaman that it might be true, he was greatly amused, and said, "Well, I'll run home and tell my wife she has a soul, and we will sit down and laugh together." We find at many points that the Bible does not reckon women as souls. It may be that because there is no future for them is the reason why they punish them here more severely than they do men for the same crimes. Here it is plainly asserted that all the souls that came out of the loins of Jacob were seventy in number. The meaning conveyed may be that the man supplies the spirit and intellect of the race, and woman the body only. Some late writers take this ground. If so, the phraseology would have been more in harmony with the idea, if the seventy souls had emanated, Minerva-like, from the brain of father Jacob, rather than from his loins.

The children of Israel multiplied so rapidly that Pharaoh became alarmed, lest the nation should become mightier than the Egyptians, so he ordered all the males at birth to be slain. To this end he had a private interview with the midwives, two women, Shiphrah and Puah, and laid his commands upon them. But they did not obey his orders, and excused themselves on the ground that the Jewish women seldom needed their services. Here we have another example of women who "feared God," and yet used deception to accomplish what they deemed right.

The Hebrew God seemed to be well pleased with the de-

ception, and gave them each a house for their fidelity in saving
the lives of his chosen children.   Such is the plain English of
the .story.   Origen ascribes a deep spiritual meaning to these
passages, as more recent writers and speakers do, making the
whole Bible a collection of symbols and allegories, but none of
them are complimentary to our unfortunate sex.   Adam Clarke
says if we begin by taking some parts of the Scriptures figuratively we shall soon figure it all away.   Though the midwives
in their comfortable homes enjoyed the approbation of God,
Pharaoh was not to be thwarted by their petty excuses, so he ordered
his own people to cast into the river every Jewish boy that was
born.   We are so accustomed to the assumption that men alone
form a nation, that we forget to resent such texts as these.
Surely daughters in freedom could perpetuate family and national
pride and honor, and if allowed to wed the men of their choice,
their children would vindicate their ancestral dignity.   The
greatest block to advancing civilization all along the line has
been the degradation of woman.   Having no independent existence, no name, holding no place of honor or trust, being mere
subjects in the family, the birth of a son is naturally considered
more important than a daughter, as the one inherits because of
sex all the rights and privileges denied the other.

Shiphrah and Puah, Aben Ezra tells us, were probably at
the head of their profession, and instructed others in the science
of obstetrics.   At this time there were five hundred midwives
among the Hebrews.   This branch of the profession was, among
the Egyptians, also in the hands of the women.   Statistics show
that the ratio of deaths among mothers and children at birth
was far less than when under male supervision exclusively.

Moses spent the first forty years of his life in Egypt, the
next forty with Jethro his father in law, and the next forty wandering in the wilderness.   One writer said the Lord must have
buried Moses, and no one ever knew where.   There is no
record of the burial place of Moses.   As his life had been
surrounded with mysteries, perhaps to verify his providential guidance in that long journey in the wilderness, he chose

to surround his death also with mystery, and arranged with members of the priesthood to keep his last resting place a profound secret. He was well versed in all the law and mythology of the Egyptians, and intended the people should no doubt think that Jehovah had taken the great leader to himself. For the purpose of controlling his followers in that long journey through the wilderness, he referred all his commands and actions to Jehovah. Moses declared that he met him face to face on Mount Sinai, veiled in a cloud of fire, received minute instructions how to feed and conduct the people, as well as to minister to their moral and spiritual necessities. In order to enforce his teachings, he said the ten commandments were written on tablets of stone by Jehovah himself, and given into his hands to convey to the people, with many ordinances and religious observances, to be sacredly kept. In this way the Jewish religion and the Mosaic code were established.

As these people had no written language at that time, and could neither read nor write, they were fitting subjects for all manner of delusions and superstitions. The question naturally suggests itself to any rational mind, why should the customs and opinions of this ignorant people, who lived centuries ago, have any influence in the religious thought of this generation?　　　　E. C. S.

CHAPTER II.

Exodus ii.

1 And there went a man of the house of Levi and took to *wife* a daughter of Levi.

2 And the woman bare a son: and when she saw that he *was* a goodly *child*, she hid him three months.

3 And when she could not longer hide him she took for him an ark of bulrushes, and daubed it with slime and with pitch, and put the child therein; and she laid *it* in the flags by the river's brink.

4 And his sister stood afar off, to wit what would be done to him.

5 ¶ And the daughter of Pharaoh came down to wash *herself* at the river; and her maidens walked along by the river's side: and when she saw the ark among the flags, she sent her maid to fetch it.

6 And when she had opened *it*, she saw the child: and, behold, the babe wept. And she had compassion on him, and said, This *is one* of the Hebrews' children.

7 Then said his sister to Pharaoh's daughter, Shall I go and call to thee a nurse of the Hebrew women, that she may nurse the child for thee?

8 And Pharaoh's daughter said to her, Go. And the maid went and called the child's mother.

9 And Pharaoh's daughter said unto her, Take this child away, and nurse it for me, and I will give *thee* thy wages. And the woman took the child, and nursed it.

10 And the child grew, and she brought him unto Pharaoh's daughter, and he became her son. And she called his name Moses: and she said, Because I drew him out of the water.

15 But Moses fled from the face of Pharaoh, and dwelt in the land of Midian: and he sat down by a well.

16 Now the priest of Midian had seven daughters: and they came and drew *water*, and filled the troughs to water their father's flock.

17 And the shepherds came and drove them away: but Moses stood up and helped them, and watered their flock.

18 And when they came to Reuel their father, he said, How *is it that* ye are come so soon to day?

19 And they said, An Egyptian delivered us out of the hand of the shepherds, and also drew *water* enough for us, and watered the flock.

20 And he said unto his daughters, And where *is* he? why *is it that* ye have left the man? call him, that he may eat bread.

21 And Moses was content to dwell with the man: and he gave Moses Zipporah his daughter.

22 And she bare *him* a son, and he called his name Gershon: for he said, I have been a stranger in a strange land.

THE account of the birth of Moses, his mother's anxiety in protecting him from the wrath of Pharaoh, and the goodness of the king's daughter, make altogether an interesting story, and is almost the first touch of sentiment with which the historian has refreshed us; a pleasant change from the continued accounts of corruption, violence, lust, war and petty falsehood, that have thus far marked the history of this people. The only value of these records to us is to show the character of the Jewish nation, and make it easy for us to reject their ideas as to the true status of woman, and their pretension of being guided by the hand of God, in all their devious wanderings. Surely such teachings as these, should have no influence in regulating the lives of women in the nineteenth century. Moses' conduct towards the seven daughters of the priest at the well, shows that there were some sparks of chivalry here and there in a few representative souls, notwithstanding the contempt for the sex in general. These Hebrew wooings and weddings were curiously similar, alike marked for the beauty and simplicity of the daughters of the land, the wells, the flocks, the handsome strangers, the strong, active young men who will prove so helpful in cultivating the lands. The father-in-law usually gets the young husband completely under his thumb, and we hear nothing of the dreaded mother-in-law of the nineteenth century. If we go through this chapter carefully we will find mention of about a dozen women, but with the exception of one given to Moses, all are nameless. Then as now names for women and slaves are of no importance; they have no individual life, and why should their personality require a life-long name? To-day the woman is Mrs. Richard Roe, to-morrow Mrs. John Doe, and again Mrs. James Smith according as she changes masters, and she has so little self-respect that she does not see the insult of the custom. We have had in this generation one married woman in England, and one in America, who had one name from birth to death, and though married they kept it. Think of the inconvenience of vanishing as it were from your friends and correspondents three times in one's natural life.

In helping the children of Israel to escape from the land of Egypt the Lord said to Moses:

Exodus iii.

19 ¶ And I am sure that the king of Egypt will not let you go, no, not by a mighty hand.

20 And I will stretch out my hand, and smite Egypt with all my wonders which I will do in the midst thereof: and after that he will let you go.

21 And I will give this people favour in the sight of the Egyptians: and it shall come to pass, that, when ye go, ye shall not go empty:

22 But every woman shall borrow of her neighbour, and of her that sojourneth in her house, jewels of silver, and jewels of gold, and raiment: and ye shall put *them* upon your sons, and upon your daughters; and ye shall spoil the Egyptians.

The role assigned the women, in helping the children of

Israel to escape in safety from bondage, is by no means complimentary to their heroism or honesty. To help bear the expenses of the journey, they were instructed to steal all the jewels
of silver and gold, and all the rich raiment of the Egyptian
ladies. The Lord and Moses no doubt went on the principle that
the Israelites had richly earned all in the years of their bondage.
This is the position that some of our good abolitionists took,
when Africans were escaping from American bondage, that the
slaves had the right to seize horses, boats, anything to help them
to Canada, to find safety in the shadow of the British lion.
Some of our pro-slavery clergymen, who no doubt often read
the third chapter of Exodus to their congregations, forgot the
advice of Moses, in condemning the abolitionists; as the Ameri-
cans had stolen the African's body and soul, and kept them in
hopeless bondage for generations—they had richly earned
whatever they needed to help them to the land of freedom.
Stretch the principle of natural rights a little further, and ask the
question, why should women, denied all their political rights,
obey laws to which they have never given their consent, either
by proxy or in person ? Our fathers in an inspired moment said,
" No just government can be formed without the consent of the
governed."

Women have had no voice in the canon law, the catechisms,
the church creeds and discipline, and why should they obey the
behests of a strictly masculine religion, that places the sex at a
disadvantage in all life's emergencies ?

Our civil and criminal codes reflect at many points the spirit
of the Mosaic. In the criminal code we find no feminine
pronouns, as " He," " His," " Him," we are arrested, tried and
hung, but singularly enough, we are denied the highest privileges of citizens, because the pronouns " She," " Hers " and
" Her," are not found in the constitutions. It is a pertinent
question, if women can pay the penalties of their crimes as " He,"
why may they not enjoy the privileges of citizens as "He"?

E. C. S.

CHAPTER III.

Exodus iv.

18 ¶ And Moses went and returned to Jethro his father in law, and said unto him, let me go, I pray thee, and return unto my brethren which *are* in Egypt, and see whether they be yet alive. And Jethro said to Moses, Go in peace.

19 And the Lord said unto Moses in Midian, Go, return into Egypt: for all the men are dead which sought thy life.

20 And Moses took his wife and his sons, and set them upon an ass, and he returned to the land of Egypt : and Moses took the rod of God in his hand.

21 And the Lord said unto Moses, when thou goest to return into Egypt, see that thou do all those wonders before Pharaoh, which I have put in thine hand : but I will harden his heart, that he shall not let the people go.

22 And thou shalt say unto Pharaoh, Thus saith the Lord, Israel *is* my son, *even* my firstborn :

23 And I say unto thee, let my son go, that he may serve me : and if thou refuse to let him go, behold, I will slay thy son, *even* thy firstborn:

24 ¶ And it came to pass by the way in the inn, that the Lord met him, and sought to kill him.

25 Then Zipporah took a sharp stone. and circumcised her son.

26 So he let him go.

WHEN Moses married Zipporah he represented himself as a stranger who desired nothing better than to adopt Jethro's mode of life, But now that he desired to see his own people, his wife has no choice but to accompany him. So Moses took his wife and his sons and set them on an ass, and he returned to the land of Egypt.

The reason the Lord met them and sought to kill the son, was readily devined by Zipporah; her son had not been circumcised; so with woman's quick intuition and natural courage to save the life of her husband, she skillfully performed the necessary operation, and the travellers went on their way rejoicing. The word circumcision seems to have a very elastic meaning "uncircumcised lips" is used to describe that want of power to speak fluently, from which Moses suffered and which he so often deplored.

As in every chapter of Jewish history this rite is dwelt upon it is worthy of remark that its prominence as a religious observance means a disparagement of all female life, unfit for offerings, and unfit to take part in religious services, incapable of consecration. The circumcision of the heart even, which women might achieve, does not render them fit to take an active part in any of the holy services of the Lord. They were per-

mitted to violate the moral code of laws to secure liberty for
their people, but they could not officiate in any of the sacraments
nor eat of the consecrated bread at meals. Although the Mosaic
code and customs so plainly degrade the female sex, and their
position in the church to-day grows out of these ancient customs, yet many people insist that our religion dignifies women.
But so long as the Pentateuch is read and accepted as the Word
of God, an undefined influence is felt by each generation that
destroys a proper respect for all womankind.

It is the contempt that the canon and civil law alike express for
women that has multiplied their hardships and intensified man's
desire to hold them in subjection. The sentiment that statesmen and bishops proclaim in their high places are responsible
for the actions of the lower classes on the highways. We scarce
take up a paper that does not herald some outrage committed
on a matron on her way to church, or the little girl gathering
wild flowers on her way to school; yet you cannot go so low
down in the scale of being as to find men who will enter our
churches to desecrate the altars or toss about the emblems of the
sacrament; because they have been educated with some respect
for churches, altars and sacraments. But where are any lessons
of respect taught for the mothers of the human family ? And yet
as the great factor in the building of the race, are they not
more sacred than churches, altars, sacraments or the priesthood?

Do our sons in their law schools, who read the old common
law of England and its commentators, rise from their studies
with higher respect for women? Do our sons in their theological seminaries rise from their studies of the Mosaic laws and
Paul's epistles with higher respect for their mothers? Alas! in
both cases they may have learned their first lessons of disrespect
and contempt. They who would protect their innocent daughters from the outrages so common to-day, must lay anew the
foundation stones of law and gospel in justice and equality, in
a profound respect of the sexes for each other.   E. C. S.

CHAPTER IV.

Exodus xii.

12 For I will pass through the land of Egypt this night, and will smite all the firstborn in the land of Egypt, both man and beast : and against all the gods of Egypt I will execute judgment. I *am* the Lord.

18 And the blood shall be to you for a token upon the houses where ye *are :* and when I see the blood, I will pass over you, and the plague shall not be upon you to destroy *you*, when I smite the land of Egypt.

43 ¶ And the Lord said unto Moses and Aaron, This *is* the ordinance of the passover : There shall no stranger eat thereof:

44 But every man's servant that is bought for money, when thou hast circumcised him, then shall he eat thereof.

45 A foreigner and a hired servant shall not eat thereof.

46 In one house shall it be eaten ; thou shalt not carry forth aught of the flesh abroad out of the house : neither shall ye break a bone thereof.

47 All the congregations of Israel shall keep it.

48 And when a stranger shall sojourn with thee, and will keep the passover to the Lord, let all his males be circumcised, and then let him come near and keep it : and he shall be as one that is born in the land : for no uncircumcised person shall eat thereof.

IN commemoration of this promise of the Lord's to pass over their homes in executing vengeance on the Egyptians, and of the prolonged battles between Jehovah and Moses on the one side, and Pharaoh and his Cabinet on the other, the Jews held an annual feast to which all circumcised males were summoned. The point of interest to us is whether women were disqualified, not being circumcised, or whether as members of the congregation they could slip in under the provision in the 47th verse, and enjoy the unleavened bread and nice roast lamb with the men of their household. It seems from the above texts that this blessed feast of deliverance from bondage must have been confined to males, that they only, could express their joy and gratitude. But women were permitted to perform a subordinate part in the grand hegira, beside carrying their respective infants they manifested their patriotism by stealing all the jewels of gold and silver, all the rich silks and velvets from their Egyptian neighbors, all they could carry, according, to the commands of Moses. And why should these women take any part in the passover ; their condition remained about the same under all dynasties in all lands. They were regarded merely as necessary factors in race building. As Jewish wives or Egyptian concubines, there was no essential difference in their social status.

As Satan, represented by a male snake, seemed to be women's counsellor from the beginning, making her skillful in cunning and tergiversation, it is fair to suppose that they were destined to commune with the spirit of evil for ever and ever, that is if women have souls and are immortal, which is thought to be doubtful by many nations.   There is no trace thus far that the Jews believed in a future state, good or bad.   No promise of immortality is held out to men even.   So far the promise to them is a purely material triumph, "their seed shall not fill the earth."

The firstborn of males both man and beast are claimed by the Lord as his own.   From the general sentiment expressed in the various texts, it is evident that Satan claims the women as his own.   The Hebrew God had very little to say in regard to them.   If the passover, the lamb and the unleavened bread, were necessary to make the males acceptable in religious services, the females could find no favor in the eyes of either God or man.

In most of the sacrifices female animals are not accepted, nor a male, born after a female by the same parent.   Males are the race, females only the creatures that carry it on.   This arrangement must be providential, as it saves men from many disabilities.   Men never fail to dwell on maternity as a disqualification for the possession of many civil and political rights. Suggest the idea of women having a voice in making laws and administering the Government in the halls of legislation, in Congress, or the British Parliament, and men will declaim at once on the disabilities of maternity in a sneering contemptuous way, as if the office of motherhood was undignified and did not comport with the highest public offices in church and state.   It is vain that we point them to Queen Victoria, who has carefully reared a large family, while considering and signing all state papers.   She has been a pattern wife and mother, kept a clean court, and used her influence as far as her position would admit, to keep peace with all nations.   Why should representative American women be incapable of discharging similar public and private duties at the same time in an equally commendable manner ?   E. C. S.

CHAPTER V.

Exodus xviii.

1 When Jethro, the priest of Midian, Moses' father in law, heard of all that God had done for Moses, and for Israel his people, *and* that the Lord had brought Israel out of Egypt ;

2 Then Jethro, Moses' father in law, took Zipporah, Moses' wife, after he had sent her back.

3 And her two sons ; of which the name of one *was* Gershom ; for he said, I have been an alien in a strange land :

4 And the name of the other *was* Eliezer ; for the God of my father, *said he, was* mine help, and delivered me from the sword of Pharaoh ;

5 And Jethro, Moses' father in law, came with his sons and his wife unto Moses into the wilderness, where he encamped at the mount of God :

6 And he said unto Moses, I thy father in law Jethro am come unto thee, and thy wife, and her sons with her.

7 ¶ And Moses went out to meet his father in law, and did obeisance, and *kissed him ;* and they asked each other of *their* welfare ; and they came into the tent.

8 And Moses told his father in law all that the Lord had done unto Pharaoh and to the Egyptians for Israel's sake, *and* all the travail that had come upon them by the way, and *how* the Lord delivered them.

AFTER a long separation the record of the meeting between Moses and his wife Zipporah is very unsatisfactory to the casual reader. There is some sentiment in the meeting of Jethro and Moses, they embraced and kissed each other. How tender and beautiful the seeming relation to a father in law, more fortunate than the mother in law in our time. Zipporah like all the women of her time was hustled about, sent forward and back by husbands and fathers, generally transported with their sons and belongings on some long-suffering jackass. Nothing is said of the daughters, but the sons, their names and their significance seem of vital importance. We must smile or heave a sigh at all this injustice, but different phases of the same guiding principle blocks woman's way to-day to perfect liberty. See the struggle they have made to gain admittance to the schools and colleges, the trades and professions, their civil and political rights. The darkest page in history is the persecutions of woman.

We take note of these discriminations of sex, and reiterate them again and again to call the attention of women to the real source of their multiplied disabilities. As long as our religion teaches woman's subjection and man's right of domination, we shall have chaos in the world of morals. Women are never referred to as persons, merely as property, and to see why, you must read the Bible until you also see how many other opportunities for the exercise of sex were given to men, and why the single one of marriage to one husband was allowed to women.

In all the directions given Moses, for the regulation of the social and civil life of the children of Israel, and in the commandments on Mount Sinai, it is rarely that females are mentioned. The regulations are chiefly for males, the offerings are male, the transgressions referred to are male.

When the Lord was about to give the ten commandments to the children of Israel he gave the most minute directions as to the preparatory duties of the people. It is evident from the text that males only were to witness Moses' ascent to Mount Sinai and the coming of the Lord in a cloud of fire.

Exodus xix.

12 And thou shalt set bounds unto the people round about, saying, Take heed to yourselves, *that ye go not* up into the mount, or touch the border of it : whosoever toucheth the mount shall be surely put to death.

13 There shall not a hand touch it, but he shall surely be stoned, or shot through ; whether *it be* beast or man, it shall not live : when the trumpet soundeth long, they shall come up to the mount.

14 ¶ And Moses went down from the mount unto the people, and sanctified the people ; and they washed their clothes.

16 And he said unto the people, Be ready against the third day : come not at *your* wives.

The children of Israel were to sanctify themselves for this great event. Besides a thorough cleaning of their persons and clothes, they were to have no affiliations or conversations with women for the space of three days. The Hebrew laws regulating the relations of men and women are never complimentary to the latter.

This feeling was in due time cultivated in the persecutions women endured under witchcraft and celibacy, when all women were supposed to be in collusion with the spirit of evil, and every man was warned that the less he had to do with the " daughters of men " the more perfect might be his communion with the Creator. Lecky in his History of Rationalism shows what women endured when these ideas were prevalent, and their sufferings were not mitigated until rationalism took the place of religion, and reason trumphed over superstition.   E. C. S.

CHAPTER VI.

Exodus xv.

20 ¶ And Miriam the prophetess, the sister of Aaron, took a timbrel in her hand ; and all the women went out after her with timbrels and with dances.

21 And Miriam answered them, Sing ye to the Lord, for he hath triumphed gloriously ; the horse and his rider hath he thrown into the sea.

AFTER many previous disappointments from Pharaoh, the children of Israel were permitted to start from Egypt and cross the Red Sea, while Pharaoh and his host in pursuit, were overwhelmed in the waters.

Then Moses and the children of Israel expressed their grati-tude to the Lord in a song, comprising nineteen verses, while Miriam and the women expressed theirs in the above two. Has this proportion any significance as to the comparative happiness of the men and the women, or is it a poor attempt by the male historian to make out that though the women took part in the general rejoicing, they were mutinous or sulky. We know that Miriam was not altogether satisfied with the management of Moses at many points of the expedition, and later on expressed her dissatisfaction. If their gratitude is to be measured by the length of their expression, the women were only one-tenth as grateful as the men. It must always be a wonder to us, that in view of their degradation, they ever felt like singing or dancing, for what desirable change was there in their lives—the same hard work or bondage they suffered in Egypt. There, they were all slaves together, but now the men, in their respective families were exalted above their heads. Clarke gives the song in metre with a chorus, and says the women, led by Miriam, answered in a chorus by themselves which greatly heightened the effect.

Exodus xvi.

23 And he said unto them, This *is that* which the Lord hath said, To morrow *is* the rest of the holy sabbath unto the Lord : bake *that* which ye will bake *to-day,* and seethe that ye will seethe ; and that which remaineth over lay up for you to be kept until the morning.

29 See, for that the Lord hath given you the sabbath, therefore he giveth you on the sixth day the bread of two days ; abide ye every man in his place, let no man go out of his place on the seventh day.

30 So the people rested on the seventh day.

In these texts we note that the work of men was done on the sixth day, but the women must work as usual on the seventh. We see the same thing to-day, woman's work is never done. What irony to say to them rest on the seventh day. The Puritan fathers would not let the children romp or play, nor give their wives a drive on Sunday, but they enjoyed a better dinner on the Sabbath than any other day; yet the xxxi chapter and 15th verse contains the following warning:

15 Six days may work be done; but in the seventh *is* the sabbath of rest, holy to the Lord: whosoever doeth *any* work in the sabbath day, he shall surely be put to death.

As the women continued to work and yet seemed to live in the flesh, it may refer to the death of their civil rights, their individuality, as nonentities without souls or personal responsibility.

A critical reading of the ten commandments will show that they are chiefly for men. After purifying themselves by putting aside their wives and soiled clothes, they assembled at the foot of Mount Sinai. We have no hint of the presence of a woman. One commandment speaks of visiting the iniquities of the fathers upon the children. There is an element of justice in this, for to talk of children getting iniquities from their mothers, in a history of males, of fathers and sons, would be as ridiculous as getting them from the clothes they wore.

"Six days shalt thou labor and do all thy work." With the majority of women this is impossible. Men of all classes can make the Sabbath a day of rest, at least a change of employment, but for women the same monotonous duties must be performed. In the homes of the rich and poor alike, most women cook, clean, and take care of children from morning till night. Men must have good dinners Sundays above all other days, as then they have plenty of time in which to eat. If the first born male child lifts up his voice at the midnight hour, the female attendant takes heed to his discontent; if in the early morning at the cock crowing, or the eventide, she is there. They who watch and guard the infancy of men are like faithful sentinels, always on duty.

The fifth commandment will take the reader by surprise. It is rather remarkable that the young Hebrews should have been told to honor their mothers, when the whole drift of the teaching thus far has been to throw contempt on the whole sex. In what way could they show their mothers honor? All the laws and customs forbid it. Why should they make any such manifestations? Scientists claim that the father gives the life, the spirit, the soul, all there is of most value in existence. Why honor the mother, for giving the mere covering of flesh. It was not her idea, but the father's, to start their existence. He thought of them, he conceived them. You might as well pay the price of a sack of wheat to the field, instead of the farmer who sowed it, as to honor the mother for giving life. According to the Jewish code, the father is the great factor in family life, the mother of minor consideration. In the midst of such teachings and examples of the subjection and degradation of all womankind, a mere command to honor the mother has no significance.   E. C. S.

CHAPTER VII.

Exodus xxxii

1 And when the people saw that Moses delayed to come down out of the mount, the people gathered themselves together unto Aaron, and said unto him, Up, make us gods, which shall go before us ; for *as for* this Moses, the man that brought us up out of the land of Egypt, we wot not what is become of him.

2 And Aaron said unto them, Break off the golden earrings, which *are* in the ears of your wives, of your sons, and of your daughters, and bring *them* unto me.

And all the people brake off the golden earrings which *were* in their ears, and brought *them* unto Aaron.

And he received *them* at their hand, and fash-ioned it with a graving tool, after he had made it a molten calf : and they said, These *be* thy gods, O Israel, which brought thee up out of the land of Egypt.

5 And when Aaron saw *it*, he built an altar before it ; and Aaron made proclamation, and said, To-morrow *is* a feast to the Lord.

6 And they rose up early on the morrow, and offered burnt offerings, and brought peace offerings, and the people sat down to eat and to drink, and rose up to play.

7 ¶ And the Lord said unto Moses, Go, get thee down ; for thy people, which thou broughtest out of the land of Egypt, have corrupted *themselves.*

S O tired were the children of Israel waiting at the foot of Mount Sinai for the return of Moses, that Aaron to pacify them made a golden calf which they worshipped. To procure the gold he took the jewelry of the women young and old, men never understanding how precious it is to them, and the great self-sacrifice required to part with it. But as the men generally give it to them during courtship, and as wedding presents, they feel that they have a vested right therein for emergencies.

It was just so in the American Revolution, in 1776, the first delicacy the men threw overboard in Boston harbor was the tea, woman's favorite beverage. The tobacco and whiskey, though heavily taxed, they clung to with the tenacity of the devil-fish. Rather than throw their luxuries overboard they would no doubt have succumbed to King George's pretensions. Men think that self-sacrifice is the most charming of all the cardinal virtues for women, and in order to keep it in healthy working order, they make opportunities for its illustration as often as possible. I would fain teach women that self-development is a higher duty than self-sacrifice.

The pillar of cloud for day and light for night, that went before the children of Israel in the wilderness, was indeed a marvel. It was an aqueous cloud that kept them well watered by day, and shadowed from the heat of the sun ; by night it showed its light side to the Israelites, and its dark side to whatever enemy might pursue them. It is supposed that about 3,200,000 started on this march with 165,000 children. They carried all their provisions, cooking utensils, flocks, herds and all the gold, silver, precious stones and rich raiment that they borrowed (stole) of the Egyptians, besides the bones of the twelve sons of Jacob. It is said the Israelites spent forty years wandering in the wilderness, kept there because of their wickedness, though they might have accomplished the journey in a few weeks. They disobeyed the commandments given them by Moses, and worshipped a golden calf, so they journeyed through deep waters, woe and tribulation. Fire was always a significant emblem of Deity, not only among the Hebrews but many other ancient nations, hence men have adopted it as a male emblem. They talk of Moses seeing God ; but Moses says : "ye saw no manner of similitude on the day the Lord spoke unto me on Mount Horeb out of the cloud of fire." E. C. S.

CHAPTER VIII.

Exodus xxxiv.

12 Take heed to thyself, lest thou make a covenant with the inhabitants of the land whither thou goest, lest it be for a snare in the midst of thee ;

13 But ye shall destroy their altars, break their images, and cut down their groves :

14 For thou shalt worship no other god : for the Lord, who *is* a jealous God.

15 Lest thou make a covenant with the inhabitants of the land, and they go after their gods, and do sacrifice unto their gods, and *one* call thee, and thou eat of his sacrifice ;

16 And thou take of their daughters unto thy sons, and their daughters go after their gods, and make thy sons go after their gods.

23 ¶ Thrice in the year shall all your men children appear before the Lord God, the God of Israel.

24 For I will cast out the nations before thee, and enlarge thy borders ; neither shall any man desire thy land, when thou shalt go up to appear before the Lord thy God thrice in the year.

25 Thou shalt not offer the blood of my sacrifice with leaven ; neither shall the sacrifice of the feast of the passover be left unto the morning.

26 The first of the first fruits of thy land thou shalt bring unto the house of the Lord thy God. Thou shalt not seethe a kid in his mother's milk.

THE Jews did not seem to have an abiding faith in the attractions of their own religion. They evidently lived in constant fear lest their sons and daughters should worship the strange gods of other nations. They seem also to have had most exaggerated fears as to the influence alien women might exert over their sons. Three times in the year all the men were to appear before the Lord. Why the women were not commanded to appear has been a point of much questioning. Probably the women, then as now, were more conscientious in their religious duties, and not so susceptible to the attractions of alien men and their strange gods.

If the Lord had talked more freely with the Jewish women and impressed some of his wise commands on their hearts, they would have had a more refined and religious influence on the men of Israel. But all their knowledge of the divine commands was second hand and through an acknowledged corrupt medium.

"Thou shalt not seethe a kid in his mother's milk." After all the learning critics have bestowed on this passage, the simple meaning, says Adam Clarke, seems to be this : Thou shalt do nothing that may have a tendency to blunt thy moral feelings, or teach thee hardness of heart. Even human nature shudders at the thought of taking the mother's milk to seethe

the flesh of her own dead lamb. With all their cruelty towards alien tribes and all their sacrifices of lambs and kids, there is an occasional touch of tenderness for animal life among the Hebrews that is quite praiseworthy.

Exodus xxxvi.

22 And they came, both men and women, as many as were willing hearted, *and* brought bracelets, and earrings, and rings, and tablets, all jewels of gold ; and every man *offered* an offering of gold unto the Lord.

23 And every man, with whom was found blue, and purple, and scarlet, and fine linen, and goats' *hair*, and red skins of rams, and badgers' skins, brought *them*.

25 And all the women that were wise hearted did spin with their hands, and brought that which they had spun, *both* of blue, and of purple, *and* of scarlet, and of fine linen.

26 And all the women whose heart stirred them up in wisdom spun goats' *hair*.

Women were always considered sufficiently clean to beg, work and give generously for the building and decoration of churches, and the support of the priesthood. They might always serve as inferiors, but never receive as equals.

Great preparations were made for building the Tabernacle, and all the willing hearted were invited to bring all their ornaments and all manner of rich embroideries, and brilliant fancy work of scarlet, blue and purple. As usual in our own day the Jewish women were allowed to give generously, work untiringly and beg eloquently to build altars and Tabernacles to the Lord, to embroider slippers and make flowing robes for the priesthood, but they could not enter the holy of holies or take any active part in the services.

Some women in our times think these unhappy Jewesses would have been much "wiser hearted" if they had kept their jewelry and beautiful embroideries to decorate themselves and their homes, where they were at least satellites of the dinner pot and the cradle, and Godesses at their own altars. Seeing they had no right inside the sacred Temple, but stood looking-glass in hand at the door, it would have indicated more self-respect to have washed their hands of all that pertained to male ceremonies, altars and temples. But the women were wild with enthusiasm, just as they are to-day with fairs and donation parties, to build churches, and they brought such loads of

bric-a-brac that at last Moses compelled them to stop, as the
supply exceeded all reasonable demand. But for the building
of the Tabernacle the women brought all they deemed most
precious, even the most necessary and convenient articles of their
toilets.

Exodus xxxviii.

8 ¶ And he made the laver *of* brass, and the | *women* assembling *at* the door of the tabernacle of
foot of it *of* brass, of the looking glasses of *the* | the congregation.

The men readily accepted the sacrifice of all their jewelry,
rich laces, velvets and silks, their looking glasses of solid
precious metal. These being made of metal could be used for
building purposes. The women carried these with them
wherever they went, and always stood with them in hand at the
door of the Tabernacle, as they were the doorkeepers standing
outside to watch and guard the door from those not permitted
to enter.

An objective view of the manner these women were imposed
upon, wheedled and deceived with male pretensions and the pat
use of the phrase "thus saith the Lord," must make every one
who reads indignant at the masculine assumption, even at this
late day.   E. C. S.

At every stage of his existence Moses was indebted to some
woman for safety and success. Miriam, by her sagacity, saved
his life. Pharaoh's daughter reared and educated him and made
the way possible for the high offices he was called to fill; and
Zipporah, his wife, a woman of strong character and decided
opinions, often gave him good advice. Evidently from the text
she criticised his conduct and management as a leader, and
doubted his supernatural mission, for she refused to go out of
Egypt with him, preferring to remain with her sons under her
father's roof—Jethro, a priest of Midian. After the destruction
of Pharaoh's host, when the expedition, led by Moses seemed to
be an assured success, she followed with her father to join the
leader of the wandering Israelites. (Chapter xviii, 2.)

In the ordinances which follow the ten commandments.

exact judgment and cruel punishment are ordained alike for man and woman ; life for life, eye for eye, tooth for tooth, hand for hand and foot for foot (Chapter xxi, 23).

In pronouncing punishments, woman's individuality and responsibility are always fully recognized, alike in the canon and civil laws, which reflect the spirit of the Mosaic code.

Exodus xxii.

21 ¶ Thou shalt neither vex a stranger, nor oppress him : for ye were strangers in the land of Egypt.

22 ¶ Ye shall not afflict any widow, or fatherless child.

23 If thou afflict them in any wise, and they cry at all unto me, I will surely hear their cry ;

24 And my wrath shall wax hot, and I will kill you with the sword, and your wives shall be widows, and your children fatherless:

This special threat against those who oppress the widow and the fatherless, has a touch of tenderness and mercy, but if the vengeance is to make more widows and fatherless, the sum of human misery is increased rather than diminished. As to the stranger, after his country has been made desolate, his cities burned, his property, cattle, lands and merchandise all confiscated, kind words and alms would be but a small measure of justice under any circumstances.

In closing the book of Exodus, the reader must wonder that the faith and patience of the people, in that long sorrowful march through the wilderness, held out as long as it did. Whether fact or fiction, it is one of the most melancholy records in human history. Whether as a mere work of the imagination, or the real experience of an afflicted people, our finer sentiments of pity and sympathy find relief only in doubts of its truth.   L. D. B.

THE BOOK OF LEVITICUS.

CHAPTER I.

Leviticus iv, vi.

22 When a ruler hath sinned and somewhat through ignorance, *against* any of the commandments of the Lord his God *concerning things* which should not be done, and is guilty.

23 Or if his sin, wherein he hath sinned, come to his knowledge ; he shall bring his offering, a kid of the goats, a male without blemish :

27 ¶ And if any one of the common people sin through ignorance, while he doeth *somewhat against* any of the commandments of the Lord *concerning things* which ought not to be done, and be guilty ;

28 Then he shall bring his offering, a kid of the goats, a female without blemish, for his sin.

14 ¶ And this *is* the law of the meat offering: the sons of Aaron shall offer it before the Lord. before the altar.

15 And he shall take of it his handful, of the flour of the meat offering, and of the oil thereof, and all the frankincense which *is* upon the meat offering, and shall burn *it* upon the altar *for* a sweet savour, *even* the memorial of it, unto the Lord.

18 All the males among the children of Aaron shall eat of it. It *shall be* a statute for ever in your generations concerning the offerings of the Lord made by fire : every one that toucheth them shall be holy.

THERE seems to have been some distinction of sex even in the offerings of male and female animals. For rulers, priests and people of distinction male animals were required, but for the common people a female lamb or goat would do. There is a difference of opinion among writers as to tne reason of this custom, some say because all female animals were considered unclean, others that the females were too valuable for wholesale slaughter. Farmers use the male fowls for the table because the hens are too valuable producing eggs and chickens. The fact has some significance, though Adam Clarke throws no light on it, he says "the whole sacrificial system in this book refers to the coming sacrifice of Christ; without this spiritual reference, the general reader can feel no spiritual interest in this book." For burnt offerings males were required, but for peace offerings and minor sins the female would answer.

As the idea of sacrifice to unknown gods, was the custom with all nations and religions, why should the Jewish have more significance than that of any other people. For swearing, an offence to ears polite, rather than eternal justice, a female creature or turtle dove might be offered.

The meat so delicately cooked by the priests, with wood and coals in the altar, in clean linen, no woman was permitted to taste, only the males among the children of Aaron. Seeing that the holy men were the cooks, it seems like a work of super-erogation to direct them to clean themselves and their cooking utensils. Perhaps the daughters of Israel were utilized for that work.

It is clearly shown that child-bearing among the Jews was not considered a sacred office and that offerings to the Lord were necessary for their purification, and that double the time was necessary after the birth of a daughter.

In several of the following chapters the sins of men and women are treated on equal grounds, hence they need no special comments. In reading many of these chapters we wonder that an expurgated edition of these books was not issued long ago. We trust the volume we propose to issue may suggest to the next Revising Committee of gentlemen the propriety of omitting many texts that are gross and obscene, especially if the Bible is to be read in our public schools.

Leviticus x.

12 ¶ And Moses spake unto Aaron, and unto Eleazar and unto Ithamar, his sons that were left, Take the meat offering that remaineth of the offerings of the Lord made by fire, and eat it without leaven beside the altar: for it *is* most holy.

13 And ye shall eat it in the *holy place*, because it *is* thy due, and thy sons' due, of the sacrifices of the Lord made by fire: for so I am commanded.

14 And the wave breast and heave shoulder shall ye eat in a *clean place;* thou, and thy sons, and thy daughters with thee: for *they be* thy due, and thy sons' due, *which* are given out of the sacrifices of peace offerings of the children of Israel.

Why the daughters cannot eat with the sons in the thirteenth verse and may in the fourteenth we cannot conjecture. We notice, however, that where the sons eat alone is called a "holy place," where the daughters eat with them it is called simply a "clean place." We are thankful, however, that in the distribution of meats the women come in occasionally for a substantial meal in a clean place.

All the directions given in the eighteenth chapter are for men and women alike, for all nations and all periods of human development. The social habits and sanitary conditions prescribed are equally good for our times as when given by Moses to the children of Israel. The virtue of cleanliness so sedulously taught cannot be too highly commended. E. C. S.

CHAPTER II.

Leviticus xix.

3 ¶ Ye shall fear every man his mother, and his father, and keep my sabbaths : I *am* the Lord your God.

20 ¶ And whosoever cohabits with a bondmaid, betrothed to a husband, and not at all redeemed, nor freedom given her ; she shall be scourged : they shall not be put to death, because she was not free.

21 And he shall bring his trespass offering unto the Lord, unto the door of the tabernacle of the congregation, *even* a ram for a trespass offering.

22 And the priest shall make an atonement for him with the ram of the trespass offering before the Lord for his sin which he hath done : and the sin which he hath done shall be forgiven him.

BY what possible chance the mother is mentioned first here, it is difficult to conjecture, but we do see the cruel injustice of the comparative severity of the punishment for man and woman for the same offence. The woman is scourged, the man presents the priest with a ram and is forgiven.

Leviticus xx.

9 ¶ For every one that curseth his father or his mother shall be surely put to death : he hath cursed his father or his mother ; his blood *shall be* upon him.

21 And if a man shall take his brother's wife, it *is* an unclean thing : he hath uncovered his brother's nakedness ; they shall be childless.

27 ¶ A man also or woman that hath a amiliar spirit, or that is a wizard, shall surely be put to death : they shall stone them with stones ; their blood *shall be* upon them.

Clarke remarks that all language that tends to lessen respect for father or mother, is included in this judgment. In this chapter we have still further directions for race and family purity. I suppose in the 21st verse we have that stumbling-block in the British Parliament whenever the deceased wife's sister's bill comes up for passage. Here, too, those who in times past have persecuted witches, will find justification for their cruelties. The actors in one of the blackest pages in human history, claim Scripture authority for their infernal deeds. Far into the eighteenth century in England, the clergy dragged innocent women into the courts as witches, and learned judges pronounced on them the sentence of torture and death. The chapter on witchcraft in Lecky's History of Rationalism, contains the most heartrending facts in human history. It is unsafe to put unquestioned confidence in all the vagaries of mortal man. While women were tortured, drowned and burned by the thousands, scarce one wizard to a hundred was ever condemned. The marked distinction in the treatment of the sexes, all through the Jewish dispensation, is curious and depressing, especially as we see the trail of the serpent all through history, wherever their form of religion has made its impress. In the old common law of our Saxon fathers, the Jewish code is essentially reproduced. This same distinction of sex appears in our own day. One code of morals for men, another for women. All the opportunities and advantages of life for education, self-support and self-development freely accorded boys, have, in a small measure, been reluctantly conceded to women after long and persevering struggles.

Leviticus xxii.

12 If the priest's daughter also be *married* unto a stranger, she may not eat of an offering of the holy things.

13 But if the priest's daughter be a widow, or divorced, and have no child, and is returned unto her father's house, as in her youth, she shall eat of her father's meat : but there shall no stranger eat thereof.

These restrictions on the priests' daughters would never be tolerated by the priests' sons should they marry strangers. The individuality of a woman, the little she ever possessed, is obliterated by marriage.

Leviticus xxiv.

10 ¶ And the son of an Israelitish woman, whose father *was* an Egyptian, went out among the children of Israel : and this son of the Israelitish *woman* and a man of Israel strove together in the camp ;

11 And the Israelitish woman's son blasphemed the name *of the LORD*, and cursed. And they brought him unto Moses : (and his mother's name *was* Shelomith, the daughter of Dibri, of the tribe of Dan :)

The interesting fact here is that a woman is dignified by a name, the only one so mentioned in the book of Leviticus. This is probably due to the fact that the son's character was so disreputable that he would reflect no lustre on his father's family, and so on his maternal ancestors rested his disgrace. If there had been anything good to tell of him, reference would no doubt have been made to his male progenitors.

Leviticus xxvi.

26 *And* when I have broken the staff of your bread, ten women shall bake your bread in one oven, and they shall deliver *you* your bread again by weight: and ye shall eat, and not be satisfied.

29 And ye shall eat the flesh of your sons, and the flesh of your daughters shall ye eat.

There could be no greater punishment in ordinary life than for ten women to bake in one oven. As every woman would necessarily look at her pies and cakes two or three times, that would involve a frequent looking in, which might make the contents heavy as lead. A current of cold air rushing in too often, would wreck the most perfect compound. But perhaps heavy bread was intended as part of the punishment of the people for their sins. Some commentators say that the labors of the ten women are symbolical of the poverty of the family. When people are in fortunate circumstances, the women are supposed, like the lilies of the valley, to neither toil nor spin, but when the adverse winds blow they suddenly find themselves compelled to use their own brains and hands or perish.

The 29th verse at last gives us one touch of absolute equality, the right to be eaten. This Josephus tells us really did occur in the sieges of Samaria by Benhadad, of Jerusalem by the Chaldeans, and also in the last siege of Jerusalem by the Romans. E. C. S.

Amid the long list of directions for sacrifices and injunctions against forbidden actions, chapter xii gives the law of purification, not only degrading motherhood by the observance of certain ceremonies and exclusion from the sanctuary, but by discriminating against sex, honoring the birth of a son above that of a daughter.

According to the Levitical law, the ewe lambs were not used for sacrifices as offerings to the Lord, because they were unclean. This was an idea put forth by the priests and Levites. But there was a better and more rational reason. To sacrifice the ewes was to speedily deplete the flocks, but beyond a certain number needed as sires for the coming generation, the males could be put to no better use than to feed the priests, the refuse of the animal, the skin, feet, etc., constituted the sacrifice to the Lord.

Bishop Colenso, in his remarkable work on the Pentateuch, gives the enormous number of lambs annually sacrificed by the Hebrews. A certain portion of the flocks were assigned to the priests, who were continually provided with the best mutton.

L. D. B.

THE BOOK OF NUMBERS.

CHAPTER I.

Numbers i.

And the Lord spake unto Moses in the wilderness of Sinai, saying,

2 Take ye the sum of all the congregation of the children of Israel, after their families, by the house of their fathers, with the number of *their* names, every male by their polls :

32 ¶ These *are* those which were numbered of the children of Israel by the house of their fathers : all those that were numbered of the camps throughout their hosts *were* six hundred thousand and three thousand and five hundred and fifty.

IN this chapter Moses is commanded to number the people and the princes of the tribe, males only, and by the houses of their fathers. As the object was to see how many effective men there were able to go to war, the priests, the women, the feeble old men and children were not counted. Women have frequently been classified with priests in some privileges and disabilities. At one time in the United States the clergy were not allowed to vote nor hold office. Like women, they were considered too good to mingle in political circles. For them to have individual opinions on the vital questions of the hour might introduce dissensions alike into the church and the home.

This census of able bodied men still runs on through chapter ii, and all these potential soldiers are called children of their fathers. Although at this period woman's chief duty and happiness was bearing children, no mention is made of the mothers of this mighty host, though some woman had gone to the gates of death to give each soldier life ; provided him with rations long before he could forage for himself, and first taught his little feet to march to tune and time. But, perhaps, if we could refer to the old Jewish census tables we might find that the able bodied males of these tribes, favorites of Heaven, had all sprung, Minerva-like, from the brains of their fathers, and that only the priests, the feeble old men and the children had mothers to care for them, in the absence of the princes and soldiers.

However, in some valuable calculations of Schencher we learn that there was some thought of the mothers of the tribes by German commentators. We find in his census such references as the following: The children of Jacob by Leah. The children of Jacob by Zilpah. The children of Jacob by Rachel. The children of Jacob by Bilhah. But even this generous mention of the mothers of the tribe of Jacob does not satisfy the exacting members of the Revising Committee. We feel that the facts should have been stated thus: The children of Leah, Zilpah, Rachel and Bilhah by Jacob, making Jacob the incident instead of the four women. Men may consider this a small matter on which to make a point, but in restoring woman's equality everywhere we must insist on her recognition in all these minor particulars, and especially in the Bible, to which people go for their authority on the civil and social status of all womankind.

E. C. S.

CHAPTER II.

Numbers v.

1 And the Lord spake unto Moses, saying,

2 Command the children of Israel, that they put out of the camp every leper, and every one that hath an issue, and whosoever is defiled by the dead ;

3 Both male and female that they defile not their camps.

11 ¶ And the Lord spake unto Moses, saying,

12 If any man's wife go aside, and commit a trespass against him.

14 And the spirit of jealousy come upon him, and she be defiled ; or if she be not defiled :

15 Then shall the man bring his wife unto the priest, and he shall bring her offering for her, the tenth *part of an ephah of barey meal ;* he shall pour no oil upon it, nor put frankincense thereon ; for it *is* no offering of jealousy.

17 And the priest shall take holy water in an earthen vessel ; *and of the dust that* is it, the floor of the tabernacle the priest shall take, and put *it* into the water:

18 And the priest shall set the woman before the Lord and *uncover the woman's* head, and put the offering of memorial in her hands, which *is* the jealousy offering, and the priest shall have in his hand the bitter water that causeth the curse :

19 And the priest shall charge her by an oath, and say unto the woman, if thou hast not gone aside be thou free from this bitter water that causeth the curse:

20 But if thou hast gone aside, and if thou hast been defiled.

21 Then the priest shall charge the woman with an oath of cursing, and the priest shall say unto the woman, The Lord make thee a curse and an oath among thy people.

24 And he shall cause the woman to drink the bitter water that causeth the curse :

25 Then the priest shall take the jealousy offering out of the woman's hand, and shall wave the offering before the Lord, and offer it upon the altar :

26 And the priest shall take a handful of the offering, *even* the memorial thereof, and burn *it* upon the altar, and afterwards shall cause the woman to drink the water.

27 And when he hath made her to drink the water, then it shall come to pass, *that* if she be defiled, and have done tresspass against her husband, that the water that causeth the curse shall enter into her, *and become* bitter.

28 And if the woman be not defiled, but be clean : then she shall be free.

AT the first blush it seems very cruel for the Jewish God to order the diseased and unfortunate to be thrown out of the camp and left in the wilderness. But commentators suggest that they must have had a sanatorium near by where the helpless could be protected. Though improbable, still the suggestion will be a relief to sensitive souls. This ordinarice of Moses probably suggested the first idea of a hospital. The above account of the unfortunate wife was called "trial by ordeal," of which Clarke gives a minute description in his commentaries. It was common at one time among many nations, the women in all cases being the chief sufferers as in the modrn trials for witchcraft. If the witch was guilty when thrown into the water she went to the bottom, if innocent she floated on the surface and was left to sink, so in either case her fate was the same. As men make and execute the laws, prescribe and administer the punishment, "trials by a jury or ordeal" for women though seemingly fair, are never based on principles of equity. The one remarkable fact in all these social transgressions in the early periods as well as in our modern civilization is that the penalties whether moral or material all fall on woman. Verily the darkest page in human history is the slavery of women!

The offering by the priest to secure her freedom was of the cheapest character. Oil and frankincense signifying grace and acceptableness were not permitted to be used in her case. The woman's head is uncovered as a token of her shame, the dust from the floor signifies contempt and condemnation, compelling the woman to drink water mixed with dirt and gall is in the same malicious spirit. There is no instance recorded of one of these "trials by ordeal" ever actually taking place, as divorce was so easy that a man could put away his wife at pleasure, so he need not go to the expense of even "a tenth part of an ephah of barley," on a wife of doubtful faithfulness. Moreover the woman upon whom it was proposed to try all these pranks might be innocent, and the jealous husband make himself ridiculous in the eyes of the people. But the publication of these ordinances no doubt had a restraining influence on the young and heedless daughters of Israel, and they serve as land-marks in man's system of jurisprudence, to show us how far back he has been consistent in his unjust legislation for woman.

E. C. S.

CHAPTER III.

Numbers xii.

And Miriam and Aaron spake against Moses because of the Ethiopian woman whom he had married.

2 And they said, Hath the Lord indeed spoken only by Moses? hath he not spoken also by us? And the Lord heard it.

3 (Now the man Moses was very meek, above all the men which were upon the face of the earth.)

5 And the Lord came down in the pillar of the cloud and stood in the door of the tabernacle and called Aaron and Miriam, and they both came forth.

6 And He said, Hear now my words: If there be a prophet among you, I, the Lord, will make myself known unto him in a vision, and will speak unto him in a dream.

8 With him will I speak mouth to mouth, even apparently, and not in dark speeches;

and the similitude of the Lord shall he behold: wherefore then were ye not afraid to speak against my servant Moses?

9 And the anger of the Lord was kindled against them: and He departed.

10 And the cloud departed from off the tabernacle; and, behold, Miriam became leprous, white as snow; and Aaron looked upon Miriam, and behold, she was leprous.

11 And Aaron said unto Moses, Alas, my lord, I beseech thee, lay not the sin upon us, wherein we have done foolishly, and wherein we have sinned.

13 And Moses cried unto the Lord, saying Heal her now, O God, I beseech thee.

15 And Miriam was shut out from the camp seven days: and the people journeyed not till Miriam was brought in again.

H ERE we have the first mention of Moses's second marriage, but the name of the woman is not given, though she is the assigned cause of the sedition. Both Aaron and Miriam had received a portion of the prophetic genius that distinguished Moses, and they naturally thought that they should have some share in the government, at least to make a few suggestions, when they thought Moses made a blunder. Miriam was older than Moses, and had at this time the experience of 120 years. When Moses was an infant on the River Nile, Miriam was intrusted by his parents to watch the fate of the infant in the bulrushes and the daughter of Pharaoh in her daily walks by the river side. It was her diplomacy that secured the child's own mother for his nurse in the household of the King of Egypt.

It is rather remarkable, if Moses was as meek as he is represented in the third verse, that he should have penned that strong assertion of his own innate modesty. There are evidences at this and several other points that Moses was not the sole editor of the Pentateuch, if it can be shown that he wrote any part of it.

Speaking of the punishment of Miriam, Clarke in his commentaries says it is probable that Miriam was chief in this mutiny; hence she was punished while Aaron was spared. A mere excuse for man's injustice; had he been a woman he would have shared the same fate. The real reason was that Aaron was a priest. Had he been smitten with leprosy, his sacred office would have suffered and the priesthood fallen into disrepute.

As women are supposed to have no character or sacred office, it is always safe to punish them to the full extent of the law. So Miriam was not only afflicted with leprosy, but also shut out of the camp for seven days. One would think that potential motherhood should make women as a class as sacred as the priesthood. In common parlance we have much fine-spun theorizing on the exalted office of the mother, her immense influence in moulding the character of her sons; "the hand that rocks the cradle moves the world," etc., but in creeds and codes, in constitutions and Scriptures, in prose and verse, we do not see these lofty pæans recorded or verified in living facts. As a class, women were treated among the Jews as an inferior order of beings, just as they are to-day in all civilized nations. And now, as then, men claim to be guided by the will of God.

In this narrative we see thus early woman's desire to take some part in government, though denied all share in its honor and dignity. Miriam, no doubt, saw the humiliating distinctions of sex in the Mosaic code and customs, and longed for the power to make the needed amendments. In criticising the discrepancies in Moses's character and government, Miriam showed a keen insight into the common principles of equity and individual conduct, and great self-respect and self-assertion in expressing her opinions—qualities most lacking in ordinary women.

Evidently the same blood that made Moses and Aaron what they were, as leaders of men, flowed also in the veins of Miriam. As daughters are said to be more like their fathers and sons like their mothers, Moses probably inherited his meekness and distrust of himself from his mother, and Miriam her self-reliance and heroism from her father. Knowing these laws of heredity, Moses should have averted the punishment of Miriam instead of allowing the full force of God's wrath to fall upon her alone. If Miriam had helped to plan the journey to Canaan, it would no doubt have been accomplished in forty days instead of forty years. With her counsel in the cabinet, the people might have enjoyed peace and prosperity, cultivating the arts and sciences, instead of making war on other tribes, and burning offerings to their gods. Miriam was called a prophetess, as the Lord had, on some occasions, it is said, spoken through her, giving messages to the women. After their triumphal escape from Egypt, Miriam led the women in their songs of victory. With timbrels and dances, they chanted that grand chorus that has been echoed and re-echoed for centuries in all our cathedrals round the globe. Catholic writers represent Miriam "as a type of the Virgin Mary, being legislatrix over the Israelitish women, especially endowed with the spirit of prophecy."

Numbers xx.
Then came the children of Israel, even the whole congregation, into the desert of Zin in the first month : and the people abode in Kadesh; and Miriam died there, and was buried there.

Eusebius says her tomb was to be seen at Kadesh, near the city of Petra, in his time, and that she and her brothers all died in the same year, it is hoped to reappear as equals in the resurrection. E. C. S.

CHAPTER IV.

Numbers vi.

1 And the Lord said unto Moses,

2 Speak unto the children of Israel, and say, When either man or woman shall separate *themselves* to vow a vow of a Nazarite, unto the Lord.

5 All the days of the vow of his separation there shall no razor come upon his head ; until the days be fulfilled, in the which he separateth *himself* unto the Lord, he shall be holy, *and* shall let the locks of the hair of his head grow.

THE Nazarites, both men and women, allowed their hair to grow long, as the hair of the Nazarine was a token of subjection, the man to God, the woman to man. St. Paul no doubt alluded to this custom when he said the woman ought to have power upon her head, that is, wear her hair and veil and bonnet in church as a proof of her subjection to man, as he is to the Lord. The discipline of the church to-day requires a woman to cover her head before entering a cathedral for worship.

The fashion for men to sit with their heads bare in our churches, while women must wear bonnets, is based on this ancient custom of the Nazarine. But as fashion is gradually reducing the bonnet to an infinitesimal fraction it will probably in the near future be dispensed with altogether. A lady in England made the experiment of going to the established church without her bonnet, but it created such an agitation in the congregation that the Bishop wrote her a letter on the impropriety and requested her to come with her head covered. She refused. He then called and labored with her as to the sinfulness of the proceedings, and at parting commanded her either to cover her head or stay away from church altogether. She choose the latter. I saw and heard that letter read at a luncheon in London, where several ladies were present. It was received with peals of laughter. The lady is the wife of a colonel in the British army.

Numbers xxv.

6 ¶ And, behold, one of the children of Israel came and brought unto his brethren a Midianitish woman in the sight of Moses and all the congregation of the children of Israel.

7 And when Phinehas, the son of Eleazar, the son of Aaron the priest, saw *it*, he rose and took a javelin in his hand ;

8 And he went after the man of Israel into the tent, and thrust both of them through, the man of Israel, and the woman.

14 Now the name of the Israelite that was slain, *even* that was slain with the Midianitish woman, *was* Zimri, the son of Salu, a prince of a chief house among the Simeonites.

15 And the name of the Midianitish woman that was slain *was* Cozbi, the daughter of Zur ; he *was* head over a people, *and* of a chief house in Midian.

Some commentators say the tie between Zimri and Cozbi was a matrimonial alliance, understood in good faith by the Midianitish woman. He was a prince and she was a princess. But the Jewish law forbade a man going outside of his tribe for a wife. It was deemed idolatry. But why kill the woman. She had not violated the laws of her tribe and was no doubt ignorant of Jewish law. Other commentators say that Zimri was notorious at the licentious feasts of Baal-poer and that the Midianitish women tempted the sons of Israel to idolatry. Hence the justice of killing both Zimri and Cozbi in one blow. It is remarkable that the influence of woman is so readily and universally recognized in leading the strongest men into sin, but so uniformly ignored as a stimulus to purity and perfection. Unless the good predominates over the evil in the mothers of the race, there is no hope of our ultimate perfection. E. C. S.

The origin of the command that women should cover their heads is found in an old Jewish or Hebrew legend which appears in literature for the first time in Genesis vi. There we are told the Sons of God, that is, the angels, took to wives the daughters of men, and begat the giants and heroes, who were instrumental in bringing about the flood. The Rabbins held that the way in which the angels got possession of women was by laying hold of their hair ; they accordingly warned women to cover their heads in public, so that the angels might not get possession of them. It was believed that the strength of people lay in their hair, as the story of Samson illustrates. Paul merely repeats this warning which he must often have heard at the feet of Gamaliel, who was at that time Prince or President of the Sanhedrim, telling women to have a "power (that is, protection) on their heads because of the angels:" I Corinthians, chapter xi, verse 10. "For this cause ought the woman to have power on her head because of the angels." Thus the command has its origin in an absurd old myth. This legend will be found fully treated in a German pamphlet—Die paulinische Angelologie und Daemonologie. Otto Everling, Gottingen, 1888.

If the command to keep silence in the churches has no higher origin than that to keep covered in public, should so much weight be given it, or should it be so often quoted as having Divine sanction?

The injunctions of St. Paul have had such a decided influence in fixing the legal status of women that it is worth our while to consider their source. In dealing with this question we must never forget that the majority of the writings of the New Testament were not really written or published by those whose names they bear. Ancient writers considered it quite permissible for a man to put out letters under the name of another, and thus to bring his own ideas before the world under the protection of an honored sponsor. It is not usually claimed that St. Paul was the originator of the great religious movement called Christianity, but there is a strong belief that he was divinely inspired. His inward persuasions, and especially his visions appeared as a gift or endowment which had the force of inspiration ; therefore, his mandates concerning women have a strong hold upon the popular mind, and when opponents to the equality of the sexes are put to bay they glibly quote his injunctions.

We congratulate ourselves that we may shift some of these biblical arguments that have such a sinister effect from their firm foundation. He who claims to give a message must satisfy us that he has himself received such message.

L. S.

CHAPTER V.

Numbers xxvii.

1 Then came the daughters of Zelophehad, the son of Hepher, the son of Gilead, the son of Machir, the son of Manasseh, of the families of Manasseh, the son of Joseph; and these are the names of his daughters: Mahlah, Noah, and Hoglah, and Milcah, and Tirzah.

2 And they stood before Moses, and before Eleazar the priest, and before the princes and all the congregation, by the door of the tabernacle of the congregation, saying,

3 Our father died in the wilderness, and he was not in the company of them that gathered themselves together against the Lord in the company of Korah.

4 Why should the name of our father be done away from among his family, because he hath no son? Give us therefore a possession among the brethren of our father.

5 And Moses brought their cause before the Lord.

6 ¶ And the Lord spake unto Moses, saying,

7 The daughters of Zelophehad speak right: thou shalt surely give them a possession of an inheritance among their father's brethren; and thou shalt cause the inheritance of their father to pass unto them.

8 And thou shalt speak unto the children of Israel, saying, If a man die, and have no son, then ye shall cause his inheritance to pass unto his daughter.

9 And if he have no daughter, then ye shall give his inheritance unto his brethren.

10 And if he have no brethren, then ye shall give his inheritance unto his father's brethren.

11 And if his father have no brethren, then ye shall give his inheritance unto his kinsman that is next to him of his family, and he shall possess it; and it shall be unto the children of Israel a statute of judgment, as the Lord commanded Moses.

THE respect paid to the daughters of Zelophehad at that early day is worthy the imitation of the rulers in our own times. These daughters were no doubt fine-looking, well-developed women, gifted with the power of eloquence, able to impress their personality and arguments on that immense assemblage of the people. They were allowed to plead their own case in person before the lawgivers, the priests, and the princes, the rulers in State and Church, and all the congregation, at the very door of the tabernacle. They presented their case with such force and clearness that all saw the justice of their claims. Moses was so deeply impressed that he at once retired to his closet to listen to the still small voice of conscience and commune with his Maker. In response, the Lord said to him: "The daughters of Zelophehad speak right, if a man die and leave no son, then ye shall cause his inheritance to pass unto his daughters." It would have been commendable if the members of the late Constitutional Convention in New York had, like Moses, asked the guidance of the Lord in deciding the rights of the daughters of the Van Rensselaers, the Stuyvesants, the Livingstons, and the Knickerbockers. Their final action revealed the painful fact that they never thought to take the case to the highest court in the moral universe. The daughters of Zelophehad were fortunate in being all of one mind ; none there to plead the fatigue, the publicity. the responsibility of paying taxes and investing property, of keeping a bank account, and having some knowledge of mathematics. The daughters of Zelophehad were happy to accept all the necessary burdens, imposed by the laws of inheritance, while the daughters of the Knickerbockers trembled at the thought of assuming the duties involved in self-government.

As soon as Moses laid the case before the Lord, He not only allowed the justice of the claim, but gave "a statute of judgment," by which the Jewish magistrates should determine all such cases in the division of property in the land of Canaan in all after ages.

When the rights of property were secured to married women in the State of New York in 1848, a certain class were opposed to the measure, and would cross the street to avoid speaking to the sisters who had prayed and petitioned for its success. They did not object, however, in due time to use the property thus secured, and the same type of women will as readily avail themselves of all the advantages of political equality when the right of suffrage is secured.　　　　　　　　　　　　E. C. S.

――――――

The account given in this chapter of the directions as to the division or inheritance of property in the case of Zelophehad, and his daughters shows them to be just, because the daughters are to be treated as well as the sons would be ; but the law thereafter given, apparently suggested by this querying of Zelophehad's daughters in reference to their father's possessions is obviously unjust, in that it gives no freedom to the owner of property as to the disposition of the same after his death, *i. e.* leaves him without power to will it to any one, and leaves unmentioned the female relatives as heirs at law. Only "brethren" and "kinsman" are the words used, and it is very plain that only males were heirs, except where a man had no son, but had one or more daughters. "The exception proves the rule." P. A. H.

CHAPTER VI.

Numbers xviii

11 And this *is* thine; the heave offering of their gift, with all the wave offerings of the children of Israel: I have given them unto thee, and to thy sons and to thy daughters with thee, by a statute for ever: every one that is clean in thy house shall eat of it.

19 All the heave offerings of the holy things, which the children of Israel offer unto the LORD, have I given thee, and thy sons and thy daughters with thee, by a statute for ever: it *is* a covenant of salt for ever before the LORD unto thee and to thy seed with thee.

THE house of Aaron was now thoroughly confirmed in the priesthood, and the Lord gives minute directions as to the provisions to be made for the priests. The people then, as now, were made to feel that whatever was given to them was given to the Lord, and that "the Lord loveth a cheerful giver." That their minds might be at peace and always in a devout frame, in communion with God, they must not be perplexed with worldly cares and anxieties about bread and raiment for themselves and families. Whatever privations they suffered themselves, they must see that their priests were kept above all human wants and temptations. The Mosaic code is responsible for the religious customs of our own day and generation. Church property all over this broad land is exempt from taxation, while the smallest house and lot of every poor widow is taxed at its full value. Our Levites have their homes free, and good salaries from funds principally contributed by women, for preaching denunciatory sermons on women and their sphere. They travel for half fare, the lawyer pleads their cases for nothing, the physician medicates their families for nothing, and generally in the world of work they are served at half price. While the common people must be careful not to traduce their neighbors lest they be sued for libel, the Levite in surplice and gown from his pulpit (aptly called the coward's castle) may smirch the fairest characters and defame the noblest lives with impunity.

This whole chapter is interesting reading as the source of priestly power, that has done more to block woman's way to freedom than all other earthly influences combined. But the chief point in this chapter centers in the above verses, as the daughters of the Levites are here to enjoy an equal privilege with the sons. Scott tells us "that covenants were generally ratified at an amiable feast, in which salt was always freely used, hence it became an emblem of friendship." Perhaps it was the purifying, refining influence of this element that secured these friendly relations between the sons and daughters of the priesthood on one occasion at least. From the present bitter, turbulent tone of our Levites, I fear the salt we both manufacture and import must all have lost its savor.   E. C. S.

CHAPTER VII.

Numbers xxii.

21 And Balaam rose up in the morning, and saddled his ass, and went with the princes of Moab.

22 ¶ And God's anger was kindled because he went : and the angel of the LORD stood in the way for an adversary against him. Now he was riding upon his ass, and his two servants *were* with him.

23 And the ass saw the angel of the LORD standing in the way, and his sword drawn in his hand : and the ass turned aside out of the way, and went into the field : and Balaam smote the ass, to turn her into the way.

24 But the angel of the LORD stood in a path of the vineyards, a wall *being* on this side, and a wall on that side.

25 And when the ass saw the angel of the LORD, she thrust herself unto the wall, and crushed Balaam's foot against the wall : and he smote her again.

26 And the angel of the LORD went further, and stood in a narrow place, where *was* no way to turn either to the right hand or to the left.

27 And when the ass saw the angel of the LORD, she fell down under Balaam : and Balaam's anger was kindled, and he smote the ass with a staff.

28 And the LORD opened the mouth of the ass, and she said unto Balaam, What have I done unto thee, that thou hast smitten me these three times?

29 And Balaam said unto the ass, Because thou hast mocked me ; I would there were a sword in mine hand, for now would I kill thee.

30 And the ass said unto Balaam, Am not I thine ass, upon which thou hast ridden ever since *I was* thine unto this day? was I ever wont to do so unto thee? And he said, Nay.

31 Then the LORD opened the eyes of Balaam, and he saw the angel of the LORD standing in the way, and his sword drawn in his hand : and he bowed down his head, and fell flat on his face.

32 And the angel of the LORD said unto him, Wherefore hast thou smitten thine ass these three times? Behold, I went out to withstand thee, because *thy* way is perverse before me :

33 And the ass saw me, and turned from me these three times : unless she had turned from me, surely now also I had slain thee, and saved her alive.

34 And Balaam said unto the angel of the LORD, I have sinned ; for I knew not that thou stoodest in the way against me : now therefore, if it displease thee, I will get me back again.

THE chief point of interest in this parable of Balaam and his ass, is that the latter belonged to the female sex. This animal has been one of the most remarkable characters in literature. Her virtues have been quoted in the stately cathedral, in the courts of justice, in the editorial sanctum, in both tragedy and comedy on the stage, to point a moral and adorn a tale. Some of the fairest of Eve's daughters bear her baptismal name, and she has been immortalized in poetry and prose. Wordsworth sends her with his Peter Bell to enjoy the first flowers of early spring. To express her love of the beautiful "upon the pivot of her skull she turned round her long left ear" while stolid Peter makes no sign—

"A primrose by a river's brim
A yellow primrose was to him,
And it was nothing more."

The courage and persistence of the ass has made her as famous in war as in literature. She is a marked feature everywhere in military stations, alike in the camp and the field, and her bray always in the minor key, gives a touch of pathos to the music of the band ! The ass accompanied Deborah and Barak when they went to fight their great battle, she has gone with pioneers in all their weary wanderings, and has taken an active part in the commerce of the world, bearing the heaviest burdens though poorly fed and sheltered. At one time this animal voted at three successive elections in the state of New York. The property qualification being $250, just the price of a jackass, Ben Franklin facetiously asked "if a man must own a jackass in order to vote,—who does the voting, the man or the jackass?" It so happened once that the same animal passed into the hands of three different owners, constituting all the earthly possessions of each at that time and thus by proxy she was represented at the polls. Yet with this world-wide fame, this is the first time the sacred historian has so richly endowed and highly complimented any living thing of the supposed inferior sex. Far wiser than the master who rode her, with a far keener spiritual insight than he possessed, and so intensely earnest and impressible, that to meet the necessities of the occasion, she suddenly exercised the gift of speech. While Balaam was angry, violent, stubborn and unreasonable, the ass calmly manifested all the cardinal virtues. Obedient to the light that was in her, she was patient under abuse, and tried in her mute way to save the life of her tormentor from the sword of the angel. But when all ordinary warnings of danger proved unavailable, she burst into speech and opened the eyes of her stolid master. Scott, who considers this parable a literal fact, says in his commentaries, "The faculty of speech in man is the gift of God and we cannot comprehend how we ourselves articulate. We need not therefore be surprised that the Lord made use of the mouth of the ass to rebuke the madness of His prophet, and to shame him by the reproof and example of a brute. Satan spoke to Eve by a subtle male serpent, but the Lord chose to speak to Balaam by a she ass, for He does not use enticing words of man's wisdom, but works by instruments and means that men despise."

Seeing that the Lord has endowed "the daughters of men" also with the gift of speech, and they may have messages from Him to deliver to "the sons of God," it would be wise for the prophets of our day to admit them into their Conferences, Synods and General Assemblies, and give them opportunities for speech.

The appeal of the meek, long suffering ass, to her master, to remember her faithfulness and companionship from his youth up, is quite pathetic and reminds one of woman's appeals and petitions to her law-givers for the last half century. In the same language she might say to her oppressors, to fathers, husbands, brothers and sons, have we not served you with faithfulness; companions from your youth up; watched you through all your infant years; and carried you triumphantly through every danger ? When at the midnight hour or the cock crowing, your first born lifted up his voice and wept, lo! we were there, with water for his parched lips; a cool place for his aching head; or patiently for hours to pace with him the chamber floor. In youth and manhood what have we not done to add to your comfort and happiness; ever rejoicing in your triumphs and sympathizing in your defeats?

This waiting and watching for half a century to recover our civil and political rights and yet no redress, makes the struggle seem like a painful dream in which one strives to fly from some impending danger and yet stands still. Balaam, unlike our masters, confessed that he had sinned, but it is evident from his conduct that he felt no special contrition for disobedience to the commands of his Creator, nor for his cruelty to the creature. So merely to save his life he sulkily retraced his steps with a determination still to consider Barak's propositions. Whether he took the same ass on the next journey does not appear.

It must have been peculiarly humiliating to that proud man, who boasted of his eyes being open and seeing the vision of the Almighty, to be reproved and silenced by the mouth of a brute. As the Lord appeared first to the ass and spake by her, he had but little reason to boast that his eyes were opened by the Lord. The keen spiritual insight and the ready power of speech with which the female sex has been specially endowed, are often referred to with ridicule and reproach by stolid, envious observers of the less impressible sex. E. C. S.

CHAPTER VIII.

Numbers xx.

1 And Moses spake unto the heads of the tribes concerning the children of Israel, saying, This *is* the thing which the Lord hath commanded.

2 If a man vow a vow unto the Lord, or swear an oath to bind his soul with a bond ; he shall not break his word, he shall do according to all that proceedeth out of his mouth.

3 If a woman also vow a vow unto the Lord, and bind *herself* by a bond, *being* in her father's house in her youth ;

4 And her father hear her vow, and her bond wherewith she hath bound her soul, and her father shall hold his peace at her ; then all her vows shall stand, and every bond wherewith she hath bound her soul shall stand.

5 But if her father disallow her in the day that he heareth, not any of her vows, or of her bonds wherewith she had bound her soul, shall stand ; and the Lord shall forgive her, because her father disallowed her.

6 And if she had at all a husband, when she vowed, or uttered aught out of her lips, wherewith she bound her soul ;

7 And her husband heard *it*, and held his peace at her in the day that he heard *it ;* then her vows shall stand, and her bonds wherewith she bound her soul shall stand.

8 But if her husband disallowed her on the day that he heard *it*, then he shall make her vow which she vowed, and that which she uttered with her lips, wherewith she bound her soul, of none effect ; and the Lord shall forgive her.

9 But every vow of a widow, and of her that is divorced, wherewith they have bound their souls, shall stand against her.

13 Every vow, and every binding oath to afflict the soul, her husband may establish it, or her husband may make it void.

14 But if her husband altogether hold his peace at her from day to day ; then he establisheth all her vows, or all her bonds, which *are* upon her: he confirmeth them, because he held his peace at her in the day that he heard *them*.

15 But if he shall any ways make them void after that he hath heard *them ;* then he shall bear her iniquity.

16 These *are* the statutes, which the Lord commanded Moses, between a man and his wife, between the father and his daughter, *being yet* in her youth in her father's house.

A VOW is a religious promise made to God, and yet in the face of such a definition is placed the authority of husband and father between the woman and her God. God seems thus far to have dealt directly with women when they sinned, but in making a religious vow, or dedication of themselves to some high purpose, their fathers and husbands must be consulted. A man's vow stands ; a woman's is always conditional. Neither wisdom nor age can make her secure in any privileges, though always personally responsible for crime. If she have sufficient intelligence to decide between good and evil, and pay the penalty for violated law, why not make her responsible for her words and deeds when obedient to moral law. To hold woman in such an attitude is to rob her words and actions of all moral character. We see from this chapter that Jewish women, as well as those of other nations, were held in a condition of perpetual tutelage or minority under the authority of the father until married and then under the husband, hence vows if in their presence if disallowed were as nothing. That Jewish men appreciate the degradation of woman's position is seen in a part of their service in which each man says on every Sabbath day, "I thank Thee, oh Lord, that I was not born a woman!" and the woman meekly responds, "I thank Thee, oh Lord, that I am what I am, according to Thy holy will."

The injunction in the above texts in regard to the interference of fathers is given only once, while the husband's authority is mentioned three times. If the woman was betrothed, even the future husband had the right to disallow her vows. It is supposed by some expositors that by a parity of reason minor sons should have been under the same restrictions as daughters, but if it were intended, it is extraordinary that daughters alone should have been mentioned. Scott, in extenuating the custom, says: "Males were certainly allowed more liberty than females; the vows of the latter might be adjudged more prejudicial to families; or the sons being more immediately under the father's tuition might be thought less liable to be inveigled into rash engagements of any kind."

E. C. S.

Woman is here taught that she is irresponsible. The father or the husband is all. They are wisdom, power, responsibility. But woman is a nonentity if still in her father's house, or if she has a husband. I object to this teaching. It is unjust to man that he should have the added responsibility of his daughter's or wife's word, and it is cruel to woman because the irresponsibility is enslaving in its influence. It is contrary to true Gospel teaching, for only in freedom to do right can a soul dwell in that love which is the fulfilling of the law.

The whole import of this chapter is that a woman's word is worthless, unless she is a widow or divorced. While an unmarried daughter, her father is her surety; when married, the husband allows or disallows what she promises, and the promise is kept or broken according to his will. The whole Mosaic law in this respect seems based upon the idea that a woman is an irresponsible being; and that it is supposed each daughter will marry at some time, and thus be continually under the control of some male—the father or the husband. Unjust, arbitrary and debasing are such ideas, and the laws based upon them. Could the Infinite Father and Mother have give them to Moses? I think not.   **P. A. H.**

CHAPTER IX.

Numbers xxxi.

9 And the children of Israel took *all* the women of Midian captives, and their little ones, and took the spoil of all their cattle, and all their flocks, and all their goods.

10 And they burnt all their cities wherein they dwelt, and all their goodly castles with fire.

12 And they brought the captives, and the prey, and the spoil, unto Moses and Eleazar the priest, and unto the congregation of the children of Israel, unto the camp, at the plains of Moab, which *are* by the Jordan *near* Jericho.

14 And Moses was wroth with the officers of the host, *with* the captains over thousands, and captains over hundreds, which came from the battle.

15 And Moses said unto them, have ye saved all the women alive?

16 Behold, these caused the children of Israel, through the counsel of Balaam, to commit tresspass against the Lord in the matter of Peor, and there was a plague among the congregation of the Lord.

17 Now therefore kill every male among the little ones, and kill every woman that hath known man.

18 But all the women children, that have not known a man keep alive for yourselves.

25 ¶ And the Lord spake unto Moses, saying,

26 Take the sum of the prey that was taken, *both* of man and of beast, thou, and Eleazar the priest , and the chief fathers of the congregation :

31 And Moses and Eleazar the priest did as the Lord commanded Moses.

32 And the booty, *being* the rest of the prey which the men of war had caught, was six hundred thousand and five thousand sheep.

33 And threescore and twelve thousand beeves.

34 And threescore and one thousand asses

35 And thirty and two thousand persons in of women that had not known man.

IT appears from the enumeration here of the booty, that the Israelites took in this war against the Midianites seventy-two thousand beeves, six hundred and seventy-five thousand sheep, sixty-one thousand asses and thirty-two thousand women virgins, beside the women and children killed, (as they said) by God's order. The thirty-two thousand wornen and women children were given to the soldiers and the priests. Why should the social purity societies in England and America who believe in the divine origin of all Scripture object to the use of wornen children by their statesmen and soldiers when the custom was permitted to the chosen people of Israel ? True, the welfare of the priests, lawgivers and soldiers was carefully guarded in selecting for them the purest of the daughters of the Midianites.

Surely such records are enough to make the most obstinate believer doubt the divine origin of Jewish history and the claim of that people to have been under the special guidance of Jehovah. Their claim to have had conversations with God daily and to have acted under His commands in all their tergiversations of word and action is simply blasphemous. We must discredit their pretensions, or else the wisdom of Jehovah himself. "Talking with God," at that period was a mere form of speech, as "tempted of the devil" was once in the records of our courts. Criminals said "tempted of the devil, I did commit the crime." This chapter places Moses and Eleazar the priest, in a most unenviable light according to the moral standard of any period of human history. Verily the revelations in the *Pall Mall Gazette* a few years ago, pale before this wholesale desecration of women and children. Bishop Colenso in his exhaustive work on the Pentateuch shows that most of the records therein claiming to be historical facts are merely parables and figments of the imagination of different writers, composed at different periods, full of contradictions, interpolations and discrepancies.

He shows geologically and geographically that a flood over the whole face of the earth was a myth. He asks how was it possible to save two of every animal, bird and creeping thing on both continents and get them safely into the ark and back again to their respective localities. How could they make their way from South America up north through the frigid zone and cross over the polar ices to the eastern continent and carry with them the necessary food to which they had been accustomed, they would all have perished with the cold before reaching the Arctic circle. While the animals from the northern latitudes would all perish with heat before reaching the equator. What a long weary journey the animals, birds and fowls would have taken from Japan and China to Mount Ararat. The parable as an historical fact is hedged with impossibilities and so is the whole journey of forty years from Egypt to Canaan; but if we make up our minds to believe in miracles then it is plain sailing from Genesis to the end of Deuteronomy. Both Ezra and Jeremiah are said to have written the last book of the Pentateuch, and some, question whether Moses was the author of either. Bishop Colenso also questions the arithmetical calculations of the historians in regard to the conquest of the Midianites, as described in the book of Numbers.   E. C. S.

But how thankful we must be that we are no longer obliged to believe, as a matter of fact, of vital consequence to our eternal hope, each separate statement contained in the Pentateuch, such for instance, as the story related in Numbers xxxi!—where we are told that a force of twelve thousand Israelites slew *all* the males of the Midianites, took captive *all* the females and children, seized *all* their cattle and flocks, (seventy-two thousand oxen, sixty-one thousand asses, six hundred and seventy-five thousand sheep,) and *all* their goods, and burnt *all* their cities, and *all* their goodly castles, without the loss of a single man,—and then, by command of Moses, butchered in cold blood all the women, except "the women-children and virgins, to be given to the priests and soldiers."

They amounted to thirty-two thousand, mostly, we suppose, under the age of sixteen. We may fairly reckon that there were as many more under the age of forty, and half as many more above forty, making altogether eighty thousand females, of whom, according to the story, Moses ordered forty-eight thousand to be killed, besides (say) twenty thousand young boys. The tragedy of Cawnpore, where three hundred were butchered, would sink into nothing, compared with such a massacre, if, indeed, we were required to believe it.

The obvious intention of Moses, as shown in these directions, was to keep the Jewish race from amalgamation. But the great lawgiver seems to have ignored the fact, or been ignorant of it, that transmission of race qualities is even greater through the female line than through the male, and if they kept the women children for themselves they were making sure the fact that in days to come there would be Jewish descendants who might be Jews in name, but, through the law of heredity, aliens in spirit. The freedom of the natural law will make itself evident, for so-called natural law is divine.   P. A. H.

Zipporah the wife of Moses was a Midianite, Jethro her father was a priest of some sagacity and consideration. When he met Moses in the desert he gave him valuable advice about the government of his people, which the great lawgiver obeyed.

The sons of Zipporah and Moses, Gershon and Eliezer, were therefore of Midianite blood, yet Moses sent an army of twelve thousand armed for war; a thousand of each tribe, with orders to slay every man. If the venerable Jethro was still alive he must have been murdered by his grandsons and their comrades. This is a most extraordinary story. If after the men, women and male children were all killed, thirty thousand maidens and young girls still remained, the Midianites must have been too large a tribe to have been wholly destroyed by twelve thousand Israelites, unless the Jewish God fought the battle.

L. D. B.

CHAPTER X.

Numbers xxxvi.

1 And the chief fathers of the families of the children of Gilead drew near, and spake before Moses, and before the princes, the chief fathers of the children of Israel:

2 And they said, The Lord commanded my lord to give the land for an inheritance by lot to the children of Israel: and my lord was commanded by the Lord to give the inheritance of Zelophehad our brother unto his daughters.

3 And if they be married to any of the sons of the *other* tribes of the children of Israel, then shall their inheritance be taken from the inheritance of our fathers, and shall be put to the inheritance of the tribe whereunto they are received: so shall it be taken from the lot of our inheritance.

4 And when the jubilee of the children of Israel shall be, then shall their inheritance be put unto the inheritance of the tribe whereunto they are received:

5 And Moses commanded the children of Israel according to the word of the Lord, saying, The tribe of the sons of Joseph hath said well.

6 ......the Lord doth command concerning the daughters of Zelophehad, saying, Let them marry to whom they think best; only to the family of the tribe of their father shall they marry.

7 So shall not the inheritance of the children of Israel remove from tribe to tribe; for every one of the children of Israel shall keep himself to the inheritance of the tribe of his fathers.

8 And every daughter, that possesseth an inheritance in any tribe of the children of Israel, shall be wife unto one of the family of the tribe of her father, that the children of Israel may enjoy every man the inheritance of his fathers.

10 Even as the Lord commanded Moses, so did the daughters of Zelophehad:

11 ......and were married unto their father's brothers' sons.

IN a former chapter there was a sense of justice shown towards the daughters of Zelophehad, but here a new complication arises. The uncles of these girls had their eyes on the property and perhaps feared that their sons had not found favor in the eyes of their cousins, as they might have seen and admired some fine looking young men from other tribes. So the crafty old uncles moved in time to get a statute passed that would compel daughters to marry in the tribe of their fathers and got a direct command from the Lord to that effect, then the young women, compelled to limit their predilections, married their cousins, setting the laws of heredity quite aside; property in all ages being considered of more importance than persons. Thus, after making some show of justice in giving the daughters of Zelophehad the inheritance of their fathers, the Israelites began to consider the loss to their tribe, if peradventure the five sisters should marry into other tribes and all this property be transferred to their enemies.

They seemed to consider these noble women destitute of the virtue of patriotism, of family pride, of all the tender sentiments of friendship, kindred and home, and so with their usual masculine arrogance they passed laws to compel the daughters of Zelophehad to do what they probably would have done had there been no law to that effect.   These daughters were known by the euphonious names of Mahlah, Tirzah, Hoglah, Milcah and Noah, and they all married their father's brothers' sons.   Cousins on the mother's side would probably have been forbidden.

If Moses, as the mouthpiece of God, aimed to do exact justice, why did he not pass an ordinance giving property in all cases equally to sons and daughters.   E. C. S.

———

Moses gave what appears to be, in the light of this Christian era, a just judgment when he decided that the daughters of Zelophehad should inherit their father's property, but he gave as the law of inheritance the direction that "if a man die, *and have no son*, then ye shall cause his inheritance to pass unto his daughter ;"   thus, as I think, unjustly discriminating between women who have brothers and women who have none, and he goes on further to deal unjustly with women when he directs that the daughters of Zelophehad marry so that the inheritance justly awarded them should not go out of the family of the tribe of their fathers.

"Let them marry to whom they think best," and those words seemingly recognize their righteous freedom.   But immediately he limits that phrase and informs the five women they must only marry in their father's tribe, and were limited also to their father's family.   The result was that each married her own cousin.   If this was contrary to physiological law, as some distinguished physiologists affirm, then they were compelled by the arbitrary law of Moses to break the law of God.
                                                P. A. H.

THE BOOK OF DEUTERONOMY.

CHAPTER I.

THIS book contains an account of what passed in the wilderness the last month of the fortieth year, which is supposed to be written by Ezra, as the history is continued several days after the death of Moses. Moses' farewell address to the children of Israel is full of wisdom, with a touch of pathos. This had been a melancholy year with the Hebrews in the death of Miriam, Aaron and Moses. The manner in which this people were kept wandering up and down on the very verge of the land of Canaan because they were rebellious does seem like child's play. No wonder they were discouraged and murmured. It is difficult from the record to see that these people were any better fitted to enter the promised land at the end of forty years than when they first left Egypt. But the promise that they should be as numerous as the stars in the heavens, according to Adam Clarke, had been fulfilled. He tells us that only three thousand stars can be seen by the naked eye, while the children of Israel numbered at this time six hundred thousand fighting men, beside all the women and children. Astronomers, however, now estimate that there are over seventy-five million stars within the range of their telescopes. If census takers had prophetic telescopes, they could no doubt see the promises to the Hebrews fully realized in that one line of their ambition.

125

Deuteronomy ii.

34 And we took all his cities at that time, and utterly destroyed the men, and the women, and the little ones, of every city, we left none to remain.

Though the women were ignored in all the civil affairs and religious observances of the Jews, yet in making war on other tribes they thought them too dangerous to be allowed to live, and so they killed all the women and children. The women might much better have helped to do the fighting, as it is far easier to die in the excitement of the battlefield than to be murdered in cold blood. In making war on neighboring tribes, the Jewish military code permitted them to take all the pure, virgins and child women for booty to be given to the priests and soldiers, thus debauching the men of Israel and destroying all feelings of honor and chivalry for women. This utter contempt for all the decencies of life, and all the natural personal rights of women as set forth in these pages, should destroy in the minds of women at least, all authority to superhuman origin and stamp the Pentateuch at least as emanating from the most obscene minds of a barbarous age.

Deuteronomy v, vi.

16 ¶ Honour thy father and thy mother, as the Lord thy God hath commanded thee; that thy days may be prolonged, and that it may go well with thee, in the land which the Lord thy God giveth thee.

17 Thou shalt not kill.

18 Neither shalt thou commit adultery.

19 Neither shalt thou steal.

20 Neither shalt thou bear false witness against thy neighbour.

21 Neither shalt thou desire thy neighbour's wife, neither shalt thou covet thy neighbour's house, his field, or his manservant, or his maidservant, his ox, or his ass, or any *thing* that *is* thy neighbour's.

2 That thou mightest fear the Lord thy God, to keep all his statutes and his commandments, which I command thee, thou, and thy son, and thy son's son, all the days of thy life; and that thy days may be prolonged.

The best commentary on these texts is that no Revising Committee of Ecclesiastics has found it necessary to make any suggestions as to whom the commandments are addressed. Suppose we reverse the language and see how one-sided it would seem addressed only to women. Suppose this were the statement. Here is a great lawgiver and he says: "Thou art to keep all God's commandments, thou and thy daughters and thy daughter's daughters, and these are the commandments: 'Thou shalt honor thy mother and thy father.' 'Thou shalt not steal nor lie.' 'Thou shalt not covet thy neighbor's husband, nor *her* field, nor *her* ox, nor anything that is thy neighbor's.'"

Would such commandments occasion no remark among Biblical scholars? In our criminal code to-day the pronouns she, her and hers are not found, yet we are tried in the courts, imprisoned and hung as "he," "him" or "his," though denied the privileges of citizenship, because the masculine pronouns apply only to disabilities. What a hustling there would be among prisoners and genders if laws and constitutions, Scriptures and commandments, played this fast and loose game with the men of any nation.

Deuteronomy iv.

5 Behold, I have taught you statutes and judgments, even as the Lord my God commanded me, that ye should do so in the land whither ye go to possess it.

6 Keep therefore and do *them;* for this *is* your wisdom and your understanding in the sight of the nations, which shall hear all these statutes, and say, Surely this great nation *is* a wise and understanding people.

7 For what nation *is there so* great, who *hath* God *so* nigh unto them, as the Lord our God *is* in all *things that* we call upon him *for?*

8 And what nation *is there so* great, that hath statutes and judgments *so* righteous as all this law, which I set before you this day?

Adam Clarke in his comments on chapter iv, says, "there was no form of worship at this time on the face of the earth that was not wicked and obscene, puerile and foolish and ridiculous, except that established by God himself among the Israelites, and every part of this taken in its connection and reference may be truly called a wise and reasonable service. Almost all the nations of the earth manifested in time their respect for the Jewish religion by copying different parts of the Mosaic code as to civil and moral customs."

As thoughtful, intelligent women, we question all this: First.—We see no evidence that a just and wise being wrote either the canon or civil laws that have been gradually compiled by ecclesiastics and lawgivers. Second.—We cannot accept any code or creed that uniformly defrauds woman of all her natural rights. For the last half century we have publicly and persistently appealed from these laws, which Clarke says all nations have copied, to the common sense of a more humane and progressive age. To-day women are asking to be delivered from all the curses and blessings alike of the Jewish God and the ordinances he established. In this book we have the ten commandments repeated.   E. C. S.

CHAPTER II.

Deuteronomy vii.

1 When the Lord thy God shall bring thee into the land whither thou goest to possess it and hath cast out many nations before thee.

2 Thou shalt smite them, *and* utterly destroy them: thou shalt make no covenant with them, nor shew mercy unto them:

3 Neither shalt thou make marriages with them; thy daughter t ou shalt not give unto his son, nor his daughter shalt thou take unto thy son.

4 For they will turn away thy son from following me.

5 But thus shall ye deal with them: ye shall destroy their altars, and break down their images,

and cut down their groves, and burn their graven images with fire.

6 For thou *art* a holy people.

7 The Lord did not set his love upon you, nor choose you, because ye were more in number than any people; for ye *were* the fewest of all people:

8 But because the Lord loved you, and because he would keep the oath which he had sworn unto your fathers, hath the Lord brought you out with a mighty hand, and redeemed you out of the house of bondmen, from the hand of Pharaoh king of Egypt.

WITH the seven nations that God cast out, the children of Israel were commanded to make no covenants, nor matrimonial alliances lest they should fall into idolatry. As men are more given to wandering in strange countries than women these injunctions are intended specially for them. Adam Clarke says, the heart being naturally inclined to evil, the idolatrous wife would more readily draw aside the believing husband, than the believing husband the idolatrous wife. That being the case, could not the believing wife with her subtle influence have brought over the idolatrous husband ? Why should she not have the power to convert to one religion as well as another, especially as there was no choice between them. There could not have been anything worse than the Jewish religion illustrated in their daily walk and conversation, as described in their books, and if the human heart naturally inclined to evil, as many converts might have been made to the faith of Moses as to any other.

With this consideration it is plain that if the Jews had offered women any superior privileges, above any other tribe, they could have readily converted the women to their way of thinking. The Jewish God seems as vacillating and tempest-tossed between loving and hating his subjects as the most. undiciplined son of Adam. The supreme ideal of these people was pitiful to the last degree and the appeals to them were all on the lowest plane of human ambition. The chief promise to the welldoer was that his descendants should be as numerous as the sands of the sea.

In chapter ix when rebellion at Horeb is described, Aaron only is refered to, and in chapter x when his death is mentioned, nothing is said of Miriam. In the whole recapitulation she is forgotten, though altogether the grandest character of the three, though cast out of the camp and stricken with leprosy, in vengeance, she harbors no resentment, but comforts and cheers the women with songs and dances, all through their dreary march of forty years.

Deuteronony x.

18 He doth execute the judgment of the fatherless and widow, and loveth the stranger, in giving him food and raiment.

19 Love ye therefore the stranger: for ye were strangers in the land of Egypt.

The sacred fabulist has failed to give us any choice examples in which the Jews executed just judgments for widows or fatherless girls; on the contrary in all their dealings with women of all ranks, classes and ages they were merciless and unjust.

As to the stranger, their chief occupation was war and wholesale slaughter, not only of the men on the battlefield, but of innocent women and children, destroying their cities and making their lands desolate. A humane person reading these books for the first time without any glamour of divine inspiration, would shudder at their cruelty and blush at their obscenity.

Those who can make these foul facts illustrate beautiful symbols must have genius of a high order.

Deuteronomy xii.

18 But thou must eat them before the Lord thy God in the place which the Lord thy God shall choose, thou, and thy son, and thy daughter, and thy manservant, and thy maidservant, and the Levite that *is* within thy gates: and thou shalt

rejoice before the Lord thy God in all that thou puttest thine hands unto.

19 Take heed to thyself that thou forsake not the Levite as long as thou livest upon the earth.

If women have been faithful to any class of the human family it has been to the Levite. The chief occupation of their lives next to bearing children has been to sustain the priesthood and the churches.

With continual begging, fairs and donation parties, they have helped to plant religious temples on every hill-top and valley, and in the streets of all our cities, so that the doleful church bell is forever ringing in our ears. The Levites have not been an unqualified blessing, ever fanning the flames of religious persecution they have been the chief actors in subjugating mankind.

E. C. S.

CHAPTER III.

Deuteronomy xiii.

6 ¶ If thy brother, the son of thy mother, or thy son, or thy daughter, or the wife of thy bosom, or thy friend, which *is* as thine own soul, entice thee secretly, saying, Let us go and serve other gods, which thou hast not known, thou, nor thy fathers;

7 *Namely*, of the gods of the people which *are* round about you, nigh unto thee, or far off from thee, from the *one* end of the earth even unto *the other* end of the earth;

8 Thou shalt not consent unto him, nor hearken unto him; neither shall thine eye pity him, neither shalt thou spare, neither shalt thou conceal him;

9 But thou shalt surely kill him; thine hand shall be first upon him to put him to death, and afterwards the hand of all the people.

HERE is the foundation of all the terrible persecutions for a change of faith so lamentable among the Jews and so intensified among the Christians. And this idea still holds, that faith in the crude speculations of unbalanced minds as to the nature of the great first cause and his commands as to the conduct of life, should be the same in the beginning, now and forever. All other institutions may change, opinions on all other subjects may be modified and improved, but the old theologies are a finality that have reached the ultimatum of spiritual thought. We imagine our religion with its dogmas and absurdities must remain like the rock of ages, forever.

Deuteronomy xvi.

11 And thou shalt rejoice before the Lord thy God, thou, and thy son, and thy daughter, and thy manservant, and thy maidservant, and the Levite that *is* within thy gates, and the stranger, and the fatherless, and the widow, that *are* among you, in the place which the Lord thy God hath chosen to place his name there.

14 And thou shalt rejoice in thy feast, thou, and thy son, and thy daughter, and thy manservant, and thy maidservant, and the Levite, the stranger, and the fatherless, and the widow, that *are* within thy gates.

15 Seven days shalt thou keep a solemn feast unto the Lord thy God in the place which the Lord shall choose.

16 ¶ Three times in a year shall all thy males appear before the Lord thy God in the place which he shall choose; in the feast of unleavened bread, and in the feast of weeks, and in the feast of tabernacles.

In the general festivities women of all ranks were invited to take part, but three times a year Moses had something special to say to the men; then women were not allowed to be present. We have no instance thus far in the Jewish economy of any direct communication from God to woman. The general opinion seemed to be that man was an all-sufficient object of worship for them, an idea not confined to that period. Milton makes his Eve with sweet humility say to Adam, "God thy law, thou mine."

This is the fundamental principle on which the canon and civil laws are based, as well as the English classics. It is only in the galleries of art that we see the foreshadowing of the good time coming. There the divine artist represents the virtues, the graces, the sciences, the seasons, day with its glorious dawn, and night with its holy mysteries, all radiant and beautiful in the form of woman. The poet, the artist, the novelist of our own day, are more hopeful prophets for the mother of the race than those who have spoken in the Scriptures.

E. C. S.

Deuteronomy xvii.

1 Thou shalt not sacrifice unto the Lord thy God *any* bullock or sheep, wherein is blemish, *or* any evil favouredness: for that *is* an abomination unto the Lord thy God.

2 ¶ If there be found among you, man or woman, that hath wrought wickedness in the sight of the Lord thy God, in transgressing his covenant:

3 And hath gone and served other gods, and worshipped them, either the sun, or the moon, or any of the host of heaven, which I have not commanded;

4 And it be told thee, and thou hast heard *of it,* and inquired diligently, and, behold, *it be* true, *and* the thing certain, *that* such abomination is wrought in Israel:

5 Then shalt thou bring forth that man or that woman unto thy gates and shalt stone them with stones, till they die.

This is certainly a very effective way of strengthening religious faith. Most people would assent to any religious dogma, however absurd, rather than be stoned to death. As all their healthy tender lambs and calves were eaten by the priests and rulers, no wonder they were so particular to get the best. To delude the people it was necessary to give a religious complexion to the sacrifices and to make God command the people to bring their choicest fruits and grains and meats. It was very easy for these accomplished prestidigitators to substitute the offal for sacrifices on their altars, and keep the dainty fruits and meats for themselves, luxuries for their own tables.

The people have always been deluded with the idea that what they gave to the church and the priesthood was given unto the Lord, as if the Maker of the universe needed anything at our hands. How incongruous the idea of an Infinite being who made all the planets and the inhabitants thereof commanding his creatures to kill and burn animals for offerings to him. It is truly pitiful to see the deceptions that have been played upon the people in all ages and countries by the priests in the name of religion. They are omnipresent, ever playing on human credulity, at birth and death, in affliction and at the marriage feast, in the saddest and happiest moments of our lives they are near to administer consolation in our sorrows, and to add blessings to our joys. No other class of teachers have such prestige and power, especially over woman. E. C. S.

CHAPTER IV.

Deuteronomy xviii.

9 ¶ When thou art come into the land which the Lord thy God giveth thee, thou shalt not learn the abominations of those nations.

10 There shall not be found among you *any one* that maketh his son or his daughter to pass through the fire, *or* that useth divination, *or* an observer of times, or an enchanter, or a witch,

11 Or a charmer, or a consulter with familiar spirits, or a wizard, or a necromancer

12 For all that do these things *are an abom*ination unto the Lord.

ONE would think that Moses with his rod taking the children of Israel through the Red Sea, bringing water out of a rock and manna from heaven, going up into a mountain and there surrounding himself with a cloud of smoke, sending out all manner of pyrotechnics, thunder and lightning, and deluding the people into the idea that there he met and talked with Jehovah, should have been more merciful in his judgments of all witches, necromancers and soothsayers. One would think witches, charmers and necromancers possessing the same power and manifesting many of the same wonders that he did, should not have been so severely punished for their delusions. Moses had taught them to believe in miracles. When the human mind is led to believe things outside the realm of known law, it is prepared to accept all manner of absurdities. And yet the same people that ridicule Spiritualism, Theosophy and Psychology, believe in the ten plagues of Egypt and the passage of the children of Israel through the Red Sea. If they did go through, it was when the tide was low at that point, which Moses understood and Pharaoh did not. Perhaps the difficulty is to be gotten over in much the same way as that employed by the negro preacher who, when his statement, that the children of Israel crossed the Red Sea on the ice, was questioned on the ground that geography showed that the climate there was too warm for the formation of ice, replied: "Why, this happened before there was any geography!" The Jews, as well as the surrounding nations, were dominated by all manner of supernatural ideas. All these uncanny tricks and delusions being forbidden shows that they were extensively practised by the chosen people, as well as by other nations.

Deuteronomy xx, xxi.

14 But the women, and the little ones, and the cattle, and all that is in the city, *even* all the spoil thereof, shalt thou take unto thyself; and thou shalt eat the spoil of thine enemies, which the Lord thy God hath given thee.

10 ¶ When thou goest forth to war against thine enemies, and the Lord thy God hath delivered them into thine hands, and thou hast taken them captive,

11 And seest among the captives a beautiful woman, and hast a desire unto her, that thou wouldest have her to thy wife;

12 Then thou shalt bring her home to thine house; and she shall shave her head, and pare her nails;

13 And she shall put the raiment of her captivity from off her, and shall remain in thine house, and bewail her father and her mother a full month: and after that she shall be thy wife.

14 And it shall be, if thou have no delight in her, then thou shalt let her go whither she will: but thou shalt not sell her at all for money, thou shalt not make merchandise of her, because thou hast *humbled* her.

15 ¶ If a man have two wives, one beloved, and another hated, and they have borne him children, *both* the beloved and the hated: and *if* the firstborn son be hers that was hated:

16 Then it shall be, when he maketh his sons to inherit *that* which he hath, *that* he may not make the son of the beloved firstborn before the son of the hated, *which is indeed* the firstborn:

17 But he shall acknowledge the son of the hated *for* the firstborn, by giving him a double portion of all that he hath: for he *is* the beginning of his strength; the right of the firstborn *is* his.

All this is done if the woman will renounce her religion and accept the new faith. The shaving of the head was a rite in accepting the new faith, the paring of the nails a token of submission. In all these transactions the woman had no fixed rights whatever. In that word "humbled" is included the whole of our false morality in regard to the equal relations of the sexes. Why in this responsible act of creation, on which depends life and immortality, woman is said to be humbled, when she is the prime factor in the relation, is a question difficult to answer, except in her general degradation, carried off without her consent as spoils of war, subject to the fancy of any man, to be taken or cast off at his pleasure, no matter what is done with her. Her sons must be carefully guarded and the rights of the first-born fully recognized. The man is of more value than the mother in the scale of being whatever her graces and virtues may be. If these Jewish ideas were obsolete they might not be worth our attention, but our creeds and codes are still tinged with the Mosaic laws and customs. The English law of primogeniture has its foundation in the above text. The position of the wife under the old common law has the same origin.

When Bishop Colenso went as a missionary to Zululand, the horror with which the most devout and intelligent of the natives questioned the truth of the Pentateuch confirmed his own doubts of the records. Translating with the help of a Zulu scholar he was deeply impressed with his revulsion of feeling at the following passage : "If a man smite his servant, or his maid, with a rod, and he die under his hand, he shall be surely punished. Notwithstanding, if he continue a day or two, he shall not be punished : for *he is his money*." Exodus xxi : 20, 21. "I shall never forget," says the Bishop, "the revulsion of feeling, with which a very intelligent Christian native, with whose help I was translating these last words into the Zulu tongue, first heard them as words said to be uttered by the same great and gracious Being, whom I was teaching him to trust in and adore. His whole soul revolted against the notion, that the Great and Blessed God, the Merciful Father of all mankind, would speak of a servant or maid as mere 'money,' and allow a horrible crime to go unpunished, because the victim of the brutal usage had survived a few hours ! "

Though they had no Pentateuch nor knowledge of our religion, their respect for the mother of the race and their recognition of the feminine element in the Godhead, as shown in the following beautiful prayer, might teach our Bishops, Priests and Levites a lesson they have all yet to learn.

EVENING PRAYER.

"O God, Thou hast let me pass the day in peace : let me pass the night in peace, O Lord, who hast no Lord ! There is no strength but in Thee : Thou alone hast no obligation. Under Thy hand I pass the day ! under Thy hand I pass the night ! Thou art my Mother, Thou my Father ! "

Placing the mother first shows they were taught by Nature that she was the prime factor in their existence. In the whole Bible and the Christian religion man is made the alpha and omega everywhere in the state, the church and the home. And we see the result in the general contempt for the sex expressed freely in our literature, in the halls of legislation, in church convocations and by leading Bishops wherever they have opportunities for speech and whenever they are welcomed in the popular magazines of the day.   E. C. S.

CHAPTER V.

Deuteronomy xxiv.

1 When a man hath taken a wife, and married her, and it come to pass that she find no favour in his eyes, then let him write her a bill of divorcement, and give *it* in her hand, and send her out of his house.

2 And when she is departed out of his house, she may go and be another man's *wife.*

3 And *if* the latter husband hate her, and write her a bill of divorcement, and giveth *it* in her hand, and sendeth her out of his house : or if the latter husband die, which took her *to be* his wife ;

4 Her former husband, which sent her away, may not take her again to be his wife, after that she is defiled ; for that *is* abomination before the Lord : and thou shalt not cause the land to sin, which the Lord thy God giveth thee *for* an inheritance.

5 ¶ When a man hath taken a new wife, he shall not go out to war, neither shall he be charged with any business : *but* he shall be free at home one year, and shall cheer up his wife which he hath taken.

ALL the privileges accorded man alone, are based on the principle that women have no causes for divorce. If they had equal rights in law and public sentiment, a large number of cruel, whiskey drinking and profane husbands, would be sued for divorce before wives endured one year of such gross companionship.

There is a good suggestion in the text, that when a man takes a new wife he shall stay at home at least one year to cheer and comfort her. If they propose to have children, the responsible duties of parents should be equally shared as far as possible. In a busy commercial life, fathers have but little time to guard their children against the temptations of life, or to prepare them for its struggles, and the mother educated to believe that she has no rights or duties in public affairs, can give no lessons on political morality from her standpoint. Hence the home is in a condition of half orphanage for the want of fathers, and the State suffers for need of wise mothers.

It was customary among the Jews to dedicate a new house, a vineyard just planted, or a betrothed wife to the Lord with prayer and thanksgiving, before going forth to public duties. This idea is enforced in several different chapters, impressing on men with families that there are periods in their lives when "their sphere is home" their primal duty to look after the wife, the house and the vineyard.

Deuteronomy xxv.

5 ¶ If brethren dwell together, and one of them die, and have no child, the wife of the dead shall not marry without unto a stranger : her husband's brother shall take her to wife.

6 And it shall be, *that* the firstborn which she beareth shall succeed in the name of his brother *which is* dead, that his name be not put out of Israel.

7 And if the man like not to take his brother's wife, then let his brother's wife go up to the gate

unto the elders, and say, my husband's brother refuseth to raise up unto his brother a name in Israel, he will not perform the duty of my husband's brother.

8 Then the elders of his city shall call him, and speak unto him : and *if* he stand *to it*, and say, I like not to take her :

9 Then shall his brother's wife come unto him in the presence of the elders, and loose his shoe from off his foot.

I would recommend these texts to the consideration of the Bishops in the English House of Lords. If a man may marry a deceased brother's wife, why not a deceased wife's sister ? English statesmanship has struggled with this problem for generations, and the same old platitudes against the deceased wife's sister's bill are made to do duty annually in Parliament.

Deuteronomy xxviii.

56 The tender and delicate woman among you, which would not adventure to set the sole of her foot upon ground for delicateness and tenderness, her eye shall be evil toward her husband of her bosom, and toward her son, and toward her daughter, and toward her children which she shall bear ; for she shall eat them for want of all *things* secretly in the siege and straitness, wherewith thine enemy shall distress thee in thy gates.

64 Blessed *shall be* the fruit of thy body, and the fruit of thy ground, and the fruit of thy cattle, the increase of thy kine, and the flocks of thy sheep.

68 And the Lord shall bring thee into Egypt again with ships, by the way whereof I spake unto thee, thou shalt see it no more again : and there ye shall be sold unto your enemies for bondmen and bondwomen, and no man shall buy *you*.

This is addressed to men as most of the injunctions are, as to their treatment of woman in general. In enumerating the good things that would come to Israel if the commandments were obeyed, nothing is promised to women, but when the curses are distributed, woman comes in for her share. Similar treatment is accorded the daughters of Eve in modern days. She is given equal privileges with man, in being imprisoned and hung, but unlike him she has no voice in the laws, the judge, the jury, nor the manner of exit to the unknown land. She is denied the right of trial by her own peers; the laws are made by men, the courts are filled with men ; the judge, the advocates, the jurors, all men!

Moses follows the usual ancient idea that in the creation of human life, man is the important factor. The child is his fruit, he is the soul. The spirit the vital spark. The woman merely the earth that warms and nourishes the seed, the earthly environment. This unscientific idea still holds among people ignorant of physiology and psychology. This notion chimes in with the popular view of woman's secondary place in the world, and so is accepted as law and gospel. The word "beget" applied only to men in Scripture is additional enforcement of the idea that the creative act belongs to him alone. This is flattering to male egoism and is readily accepted.   E. C. S.

In the early chapters of this book Moses' praises of Hebrew valor in marching into a land already occupied and utterly destroying men, women and children, seems much like the rejoicing of those who believe in exterminating the aboriginees in America. Evidently Moses believed in the survival of the fittest and that his own people were the fittest. He teaches the necessity of exclusiveness, that the hereditary traits of the people may not be lost by intermarriage. Though the Israelites, like the Puritans, had notable foremothers as well as forefathers, yet it was not the custom to mention them. Perhaps the word fathers meant both, as the word man in Scripture often includes woman. In the preface by Lord Bishop Ely, to what is popularly known as the Speaker's Bible, the remark is made that "whilst the Word of God is one, and does not change, it must touch at new points the changing phases of physical, philological and historical knowledge, and so the comments that suit one generation are felt by another to be obsolete." So, also, it is that with the higher education of women, their wider opportunities and the increasing sense of justice, many interpretations of the Bible are felt to be obsolete, hence the same reason exists for the Woman's Commentary, which is already popularly known as the Woman's Bible.

Deuteronomy is a name derived from the Greek and signifies that this is the second or duplicate law, because this, the last book of the Pentateuch, consists partly in a restatement of the law, as already given in other books. Deuteronomy contains also, besides special commands and advice not previously written, an account of the death of Moses. Johnson's Universal Cyclopedia states that "the authority of this book has been traditionally assigned to Moses, but, of course, the part relating to his death is not supposed to be written by himself, and indeed the last four chapters may have been added by another hand." DeWette declares that Moses could not have been the author. He not only points to the closing chapters as containing proof, but he refers to the anachronisms in earlier chapters, and insists that the general manner in which the Mosaic history is treated belongs to a period after the time of Moses. And Rev. John White Chadwick in his "Bible of To-day" declares that "Prophetism created Deuteronomy." He speaks of Malachi, the last of the Prophets, as the first to mention the Mosaic law, and says that in the eighth century before Christ there was no Mosaic law in any modern sense. The Pentateuch in anything like its present form was still far in the future. Deuteronomy more than a hundred years ahead. Leviticus and Numbers nearly three hundred. * * * The book of Deuteronomy was much more of a manufacture than any previous portion of the Pentateuch. * * * Not Sinai and Wilderness, but Babylon and Jerusalem, witnessed the promulgation of the Levitical law. Its priest was Ezra and not Aaron; but who was its Moses the most patient study is not likely ever to reveal. The roar of Babylon does not give up its dead. It would seem as if the Rev. Dr. George Lansing Taylor shared some of these ideas when, in his poem at the centennial of Columbia College, he said:

> "Great Ezra, Artaxerxes' courtly scholar—
> Doctor, ere old Bologna gave that collar,
> A ready scribe in all the laws of heaven,
> From Babylon ascends, to Zion given,
> Armed with imperial power and proclamation,
> To rear God's house and educate a nation.

As editor for God, the first in story,
He crowns the editorial chair with glory.
Inspired to push Jehovah's mighty plan on
He lays its corner-stone, the Bible canon.
His Bible college, Bible publication,
Convert the city, crown the Restoration,
And fix the beacon date for History's pages
The chronologic milestone of the ages."

This chapter of Deuteronomy in the solemnity and explicitness of its blessing and cursings must produce a deep impression on those who are desirous of pursuing a course which would promote personal and national prosperity. Reading chapter xix and remembering the history of the Jews from Moses to this day I reverently acknowledge the sure word of prophecy therein recorded. Chapter xxx also has high literary merit. Its euphony is in accordance with its solemn but encouraging warnings and promises. It touches the connection divinely ordained and eternally existing between life and goodness, death and sin, emphasizing the apostolic injunction, "cease to do evil, learn to do well." This chapter, giving the last directions of Moses and intimations of his departure from earth, is one of deep interest. How the Lord communicated to him that his end approached does not appear, but deeply impressed with the belief, he naturally called together Joshua and the Levites and gave his final charge. Whether fact or fiction this farewell is deeply interesting. The closing chapters, containing the "song of blessing," comes to all lovers of religious poetry as the swan song of Moses. Though doubting its authorship, one may enjoy its beauty and grandeur. Chapter xxxiv narrates the death of Moses :

"By Nebo's lonely mountain,
On this side Jordan's wave."

It tells briefly the mourning of the children of Israel over their great leader's departure and affirms the appointment of

Joshua, the son of Nun, as his successor, and fitly closes the valuable collection of writings called the Pentateuch.

Since I have proposeed the elimination of some of the coarser portions of Deuteronomy, I wish to add the testimony of Stevens in his "Scripture Speculations," as to the general morality of this ancient code. " Barbarous as they were in many things, childish in more, their laws are as much in advance of them as of their contemporaries,—were even singular for humanity in that age, and not always equaled in ours.   We forget that there were contemporary nations which justified stealing, authorised infanticide, legalized the murder of aged parents, associated lust with worship. None of these blots can be traced on the Jewish escutcheon. By preventing imprisonment for debt, Moses anticipated the latest discovery of modern philanthropy. * * * Even the mercy of Christianity was foreshadowed in his provision for the poor, who were never to cease out of the land; the prospered were to lend without interest, and never to harden their heart against a brother.   The hovel of the poor was a sanctuary, and many a minute safeguard like the return of the debtor's garment at nightfall, to save him from suffering during the chilliness of the night, has waited to be brought to light by our more perfect knowledge of Jewish customs."   But that the Scriptures, rightly interpreted, do not teach the equality of the sexes, I must be permitted to doubt.   We who love the Old and New Testaments take "Truth for authority, and not authority for truth," as did our sainted Lucretia Mott, whose earnest appeals for liberty were often jewelled, as were Daniel Webster's most eloquent speeches, with some texts from the old Hebrew Bible.

P. A. H.

CHAPTER VI.

THE PENTATEUCH.

THE primal requisite for the more accurate understanding of the Bible is its translation from the past to the present tense. It has been studied as history, as the record of a remote past whose truth it has been well-nigh impossible to verify. It should be studied as a record of the present, the present experience of the individual and the race which is to ultimate in the perfect actualization of generic possibilities.

Like the tables of stone the Bible is written on both sides ; or it has a letter which is its exterior and an interior spirit or meaning. The history which constitutes its letter illustrates those principles which constitute its meaning. The formless must be put into form to be apprehended. Mistaking the form for that substance which has been brought to the level of human apprehension by its means, is the error which constitutes the basis of dogmatic theology. Error in a premise compels error in conclusions. It is no wonder that woman's true relation to man and just position in the social fabric has remained unknown. A Moses on Pisgah's height is needed to-day to see and declare this promised land ; and he must be revelator, first, to women themselves, for they especially need enlightenment upon the true nature of the Bible.

So long as they mistake superstition for religious revelation, they will be content with the position and opportunities assigned them by scholastic theology. They will remember and "keep their place" as thus defined. Their religious nature is warped and twisted through generations of denominational conservatism ; which fact, by the way, is the greatest stumbling block in the path of equal suffrage to-day, and one to which the leaders of that movement have seemed unaccountably blind.

Thus woman's strongest foes have been of her own sex ; and

because her sense of duty and religious sentiment have been operative according to a false ideal, unintentionally women have been and will continue to be bigoted until they allow a higher ideal to penetrate their minds; until they see with the eye of reason and logic, as well as with the sentiment which has so long kept them the dependent class. The Bible from beginning to end teaches the equality of man and woman, their relation as the two halves of the unit, but also their distinctiveness in office. One cannot take the place of the other because of the fundamental nature of each. The work of each half in its own place is necessary to the perfect whole.

The man has more prominence than the woman in the Bible because the masculine characters in their succession represent man as a whole—generic man. The exterior or male half is outermost, the interior or female half is covered by the outer. One is seen, the other has to be discerned, and can be discerned by following the harmonious relativity between the two halves of the unit. There is a straight line of ascent from the Adam to the Christ, within which is the straight line of ascent from the Eve to the Mary. The book of Genesis is the substance of the whole Bible, its meaning is the key to the meaning of the whole; it is the skeleton around which the rest is builded. If the remainder of the Old Testament were destroyed its substance could be reconstructed from Genesis. As the bony structure of the physical body is the framework which is filled in and rounded to symmetrical proportions by the muscular tissue, so Genesis is the framework which is symmetrically rounded and filled by the other books, which supply the necessary detail involved in basic principles.

The first chapter of Genesis is not the record of the creation of the world. It is a symbolical description of the composite nature of man, that being which is male and female in one. The personal pronoun "He" belongs to his exterior nature; and the characters which illustrate this nature and the order of its development are men. The pronoun "She" belongs to the interior nature, and all characters—fewer in number—which illustrate it, are women. "Male and female created he them." The second chapter describes the nature and origin of the visible world, the nature and origin of the soul, their relation to each other and to this dual being. With the third chapter begins the symbolical illustration of the soul's existence—of its continuity of existence which is unbroken till its highest possibilities are actualized, till all the inherent capabilities of the dual being are fully manifested.

The leading characters of Genesis—Adam, Enos, Noah, Abraham, Isaac, Jacob and Joseph—seven in number, represent the seven chief stages of the soul's existence which follow each other like the notes in the musical scale. It is our own experience that is there portrayed, both present and prospective. What we as individuals, and nations are now going through in our efforts for betterment, is told in the story of Genesis. More than this, the clue to assured betterment is found there also. This experience is on two lines which are always distinct but never separate—the male and the female. These are indissolubly bound together "from the beginning," the same principles, necessitating the same moral standards and spiritual ideals, and governing both. The largest measure of our individual and national perplexities and sufferings has come from the ignorant straining apart of that which "God hath joined together" and which we can not successfully and permanently "put asunder."

The remaining four books of the Pentateuch, supply the detail beginning between the Adam and Noah of Genesis, rounding out that part of the skeleton. The Exodus from Egypt under the leadership of Moses, represents the soul's growth out of purely sense-consciousness by the help of spiritual perception. Moses is the personification of this faculty inherent in and operative from the eternal *ego*, the dual being, which is "the Lord" of the Bible. The Old Testament presents the outer or masculine nature of this "Lord" as the Jehovah. The New Testament presents the inner or feminine nature as the Virgin.

The children of Israel according to their tribes, represent the ranging characteristics or parts which make up the soul of self-consciousness. They are the "chosen people" because when the soul sees with its spiritual insight as well as with its sensuous outsight, it can, if it will, choose between the two as guides. Their experiences in the wilderness are what we are passing through to-day; for there is now a people who have made this choice and are following the higher leader in their work for the human race, which is the only satisfactory way of working for themselves. But this leader—spiritual perception—cannot put the soul in possession of its promised land—a higher state of existence or quality of self-consciousness. It sees the higher and leads in its direction; but understanding of fundamental, therefore unvarying and always applicable, principles is necessary for that realization which is the attainment of the higher, or its possession.

Moses' death before crossing Jordan illustrates this limitation, which is also the limitation of earnest reformers to-day. They can see for us and point out that which awaits them; but they can never take those others "into the land." They must travel on their own feet.

Joshua, as the leader after Moses, is the personification of this understanding. He is Moses' sepulchre, for Moses is buried in him. Spiritual insight develops understanding which is its continuity. Hence the continuation of experiences under Joshua the "Saviour" through whom the soul takes "possession" of its higher state. In the "wilderness" of transition from the old to the new, mistakes occur which mar their consequences. In this illustration of the Pentateuch, Miriam "speaks against" Moses, is stricken with leprosy and "set without the camp," and the people cannot journey till all is "brought in again."

Woman's intellectual development after ages of repression, has resulted with many of the sex, in an agnosticism which, at first liberal, has grown to be a dogmatic materialism. She "speaks against" spiritual insight and its revelations. In forsaking her dogmas and creeds she has forsaken religion. She is to be "brought in again"—brought to see that religion is of the soul and is individual; while dogma and doctrine are from the sensuous out-side alone. The one tends to true freedom, the other generates bondage. Broadly, women of to-day are of two classes; those who are still held by the conservatism of creeds, and those who have gone to the other extreme through the exhilaration of intellectual activity. Both classes must meet upon a common ground, recognition of fundamental principles and effort to apply them—before the New Testament can become the practical ethical standard.

An outline of a subject so vast and profound as the nature and meaning of the Pentateuch, must necessarily be more or less unsatisfactory. It cannot be detached from the rest of the Bible which is a complete organic body. Its meaning is consecutive and harmonious with first premises, from beginning to end. The obvious inconsistencies and absurdities involve only its letter, which may or may not be true as history without affecting the truth of the book itself which lies in its meaning.

The projectors of "The Woman's Bible" must not avoid the whirlpool of a masculine Bible only, to split upon the rock of a feminine Bible alone. This would be an attempt to separate what is intensely joined together and defeat the end desired. The book is the soul's guide in the fulfilling of its destiny—that destiny which is involved in its origin ; and the soul, in sleep, is sexless. Its faculties and powers are differentiated are masculine and feminine.

If the question is asked "What is your authority for this view of the Bible?" the answer is "I have none but the internal evidence of the book itself. When joined it is self-evident truth, requiring no external authority to give it support."

U. N. G.

APPENDIX.

As the Revising Committee refer to a woman's translation of the Bible as their ultimate authority for the Greek, Latin and Hebrew text, a brief notice of this distinguished scholar is important:

Julia Smith's translation of the Bible stands out unique among all translations. It is the only one ever made by a woman, and the only one, it appears, ever made by man or woman without help. Wyclif, "the morning star of the Reformation," made a translation from the Vulgate, assisted by Nicholas of Hereford. He was not sufficiently familiar with Hebrew and Greek to translate from those tongues. Coverdale's translation was not done alone. In his dedication to the king he says he has humbly followed his interpreters and that under correction. Tyndale, in his translation, had the assistance of Frye, of William Roye, and also of Miles Coverdale. Julia Smith translated the whole Bible absolutely alone, without consultation with any one. And this not once, but five times—twice from the Hebrew, twice from the Greek and once from the Latin. Literalness was one end she kept constantly in view, though this does not work so well with the Hebrew tenses. But she did not mind that. Frequently her wording is an improvement, or brings one closer to the original than the common translation. Thus in I. Corinthians viii, 1, of the King James translation, we have: "Knowledge puffeth up, but charity edifieth." Julia Smith version: "Knowledge puffs up and love builds the house." She uses "love" in place of "charity" every time. And her translation was made nearly forty years before the revised version of our day, which also does the same. Tyndale, in his translation nearly three hundred and seventy-five years ago, made the same translation of this word ; but Julia Smith did not know that and never saw his translation. This word "charity" was one of the words that Sir Thomas More, Lord Chancellor of England, charged Tyndale with mistranslating. The other two words were "priest" and "church," Tyndale calling priests "seniors," and church "congregation." Both Julia Smith and the revised version call them priests and church. And she gives the word "Life" for "Eve:" "And Adam will call his wife's name Life, for she was the mother of all living."

One more illustration : "Now when Jesus was born in Bethlehem of Judea in the days of Herod the king, behold there came wise men from the east to Jerusalem." King James translation. "Now when Jesus was born, etc., behold there came wise men from the sunrisings to Jerusalem." Julia Smith version. She claims to have made a perfectly literal translation, and according to the verdict of competent authorities, Hebrew scholars who have examined her Bible, she has done so. Her work has had the endorsement of various learned men. A Hebrew professor of Harvard College (Prof. Young) called on her soon after her Bible was issued and examined it. He was much astonished that she had translated so correctly without consulting some learned man. He expressed surprise that she should have put the tenses as she did. She said to him : "You acknowledge that I have translated according to the Hebrew idiom?" He replied : "O yes, you have translated literally." That was just what she aimed at, to get an exact literal translation, without regard to smoothness. She received many letters from scholars, all speaking of the exact, or literal translation. Some people have criticised this feature, which is the great merit of the book.

Julia Smith was led to make the translation at the time of the Miller excitement in 1843, when the world was to come to a sudden termination ; when the saints were preparing their robes for ascension into the empyrean, and wicked unbelievers (the vast majority) were to descend as far the other way. She and her family were much interested in Miller's predictions, and she was anxious to see for herself if, in the original Hebrew text of the Bible there was any warrant for Miller's predictions. So she set to work and studied Hebrew, having previously translated the New Testament, and also the Septuagint from the Greek. So absorbed did she become in her work that the dinner bell was unheeded, and she would undoubtedly have many times gone to bed both dinnerless and supperless had not the family called her off from her work.. Once a week she met with, the family and a friend and neighbor, Miss Emily Moseley, to read over and discuss what she had translated during the week. This practice was kept up for several years. When she came to publish the work, (the manuscripts of which had lain in the garret some twenty-five or thirty years) the cashier of the Hartford bank, where the sisters had kept their money, told her she was very foolish to throw away her money printing this Bible ; that she would never sell a copy. She told him it didn't matter whether she did or not ; that she was not doing it to make money ; that she found more satisfaction in spending her money in this way than in spending it all on dress. Thanks to our more enlightened age, this translation did not meet with the opposition the early translators had to contend with. The scholars of those days thought learning should be confined to a select few ; it was, in their view, dangerous to put the Bible into a language the common people could understand, especially women. Here is what one Henry de Knyghton, a learned monk of that day, said : "This Master John Wiclif hath translated the gospel out of Latin into English, which Christ had intrusted with the *clergy and doctors* of the Church that *they* might minister it to the laity and weaker sort, according to the state of the times and the wants of men. But now the gospel is made vulgar and more open to the laity, and *even to women* who can read, than it used to be to the *most learned* of the clergy and those of the best understanding." To say nothing of reading the Bible, what would this learned man have thought of a woman translating it, and five times at that ! It would seem as if the bare suggestion must have stirred his dry bones with indignation.

King James appointed fifty-four men of learning to translate the Bible. Seven of them died and forty-seven carried the work on. Compare this corps of workers with one little woman performing the Herculean task without one suggestion or word of advice from mortal man ! This Bible is ten by seven inches, and is printed in large,

clear type. There are two styles of binding, cloth and sheepskin. The cloth binding was $2.50 at the time it was issued and while Julia Smith lived, and the other
was $3.00, but as they are getting scarcer the price may have gone up. They will
be a rarity in the next century and will be much sought after by bibliomaniacs, to
say nothing of scholars who will want it for its real value. Julia Smith had the plates
of her Bible preserved, but where they are now is more than I know. It was published by the American Publishing Company, of Hartford, in 1876.

Julia Evelina Smith, of Glastonbury, Conn., was one of five sisters of a somewhat
notable family, the father and mother both having strong traits of character and
marked individuality. The mother, Hannah Hickok, was a fine linguist and mathe-
matician. She once made an almanac for her own convenience, almanacs being
rather scarce in those days. She could tell the time of night whenever she happened
to awake by the position of the stars. She was an omnivorous reader and a great
student, and in those days before the invention of stoves, her father, in order to allow
her the requisite retirement to gratify her studious tastes, built her a small glass room.
In the days of the Abby and Julia Smith excitement, when they refused to pay their
taxes, some writer was so wicked as to say that Julia Smith's grandfather shut her
mother up in a glass cage. Seated in this glass enclosure, placed in a south room,
with the sun's rays beating down upon her, as upon a plant in a conservatory, she
could pursue her studies to her heart's content. She was an only child and adored by
her father; and so much did she think of him that in his last illness, when she was
away at school, she rode four hundred miles on horseback in order to see him before
he died.

Julia Smith's father, the Rev. Zephaniah H. Smith, a graduate of Yale, was
settled in Newtown, Conn., near South Britain, where he married Hannah Hickok.
He preached but four years, resigning his position on the ground that the gospel
should be free; that it was wrong to preach for money—ideas promulgated by the
Sandemanians of those days, the followers of Robert Sandeman, a Scotchman, who
organized the sect in England and in this country, it having originated with his
father-in-law, John Glas, the sect being called either Glassites or Sandemanians, the
former being given the preference in Scotland and England. The ideas of these
people were followed out by the Smith family, and at Abby and Julia Smith's funeral,
as at the funerals of those who had gone before them, there was no officiating minister
and no services. Simply a chapter of the Bible was read, and one or two who wished,
made remarks. On a fly-leaf of the Bible Julia Smith read every day was written
the request that she should be buried by her sisters in Glastonbury, and with no name
on the tombstone but that of her own maiden name. This request was followed out.
The names of the Smith sisters are so unique, and inasmuch as they have never been
known to be printed correctly, it may not be out of place to give them here, preceding
them by those of their parents, making a short family record for future reference :

Zephaniah H. Smith, born August 19, 1758. Died February 1, 1836.

Hannah Hickok, born August 7, 1767. Died December 27, 1850.

They were married May 31, 1786.

DAUGHTERS OF THE ABOVE :

Hancy Zephina, born March 16, 1787. Died June 30, 1871.

Cyrinthia Sacretia, born May 18, 1788. Died August 19, 1864.

Laurilla Aleroyla, born November 26, 1789. Died March 19, 1857.

Julia Evelina, born May 27, 1792.   Died March 6, 1886.

Abby Hadassah, born June 1, 1797.   Died July 23, 1878.

Julia was educated at Mrs. Emma Willard's far-famed seminary at Troy, New York.   Abby, the youngest of the family, was the one who added to their fame, when, in November, 1873, at a town meeting in Glastonbury, she delivered a speech against taxation without representation.   She had just attended the first Woman's Congress in New York, and on her way back said she was going to make a speech on taxation ; that she should apply to the authorites to speak in town hall on town meeting day. She and Julia owned considerable property in Glastonbury and their taxes were being increased while those of their neighbors (men) were not.   She applied to the authorities, but they would not let her speak in the hall, so she spoke from a wagon outside to a crowd of people.   This speech was printed in a Hartford paper (the *Courant*) and was copied all over the country, and the cry: "Abby Smith and her cows" was caught up everywhere.   Abby Smith's quaint, simple speeches attracted attention, and the sale of the cows at the sign-post aroused sympathy, and from that time on their fame grew apace.   The hitherto light mail-bags of Glastonbury came loaded with mail matter from all quarters for the Smith sisters.   And this continued for some years, or till the death of Abby in 1878, which was followed by the marriage of Julia the following spring, and the discontinuance of the sale of the cows at the public sign-post.   She married Mr. Amos A. Parker, both being eighty-seven years of age. Julia Smith sold the old family mansion in Glastonbury and bought a house at Parkville, Hartford.   She died there in 1886 and her husband died in 1893, nearly one hundred and two years of age.   F. E. B.

THE WOMAN'S BIBLE

PART II

COMMENTS ON THE OLD AND NEW TESTAMENTS

FROM

JOSHUA TO REVELATION

"OH! RATHER GIVE ME COMMENTATORS PLAIN,
WHO WITH NO DEEP RESEARCHES VEX THE BRAIN;
WHO FROM THE DARK AND DOUBTFUL LOVE TO RUN,
AND HOLD THEIR GLIMMERING TAPERS TO THE SUN."
                                                    —*The Parish Register.*

REVISING COMMITTEE.

"We took sweet counsel together."—Ps. lv., 14.

ELIZABETH CADY STANTON,
REV. PHEBE A. HANAFORD,
CLARA BEWICK COLBY,
REV. AUGUSTA CHAPIN,
URSULA N. GESTEFELD,
MARY SEYMOUR HOWELL,
JOSEPHINE K. HENRY,
MRS. ROBERT G. INGERSOLL,
SARAH A. UNDERWOOD,
ELLEN BATTELLE DIETRICK,*

LILLIE DEVEREUX BLAKE,
MATILDA JOSLYN GAGE,
REV. OLYMPIA BROWN,
FRANCES ELLEN BURR,
CLARA B. NEYMAN,
HELEN H. GARDENER,
CHARLOTTE BEEBE WILBOUR,
LUCINDA B. CHANDLER,
CATHARINE F. STEBBINS,
LOUISA SOUTHWORTH.

FOREIGN MEMBERS.

BARONESS ALEXANDRA GRIPENBERG,   Finland,
URSULA M. BRIGHT,   England,
IRMA VON TROLL-BOROSTYANI,   Austria,
PRISCILLA BRIGHT MCLAREN,   Scotland,
ISABELLE BOGELOT,   France.

---

*Deceased.

COMMENTS ON THE OLD AND NEW TESTAMENTS

FROM

JOSHUA TO REVELATION, BY

ELIZABETH CADY STANTON,

ELLEN BATTELLE DIETRICK, MATILDA JOSLYN GAGE,
LOUISA SOUTHWORTH, FRANCES ELLEN BURR,
LUCINDA B. CHANDLER, REV. PHEBE A. HANAFORD,
ANONYMOUS, CLARA B. NEYMAN.

———

APPENDIX,

LETTERS AND COMMENTS BY

Elizabeth Cady Stanton, Josephine K. Henry, Frances E. Willard, Eva A. Ingersoll, Mary A. Livermore, Irma von Troll-Borostyani, Mrs. Jacob Bright, Rev. Antoinette Brown Blackwell, Anonymous, Rev. Phebe A. Hanaford, Ednah D. Cheney, Sarah A. Underwood, Dr. Elizabeth Blackwell, Alice Stone Blackwell, Ursula N. Gestefeld, E. M., Matilda Joslyn Gage, Sarah M. Perkins, and Catharine F. Stebbins.

———

RESOLUTION

OF

National-American Woman Suffrage Association repudiating "The Woman's Bible," and Speech of
SUSAN B. ANTHONY.

DEDICATED

TO THE MEMORY OF

ELLEN BATTELLE DIETRICK,

IN WHOSE DEATH WE LOST THE ABLEST MEMBER OF OUR

REVISING COMMITTEE.

PREFACE TO PART II.

THE criticisms on "The Woman's Bible" are as varied as they are unreasonable. Both friend and foe object to the title. When John Stuart Mill wrote his "Subjection of Woman" there was a great outcry against that title. He said that proved it to be a good one. The critics said: "It will suggest to women that they are in subjection and make them rebellious." "That," said he, "is just the effect I wish to produce." Rider Haggard's "She" was denounced so universally that every one read it to see who "She" was. Thus the title in both cases called attention to the book.

The critics say that our title should have been "Commentaries on the Bible." That would have been misleading, as the book simply contains short comments on the passages referring to woman. Some say that it should have been "The Women of the Bible;" but several books with that title have already been published. The Rev. T. DeWitt Talmage says: "You might as well have a 'Shoemakers' Bible'; the Scriptures apply to women as well as to men." As the Bible treats women as of a different class, inferior to man or in subjection to him, which is not the case with shoemakers, Mr. Talmage's criticism has no significance.

> "There's nothing so becomes a man
> As modest stillness and humility."

Another clergyman says: "It is the work of women, and the devil." This is a grave mistake. His Satanic Majesty was not invited to join the Revising Committee, which consists of women alone. Moreover, he has been so busy of late years attending Synods, General Assemblies and Conferences, to prevent the recognition of

7

women delegates, that he has had no time to study the languages and "higher criticism."

Other critics say that our comments do not display a profound knowledge of Biblical history or of the Greek and Hebrew languages. As the position of woman in all religions is the same, it does not need a knowledge of either Greek, Hebrew or the works of scholars to show that the Bible degrades the Mothers of the Race. Furthermore, "The Woman's Bible" is intended for readers who do not care for, and would not be convinced by, a learned, technical work of so-called "higher criticism."

The Old Testament makes woman a mere after-thought in creation; the author of evil; cursed in her maternity; a subject in marriage; and all female life, animal and human, unclean. The Church in all ages has taught these doctrines and acted on them, claiming divine authority therefor. "As Christ is the head of the Church, so is man the head of woman." This idea of woman's subordination is reiterated times without number, from Genesis to Revelations; and this is the basis of all church action.

Parts I. and II. of "The Woman's Bible" state these dogmas in plain English, as agreeing fully with Bible teaching and church action. And yet women meet in convention and denounce "The Woman's Bible," while clinging to the Church and their Scriptures. The only difference between us is, we say that these degrading ideas of woman emanated from the brain of man, while the Church says that they came from God.

Now, to my mind, the Revising Committee of "The Woman's Bible," in denying divine inspiration for such demoralizing ideas, shows a more worshipful reverence for the great Spirit of All Good than does the Church. We have made a fetich of the Bible long enough. The time has come to read it as we do all other books, accepting the good and rejecting the evil it teaches.

> "There lives more faith in honest doubt,
> Believe me, than in half the creeds."

Hon. Andrew D. White, formerly President of Cornell University, shows us in his great work, "A History of the Warfare of Science with Theology," that the Bible, with its fables, allegories and endless contradictions, has been the great block in the way of civilization. All through the centuries scholars and scientists have been imprisoned, tortured and burned alive for some discovery which seemed to conflict with a petty text of Scripture. Surely the immutable laws of the universe can teach more impressive and exalted lessons than the holy books of all the religions on earth.

January, 1898.   ELIZABETH CADY STANTON.

THE BOOK OF JOSHUA.

Joshua ii.

1 And Joshua the son of Nun sent out of Shittim two men to spy secretly, saying, Go view the land, even Jericho. And they went, and came into a harlot's house, named Rahab, and lodged there.

2 And it was told the king of Jericho, saying, Behold, there came men in hither to-night of the children of Israel to search out the country.

3 And the king of Jericho sent unto Rahab, saying, Bring forth the men that are come to thee which are entered into thine house: for they be come to search out all the country.

4 And the woman took the two men, and hid them and said thus, There came men unto me, but I wist not whence they *were*.

5 And it came to pass *about the time* of shutting of the gate when it was dark, that the men went out; whither the men went I wot not; pursue after them quickly; for ye shall overtake them.

THIS book gives an account of the final entrance of the children of Israel into the Promised Land. Joshua was the successor of Moses, and performed the same miracle in parting the waters of the Jordan that Moses did to enable his people to pass through the Red Sea. He was seven years fighting his way into the land of Canaan, where he spent the closing years of his life in peace.

There is mention of two women only in this book, though a casual reference is again made to the daughters of Zelophehad, as described in a former chapter.

In saving the spies from their pursuers, Rahab made them promise that when Jericho fell into the hands of Joshua, they would save her and her kinsmen. From the text, it seems that Rahab fully understood the spirit of her time, and with keen insight and religious fervor, marked characteristics of women, she readily entered into the plans of the great general of Israel.

Rahab was supposed to have been a great sinner, her life in many respects questionable; but seeing that victory was with the Israelites, she cast her lot with them. From the text and what we know of humanity in general, it is difficult to decide Rahab's real motive, whether to serve the Lord by helping Joshua to take the land of Canaan, or to save her own life and that of her kinsmen. It is interesting to see that in all national emergencies, leading men are quite willing to avail themselves of the craft and cunning of women, qualities uniformly condemned when used for their own advantage.

There is no more significance, as one of our critics says, in commenting on the myths of the Bible than on Æsop's fables. The difference, however, is this: that in the latter case we admit that they were written by a man; while in the former, they are claimed to have been inspired by God. Though at variance with all natural laws, it is claimed that our eternal salvation depends on believing in the plenary inspiration of the myths of the Scriptures; as the "higher criticisms," written by learned scholars and scientists, are not familiar to women, our comments in plain English may rid them of some of their superstitions.

Though the injustice to woman is the blackest page in sacred history, the distinguished Biblical writers take no note of it whatever. Even Hon. Andrew D. White, though he devotes several pages of his work to the statue of Lot's wife in salt, vouchsafes no criticism on the position of Lot's wife in the flesh, nor of Lot's outrageous treatment of his daughters. The wonder is that women themselves should either believe that such unholy proceedings were inspired by God, or make a fetich of the very book which is responsible for their civil and social degradation.

Joshua x.

11 And it came to pass, as they fled from before Israel, and were in the going down to Beth-horon, that the Lord cast down great stones from heaven upon them unto Azekah, and they died: they were more which died with hailstones than they whom the children of Israel slew with the sword.

12 Then spake Joshua to the Lord in the day when the Lord delivered up the Amorites before the children of Israel, and he said in the sight of Israel, Sun, stand thou still upon Gibeon; and thou, Moon, in the valley of Ajalon.

13 And the Sun stood still, and the Moon stayed, until the people had avenged themselves upon their enemies. Is not this written in the book of Jasher? So the Sun stood still in the midst of heaven, and hasted not to go down about a whole day.

14 And there was no day like that before it or after it, that the Lord hearkened unto the voice of a man: for the Lord fought for Israel.

According to the sacred fabulist, Joshua surpassed Moses in

the wonders which he performed. In taking the city of Jericho, as recorded in Chapter viii., he did not use the ordinary enginery of war, but told his soldiers to blow a simultaneous blast upon their trumpets, while all the people with united shouts should produce such a violent concussion of the air as to bring down the walls of the city. He not only subsidized the atmosphere to overpower his enemies, but he commanded the sun and the moon to stand still to lengthen the day and to lighten the night until this victory was complete.

It seems that the Lord was so well pleased with Joshua's refined military tactics that he suspended the laws of the vast solar system to vindicate the superior prowess of one small tribe on the small planet called the earth. The Lord also resorted to more material and forcible means, sending down tremendous hailstones from heaven, and thus with one fell blow destroyed more of his enemies than the children of Israel did with the sword.

There are no events recorded in secular history that strain the faith of the reader to such a degree as the feats of Joshua. Moses, with his manna and pillar of light in the wilderness and his dazzling pyrotechnics on Mount Sinai, fades into insignificance before these marvellous manifestations by Joshua, with the Canaanites, Jericho, and the sun and moon under his feet. Though teaching the people that all these fables are facts, still the Church condemns prestidigitators, soothsayers, fortune tellers, Spiritualists, witches, and the assumptions of Christian Scientists.

Joshua xv.

16 And Caleb said, He that smiteth Kirjathesepher and taketh it, to him will I give Achsah my daughter to wife.

17 And Othniel, the son of Kenez, the brother of Caleb, took it; and he gave him Achsah his daughter to wife.

18 And it came to pass, as she came unto him, that she moved him to ask of her father a field: and she lighted off her ass; and Caleb said unto her, What wouldest thou?

19 Who answered, Give me a blessing; for thou hast given me a south land; give me also springs of water. And he gave her the upper springs, and the nether springs.

In giving Achsah her inheritance it is evident that the Judges of

Israel had not forgotten the judgment of the Lord in the case of Zelophehad's daughters. He said to Moses, "When a father dies leaving no sons, the inheritance shall go to the daughters. Let this henceforth be an ordinance in Israel." Very good as far as it goes; but in case there were sons, justice demanded that daughters should have an equal share in the inheritance.

As the Lord has put it into the hearts of the women of this Republic to demand equal rights in everything and everywhere, and as He is said to be immutable and unchangeable, it is fair to infer that Moses did not fully comprehend the message, and in proclaiming it to the great assembly he gave his own interpretation, just as our judges do in this year of the Lord 1898.

Achsah's example is worthy the imitation of the women of this Republic. She did not humbly accept what was given her, but bravely asked for more.   We should give to our rulers, our sires and sons no rest until all our rights—social, civil and political—are fully accorded.   How are men to know what we want unless we tell them? They have no idea that our wants, material and spiritual, are the same as theirs; that we love justice, liberty and equality as well as they do; that we believe in the principles of self-government, in individual rights, individual conscience and judgment, the fundamental ideas of the Protestant religion and republican government.

E. C. S.

THE BOOK OF JUDGES.

CHAPTER I.

Judges i.

19 And the Lord was with Judah; and he drave out the inhabitants of the mountain: but could not drive out the inhabitants of the valley, because they had chariots of iron.

Judges ii.

6 And when Joshua had let the people go, the children of Israel went every man unto his inheritance to possess the land.

7 And the people served the Lord all the days of Joshua, and all the days of the elders that outlived Joshua, who had seen all the great works of the Lord, that he did for Israel.

8 And Joshua the son of Nun, the servant of the Lord, died, being a hundred and ten years old.

THIS book, supposed to have been written by Samuel the Prophet, covers a period of 300 years. During all of this time the children of Israel are in constant friction with the Lord and neighboring tribes, never loyal to either. When at peace with the Lord, they are fighting with their neighbors; when at peace with them, worshiping their gods and giving them their daughters in marriage, then the Lord is angry, and vents His wrath on them. Thus, they are continually between two fires; now repenting in sackcloth and ashes, and now, with the help of the Lord, blessed with victories.

Life with them was a brief period of success and defeat. It seems that the Lord, according to their ideas, had His limitations, and could not fight tribes who had iron chariots.

What could iron chariots be in the way of that Great Force which creates cyclones, hurricanes and earthquakes, or the pyrotechnics of a thunderstorm. How little these people knew of the Great Intelligence behind the laws of the universe, with whom they pretended to talk in the Hebrew language, and from whom they claimed to have received directions as to their treatment of women?

In the opening of this book Joshua still governs Israel. After

15

his death, the Lord raised up a succession of Judges, remarkable
for their uprightness and wisdom; but they found it impossible
to keep the chosen people in the straight and narrow path. The
children of Israel did not learn wisdom by experience. They tired
of a rigid code of morals, of a mystical system of theology, and
of the women of their own tribe. There was a fascination in the
manners and the appearance of a new type of womanhood which
they could not resist. There should have been some allowance for
these human proclivities. If the Jews of our day had followed this
tendency of their ancestors and intermarried with other nations, there
would have been by this time no peculiar people to persecute.

The most important feature of this book is the number of remarkable women herein described; six in number, Achsah, Deborah,
Jael, Jephthah's daughter, Delilah, and two whose names are not
mentioned—she who slew Abimelech, and the concubine of a Levite,
whose fate was terrible and repulsive. There are many instances in
the Old Testament where women have been thrown to the mob, like
a bone to dogs, to pacify their passions; and women suffer to-day
from these lessons of contempt, taught in a book so revered by the
people.   E. C. S.

The writer of the Book of Judges is unknown. Professor Moore,
of Andover Theological Seminary, supposes that the author used as
a basis for his work an older collection of tales wherein the heroes
of Israel and the varying fortunes of the people were related, and
which, like all good tales, pointed a moral. In all Jewish literature is to be found the same moral—namely, that the prime cause of
all of the evils which befell the Jewish people was unfaithfulness to
Jehovah. "Adherence to the written law brings God's favor, while
disobedience is followed by God's wrath and punishment."

It is not obedience to the inner truth of the individual soul that is
made the spring of action, but obedience to an external authority, to
a book, to a prophet, to a judge or to a king. In Judges, to woman
in various ways is given an exalted position; she is not the abject

slave or unclean vessel, the drudge, the servile sinner, the nonentity, as depicted in other parts of the Bible.

Woman has at no time of the world's history maintained the high position which she commands to-day in the hearts of the best and most enlightened; but there were stages when her independence was an assured fact. With Christianity came the notion of man's dual nature; the physical was looked upon as sinful; this earth was merely preparatory for a life beyond. Woman, as the mother of the race, was not honored and revered as such, the monastic idea being considered more God-like, she was made the instrument of sin. To be born into this life was not a blessing so long as ascetism ruled supreme.

The Bible has been of service in some respects; but the time has come for us to point out the evil of many of its teachings. It now behooves us to throw the light of a new civilization upon the women who figure in the Book of Judges. We begin with Achsah, a woman of good sense. Married to a hero, she must needs look out for material subsistence. Her husband being a warrior, had probably no property of his own, so that upon her devolved the necessity of providing the means of livelihood. Great men, heroic warriors, generally lack the practical virtues, so that it seems befitting in her to ask of her father the blessing of a fruitful piece of land; her husband would have been satisfied with the south land. She knew that she required the upper and the nether springs to fertilize it, so that it might yield a successful harvest.   C. B. N.

CHAPTER II.

Judges iv.

4 And Deborah, a prophetess, the wife of Lapidoth, judged Israel at that time.

5 And she dwelt under the palm tree of Deborah, between Ramah and Beth-el in Mount Ephraim; and the children of Israel came up to her for judgment.

6 And she sent and called Barak, the son of Abinoam, out of Kedesh-naphtali, and said unto him, Hath not the Lord God of Israel commanded, saying, Go and draw toward Mount Tabor, and take with thee ten thousand men of the children of Naphtali and of the children of Zebulun?

7 And I will draw unto thee, to the river Kishon, Sisera the captain of Jabin's army, with his chariots and his multitude; and I will deliver him into thine hand.

8 And Barak said unto her, If thou wilt go with me, then I will go; but if thou wilt not go with me, then I will not go.

9 And she said, I will surely go with thee; notwithstanding the journey that thou takest shall not be for thine honor; for the Lord shall sell Sisera into the hand of a woman. And Deborah arose, and went with Barak to Kedesh.

10 And Barak called Zebulon and Naphtali to Kedesh; and he went up with ten thousand men at his feet; and Deborah went up with him.

SOME commentators say that Deborah was not married to a man by the name of Lapidoth, that such a terminology is not customary to the name of a person, but of a place. They think that the text should read, Deborah of Lapidoth. Indeed, Deborah seems to have had too much independence of character, wisdom and self-reliance to have ever filled the role of the Jewish idea of a wife.

"Deborah" signifies "bee;" and by her industry, sagacity, usefulness and kindness to her friends and dependents she fully answers to her name. "Lapidoth" signifies "lamps." The Rabbis say that Deborah was employed to make wicks for the lamps in the Tabernacle; and having stooped to that humble office for God's service, she was afterward exalted as a prophetess, to special illumination and communion with God—the first woman thus honored in Scripture.

Deborah was a woman of great ability. She was consulted by the children of Israel in all matters of government, of religion and of war. Her judgment seat was under a palm tree, known ever after as "Deborah's Palm." Though she was one of the great judges of Israel for forty years, her name is not in the list, as it should have been, with Gideon, Barak, Samson and Jephthah. Men have always been slow to confer on women the honors which they deserve.

Deborah did not judge as a princess by any civil authority conferred upon her, but as a prophetess, as the mouthpiece of God, redressing grievances and correcting abuses. The children of Israel appealed to her, not so much to settle controversies between man and man as to learn what was amiss in their service to God; yet she did take an active part in the councils of war and spurred the generals to their duty.

The text shows Barak hesitating and lukewarm in the last eventful battle with Sisera and his host. He flatly refused to go unless Deborah would go with him. She was the divinely chosen leader; to her came the command, "Go to Mount Tabor and meet Sisera and his host." Not considering herself fit to lead an army, she chose Barak, who had already distinguished himself. He, feeling the need of her wisdom and inspiration, insisted that she accompany him; so, mounted on pure white jackasses, they started for the field of battle. The color of the jackass indicated the class to which the rider belonged. Distinguished personages were always mounted on pure white and ordinary mortals on gray or mottled animals.

As they journeyed along side by side, with wonderful insight Deborah saw what was passing in Barak's mind; he was already pluming himself on his victory over Sisera. So she told him that the victory would not be his, that the Lord would deliver Sisera into the hands of a woman. It added an extra pang to a man's death to be slain by the hand of a woman. Fortunately, poor Sisera was spared the knowledge of his humiliation. What a picture of painful contrasts his death presents—a loving mother watching and praying at her window for the return of her only son, while at the same time Jael performs her deadly deed and blasts that mother's hopes forever! What a melancholy dirge to her must have been that song of triumph, chanted by the army of Deborah and Barak, and for years after, by generation after generation.

We never hear sermons pointing women to the heroic virtues of Deborah as worthy of their imitation. Nothing is said in the pulpit to rouse them from the apathy of ages, to inspire them to do and dare

great things, to intellectual and spiritual achievements, in real communion with the Great Spirit of the Universe. Oh, no! The lessons
doled out to women, from the canon law, the Bible, the prayer-books
and the catechisms, are meekness and self-abnegation; ever with
covered heads (a badge of servitude) to do some humble service for
man; that they are unfit to sit as a delegate in a Methodist conference, to be ordained to preach the Gospel, or to fill the office of elder,
of deacon or of trustee, or to enter the Holy of Holies in cathedrals.

Deborah was a poetess as well as a prophetess, a judge as well as
a general. She composed the famous historical poem of that period
on the eventful final battle with Sisera and his hosts; and she ordered
the soldiers to sing the triumphant song as they marched through the
the land, that all the people might catch the strains and that generations might proclaim the victory.

Judges iv.

18 And Jael went out to meet Sisera, and said unto him, Turn in, my Lord, turn in to me; fear not. And when he had turned in unto her into the tent, she covered him with a mantle.

19 And he said unto her, Give me, I pray thee, a little water to drink: for I am thirsty. And she opened a bottle of milk, and gave him to drink, and covered him.

20 Again he said unto her, Stand in the door of the tent, and it shall be, when any man doth come and inquire of thee, and say, Is there any man here? that thou shalt say, No.

21 Then Jael, Heber's wife, took a nail of the tent, and took a hammer in her hand and went softly unto him, and smote the nail into his temples, and fastened it into the ground; for he was fast asleep and weary. So he died.

22 And behold, as Barak pursued Sisera, Jael came out to meet him, and said unto him, Come, and I will show thee the man whom thou seekest. And when he came into her tent, behold, Sisera lay dead, and the nail was in his temples.

The deception and the cruelty practised on Sisera by Jael under
the guise of hospitality is revolting under our code of morality. To
decoy the luckless general fleeing before his enemy into her tent,
pledging him safety, and with seeming tenderness ministering to his
wants, with such words of sympathy and consolation lulling him to
sleep, and then in cold blood driving a nail through his temples,
seems more like the work of a fiend than of a woman.

The song of Deborah and Barak, in their triumph over Sisera,
has been sung in cathedrals and oratorios and celebrated in all time
for its beauty and pathos. The great generals did not forget in the

hour of victory to place the crown of honor on the brow of Jael for what they considered a great deed of heroism. Jael imagined herself in the line of her duty and specially called by the Lord to do this service for his people.

Nations make their ideal gods like unto themselves. At this period He was the God of battles. Though He had made all the tribes, we hope, to the best of His ability; yet He hated all, the sacred fabulist tells us, but the tribe of Israel, and even they were objects of His vengeance half the time. Instead of Midianites and Philistines, in our day we have saints and sinners, orthodox and heterodox, persecuting each other, although you cannot distinguish them in the ordinary walks of life. They are governed by the same principles in the exchanges and the marts of trade.   E. C. S.

Judges v.

Then sang Deborah and Barak, the son of Abinoam, on that day, saying,

2 Praise ye the Lord for the avenging of Israel, when the people willingly offered themselves.

3 Hear, O ye kings; give ear, O ye princes; I, even I will sing unto the Lord; I will sing praise to the Lord God of Israel.

4 Lord, when thou wentest out of Seir, when thou marchedst out of the field of Edom, the earth trembled, and the heavens dropped, the clouds also dropped water.

5 The mountains melted from before the Lord even that Sinai from before the Lord God of Israel.

6 In the days of Shamgar the son of Anath, in the days of Jael, the highways were unoccupied and the travellers walked through byways.

7 The inhabitants of the villages ceased, they ceased in Israel, until that I, Deborah, arose, that I arose a mother in Israel.

The woman who most attracts our attention in the Book of Judges is Deborah, priestess, prophetess, poetess and judge. What woman is there in modern or in ancient history who equals in loftiness of position, in public esteem and honorable distinction this gifted and heroic Jewish creation? The writer who compiled the story of her gifts and deeds must have had women before him who inspired him with such a wonderful personality. How could Christianity teach and preach that women should be silent in the church when already among the Jews equal honor was shown to women? The truth is that Christianity has in many instances circumscribed woman's sphere of action, and has been guilty of great injustice toward the whole sex.

Deborah was, perhaps, only one of many women who held such high and honorable positions. Unlike any modern ruler, Deborah dispensed justice directly, proclaimed war, led her men to victory, and glorified the deeds of her army in immortal song. This is the most glorious tribute to woman's genius and power. If Deborah, way back in ancient Judaism, was considered wise enough to advise her people in time of need and distress, why is it that at the end of the nineteenth century, woman has to contend for equal rights and fight to regain every inch of ground she has lost since then? It is now an assured fact that not only among the Hebrews, but also among the Greeks and the Germans, women formerly maintained greater freedom and power.

The struggle of to-day among the advanced of our sex is to regain and to reaffirm what has been lost since the establishment of Christianity. Every religion, says a modern thinker, has curtailed the rights of woman, has subjected her to man's ruling; in emphasizing the life beyond, the earthly existence became a secondary consideration. We are learning the great harm which comes from this one-sided view of life; and by arousing woman to the dignity of her position we shall again have women like Deborah, honored openly and publicly for political wisdom, to whom men will come in time of need.

Genius knows no sex; and woman must again usurp her Divine prerogative as a leader in thought, song and action. The religion of the future will honor and revere motherhood, wifehood and maidenhood. Asceticism, an erroneous philosophy, church doctrines based not upon reason or the facts of life, issued out of crude imaginings; phantasms obstructed the truth, held in check the wheel of progress. Let our church women turn their gaze to such characters as Deborah, and claim the same recognition in their different congregations.

The antagonism which the Christian church has built up between the male and the female must entirely vanish. Together they will slay the enemies—ignorance, superstition and cruelty. United in every enterprise, they will win; like Deborah and Barak, they will clear the highways and restore peace and prosperity to their people. Like Deborah, woman will forever be the inspired leader, if she will have the courage to assert and maintain her power. Her aspirations must keep pace with the demands of our civilization. "New times teach new duties."

God never discriminates; it is man who has made the laws and compelled woman to obey him. The Old Testament and the New are books written by men; the coming Bible will be the result of the efforts of both, and contain the wisdom of both sexes, their combined spiritual experience. Together they will unfold the mysteries of life, and heaven will be here on earth when love and justice reign supreme.   C. B. N.

———

Judges viii.

30 And Gideon had three score and ten sons: for he had many wives.

31 And his concubine that was in Shechem, she also bare him a son, whose name he called Abimelech.

Judges ix.

52 And Abimelech came unto the tower, and fought against it, and went hard unto the door of the tower to burn it with fire.

53 And a certain woman cast a piece of a millstone upon Abimelech's head, and all to break his skull.

54 Then he called hastily unto the young man, his armour-bearer, and said unto him, Draw thy sword, and slay me, that men say not of me, A woman slew him. And his young man thrust him through, and he died.

Abimelech destroyed the city of Thebez, drove all the people into a tower and then tried to set it on fire, as he had done in many places before in his war on other tribes; but here he lost his life, and at the hand of a woman, which was considered the greatest disgrace which could befall a man. Commentators say that as Sisera and Abimelech were exceptionally proud and lofty, they were thus degraded in their death. Sisera was spared the knowledge of his fate by being taken off when asleep; but Abimelech saw the stone coming and knew that it was from the hand of a woman, an added pang to his death agony. He had no thoughts of his wicked life nor his eternal welfare, but with his dying breath implored his armor-bearer to thrust him through with his sword, that it might not be said that he was slain by the hand of a woman.

Abimelech had three score and ten brethren. It is said that his mother roused his ambition to be one of the judges of Israel. To at-

tain this he killed all his brethren but one, who escaped.   He enjoyed
his ill-gotten honors but a short space of time.   We find many such
stories in the Hebrew mythology which have no foundation in fact.

Judges xi.

30 And Jephthah vowed a vow unto the
Lord, and said, If thou shalt without fail
deliver the children of Ammon into mine
hands,

31 Then it shall be that whatsoever cometh forth of the doors of my house to meet
me, when I return in peace from the children of Ammon, shall surely be the Lord's,
and I will offer it up for a burnt offering.

33 And he smote them from Aroer, even
till thou come to Minnith, even twenty
cities, and unto the plain of the vineyards,
with a very great slaughter. Thus the children of Ammon were subdued before the
children of Israel.

34 And Jephthah came to Mizpeh unto
his house, and, behold, his daughter came
out to meet him with timbrels and with
dances; and she was his only child; beside
her he had neither son nor daughter.

35 And it came to pass, when he saw her,
that he rent his clothes, and said, Alas, my
daughter! thou has brought me very low,
and thou art one of them that trouble me:
for I have opened my mouth unto the
Lord, and I cannot go back.

36 And she said unto him, My father, if
thou hast opened thy mouth unto the Lord,
do to me according to that which hath pro-
ceeded out of thy mouth; forasmuch as the
Lord hath taken vengeance for thee of thine
enemies, even of the children of Ammon.

37 And she said unto her father, Let this
thing be done for me: let me alone two
months, that I may go up and down upon
the mountains, and bewail my virginity, I
and my fellows.

A woman's vow, as we have already seen, could be disallowed at
the pleasure of any male relative; but a man's was considered sacred
even though it involved the violation of the sixth commandment, the
violation of the individual rights of another human being.   These
loving fathers in the Old Testament, like Jephthah and Abraham,
thought to make themselves specially pleasing to the Lord by sacrificing their children to Him as burnt offerings.   If the ethics of their
moral code had permitted suicide, they might with some show of
justice have offered themselves, if they thought that the first-born kid
would not do; but what right had they to offer up their sons and
daughters in return for supposed favors from the Lord?

The submission of Isaac and Jephthah's daughter to this violation
of their most sacred rights is truly pathetic.   But, like all oppressed
classes, they were ignorant of the fact that they had any natural, in-
alienable rights.   We have such a type of womanhood even in our
day.   If any man had asked Jephthah's daughter if she would not
like to have the Jewish law on vows so amended that she might dis-

allow her father's vow, and thus secure to herself the right of life, she would no doubt have said, "No; I have all the rights I want," just as a class of New York women said in 1895, when it was proposed to amend the constitution of the State in their favor.

The only favor which Jephthah's daughter asks, is that she may have two months of solitude on the mountain tops to bewail the fact that she will die childless. Motherhood among the Jewish women was considered the highest honor and glory ever vouchsafed to mortals. So she was permitted for a brief period to enjoy her freedom, accompanied by young Jewish maidens who had hoped to dance at her wedding.

Commentators differ as to the probable fate of Jephthah's daughter. Some think that she was merely sequestered in some religious retreat, others that the Lord spoke to Jephthah as He did to Abraham forbidding the sacrifice. We might attribute this helpless condition of woman to the benighted state of those times if we did not see the trail of the serpent through our civil laws and church discipline.

This Jewish maiden is known in history only as Jephthah's daughter—she belongs to the no-name series. The father owns her absolutely, having her life even at his disposal. We often hear people laud the beautiful submission and the self-sacrifice of this nameless maiden. To me it is pitiful and painful. I would that this page of history were gilded with a dignified whole-souled rebellion. I would have had the daughter receive the father's confession with a stern rebuke, saying: "I will not consent to such a sacrifice. Your vow must be disallowed. You may sacrifice your own life as you please, but you have no right over mine. I am on the threshold of life, the joys of youth and of middle age are all before me. You are in the sunset; you have had your blessings and your triumphs; but mine are yet to come. Life is to me full of hope and of happiness. Better that you die than I, if the God whom you worship is pleased with the sacrifice of human life. I consider that God has made me the arbiter of my own fate and all my possibilities. My first duty is to develop all the powers given to me and to make the most of myself and my own life. Self-development is a higher duty than self-sacrifice. I demand the immediate abolition of the Jewish law on vows. Not with my consent can you fulfill yours." This would have been a position worthy of a brave woman.   E. C. S.

———

The ideal womanhood portrayed by ancient writers has had by far too much sway. The prevailing type which permeates all literature is that of inferiority and subjection. In early times Oriental poets often likened woman to some clear, flawless jewel, and made them serve simply as ornaments, while, on the other hand, they were made subordinate by the legislation of barbarous minds; and men, because of their selfish passion, have inflicted woe after woe upon them. Ancient literature is wholly against the equality of the sexes or the rights of women, and subordinates them in every relation of life.

The writings of the Bible, especially the Old Testament, are no exception to this rule. The reference, "The sons of God and daughters of men," while it admits of many interpolations, legendary or mythical as it may be, portrays the real animus of the Scriptures. To what extent the sentiment of the Hebrews favored sons rather than daughters, and the injustice of this distinction is fully exemplified by the stories of Abraham and Isaac, and of Jephthah and his daughter. Abraham was commanded by his God to sacrifice his son Isaac, after the manner of the Canaanites, who often slew their children and burnt them upon their altars in honor of their deities. But when all was made ready for the sacrifice an angel of Jehovah appeared, the hand of Abraham was stayed, and a ram was made a substitute for the son of promise.

The conditions were quite different in the case of Jephthah and his daughter. The Israelites had been brought very low in their contest with the Ammonites, and they chose the famous warrior, Jephthah, to lead them against their foe, who with warlike zeal summoned the hosts to battle. The risk was enormous, the enemy powerful, and the general, burning for victory, intent on securing the assistance of the Deity, made a solemn and fatal vow.

In the first case it was a direct command of God, but means were found to revoke this explicit command with regard to a son; in the second case it was only a hasty and unwise promise of a general going to war, and the prevailing sentiment of the age felt it unnecessary to evade its fulfillment—the victim was only a girl. The unhappy father must sacrifice his daughter!

What a masculine coloring is given to the rest of the narrative: "A maiden who did not mourn her death, but wandered up and down the mountain mourning her virginity." So much glamor has been thrown by poetry and by song, over the sacrifice of this Jewish maiden, that the popular mind has become too benumbed to perceive its great injustice. The Iphigenias have been many and are still too numerous to awaken compassion. We must destroy the root of this false and pernicious teaching, and plant in its place a just and righteous doctrine.

What women have to win for the race is a theory of conduct which shall be more equitable. The unalterable subserviency of woman in her natural condition can never be overcome and social development progress so long as there is a lack of distributive justice to every living soul without discrimination of sex.   L. S.

CHAPTER III.

Judges xiii.

2 And there was a certain man of Zorah, of the family of the Danites, whose name was Manoah; and his wife was barren.

3 And the angel of the Lord appeared unto the woman, and said unto her, Behold now, thou art barren; but thou shalt conceive, and bear a son.

4 Now therefore beware, I pray thee, and drink not wine nor strong drink, and eat not any unclean thing:

5 For, lo, thou shalt bear a son; and no razor shall come on his head: for the child shall be a Nazarite unto God; and he shall begin to deliver Israel out of the hands of the Philistines.

6 Then the woman came and told her husband, saying, A man of God came unto me, and his countenance was like the countenance of an angel of God, very terrible: but I asked him not whence he was, neither told he me his name:

7 But he said unto me, Behold, thou shalt bear a son; and now drink no wine nor strong drink, neither eat any unclean thing: for the child shall be a Nazarite to God to the day of his death.

8 Then Manoah entreated the Lord, and said, O my Lord, let the man of God which thou didst send come again unto us, and teach us what we shall do unto the child that shall be born.

9 And God hearkened to the voice of Manoah: and the angel of God came again unto the woman as she sat in the field: but Manoah her husband was not with her.

10 And the woman made haste, and ran, and shewed her husband, and said unto him, Behold, the man hath appeared unto me, that came unto me the other day.

11 And Manoah arose, and went after his wife, and came to the man, and said unto him, Art thou the man that spakest unto the woman? And he said, I am.

12 And Manoah said, Now let thy words come to pass. How shall we order the child, and how shall we do unto him?

13 And the angel of the Lord said unto Manoah, Of all that I said unto the woman let her beware.

WE come now to a very interesting incident, giving proof of the remarkable knowledge which the writers had of some intrinsic laws and the power of transmission which, even to-day, are known and adhered to only by a very small minority of wise, thoughtful mothers.   However, the wife of Manoah, the future mother of Samson, is visited by an angel, giving her instructions as to her way of living during pregnancy.   It appears that the writer was acquainted with some pre-natal influences and their effect upon the unborn.

We are just now beginning to investigate the important problem of child culture.   Many good thoughts have been given on this subject by earnest thinkers. A knowledge of these important laws of life will do away with the most harassing evils and sins which human flesh is heir to. Intelligent, free mothers will be enabled to forecast not only the physical, but also the psychical, traits of their offspring. How and why this once recognized knowledge was lost we know not. We may, however, rightly infer that so long as woman was not the arbiter of her own destiny she had no power to make use of this knowledge. Only the thoughful, independent wife can administer the laws and the rules necessary for her own wellbeing and that of her offspring. Freedom is the first prerequisite to a noble life.

Observe how simple and trustful the relation is between this husband and wife. Manoah is thoughtful and ready to unite with his wife in all that the angel had commanded. There is no trace of disunion or of disobedience to the higher law which his wife had been instructed to follow. To her the law was revealed, and he sustained her in its observance. Mark, however, one difference from our interpretation of to-day, and how the omission of it worked out the destruction of the child. All the injunctions received were of a physical nature; strength of body and faith in God were to be the attributes through which Samson was to serve his people. The absence of moral traits is very evident in Samson; and this is the reason why he fell an easy prey to the wiles of designing women. It was not moral, but physical heroism which distinguished Samson from his combatants. Vengeance, cruelty, deceit, cunning devices were practised not only by the Philistines, but likewise by the Nazarite.

The angel who appeared to Manoah's wife was probably her own inner sense, and the appearance is to be understood rather as a figure of speech than as an actual occurrence, although there may have been, as there are to-day, people who were so credulous as to believe that such things actually occurred. The angel who whispers into our ears is knowledge, foresight, high motive, ideality, unselfish love. A conscious attitude towards the ideal still unattained, a lofty standard of virtue for the coming offspring, an intelligent, pure fatherhood, and a wise, loving motherhood must take the place of a mysterious, instinctive trust—the blind faith of the past.   C. B. N.

One would suppose that this woman, so honored of God, worthy
to converse with angels on the most delicate of her domestic relations, might have had a name to designate her personality instead of
being mentioned merely as the wife of Manoah or the mother of
Samson. I suppose that it is from these Biblical examples that the
wives of this Republic are known as Mrs. John Doe or Mrs. Richard
Roe, to whatever Roe or Doe she may belong. If she chance to
marry two or three times, the woman's identity is wholly lost. To
make this custom more ludicrous, women sometimes keep the names
of two husbands, clinging only to the maiden name, as Dolly Doe
Roe, ignoring her family name, the father from whom she may have
derived all of her talent. Samson's wife had no name, nor had the
second woman on whom he bestowed his attentions; to the third one
is vouchsafed the name of Delilah, but no family name is mentioned.
All three represented one type of character and betrayed the "consecrated Nazarite," "the canonized Judge of Israel."

It would be a great blessing to the race, if parents would take heed
to the important lesson taught in the above texts. The nine months
of ante-natal life is the period when the mother can make the deepest
impression in forming future character, when she has absolute
power for weal or for woe over the immortal being. Locke, the
philosopher, said, "Every child is born into the world with a mind like
a piece of blank paper, and we may write thereon whatever we will;"
but Descartes said, "Nay, nay; the child is born with all its possibilities. You can develop all you find there, but you cannot add genius
or power." *"Nascitur, non fit,"* although our learned blacksmith,
Elihu Burritt, always reversed this motto.   E. C. S.

No body of ecclesiastics has taught the message of the angel of
the Lord to Manoah's wife as a message of direction from the Lord
to save the race from the disastrous results of strong drink and im-
pure food. And although the degree of enlightenment attained
shows that science and the instructions of the angel to Manoah's wife
agree, this knowledge does not protect the unborn child from the

effects of the use by the mothers of to-day of wine, strong drink and unclean food.

Could the light which reveals to the mother what would be a saving power to her child, be followed carefully by both herself and the father during ante-natal life, the race would more rapidly be brought to the full stature of its destined perfection. Not only is physical endowment available to the child through the wholesome sustenance of the mother, but the qualities of the higher nature may also be transmitted, and moral grandeur be an inheritance equally with grand physical powers.

The theological teaching that has made human nature depraved and cut off from the divine source of all perfection, has hindered the development of the higher faculties of understanding. It has led to a misapprehension of the creative power of parenthood. From the idea that the creation of humanity was finished "in the beginning," and that man fell from his high estate as the image of God, has resulted a demoralized race. The instruction of the angel to Samson's mother, was in accord with the dominant spirit that wrought the victories of Israel over enemies, and the reign of physical force that characterized the people of that age.

The woman, having had no experience of motherhood, had not been subject to the deep soul-stirring that belongs to the mystery of life in a developed womanhood. Nor did that experience evidently transmit to Samson a high degree of moral strength. He was but a well developed physical organism, which the spirit of life could act through without limitation. He consorted with the harlot, but it was the woman whom he loved who succeeded in wringing from him the secret of his strength, and thus the possibility of delivering him to his enemies.

In the relation of women to this man of might there is illustrated the dominant characteristics of the purely animal man. The father of Samson's first wife gave her to another man after Samson had gone in anger to his father's house, and when he returned and proposed to resume his conjugal relations, this father proposed that he should take the younger sister, who "was fairer than she."

It is a significant suggestion of the quality of the relation that

Samson's first wife (who had also no name of her own) and Delilah, whom he loved, were both more loyal to their own people, and had more regard for them, than for the man to whom they had been "given."   L. B. C.

Judges xiv.

1 And Samson went down to Timnath, and saw a woman in Timnath of the daughters of the Philistines.

2 And he came up, and told his father and his mother, and said, I have seen a woman in Timnath of the daughters of the Philistines: now therefore get her for me to wife.

3 Then his father and his mother said unto him, Is *there* never a woman among the daughters of thy brethren, or among all my people, that thou goest to take a wife of the uncircumcised Philistines? And Samson said unto his father, Get her for me; for she pleaseth me well.

So the father and the mother, much against their wishes, went down to Timnath and secured for Samson the desired wife. He conformed to the custom of the Philistines; and on the occasion of the nuptial solemnities he made a great feast, and invited thirty young men to join in the festivities, which lasted seven days. These feasts were enlivened with interesting discussions, stories and riddles. Samson propounded one, with promises of valuable gifts to those who guessed the riddle: "Out of the eater came forth meat, out of the strong came forth sweetness."

It seems that on one occasion, being attacked by a lion, Samson, without any weapon of defense, tore the lion to pieces. Passing the vineyard some time after, he went in to see if the lion still rested there; and lo! the skeleton was a hive of bees. He partook freely of the honey and carried some to his parents. Being proof against the lion's paws, he had no fear of the bees. Day after day passed, and the young men could not guess the riddle. So they persuaded the wife to coax him for the answer, with promises of silver if she succeeded, and threatenings of wrath if she failed. So, with constant weeping and doubts of his love, she at last worried the answer out of him, with promises of secrecy.

As soon as Samson saw that he was betrayed he sent his wife back to her father's house, who gave her at once to one of the leaders at the festivities. As Samson loved the woman, he forgave her, and sought to bring her back to his own home. The father informed him that he had already given her to another, and that he might have the younger daughter, if he chose, who had far more grace and beauty. The commentators say that it was very generous in Samson to make this concession, as he was the party offended. But Samson was himself a riddle and a paradox of a man. "He saw something in her face which pleased him well." "He that in the choice of a wife is guided by his eye, and governed by his fancy, must afterwards blame himself if he find a Philistine in his arms." It is a great calamity that even able men are so easily influenced by weak and wicked women to do what they know is dangerous; and yet they feel it a disparagement to follow the advice of a good wife in what is virtuous and praiseworthy.

Samson was most unfortunate in all his associations with women. It is a pity that the angel who impressed on his parents the importance of considering everything that pertained to the physical development of the child, had not made some suggestions to them as to the formation of his moral character. Even his physical prowess was not used by him for any great purpose. To kill a lion, to walk off with the gates of the city, to catch three hundred foxes and to tie them together by their tails two by two, with firebrands to burn the cornfields and the vineyards—all this seems more like the frolics of a boy, than the military tactics of a great general or the statesmanship of a Judge in Israel.

Samson does not seem to have learned wisdom from expcrience in his dealings with women. He foolishly trusted another woman, "whose face pleased him," with the secret of his great strength, which she, too, worried out of him with tears and doubts of his affection. For the betrayal of his secret the Philistines paid her eleven hundred pieces of silver.

In the last act of this complicated tragedy, it is said that Samson at his death killed more people than in all his life before. After Delilah betrayed him into the hands of the Philistines, they put out his eyes, and left him to grind in the prison house. As was their custom, they brought him out to make sport for the people assembled in a spacious building. As his hair bad begun to grow, he braced himself against the door posts, overturned the building, and killed all of its occupants, and himself, gladly ending his own sad life.

The name Delilah is fitly used to describe those who with flattery bring destruction on those whom they pretend to love. Many a strong man has been slain by this type of designing woman. Commentators do not agree as to whether Delilah was an Israelite or a Philistine, probably the latter, as Samson seemed to be more pleased with the women of that tribe than with those of his own. One hesitates to decide which is most surprising—Samson's weakness or Delilah's wickedness.   E. C. S.

The writer of the Book of Judges would fail in his endeavor to present a complete picture of his time, did he omit the important characteristic of a woman and her influence upon man therein portrayed.

In Delilah, the treacherous, the sinister, the sensuous side of woman is depicted. Like Vivian, in the Idyls of King Arthur, Delilah uses—nay, abuses—the power which she had gained over Samson by virtue of her beauty and her personal attractions. She uses these personal gifts for a sinister purpose. They serve her as a snare to beguile the man whose lust she had aroused.

What a lesson this story teaches to men as well as to women! Let man overcome the lust of his eyes and prostitution will die a natural death. Let woman beware that her influence is of the purest and highest; let her spiritual nature be so attractive that man will be drawn toward it. Forever "the eternal womanly draweth man" onward and upward. Soul unity will become the rule when the same chastity and purity are demanded of the sexes alike. Woman's chastity is never secure as long as there are two standards of morality.

C. B. N.

"Colonial days" is the felicitous term given by Rev. Dr. Lyman Abbott to the period of nearly three centuries following the campaign against the inhabitants of Canaan, when the Israelites took possession of their land. The Book of Judges is a record of those "colonial days;" and they are described also in the first part of the book which bears the name of the prophet Samuel. During those Hebrew "colonial days," as Dr. Abbott states, "there was no true Capital—indeed, no true Nation. There were a variety of separate provinces, having almost as little common life as had the American colonies before the formation of the Constitution of the United States. In war these colonies united; in peace they separated from each other again."

But in one thing they were united. They clung to the teachings of their great law-giver, Moses, and emphasized a belief in one righteous God. Whether expressed by priestly ritual or in prophetic declaration, the truth was clearly revealed that the Jews were a people who worshiped one God, and that they accorded to Him the attribute of righteousness. He was a sovereign, but a just one. And to this belief they clung tenaciously, believing themselves justified in conquering the nations about them, because their God was the only ruler.

The Book of Judges contains the record of many harrowing events; but what besides savagery can be expected of a warring people whose Deity is invoked as the "God of battles," and who believed themselves Divinely commissioned to drive other tribes from off the face of the earth! The book is as sensational as are our newspapers; and if each chapter and verse were illustrated as are the papers of what is termed the "New Journalism," they would present an appearance of striking and painful similarity.

The fate of Adoni-besek, an example of retributive justice; the treacherous act of the left-handed Ehud, causing the death of the fat King Eglon of Moab; the inhospitable cruelty—or cruel inhospitality—of Jael, the wife of Heber, whose hammer and nail are welded fast in historical narration with the brow of the sleeping guest, Sisera, the captain of Jabin's army; the famous exploits of Gideon, who, if he was a superior strategist and warrior, gave little evidence, by his seventy sons, of his morality according to Christian standards; the death of Abimelech, which was half suicidal lest it should be said that a woman's hand had slain him; these, and more also of the same sort, leave the impression on the mind that those "colonial days" of the Hebrew nation were far from days of peace or of high morality;

and the record of them is certainly as unfit for the minds of children and of youth as are the illustrated and graphic accounts of many unholy acts which are to found in our daily newspapers.

General Weyler, in his Cuban warfare, has, in many respects, a prototype in General Gideon, and also in General Jephthah, "a mighty man of valor" and "the son of a harlot," as the author of the Book of Judges declares him to have been. We deprecate the savage butchery of the one—what ought we to say of the renown of the others? War is everywhere terrible, and "deeds of violence and of blood" are sad reminders of the imperfections of mankind. The men of those "colonial days" were far from being patterns of excellence; and the women "matched the men," in most instances. Deborah, as a "mother in Israel," won deserved renown, so that her song of victory is even now rehearsed, but it is a query that can have but one answer, whether her anthem of triumph is not a musical rehearsal of treacherous and warlike deeds, unworthy of a woman's praise?

In the Book of Judges Delilah appears, and if the mother of her strong lover, Samson, was not a perfect woman, in the modern sense, she has helped to make some readers feel that the law of heredity is a revealer of secrets, and that the story of the angel of the Lord may be received with due caution. The name "Delilah" has become a synonym for a woman tempting to sin, and the moral weakness and physical strength of Samson show the power of heredity. But whether the stories should be in the hands of our youth, without sufficient explanation and wise commentaries, is a question which coming days will solve to the extent of a wise elimination. Solemn lessons, and those of moral import, are given in the Book of Judges; yet, as a whole, the book does not leave one with an exalted opinion of either the men or the women of those days. But it certainly gives no evidence that in shrewdness, in a wise adaptation of means to ends, in a persistent effort after desired objects, in a successful accomplishment of plans and purposes, the women were the inferiors of the men in that age. They appear to have been their equals, and occasionally their superiors.   P. A. H.

THE BOOK OF RUTH.

1 Now it came to pass in the days when the Judges ruled, that there was a famine in the land. And a certain man of Beth-lehem-judah, went to sojourn in the country of Moab, he, and his wife, and his two sons.

2 And the name of the man was Elimelech, and the name of his wife Naomi, and the name of his two sons Mahlon and Chilion. And they came into the country of Moab, and continued there.

3 And Elimelech, Naomi's husband, died; and she was left, and her two sons.

4 And they took them wives of the women of Moab; the name of the one was Orpah, and the name of the other Ruth: and they dwelt there about ten years.

5 And Mahlon and Chilion died also both of them; and the woman was left of her two sons and her husband.

6 Then she arose with her daughters in law, that she might return from the country of Moab; for she had heard in the country of Moab how that the Lord had visited his people in giving them bread.

7 Wherefore she went forth out of the place where she was, and her two daughters in law with her.

8 And Naomi said unto her daughters in law, Go, return each to her mother's house;

The Lord deal kindly with you, as ye have dealt with the dead, and with me.

10 And they said unto her, Surely we will return with thee unto thy people.

14 And they lifted up their voice, and wept: and Orpah kissed her mother in law; but Ruth clave to her.

15 And she said, Behold, thy sister in law is gone back unto her people, and unto her gods: return thou after thy sister in law.

16 And Ruth said, Entreat me not to leave thee: for whither thou goest, I will go; and where thou lodgest, I will lodge: thy people shall be my people, and thy God my God:

19 So they two went until they came to Beth-lehem. And it came to pass, when they were come to Beth-lehem, that all the city was moved about them, and they said, Is this Naomi?

20 And she said unto them, Call me not Naomi, call me Mara: for the Almighty hath dealt very bitterly with me.

21 I went out full, and the Lord hath brought me home again empty: why then call ye me Naomi, seeing the Lord hath testified against me, and the Almighty hath afflicted me.

22 So Naomi returned, and Ruth the Moabitess, her daughter in law, with her.

COMMENTATORS differ as to the exact period when this book was written and as to the Judge who ruled Israel at that time. It must have been, however, in the beginning of the days when the Judges ruled, as Boaz, who married Ruth, was the son of Rahab, who protected the spies in Joshua's reign. Some say that it was in the reign of Deborah. Tradition says that the Messiah was descended from two Gentile maidens, Rahab and Ruth, and that Ruth was the daughter of Eglon, King of Moab; but this is denied, as Boaz, whom Ruth married, judged Israel two hundred years after Eglon's death. However widely the authorities differ as to Ruth's genealogical tree, they all agree that she was a remarkably sincere, refined, discreet maiden, a loving daughter and an honored wife.

Elimelech, the husband of Naomi, is severely criticised by Biblical writers for leaving his people and his country when in distress and seeking his fortune among the heathen Moabites, thus leading his sons into the temptation of taking strange wives. They say that the speedy deaths of the father and the sons were a proof of God's disapprobation. Naomi manifested such remarkable goodness and wisdom as a widow, that one wonders that she did not use her influence to keep her husband in his native land to share the trials of his neighbors.

The tender friendship between Ruth and Naomi, so unusual with a mother-in-law, has been celebrated in poetry, in prose and in art the world round. The scene between Naomi and her daughters in parting was most affectionate. As soon as Naomi decided to return to her own country, her daughters assisted her in making the necessary preparations. Ruth secretly made her own, having decided to go with Naomi to the land of Judea.

When the appointed day arrived, mounted on three gray jack-asses, they departed. A few miles out Naomi proposed to rest by the roadside and to say farewell, and, after thanking them for all the love and kindness they had shown her, advised them to go no farther, but return to their home in that land of plenty. She told them frankly that she had no home luxuries to offer, life with her would for them be poverty and privation in a strange land, and she was not willing that they should sacrifice all the pleasures of their young lives for her. Sad and lonely with the loss of their husbands, parting with Naomi seemed to intensify their grief. United in a common sorrow, the three women stood gazing in silence into each other's faces, until Naomi, with her usual self-control and common sense, again pointed out to them all the hardships involved in the change which they proposed.

Her words made a deep impression on Orpah. She hesitated,

and at last decided to abide by Naomi's advice; but not so with Ruth. Naomi had a peculiar magnetic attraction for her, a charm stronger than kindred, country or ease. Her expressions of steadfast friendship in making her decision were so tender and sincere that they have become household words. She said: "Entreat me not to leave thee; for whither thou goest I will go, and where thou lodgest I will lodge; thy people shall be my people, and thy God my God; where thou diest will I die, and there will I be buried. The Lord do so to me, and more also, if aught but death part thee and me." (These words are on a bronze tablet on the stone over the grave of Robert Louis Stevenson at Samoa.)

Having bade farewell to Orpah, they journeyed together and made a home for themselves in Bethlehem. Naomi owned a small house, lot and spring of water on the outskirts of the town. After a few days of rest, Ruth said to Naomi, I must not sit here with folded hands, nor spend my time in visiting neighbors, nor in search of amusement, but I must go forth to work, to provide food and clothes, and leave thee to rest. As it was the season for the wheat and barley harvests, Ruth heard that laborers were needed in the fields. It was evident that Ruth believed in the dignity of labor and of self-support. She thought, no doubt, that every one with a sound mind in a sound body and two hands should earn her own livelihood. She threw her whole soul into her work and proved a blessing to her mother. So Naomi consented that she might go and glean in the fields with other maidens engaged in that work.

When Naomi was settled in Bethlehem she remembered that she had a rich kinsman, Boaz, whose name means strength, a man of great wealth as well as wisdom. Ruth was employed in the field of Boaz; and in due time he took note of the fair maiden from Moab. In harvest time he needed many extra hands, and he came often among the reapers to see how the work went forward. He heard such good accounts of Ruth's industry, dignity and discretion that he ordered his men to make her work as easy as possible, to leave plenty for her to glean and to carry home in the evening. This she often sold on the way, and bought something which Naomi needed.

Naomi and Ruth enjoyed their evenings together. Naomi did

not spend the day in idleness either. She had her spinning-wheel
and loom to make their garments; she worked also in her garden,
raising vegetables, herbs and chickens; and they talked over their
day's labor as they enjoyed their simple supper of herb tea, bread and
watercresses. Their menu was oft times more tempting, thanks to
Ruth's generous purchases on her way home. Being busy, practical women, their talk during the evening was chiefly on "ways and
means;" they seldom rose to the higher themes of pedagogics and
psychology, subjects so familiar in the clubs of American women.

E. C. S.

Ruth ii.

1 And Naomi had a kinsman of her husband's, a mighty man of wealth, of the family of Elimelech; and his name was Boaz.

2 And Ruth the Moabitess said unto Naomi, Let me now go to the field, and glean
ears of corn after him in whose sight I shall
find grace. And she said unto her, Go, my
daughter.

4 And, behold, Boaz came from Bethlehem . . .

7 And she said, I pray you, let me glean
and gather after the reapers among the
sheaves: so she came.

8 Then said Boaz unto Ruth, Hearest
thou not, my daughter? Go not to glean in
another field, neither go from hence, but
abide here fast by my maidens: . . . .
It hath fully been shewed me, all that thou
hast done unto thy mother-in-law since the
death of thine husband; and how thou hast
left thy father and thy mother.

19 And her mother-in-law said unto her,
Where hast thou gleaned to-day? and where
wroughtest thou? blessed be he that did
take knowledge of thee. . . . And Ruth
said, the man's name is Boaz. . . . And
Naomi said unto her, The man is near of
kin unto us, one of our next kinsmen.

It was a custom among the Israelites, in order to preserve their
own line, that the nearest kinsman should marry the young widow
on whom their hopes depended. So when Naomi remembered that
Boaz was her kinsman, and that as age made marriage with her un-
desirable, Ruth would be the proper person to fill her place. With
great tact on their part Naomi's wishes were accomplished.

Boaz was the son of Salmon and Rahab, and according to the
Chaldee was not only a mighty man in wealth but also in wisdom, a
most rare and excellent conjunction. Boaz was of the family of
Elimelech, of which Ruth, by marriage, was a part also. Moreover,
as she had adopted the country of Naomi and was a proselyte to her
faith, her marriage with Boaz was in accordance with Jewish custom.
Naomi was told by the spirit of prophecy, says the Chaldee, that from

her line should descend six of the most righteous men of the age, namely, David, Daniel, his three compeers and the King Messiah.

Commentators say that Boaz was probably himself one of the elders, or the aldermen, of the city, and that he went up to the gates as one having authority, and not as a common person. They say that Ruth was neither rich nor beautiful, but a poor stranger, "whose hard work in the fields" had withered her "lilies and roses." But Boaz had heard her virtue and dignity extolled by all who knew her. The Chaldee says, "house and riches are the inheritance from fathers; but a prudent wife is more valuable than rubies and is a special gift from heaven." Boaz prized Ruth for her virtues, for her great moral qualities of head and heart. He did not say like Samson, when his parents objected to his choice, "her face pleaseth me."

In narrating the story of Ruth and Naomi to children they invariably ask questions of interest, to which the sacred fabulist gives no answer. They always ask if Ruth and Naomi had no pets when living alone, before Obed made his appearance. If the modern historian may be allowed to wander occasionally outside of the received text, it may be said undoubtedly that they had pets, as there is nothing said of cats and dogs and parrots, but frequent mention of doves, kids and lambs, we may infer that in these gentle innocents they found their pets. No doubt Providence softened their solitude by providing them with something on which to expend their mother love.

Ruth iv.

1 Then went Boaz up to the gate, and sat him down there; and, behold, the kinsman of whom Boaz spake came by; unto whom he said, Ho, such a one! turn aside, sit down here. And he turned aside, and sat down.

2 And he took ten men of the elders of the city, and said, Sit ye down here.

3 And he said unto the kinsman, Naomi, that is come again out of the country of Moab, selleth a parcel of land, which was our brother Elimelech's:

4 And I thought to advertise thee, saying, Buy it before the inhabitants, and before the elders of my people. If thou wilt redeem it, redeem it; but if thou wilt not redeem it, then tell me, that I may know; for there is none to redeem it beside thee; and I am after thee. And he said, I will redeem it.

5 Then said Boaz, What day thou buyest the field of the hand of Naomi, thou must buy it also of Ruth the Moabitess, the wife of the dead, to raise up the name of the dead upon his inheritance.

6 And the kinsman said, I cannot redeem it for myself, lest I mar mine own inheritance; redeem thou my right to thyself; for I cannot.

Boaz was one of the district judges, and he held his court in the town hall over the gates of Bethlehem. The kinsman who was summoned to appear there and to settle the case readily agreed to the proposal of Boaz to fill his place, as he was already married. He was willing to take the land; but as the widow and the land went together, according to the Jewish law of inheritance, Boaz was in a position to fill the legal requirements; and as he loved Ruth, he was happy to do so. Ruth was summoned to appear before the grave and reverend seigniors; the civil pledges were made and the legal documents duly signed. The reporter is silent as to the religious observances and the marriage festivities. They were not as vigilant and as satisfying as are the skilled reporters of our day, who have the imagination to weave a connected story and to give to us all the hidden facts which we desire to know. Our reporters would have told us how, when and where Ruth was married, what kind of a house Boaz had, how Ruth was dressed, etc., etc., whereas we are left in doubt on all of these points.

The historian does vouchsafe to give to us further information on the general feeling of the people. They all joined in the prayer of the elders that the Lord would "make the woman that is come into thine house like Rachel and like Leah, which two did build the house of Israel;" they prayed for Boaz that he might be more famous and powerful; they prayed for the wife that she might be a blessing in the house, and the husband in the public business of the town; that all of their children might be faithful in the church, and their descendants be as numerous as the sands of the sea.

In due time one prayer was answered, and Ruth bore a son. Naomi loved the child and shared in its care. But Ruth said: "The love of Naomi is more to me than that of seven sons could be." Naomi was a part of Ruth's household to the day of her death and shared all of her luxuries and her happiness.

The child's name was Obed, the father of Jesse, the father of David. The name Obed signifies one who serves. The motto of the Prince of Wales is (ich dien) "I serve." It is to be hoped that Obed was more profoundly interested in the problems of industrial economics than the Prince seems to be, and that he spent a more useful and practical life. If the Bethlehem newspapers had been as enterprising as our journals they would have given us some pictorial representations of Obed on Naomi's lap, or at the baptismal font, or in the arms of Boaz, who, like Napoleon, stood contemplating in silence his firstborn.

Some fastidious readers object to the general tenor of Ruth's courtship. But as her manners conformed to the customs of the times, and as she followed Naomi's instructions implicitly, it is fair to assume that Ruth's conduct was irreproachable. E. C. S.

BOOKS OF SAMUEL.

CHAPTER I.

1. Samuel i.

1 Now there was a certain man of Ramathaim-zophim, of mount Ephraim, and his name was Elkanah.

2 And he had two wives; the name of the one was Hannah, and the name of the other Peninnah; and Peninnah had children, but Hannah had no children.

3 And this man went up out of his city yearly to worship and to sacrifice unto the Lord of hosts in Shiloh.

4 And when the time was that Elkanah offered, he gave to Peninnah his wife, and to all her sons and her daughters, portions:

5 But unto Hannah he gave a worthy portion; for he loved Hannah; but Peninnah mocked her.

7 And as he did so year by year, when she went up to the house of the Lord; so she provoked her, therefore she wept, and did not eat.

8 Then said Elkanah her husband to her, Hannah, why weepest thou? and why eatest thou not? and why is thy heart grieved? am not I better to thee than ten sons?

Now Eli the priest sat upon a seat by a post of the temple of the Lord.

10 And she was in bitterness of soul, and prayed unto the Lord, and wept sore.

11 And she vowed a vow, and said, O Lord of hosts, if thou wilt indeed look on the affliction of thine handmaid, and wilt give unto me a man child, then I will give him unto the Lord all the days of his life.

17 Then Eli answered and said, Go in peace; and the God of Israel grant thee thy petition that thou hast asked of him. And she bare a son, and called his name Samuel, saying, Because I have asked him of the Lord.

26 And she said, O my lord, as thy soul liveth, I am the woman that stood by thee here, praying unto the Lord.

27 For this child I prayed; and the Lord hath given me my petition which I asked of him.

28 Therefore also I have lent him to the Lord, as long as he liveth.

THESE books contain the history of the last two of the judges of Israel. Eli and Samuel were not as the rest, men of war, but priests. It is uncertain who wrote these books. Some say that Samuel wrote the history of his times, and that Nathan the Prophet continued it. Elkanah, though a godly man, had sore family trials, the result of having married two wives, just as Abraham and Jacob did before him. It is probable that Elkanah married Hannah from pure love; but she had no children, and as at that time every man had great pride in building up a family, he married Peninnah, who bare him children, but in other respects was a constant vexation.

Peninnah was haughty and insolent because she had children, while Hannah was melancholy and discontented because she had none, hence Elkanah had no pleasure in his daily life with either. He had a difficult part to act. Hoping much from the consolations of religion, he took his wives and children annually up to the temple of the Lord in Shiloh to worship. Being of a devout spiritual nature, he thought that worshiping at the same altar must produce greater harmony between his wives. But Peninnah became more peevish and provoking, and Hannah more silent and sorrowful, weeping most of the time. Elkanah's love and patience with Hannah was beautiful to behold. He paid her every possible attention and gave her valuable gifts.

Appreciating his own feelings, he said to her one day in an exuberant burst of devotion, "Am I not more to thee than ten sons?" He made peace offerings to the Lord, gave Hannah the choice bits at the table, but all his delicate attentions made Hannah more melancholy and Peninnah more rebellious. He and Hannah continued to pray earnestly to the Lord to remove her reproach, and their prayers were at last answered.

Eli was presiding at the temple one day when he noticed Hannah in a remote corner wrestling in prayer with the Lord. Though her manner was intense, and her lips moved, he heard no sound, and inferred that she was intoxicated. Hannah, hearing of his suspicion, said that naught but the debauchery of his own sons could have made such a suspicion possible. But Eli made atonement for his rash, unfriendly censure by a kind of fatherly benediction. With all these adverse winds in this visit to Shiloh, Elkanah must have felt as if his family had been possessed by the spirit of evil. When the sons of God come "to present themselves before the Lord, Satan will be seen to come also." Peninnah behaved worse during these religious festivities because she saw more of Elkanah's devotion to Hannah. Hannah became more sad because she was losing faith in prayer. "Hope deferred maketh the heart sick."

An endless discord in the harmony of the family joys was a puzzling problem for the sweet tempered Elkanah. But the ever-turning wheel of fortune brought peace and prosperity to his domestic altar at last. Hannah bore a son and named him Samuel, which signifies "heard of the Lord," or given by the Lord. Hannah was very modest in her petition; she said, "O Lord, give me a son," while Rachel said, "give me children."

The one sorrow which overtopped all others with these Bible women was in regard to children. If they had none, they made everybody miserable. If they had children, they fanned the jealousies of one for the other. See how Rebekah deceived Isaac and defrauded Esau of his birthright. The men, instead of appealing to the common sense of the women, join in constant prayer for the Lord to do what was sometimes impossible.

Hannah in due time took Samuel up to the temple at Shiloh. In presenting Samuel to Eli the priest she reminded him that she was the woman on whom he passed the severe comment; but now she came to present the child the Lord had given to her. She offered three bullocks, one for each year of his life, one for a burnt offering, one for a sin offering and one for a peace offering. So Hannah dedicated him wholly to the Lord and left him in Shiloh to be educated with the sons of the priests. Although Samuel was Hannah's only child and dearly loved, she did not hesitate to keep her vow unto the Lord.

1 Samuel ii.

11 And Elkanah went to Ramah to his house. And the child did minister unto the Lord before Eli the priest.

18 But Samuel ministered before the Lord, being a child, girded with a linen ephod.

19 Moreover his mother made him a little coat, and brought it to him from year to year, when she came up with her husband to offer the yearly sacrifice.

20 And Eli blessed Elkanah and his wife. And they went unto their own home.

21 And Hannah bare three sons and two daughters. And the child Samuel grew before the Lord.

The historians and commentators dwell on the fact that Hannah made her son "a little coat," and brought one annually. It is more probable that she brought to him a complete suit of clothes once in three months, especially trousers, if those destined to service in the temple were allowed to join in any sports. Even devotional genuflections are severe on that garment, which must have often needed Hannah's care. Her virtue and wisdom as a mother were in due time rewarded by five other children, three sons and two daughters.

And Samuel judged Israel all the days of his life. Saul was made king at the request of the people. The ark of the Lord fell into the hands of the Philistines. This event, with the death of Eli and his sons, had most tragic results, viz., in the killing of thirty thousand people and the death of the wife of Phinehas, who was said to have been a woman of gracious spirit, though the wife of a wicked husband. Her grief for the death of her husband and father-in-law proved her strong natural affection, but her much greater concern for the loss of the ark of the Lord was an evidence of her devout affection to God. Her dying words, "the glory has departed from Israel," show that her last thought was of her religion. She named her son Ichabod, whose premature birth was the result of many calamities, both public and private, crowning all with the great battle with the Philistines. Samuel was the last judge of Israel. As the people clamored for a king, Saul was chosen to rule over them. The women joined in the festivities of the occasion with music and dancing.

1 Samuel xviii.

6 And it came to pass when David was returned from the slaughter of the Philistines that the women came out of all the cities of Israel, singing and dancing, to meet King Saul, with tabrets and instruments of music.

7 And the women answered *one another* as they played, and said, Saul hath slain his thousands, and David his ten thousands.

8 And Saul was very wroth, and the saying displeased him; and he said, They have ascribed unto David ten thousands, and to me they have ascribed *but* thousands; and *what* can he have more than the kingdom?

It was the custom among women to celebrate the triumphs of their warriors after a great battle in spectacular performances. Decked with wreaths, they danced down the public streets, singing the songs of victory in praise of their great leaders. They were specially enthusiastic over David, the chorus, "Saul hath killed his thousands, but David his ten thousands," chanted with pride by beautiful maidens and wise matrons, stirred the very soul of Saul to deadly jealousy, and he determined to suppress David in some way or to kill him outright. It is not probable that any of these battle hymns, so much admired, emanated from the brain of woman; the blood and thunder style shows clearly that they were all written by the pen of a warrior, long after the women of their respective tribes were at rest in Abraham's bosom.

David was a general favorite; even the Philistines admired his courage and modesty. The killing of Goliath impressed the people generally that David was the chosen of the Lord to succeed Saul as King of Israel.

But on the heels of his triumphs David's troubles soon began. Saul was absorbed in plotting and in planning how to circumvent David, and looked with jealousy on the warm friendship maturing between him and his son Jonathan.

17 And Saul said to David, Behold my elder daughter Merab; her will I give thee to wife: only be thou valiant for me, and fight the Lord's battles. For Saul said, Let not mine hand be upon him, but let the hand of the Philistines be upon him.

18 And David said unto Saul, Who am I? and what is my life, or my father's family in Israel, that I should be son-in-law to the king?

19 But it came to pass at the time when Merab, Saul's daughter, should have been given to David, that she was given unto Adriel, the Meholathite, to wife.

20 And Michal, Saul's daughter, loved David: and they told Saul, and the thing pleased him.

21 And Saul said, I will give him her, that she may be a snare to him, and that the hand of the Philistines may be against him. Wherefore Saul said to David, Thou shalt this day be my son in law in the one of the twain.

22 And Saul commanded his servants, saying, Commune with David secretly, and say, Behold the king hath delight in thee, and all his servants love thee: now therefore be the king's son-in-law.

24 And Saul's servants spake those words in the ears of David. And David said, Seemeth it to you a light thing to be a king's son-in-law, seeing that I am a poor man, and lightly esteemed?

28 And Saul saw and knew that the Lord was with David, and that Michal, Saul's daughter, loved him.

Saul thought if he could get David to marry his daughter he would make her a snare to entrap him. He promised David his daughter, and then married her to another to provoke him to some act of violence, that he might have an excuse for whatever he chose to do. But when Saul offered to give him Michal, David modestly replied that he belonged to a humble shepherd family and was not worthy to be the son-in-law of a king.

In due time David did marry Michal, who loved him and proved a blessing rather than a snare. On one occasion when Saul had made secret plans to capture David, Michal with her diplomacy saved him. Saul surrounded his house with guards and ordered them to kill David the moment he appeared in the morning. Michal, seeing their preparations, knew their significance, and at night, when all was still, she let David down through a window and told him to flee. In the morning, as David did not appear, they searched the house. Michal told them that David was ill and in bed. She had covered the head of a wooden image with goat's hair and tucked the supposed David up snug and warm. The guards would not wake a sick man in order to kill him, and they reported what they saw to Saul, but he ordered them to return and to bring David, sick or well.

When Saul found that he had escaped, he was very wroth and upbraided Michal for her disrespect to him. Though she had saved the man she loved, yet she marred her noble deed by saying that David would have killed her if he suspected she had connived with her father to kill him. But alas! the poor woman was between two fires—the husband whom she loved on one side, and the father whom she feared on the other. Most of the women in the Bible seem to have been in a quandary the chief part of the time.

Saul made a special war on the soothsayers and the fortune-tellers, because they were divining evil things of him. But losing faith in himself and embittered by many troubles, he went to the witch of Endor to take counsel with Samuel, hoping to find more comfort with the dead than with the living. The witch recognized him and asked him why he came to her, having so cruelly persecuted her craft. However, she summoned Samuel at his request, who told him that on the morrow, in the coming battle with the Philistines, he and his sons would be slain by the enemy. When the witch saw Saul's grief and consternation she begged him to eat, placing some tempting viands before him, which he did, and then hastened to depart while it was yet dark, that he might not be seen coming from such a house. Commentators say it was not Samuel who appeared, but Satan in the guise of the prophet, as he especially enjoys all psychical mysteries. Josephus extols the witch for her courtesy, and Saul for his courage in going forth to the battle on the next day to meet his doom.

The poet says that the heart from love to one grows bountiful to all. This seems to have been the case with David as he adds wife to wife, Michal, Ahinoam the Jezreelitess, and Abigail the Carmelitess. His meeting with Abigail in the hills of Carmel was quite romantic.

She made an indelible impression on his heart, and as soon as her husband was gathered to his fathers David at once proposed and was accepted. Though the women who attracted David were "beautiful to look upon," yet they had great qualities of head and heart, and he seemed equally devoted to all of them. When carried off captives in war he made haste to recapture them. Michal's steadfastness seems questionable at one or two points of her career, but the historian does not let us into the secret recesses of her feelings.

David's time and thoughts seem to have been equally divided between the study of government and social ethics, and he does not appear very wise in either. His honor shines brighter in his psalms than in his ordinary, everyday life.   E. C. S.

CHAPTER II.

1 Samuel xxv.

2 And there was a man in Maon, whose possessions were in Carmel; and the man was very great, and he had three thousand sheep, and a thousand goats: and he was shearing his sheep in Carmel.

3 Now the name of the man was Nabal, and the name of his wife Abigail; and she was a woman of good understanding, and of a beautiful countenance: but the man was churlish and evil in his doings.

4 And David heard in the wilderness that Nabal did shear his sheep.

5 And David sent out ten young men, and David said unto the young men, Get you up to Carmel, and go to Nabal, and greet him in my name:

6 And thus shall ye say to him that liveth in prosperity, Peace be both to thee, and peace be to thine house, and peace be unto all that thou hast.

8 . . . Give, I pray thee, whatsover cometh to thine hand unto thy servants.

10 And Nabal said, Who is David? and who is the son of Jesse?

11 Shall I then take my bread, and my water, and my flesh that I have killed for my shearers, and give unto men, whom I know not whence they be?

12 So David's young men came and told him all these sayings.

13 And David said unto his men, Gird ye on every man his sword; and David also girded on his sword: and there went up after David about four hundred men; and two hundred abode by the stuff.

14 But one of the young men told Abigail, Nabal's wife, saying, Behold, David sent messengers out of the wilderness to salute our master; and he railed on them.

18 Then Abigail made haste, and took two hundred loaves, and two bottles of wine, and five sheep ready dressed, and five measures of parched corn, and a hundred clusters of raisins, and two hundred cases of figs, and laid them on asses.

23 And when Abigail saw David, she hasted, and lighted off the ass, and fell before David on her face, and bowed herself to the ground.

25 Let not my lord, I pray thee, regard this man of Belial, even Nabal: for as his name is, so is he; Nabal is his name, and folly is with him: but I thine handmaid saw not the young men of my lord, whom thou didst send.

32 And David said to Abigail, Blessed be the Lord God of Israel, which sent thee this day to meet me:

35 So David received of her hand that which she had brought him, and said unto her, Go up in peace to thine house;

38 And it came to pass about ten days after, that the Lord smote Nabal, that he died.

39 . . . And David sent and communed with Abigail, to take her to him to wife.

42 And Abigail hasted, and arose, and rode upon an ass, with five damsels of hers that went after her; and she went after the messengers of David, and became his wife.

THE chief business of the women in the reigns of Kings Saul and David seems to have been to rescue men from the craft and the greed of each other. The whole interest in this story of Nabal centres in the tact of Abigail in saving their lives and possessions from threatened destruction, owing to the folly and the ignorance of her husband. His name, Nabal, signifying folly, describes his character.

It is a wonder that his parents should have given to him such a
name, and a greater wonder that Abigail should have married him.
He inherited Caleb's estate; but he was far from inheriting his virtues.   His wealth was great; but he was a selfish, snarling cynic.
Abigail's name signifies "the joy of her father;" but he could not
have promised himself much joy in her, caring more for the wealth
than for the wisdom of her husband.   Many a child is thus thrown
away—married to worldly wealth and to nothing else which is desirable.   Wisdom is good with an inheritance; but an inheritance
without wisdom is good for nothing.   Many an Abigail is tied to a
Nabal; but even if they have her understanding they will find it hard
enough to fill such a relation.

David and his men were returning from Samuel's funeral through
the wilderness of Paran and were in sore need of provisions, and
knowing that Nabal had immense wealth, and, moreover, that it was
the season for sheep shearing, David thought that he would be happy
to place the king under obligations to him, and was surprised to find
him so disloyal.   Abigail, however, appreciated the situation, and
by her courtesy and her generosity made amends for the rudeness
of her husband.   She did not stop to parley with him, but hastened
to meet the king with the needed provisions.   She wasted no words
of excuse for Nabal, but spoke of him with marked contempt.   Her
conduct would have shocked the Apostle who laid such stress on the
motto, "Wives, obey your husbands."   "What little reason we have
to value the wealth of this world," says the historian, "when such a
churl as Nabal abounds in plenty, while such a saint as David suffers
want."

David sent to him most gracious messages; but he replied in his
usual gruff manner, "Who is David, that I should share with him my
riches?   What care I for the son of Jesse?"   The servant did not
return to Nabal with David's outburst of wrath nor his resolution
of vengeance; but he told all to Abigail, who made haste to avert
the threatened danger.   She did what she saw was to be done,
quickly.   Wisdom in such a case was better than weapons of war.

Nabal begrudged the king and his retinue water; but Abigail
gave them two casks of wine and all sorts of provisions in abun-

dance. She met David on the march big with resentment, medi-
tating the destruction of Nabal. But Abigail by her humility completely disarmed the king. With great respect and complaisance
she urges him to lay all of the blame on her; and to attribute Nabal's
faults to his want of wit, born simple, not spiteful. Abigail puts
herself in the attitude of a humble petitioner.

David received all that Abigail brought him with many thanks.
It is evident from the text that she gave to him many of the delicacies
from her larder. Ten days after this Nabal died. David immediately sent messengers to Abigail asking her to be his wife. She
readily accepted, as David had made a deep impression on her heart.
So, with her five damsels, all mounted on white jackasses, she accompanied the messengers to the king and became his wife.

The Hebrew mythology does not gild the season of courtship
and marriage with much sentiment or romance. The transfer of a
camel or a donkey from one owner to another, no doubt, was often
marked with more consideration than that of a daughter. One loves
a faithful animal long in our possession and manifests more grief in
parting than did these Hebrew fathers in giving away their daughters, or than the daughters did in leaving their family, their home or
their country.

We have no beautiful pictures of lovers sitting in shady groves,
exchanging their tributes of love and of friendship, their hopes and
fears of the future; no temples of knowledge where philosophers and
learned matrons discussed great questions of human destiny, such
as Greek mythology gives to us; Socrates and Plato, learning wisdom at the feet of the Diametias of their times, give to us a glimpse of
a more exalted type of womanhood than any which the sacred fabulists have vouchsafed thus far.

2 Samuel iii.

2 And unto David were sons born in
Hebron: and his firstborn was Amnon, of
Ahinoam the Jezreelitess:

3 And his second, Chileab, of Abigail
the wife of Nabal the Carmelite; and the
third, Absalom the son of Maacah the
daughter of Talmai king of Geshur:

4 And the fourth, Adonijah the son of
Haggith; and the fifth, Shephatiah the son
of Abital;

5 And the sixth, Ithream, by Eg'ah David's wife. These were born to David in
Hebron.

The last is called David's wife, his only rightful wife, Michal. It was a fault in David, say the commentators, thus to multiply wives contrary to Jewish law. It was a bad example to his successors. Men who make the laws should not be the first to disobey them. None of his sons was famous, but three were infamous, due in part to their father's nature and example.

14 And David danced before the Lord with all his might; and David was girded with a linen ephod.

15 So David and all the house of Israel brought up the ark of the Lord with shouting, and with the sound of the trumpet.

16 And as the ark of the Lord came into the city of David, Michal Saul's daughter looked through a window, and saw king David leaping and dancing before the Lord; and she despised him in her heart.

20 Then David returned to bless his household. And Michal the daughter of Saul came out to meet David, and said, How glorious was the king of Israel to-day, who uncovered himself in the eyes of his servants, as one of the vain fellows.

21 And David said unto Michal, It was before the Lord, which chose me before thy father.

Michal, like Abigail, does not seem to have been overburdened with conjugal respect. She was so impatient to let the king know how he appeared in her sight that she could not wait at home, but went out to meet him. She even questions the wisdom of such a parade over the ark, and tells the king that it would have been better to leave it where it had been hidden for years.

Neither Michal nor Abigail seem to have made idols of their husbands; they did not even consult them as to what they should think, say or do. They furnish a good example to wives to use their own judgment and to keep their own secrets, not make the family altar a constant confessional.

2 Samuel xi.

2 And it came to pass in an eveningtide, that David arose from off his bed, and walked upon the roof of the king's house, and saw a woman washing herself; and the woman was very beautiful to look upon.

3 And David sent and inquired after her. And one said, Is not this Bath-she-ba, the wife of Uriah the Hittite?

4 And David sent messengers, and took her; and she came in unto him.

6 And David sent to Joab, saying, Send me Uriah the Hittite. And Joab sent Uriah to David.

7 And when Uriah was come unto him, David demanded of him how Joab did, and how the people did, and how the war prospered.

9 And Uriah slept at the door of the king's house with all the servants of his lord, and went not down to his house.

14 And it came to pass in the morning, that David wrote a letter to Joab, and sent it by the hand of Uriah.

15 And he wrote in the letter saying, Set ye Uriah in the forefront of the hottest battle, and retire ye from him, that he may be smitten, and die.

16 And it came to pass, when Joab ob-

served the city, that he assigned Uriah unto a place where he knew that valiant men
were.

17 And the men of the city went out, and
fought with Joab: and there fell some of
the people of the servants of David; and
Uriah the Hittite died also.

26 And when the wife of Uriah heard

that her husband was dead, she mourned
for her husband.

27 And when the mourning was past,
David sent and fetched her to his house,
and she became his wife, and bare him a
son. But the thing that David had done
displeased the Lord.

This book contains but little in regard to women. What is worthy of mention in the story of Bath-sheba is finished in the following book. David's first vision of her is such a reflection on his honor that, from respect to the "man after the Lord's own heart," we pass it in silence.

David's social ethics were not quite up to the standard even of his own times. It is said that he was a master of his pen as well as of his sword. His poem on the death of Saul and Jonathan has been much praised by literary critics. But, alas! David was not able to hold the Divine heights which he occasionally attained. As in the case of Bath-sheba, he remained where he could see her; instead of going with his army to Jerusalem to attend to his duties as King of Israel and general of the army, he delegated them to others. Had he been at his post he would have been out of the way of temptation. He used to pray three times a day, not only at morning and evening, but at noon also. It is to be feared than on this day he forgot his devotions and thought only of Bath-sheba.

Uriah, the husband of Bath-sheba, was one of David's soldiers, a man of strict honor and virtue. To get rid of him for a season, David sent him with a message to one of the officers at Jerusalem, telling him that in the next battle to place Uriah in the front rank that he might distinguish himself. Uriah was a poor man and tenderly loved his wife. He little knew the fatal contents of the letter which he carried. When Joab received the letter, he took it for granted that he was guilty of some crime and that the king wished him to be punished. So Joab obeyed the king and Uriah was killed. In due time all this was known, and filled the people with astonishment and greatly displeased the Lord.

It is to be hoped that he did not commune with God during this period of humiliation or pen any psalms of praise for His goodness

and mercy.   He married Bath-sheba, and she bore him a son and
called his name Solomon.   But this did not atone for his sin.   "His
heart was sad, his soul," says a commentator, "was like a tree in
winter which has life in the root only."

2 Samuel xii.

And the Lord sent Nathan unto David.
And he came unto him, and said unto him:
There were two men in one city; the one
rich, and the other poor.

2 The rich man had exceeding many
flocks and herds:

3 But the poor man had nothing, save
one little ewe lamb, which he had bought
and nourished: and it grew up together
with him, and with his children: it did eat
of his own meat, and drank of his own cup,
and lay in his bosom, and was unto him as
a daughter.

4 And there came a traveller unto the
rich man, and he spared to take of his own
flock and of his own herd, to dress for the
wayfaring man, but took the poor man's
lamb and dressed it.

5 And David's anger was greatly kindled

against the man; and he said to Nathan,
As the Lord liveth, the man that hath done
this thing shall surely die:

6 And he shall restore the lamb fourfold,
because he did this thing.

7 And Nathan said to David, Thou art
the man. Thus saith the Lord God of Israel, I anointed thee king over Israel, and
I delivered thee out of the hand of Saul;

9 Wherefore hast thou despised the commandment of the Lord, to do evil in his
sight? Thou hast killed Uriah the Hittite
with the sword, and hast taken his wife to
be thy wife, and hast slain him with the
sword of the children of Ammon.

10 Now therefore the sword shall never
depart from thine house; because thou hast
despised me, and hast taken the wife of
Uriah the Hittite to be thy wife.

And the Lord said unto Nathan the Prophet, David's faithful
friend, "Go thou and instruct and counsel him."   Nathan judiciously
gives his advice in the form of a parable, on which David gives his
judgment as to the sin of the chief actor and denounces him in un-
measured terms, and says that he should be punished with death—
"he shall surely die."   David did not suspect the bearing of the fable
until Nathan applied it, and, to David's surprise and consternation,
said, "Thou art the man."

Uriah the Hittite had but "one little ewe lamb," one wife whom
he loved as his own soul, while King David had many; yet he robbed
Uriah of all that he had and made him carry his own message of death
to Joab, the general of the army, who gave to him the most dangerous place in the battle, and, as the king desired, he was killed.

When the king first recalled Uriah from the field, Uriah went not
to his own house, as he suspected foul play, having heard that Bath-
sheba often appeared at court.   Both the king and Bath-sheba urged
him to go to his own house; but he went not.   Bath-sheba had been
to him all that was pure and beautiful in woman, and he could not

endure even the suspicion of guilt in her. He understood the king's plans, and probably welcomed death, as without Bath-sheba's love, life had no joy for him. But to be transferred from the cottage of a poor soldier to the palace of a king was a sufficient compensation for the loss of the love of a true and faithful man.

This was one of the most cruel deeds of David's life, marked with so many acts of weakness and of crime. He was ruled entirely by his passions. Reason had no sway over him. Fortunately, the development of self-respect and independence in woman, and a higher idea of individual conscience and judgment in religion and in government, have supplied the needed restraint for man. Men will be wise and virtuous just in proportion as women are self-reliant and able to meet them on the highest planes of thought and of action.

No magnet is so powerful as that which draws men and women to each other. Hence they rise or fall together. This is one lesson which the Bible illustrates over and over—the degradation of woman degrades man also. "Her face pleaseth me," said Samson, who, although he could conquer lions, was like putty in the hands of women.
E. C. S.

BOOKS OF KINGS.

Chapter I.

1 Kings i.

11 Wherefore Nathan spake unto Bath-sheba the mother of Solomon, saying, Hast thou not heard that Adonijah the son of Haggith doth reign. Go . . . unto King David, and say unto him, Didst thou not swear unto thine handmaid, saying, Assuredly Solomon thy son shall reign after me, and he shall sit upon my throne? Why then doth Adonijah reign?

15 And Bath-sheba went in unto the king. . . . And the king said, What wouldst thou?

17 And she said unto him, Thou swarest unto thine handmaid, saying, Assuredly Solomon thy son shall reign after me, and he shall sit upon my throne.

18 And now, behold, Adonijah reigneth.

22 And lo, while she yet talked with the king, Nathan the prophet also came in.

21 And Nathan said, My lord, O king, hast thou said, Adonijah shall reign after me, and he shall sit upon my throne?

28 Then King David answered and said, Call me Bath-sheba. And she came and stood before the king.

29 And the king sware, and said, As the Lord liveth, that hath redeemed my soul out of all distress,

30 Even as I sware unto thee by the Lord. God of Israel, saying, Assuredly Solomon thy son shall reign after me, and he shall sit upon my throne in my stead; even so will I certainly do this day.

31 Then Bath-sheba bowed with her face to the earth, and did reverence to the king, and said, Let my lord, King David, live for ever.

32 And King David said, Call me Zadok the priest, and Nathan the prophet, and Benaiah the son of Jehoiada. And they came.

33 The king also said unto them, Take with you the servants of your lord, and cause Solomon my son to ride upon mine own mule, and bring him down to Gihon:

34 And let Zadok the priest and Nathan the prophet anoint him there king over Israel: and blow ye with the trumpet, and say, God save King Solomon.

THESE books give an account of David's death, of his successor Solomon, of the division of his kingdom between the kings of Judah and of Israel, with an abstract of the history down to the captivity.

Neither the king nor Bath-sheba knew that Adonijah was making preparations to be crowned king the moment when he heard of David's death. He made a great feast, inviting all the king's sons except Solomon. He began his feast by a show of devotion, sacrificing sheep and oxen. But Nathan the Prophet warns the king and

Bath-sheba. In his anxiety he appeals to Bath-sheba as the one who has the greatest concern about Solomon, and can most easily get an audience with the king. He suggests that Solomon is not only in danger of losing his crown, but both he and she of losing their lives.

Accordingly, Bath-sheba, without being announced, enters the presence of the king. She takes no notice of the presence of Abishag, but makes known the object of her visit at once. She reminds the king of his vow to her that Solomon, her son, should be his successor to his throne. Nathan the Prophet is announced in the audience chamber and tells the king of the preparations that Adonijah is making to usurp the crown and throne, and appeals to him to keep his vow to Bath-sheba. He reminds him that the eyes of all Israel are upon him, and that David's word should be an oracle of honor unto them. He urged the king to immediate action and to put an end to all Adonijah's pretensions at once, which the king did; and Solomon was anointed by the chief priests and proclaimed king.

Adonijah had organized a party, recognizing him as king, as if David were already dead; but when a messenger brought the news that Solomon had been anointed king, in the midst of the feast their jollities were turned to mourning.

Nathan's visits to the king were always welcome, especially when he was sick and when something lay heavy on his heart. He came to the king, not as a petitioner, but as an ambassador from God, not merely to right the wrongs of individuals, but to maintain the honor of the nation.

As David grew older he suffered great depression of spirits, hence his physicians advised that he be surrounded with young company, who might cheer and comfort him with their own happiness and pleasure in life. He was specially cheered by the society of Abishag, the Shunammite, a maiden of great beauty and of many attractions in manner and conversation, and who created a most genial atmosphere in the palace of the king. Bath-sheba's ambition for her son was so all absorbing that she cared but little for the attentions of the king. David reigned forty years, seven in Hebron and thirty-three in Jerusalem.

1 Kings ii.

Now the days of David drew nigh that he should die; and he charged Solomon his son, saying,

2 I go the way of all the earth: be thou strong therefore, and show thyself a man.

It is a great pity that David's advice could not have been fortified by the honor and the uprightness of his own life. "Example is stronger than precept."

1 Kings iii.

16 Then came there two women unto the king, and stood before him.

17 And the one woman said, O my lord. I and this woman dwell in one house: and I was delivered of a child.

18 And it came to pass the third day after, this woman was delivered also:

19 And her child died in the night; because she overlaid it.

20 And she arose at midnight, and took my son from beside me, while thine handmaid slept, and laid it in her bosom, and laid her dead child in my bosom.

21 And when I rose in the morning it was dead; but when I had considered it, behold, it was not my son.

22 And the other woman said, Nay; but the living is my son, and the dead is thy son. And this said, No; but the dead is

thy son, and the living is my son. Thus they spake before the king.

24 And the king said, Bring me a sword. And they brought a sword before the king.

25 And he said, Divide the living child in two, and give half to the one, and half to the other.

26 Then spake the woman whose the living child was unto the king, and she said, O my lord, give her the living child, and in no wise slay it. But the other said, Let it be neither mine nor thine, but divide it.

27 Then the king answered and said, Give her the living child, and in no wise slay it: she is the mother thereof.

28 And all Israel heard of the judgment which the king had judged; and they feared the king for they saw that the wisdom of God was in him to do judgment.

This case was opened in court, not by lawyers, but by the parties themselves, though both plaintiff and defendant were women. Commentators thing that it had already been tried in the lower courts, and the judges not being able to arrive at a satisfactory decision, preferred to submit the case to Solomon the King. It was an occasion of great interest; the halls of justice were crowded, all waiting with great expectation to hear what the king would say. When he said, "bring me my sword," the sages wondered if he intended to kill the parties, as the shortest way to end the case; but his proposition to kill only the living child and give half to each, showed such an intuitive knowledge of human nature that all were impressed with his wisdom, recognizing at once what the natural feelings of the mother would be. Solomon won great reputation by this judgment. The people feared his piercing eye ever after, knowing that he would see the real truth through all disguises and complications.   E. C. S.

In Bath-sheba's interview with David one feature impresses me unfavorably, that she stood before the king instead of being seated during the conference. In the older apostolic churches the elder women and widows were provided with seats—only the young women stood; but in the instance which we are considering the faithful wife of many years, the mother of wise Solomon, stood before her husband. Then David, with the fear of death before his eyes and the warning words of the prophet ringing in his ears, remembered his oath to Bath-sheba. Bath-sheba, the wife of whom no moral wrong is spoken, except her obedience to David in the affairs of her first husband, bowed with her face to the earth and did reverence to the king.

This was entirely wrong: David should have arisen from his bed and done reverence to this woman, his wife, bowing his face to the earth. Yet we find this Bible teaching the subservience of woman to man, of the wife to the husband, of the queen to the king, ruling the world to-day. During the recent magnificent coronation ceremonies of the Czar, his wife, granddaughter of Victoria, Queen of England and Empress of India, who changed her religion in order to become Czarina, knelt before her husband while he momentarily placed the crown upon her brow. A kneeling wife at this era of civilization is proof that the degradation of woman continues from the time of Bath-sheba to that of Alexandria.

In I Kings ii. 13-25, we have a record of Solomon's treatment of that mother to whom he was indebted not only for his throne, but also for life itself. Adonijah, who had lost the kingdom, requested Bath-sheba's influence with Solomon that the fair young Abishag should be given to him for a wife. Having lost his father's kingdom, he thought to console himself with the maiden.

19 So Bath-sheba therefore went unto King Solomon to speak unto him for Adonijah. And the king rose up to meet her, and bowed himself unto her, and sat down on his throne and caused a seat to be set for the king's mother; and she sat on his right hand.

All very well thus far; and the king, in his reception of his mother, showed to her the reverence and the respect which was due to her. Thus emboldened, Bath-sheba said:

20 I desire one small petition of thee; say me not nay. And the king said unto her, Ask on, my mother; for I will not say thee nay.

21 And she said, Let Abishag the Shunammite be given to Adonijah, thy brother, to wife.

But did King Solomon, who owed both throne and life to his mother, keep his word that he had just pledged to her, "Ask on, my mother; for I will not say thee nay?"

No indeed, for was she not a woman, a being to whom it was customary to make promises for the apparent purpose of breaking them; for the king, immediately forgetting his promise of one moment previously, cried out:

22 And why dost thou ask Abishag the Shunammite for Adonijah? ask for him the kingdom also: for he is mine elder brother.

23 Then King Solomon sware by the Lord, saying, God do so to me, and more also, if Adonijah have not spoken this word against his own life.

24 Now therefore, as the Lord liveth, who hath established me, and set me on the throne of David my father, and who hath made me an house, as he promised, Adonijah shall be put to death this day.

Solomon was anxious to give credit to the Lord instead of his mother for having set him on the throne, and also to credit him with having kept his promise, while at the very same moment he was breaking his own promise to his mother. And this promise-breaking to women, taught in the Bible, has been incorporated into the laws of both England and the United States—a true union of Church and State where woman is concerned.

It is only a few years since that a suit was brought in England by a wife against a husband in order to compel the keeping of his ante-nuptial promise that the children of the marriage should be brought up in the mother's religious faith. Having married the woman, this husband and father found it convenient to break his word, ordering her to instruct the children in his own faith, and the highest court in England, that of Appeals, through the vice-chancellor, decided against her upon the ground that a wife has no rights in law against a husband. While a man's word broken at the gaming table renders him infamous, subjecting him to dishonor through life, a husband's pledged word to his wife in this nineteenth century of the Christian era is of no more worth than was the pledged word of

King Solomon to Bath-sheba in the tenth century before the Christian era.

The Albany Law Journal, commenting upon the Agar-Ellis case, declared the English decision to be in harmony with the general law in regard to religious education—the child is to be educated in the religion of its father. But in the case of Bath-sheba, Solomon's surprising acrobatic feat is the more remarkable from the reception which he at first gave to his mother. Not only did Solomon "say her nay," but poor Adonijah lost not only wife, but life also, because of her intercession.

This chapter closes with an account of Solomon's judgment between two mothers, each of whom claimed a living child as her own and the dead child as that of her rival. This judgment has often been referred to as showing the wisdom of Solomon. He understood a mother's boundless love, that the true mother would infinitely prefer that her rival should retain her infant than that the child should be divided between them.

However, this tale, like many another Biblical story, is found imbedded in the folk-lore-myths of other peoples and religions. Prof. White's "Warfare of Science and Theology" quotes Fansböll as finding it in "Buddhist Birth Stories." The able Biblical critic, Henry Macdonald, regards the Israelitish kings as wholly legendary, and Solomon as unreal as Mug Nuadat or Partholan; but let its history be real or unreal, the Bible accurately represents the condition of women under the Jewish patriarchal and the Christian monogamous religions.   M. J. G.

CHAPTER II.

1 Kings x.

1 And when the Queen of Sheba heard of the fame of Solomon concerning the name of the Lord, she came to prove him with hard questions.

2 And she came to Jerusalem with a very great train, with camels that bare spices, and very much gold, and precious stones: and when she was come to Solomon, she communed with him of all that was in her heart.

3 And Solomon told her all her questions.

4 And when the Queen of Sheba had seen all Solomon's wisdom, and the house that he had built,

5 And the meat of his table, and the sitting of his servants, and the attendance of his ministers, and their apparel, and his cup-bearers, and his ascent by which he went up unto the house of the Lord; there was no more spirit in her.

6 And she said to the king, It was a true report that I heard in mine own land of thy acts and of thy wisdom.

7 Howbeit I believed not the words, until I came, and mine eyes had seen it; and, behold, the half was not told me; thy wisdom and prosperity exceedeth the fame which I heard.

9 Blessed be the Lord thy God, which delighteth in thee, to set thee on the throne of Israel.

10 And she gave the king a hundred and twenty talents of gold, and of spices very great store, and precious stones: . . .

13 And King Solomon gave unto the Queen of Sheba all her desire, whatsoever she asked. So she turned and went to her own country.

———

IN the height of Solomon's piety and prosperity the Queen of Sheba came to visit him. She had heard of his great wealth and wisdom and desired to see if all was true. She was called the Queen of the South, supposed to be in Africa. The Christians in Ethiopia say to this day that she came from their country, and that Candace, spoken of in Acts viii., 27, was her successor. She was queen regent, sovereign of her country. Many a kingdom would have been deprived of its greatest blessing if the Salic law had been admitted into its constitution.

It was a great journey for the queen, with her retinue, to undertake. The reports of the magnificence of Solomon's surroundings, the temple of the Lord and the palace for the daughter of Pharaoh, roused her curiosity to see his wealth. The reports of his wisdom inspired her with the hope that she might obtain new ideas on the science of government and help her to establish a more perfect system in her kingdom. She had heard of his piety, too, his religion and the God whom he worshiped, and his maxims of policy in morals and public life. She is mentioned again in the New Testament in Matthew xii., 42. She brought many valuable presents of gold, jewels, spices and precious stones to defray all the expenses of her retinue at Solomon's court, to show him that her country was worthy of honor and of respect.

The queen was greatly surprised with all that she saw, the reality surpassed her wildest imagination. Solomon's reception was most cordial and respectful, and he conversed with her as he would with a friendly king coming to visit from afar. This is the first account which we have in the Bible of a prolonged rational conversation with a woman on questions of public policy. He answered all her questions, though the commentators volunteer the opinion that some may have been frivolous and captious. As the text suggests no such idea, we have a right to assume that her conduct and conversation were pre-eminently judicious. Solomon did not suggest to the queen that she was out of her sphere, that home duties, children and the philosophy of domestic life were the proper subjects for her consideration; but he talked with her as one sovereign should with another.

She was deeply impressed by the elegance of his surroundings, the artistic effect of his table, and the gold, silver and glass, the skill of his servants, the perfect order which reigned throughout the palace, but more than all with his piety and wisdom, and his reverence when he went up to the temple to worship God or to make the customary offering. She wondered at such greatness and goodness combined in one man. Her visit was one succession of surprises; and she rejoiced to find that the truth of all that she had heard exceeded her expectations. She is spoken of in Psalms lxxii., 15, as a pattern for Solomon.

E. C. S.

1 Kings xi.

1 But King Solomon loved many strange women, together with the daughter of Pharaoh, women of the Moabites, Ammonites, Edomites, Zidonians and Hittites:

2 Of the nations concerning which the Lord said unto the children of Israel, Ye shall not go in to them, neither shall they come in unto you: for surely they will turn away your heart after their gods: Solomon clave unto these in love.

3 And he had seven hundred wives, princesses, and three hundred concubines:

4 It came to pass, when Solomon was old, that his wives turned away his heart after other gods: and his heart was not perfect with the Lord his God.

This is a sad story of Solomon's defection and degeneracy. As the Queen of Sheba did not have seven hundred husbands, she had time for travel and the observation of the great world outside of her domain. It is impossible to estimate the *ennui* a thousand women must have suffered crowded together, with only one old gentleman to contemplate; but he probably solaced their many hours with some of his choice songs, so appreciative of the charms of beautiful women. It is probable that his little volume of poems was in the hand of every woman, and that Solomon gave them occasional recitations on the imaginative and emotional nature of women. We have reason to believe that with his wisdom he gave as much variety to their lives as possible, and with fine oratory, graceful manners and gorgeous apparel made himself as attractive as the situation permitted.

E. C. S.

There have been a great number of different views held in regard to the Queen of Sheba, both in reference to the signification of the name "Sheba," and also in relation to the country from which this famous personage made a visit to Solomon. Abyssinia, Ethiopia, Persia and Arabia have each laid claim to this wise woman. Menelik, the present king of the former country, who so effectually defeated Italy in his recent war with that country, possesses the same name as, and claims descent from, the fabled son of this wise woman and of the wise king Solomon, one of whose numerous wives, it is traditionally said, she became. Ethiopia, the seat of a very ancient and great civilization, and whose capital was called Saba; Persia, where the worship of the sun and of fire originated; and Arabia, the country of gold, of frankincense and of myrrh, also claim her. It is to the latter country that this queen belonged.

Whether we look upon the Bible as a historical work, a mythological work, or, as many now do regard it, as "A Book of the Adepts, written by Initiates, for Initiates," a record of ancient mysteries hidden to all but initiates, the Queen of Sheba is a most interesting character.

The words Sab, Saba, Sheba, all have an astronomical or astrological meaning, signifying the "Host of Heaven," "The Planetary System." Saba, or Sheba, was especially the home of astronomical wisdom; and all words of this character mean wise in regard to the stars. The wisdom of Saba and of the Sabeans was planetary wisdom, the "Sabean language" meaning astronomy, or astrology, the latter being the esoteric portion of the science. At the time of the mysteries, astrology was a sacred or secret science, the words "sacred" and "secret" meaning the same thing. Among the oldest mysteries, when all learning was confined to initiates, were those of Sabasia, whose periodic festivals of a sacred character were so extremely ancient that their origin is now lost.

Solomon, also, whether looked upon as a historical or a mythical character, is philologically shown to have been connected with the planetary system, Sol-Om-On signifying "the sun." It is singular to note how closely the sun, the moon and the stars are connected with ancient religions, even that of the Jewish. In the Old Testament the new moon and the Sab-bath are almost invariably mentioned together. The full moon also possessed a religious signification to the Jews, the agricultural feasts taking place at the full moon, which were called Sab-baths. Even in the Old Testament we find that Sab has an astronomical or astrological meaning, connected with the planetary system.

The Sabeans were an occult body, especially devoted to a study of the heavens; at their head, the wisest among them, the chief astronomer and astrologer of the nation, the wisest person in a nation of wisdom, was that Queen of Sheba, who visited that other planetary dignitary, Solomon, to prove him with hard astronomical and astrological questions.

There is historic proof that the city of Saba was the royal seat of the kings of Arabia, which country, Diodorus says, was never conquered. Among ancient peoples it bore the names of "Araby the Happy," "Araby the Blest." It was a country of gold and spices whose perfume was wafted far over the sea. All cups and utensils were of the precious metals; all beds, chairs and stools having feet of silver; the temples were magnificently adorned; and the porticoes of even the private houses were of gold inlaid with ivory and precious stones.

Among the presents carried by the Queen of Sheba to Sol-Om-On were the famous balsam trees of her country. The first attempt at plant acclimatizing of which the world has record was made with this tree by the magnificent Pharaoh, Queen Hatasu, of the brilliant eighteenth Egyptian dynasty. A thousand years before she of Sheba, Queen Hatasu, upon her return from a naval expedition to the Red Sea, carried home with her twelve of these trees in baskets of earth, which lived and became one of the three species of sacred trees of Egypt.

Arabia was the seat of Eastern wisdom, from which it also radiated to the British Isles of Europe at the time of the Celtic Druids, with whom Sabs was the day when these lords of Sabaoth rested from study and gave instructions to the people. As previously among the Jews, this day of instruction became known as one of rest from physical labor, Sab-bath and rest becoming synonymous. Seven being a sacred number among initiates, every seventh day was devoted to instruction. When a knowledge of the mysteries became lost, the words "Sab-bath," "rest" and "seven" began to have a very wrong meaning in the minds of people; and much injury has been done to the world through this perversion.

But later than Druidical times, Arabian wisdom made the southwestern portion of the European continent brilliant with learning, during the long period of the Christian dark ages, a time when, like the Bourbons of later date, Christians learned nothing, a time when no heresy arose because no thought was allowed, when there was no progress because there was no doubt.

From these countrymen of the Queen of Sheba, the Spanish Arabs, Columbus first learned of a world beyond the Pillars of Hercules. Architecture rose to its height in the beautiful Alhambra, with its exquisite interlaced tracery in geometric design; medicine had its profound schools at various points; poetry numbered women among its most famous composers; the ballad originated there; and the modern literature of Europe was born from a woman's pen upon the hearth of the despised Ishmaelite, whose ancestral mother was known as Hagar, and whose most brilliant descendant was the Queen of Sheba.

Nowhere upon the earth has there existed a race of improvisatores equal to the daughters of that despised bondwoman, the countrywoman of the Queen of Sheba. As storytellers the world has not their equal. Scherezade is a name upon the lips of Jews, of Gentiles, of Mohammedans and of Christians. A woman's "Thousand and One Nights" is famous as a combination of wit, wisdom and occultism wherever the language of civilization is spoken. With increasing knowledge we learn somewhat of the mysteries of the inner, higher life contained in those tales of genii, of rings and of lamps of wondrous and curious power. The race descended from Hagar, of which the Queen of Sheba is the most brilliant reminder, has given to the world the most of its profound literature, elegant poetry, art, science and occultism. Arabia is the mother of mathematics; from this country was borrowed our one (1) and our cipher (o), from which all other notation is evolved.

Astronomy and astrology being among the oldest sciences, the moon early became known as "the Measurer," her varied motions, her influence upon the tides, her connection with the generative functions, all giving her a high place in the secret sciences. While in a planetary sense the Queen of Sheba has in a manner been identified with the moon, as Sabs, she was also connected with the sun, the same as Solomon and the serpent. When Moses lifted up the brazen serpent in the wilderness it was specifically a part of sun worship. The golden calf of Aaron was more closely connected with moon worship, although the serpentine path of both these bodies in the heavens identified each with the serpent.

The occult knowledge which the Jews possessed in regard to those planets was borrowed by them from Egypt, where for many ages the sun and the moon had been studied in connection with their movements in the zodiac. In that country these serpentine movements were symbolized by the urœus, or asp, worn upon the crown above the head of every Pharaoh. So closely was the Jewish religion connected with worship of the planetary bodies that Moses is said to have disappeared upon Mount Nebo, a word which shows the mountain to have been sacred to the moon; while Elijah ascending in a chariot of fire is a record of sun worship. When the famous woman astronomer and astrologer, Queen of Sheba, visited the symbolic King Solomon, it was for the purpose of proving him with hard planetary questions and thus learning the depth of his astronomical and his astrological knowledge, which, thanks to the planetary worship of the Jews, she found equal to her own.

We are further told that Solomon, not content with a princess from the royal house of Pharaoh as wife, married seven hundred wives, all princesses, besides taking to himself three hundred concubines. It is upon teachings of the Old Testament, and especially from this statement in regard to Solomon, that the Mormons of Utah largely base their polygamous doctrines, the revelations of Joseph Smith being upon the Solomon line. Yet the Mormons have advanced in their treatment of women from the time of Solomon. While the revelations of Joseph Smith commended plural marriages, the system and the name of concubinage was entirely omitted, each woman thus taken being endowed with the name of "wife."

The polygamy of New York, of Chicago, of London, of Paris, of Vienna and of other parts of the Christian world, like that of Solomon's three hundred, is a system of concubinage in which the woman possesses no legal rights, the mistress neither being recognized as wife, nor her children as legitimate; whereas Mormon polygamy grants Mormon respect to the second, the third, and to all subsequent wives.

The senility of old men is well illustrated in the case of Solomon, despite Biblical reference to his great wisdom, as we learn that when he became "old" he was led away by "strange" women, worshiping strange gods to whom he erected temples and offered sacrifices. To those who believe in the doctrine of re-incarnation, and who look upon the Bible as an occult work written in symbolic language,

Solomon's reputed "wives" and "concubines" are regarded as symbolic of his incarnations, the wives representing good incarnations and the concubines evil ones.   M. J. G.

---

1 Kings xvii.

8 And the word of the Lord came unto him, saying,

9 Arise, get thee to Zarephath, and dwell there: behold, I have commanded a widow there to sustain thee.

10 So he arose and went to Zarephath. And when he came to the gate of the city, behold, the widow was there gathering sticks: and he called to her, and said, Fetch me, I pray thee, a little water and a morsel of bread.

12 And she said, I have not a cake, but a handful of meal in a barrel, and a little oil in a cruse: and I am gathering sticks, that I may dress it for me and my son, that we may eat it, and die.

13 And Elijah said unto her, Fear not; go and do as thou hast said: but make me thereof a little cake first, and after make for thee and for thy son.

14 For thus saith the Lord God of Israel, The barrel of meal shall not waste, neither shall the cruse of oil fail, until the day that the Lord sendeth rain upon the earth.

15 And she went and did according to the saying of Elijah: and she, and he, and her house, did eat many days.

16 And the barrel of meal wasted not, neither did the cruse of oil fail.

17 And it came to pass after these things, that the son of the woman fell sick; and there was no breath left in him.

18 And she said unto Elijah, What have I to do with thee, O thou man of God? art thou come unto me to call my sin to remembrance, and to slay my son?

19 And he said unto her, Give me thy son. And he carried him up and laid him upon his own bed.

20 And he cried unto the Lord and said, O Lord my God, hast thou also brought evil upon the widow by slaying her son?

21 And he stretched himself upon the child three times, and cried unto the Lord, and said, O Lord my God, I pray thee, let this child's soul come into him again.

22 And the Lord heard the voice of Elijah; and the soul of the child came into him again, and he revived.

23 And Elijah took the child and delivered him unto his mother, and said, See, thy son liveth.

24 And the woman said, Now I know that thou art a man of God.

The history of Elijah the prophet begins somewhat abruptly, without any mention of father, of family or of country. He seems, as it were, suddenly to drop from the clouds. He does not come with glad tidings of joy to the people; but with prophecies of a prolonged famine, in which there shall be neither rain nor dew to moisten the earth, until King Ahab and his people repent of their sins. Elijah himself was fed by ravens in a miraculous manner, and later by a poor widow who had only just enough in her larder to furnish one meal for herself and her son. Here are a series of complications enough to stagger the faith of the strongest believer in the supernatural. But the poor widow meets him at the gates of the city as directed by the Lord, improvises bread and water, takes him to her home and for two years treats him with all the kindness and the attention which she would naturally give to one of her own kinsmen. "Oh! woman, great is thy faith," exclaimed the prophet. Women are so easily deluded that most of the miracles of the Bible are performed for their benefit; and, as in the case of the witch of Endor, she occasionally performs some herself.

The widow believed that Elijah was "a man of God," and that she could do whatever he ordered; that she could get water, though there had been a drought for a long time; that although she had only a handful of meal and a little cruse of oil, yet they would increase day by day. "Never did corn or olives in the growing," says Bishop Hall, "increase as did that of the widow in the using." During the two years in which she entertained the prophet, she enjoyed peace and prosperity; but when she supposed that her son was dead, her faith wavered; and she deplored her kindness to the prophet, and reproved him for bringing sorrow upon her household. However, as the prophet was able to restore him to life, her faith was restored also.

This is the first record which we have of the restoration of the dead to life in the Bible; and it is the first also of any one ascending into heaven "in a chariot of fire with horses of fire." Probably Elijah knew how to construct a balloon. Much of the ascending and the descending of seers, of angels and of prophets which astonished the ignorant was accomplished in balloons—a lost art for many centuries. No doubt that the poor widow, when she saw Elijah ascend, thought that he went straight to heaven, though in all probability he landed at twilight in some retired corn field or olive grove, at some distance from the point where his ascent took place.

The question is often asked where the ravens got the cooked meat and bread for the prophet. Knowing their impelling instinct to steal, the Creator felt safe in trusting his prophet to their care, and they proved themselves worthy his confidence. Their rookeries were near the cave where Elijah was sequestered. Having keen olfactories, they smelt the cooking of dainty viands from afar. Guided by this sense, they perched on a fence near by where they could watch the movements of the cook, and when her back was turned they flew in and seized the little birds and soft shell crabs and carried them to Elijah, halting by the way only long enough to satisfy their own imperative hunger.

Jezebel was Elijah's greatest enemy; yet the Lord bade him hide in her country by the brook Cherith, that he might have plenty of water. The Lord hid him so that the people should not besiege him to shorten the drought. So he was entirely alone with the ravens, and had all his time for prayer and contemplation. When removed from the care of the ravens, the Lord did not send him to the rich and the prosperous, but to a poor widow, who, believing him a man of God, ministered to his necessities. She did not suggest that he was a stranger to her and that water cost money, but hastened to do whatever he ordered. She had her recompense in the restoration of her son to life. In the prophet's struggle with God for this blessing to the widow, the man appears to greater advantage than does the Master.

It appears from the reports in our metropolitan journals that a railroad is now about to be built from Tor to the summit of Mount Sinai. The mountain is only accessible on one side. A depot, it is said, will be erected near the spot where a stone cross was placed by the Russian Empress Helena, and where, according to tradition, Moses stood when receiving the commandments. The railroad will also pass the cave in which the prophet Elijah remained in hiding while fleeing from the priest of Baal.

1 Kings xxi.

And it came to pass after these things, that Naboth the Jezreelite had a vineyard, hard by the palace of Ahab king of Samaria.

2 And Ahab spake unto Naboth, saying, Give me thy vineyard, because it is near unto my house: and I will give thee the worth of it.

3 And Naboth said to Ahab, The Lord forbid that I should give the inheritance of my fathers unto thee.

4 And Ahab came into his house heavy and displeased because of the word which Naboth had spoken to him. And he laid him down upon his bed, and turned away his face, and would eat no bread.

5 But Jezebel his wife came to him, and said unto him, Why is thy spirit so sad?

6 And he said unto her, Because I spake unto Naboth, and said unto him, Give me thy vineyard for money; and he answered, I will not.

7 And Jezebel his wife said unto him, Dost thou now govern the kingdom of Israel? arise, and let thine heart be merry: I will give thee the vineyard of Naboth.

8 So she wrote letters in Ahab's name, and sealed them with his seal, and sent the letters unto the elders and to the nobles that were in his city.

9 And she wrote in the letters, saying,

Proclaim a fast, and set Naboth on high among the people:

10 And set two men, sons of Belial, before him, to bear witness against him, saying, Thou didst blaspheme God and the king. And then carry him out, and stone him, that he may die.

11 And the men of his city did as Jezebel had sent unto them.

12 They proclaimed a fast, and set Naboth on high among the people.

13 And there came in two men and sat before him: and the men witnessed against him, saying, Naboth did blaspheme God and the king. Then they carried him forth and stoned him with stones, that he died.

14 Then they sent to Jezebel, saying, Naboth is dead.

15 And it came to pass, when Jezebel heard that Naboth was dead, she said to Ahab, Arise, take possession of the vineyard.

Jezebel, the daughter of the king of the Zidonians and the wife of Ahab, is generally referred to as the most wicked and cruel woman on record; and her name is the synonym of all that is evil. She came honestly by these characteristics, if it is true "that evil communications corrupt good manners," as her husband Ahab was the most wicked of all the kings of Israel. And yet he does not seem to have been a man of much fortitude; for in a slight disappointment in the purchase of land he comes home in a hopeless mood, throws himself on his bed and turns his face to the wall. According to the text, Jezebel was equal to the occasion. She not only infused new life into Ahab, but got possession of the desired land, though in a most infamous manner. The false prophetess spoken of in Rev. ii., 20, is called Jezebel. She was a devout adherent and worshiper of Baal and influenced Ahab to follow strange gods. He reigned twenty-two years without one worthy action to gild his memory. Jezebel's death, like her life, was a tragedy of evil.

E. C. S.

All we know about Jezebel is told us by a rival religionist, who hated her as the Pope of Rome hated Martin Luther, or as an American A. P. A. now hates a Roman Catholic. Nevertheless, even the Jewish historian, evidently biassed against Jezebel by his theological prejudices as he is, does not give any facts whatever which warrant the assertion that Jezebel was any more satanic than the ancient Israelitish gentleman, to whom her theological views were opposed. Of course we, at this stage of scientific thought, know that Jezebel's religion was not an admirable one. Strangely enough, for a religion, it actually made her intolerant! But to Jezebel it was a truth, for which she battled as bravely as Elijah did for what he imagined to be eternal verity. The facts, admitted even by the historian who hated her, prove that, notwithstanding her unfortunate and childish conception of theology, Jezebel was a brave, fearless, generous woman, so wholly devoted to her own husband that even wrong seemed justifiable to her, if she could thereby make him happy. (In that respect she seems to have entirely fulfilled the Southern Methodist's ideal of the pattern wife absorbed in her husband.) Four hundred of the preachers of her own faith were fed at her table (what a pity we have not their opinion of their benefactor!). Elijah was the preacher of a new and rival religion, which Jezebel, naturally, regarded with that same abhorrence which the established always feel for the innovating. To her, Elijahism doubtless appeared as did Christianity to the Jews, Lutheranism to the Pope, or John Wesleyism to the Church of England; but in the days of the Israelites the world had not developed that sweet patience with heresy which animates the Andover theologians of our time, and Jezebel had as little forbearance with Elijah as had Torquemada with the Jews or Elizabeth with the Puritans.

Yet, to do Jezebel justice, we must ask ourselves, how did the assumedly good Elijah proceed in order to persuade her of the superiority of his truth? It is painful to have to relate that that much-overestimated "man of God" invited four hundred and fifty of Jezebel's preachers to an open air exhibition of miracles, but, not satisfied with gaining a victory over them in this display, he pursued his defeated rivals in religion, shouting, "Let not one of them escape!" and thus roused the thoughtless mob of lookers-on to slaughter the whole four hundred and fifty in cold blood! Jezebel had signalized her advent as queen by slaying Israelitish preachers in order to put her own preachers in office. Elijah promptly retaliated at his earliest opportunity.

It seems to me that it would puzzle a disinterested person to decide which of those savage deeds was more "satanic" than the other, and to imagine why Jezebel is now dragged forth to "shake her gory locks" as a frightful example to the American women who ask for recognized right to self-government. I submit, that if Jezebel is a

disgrace to womankind, our dear brethren at any rate have not much
cause to be proud of Elijah, so, possibly, we might strike a truce over
the character of these two long-buried worthies. It may be well,
though, to note here that the now most offensive epithet which the
English translators attached to Jezebel's name, originally signified
nothing more than that she was consecrated to the worship of a religion, rival to that which ancient Israel assumed to be "the only true
one."   E. B. D.

CHAPTER III.

2 Kings iv.

1 Now there cried a certain woman of the wives of the sons of the prophets unto Elisha, saying, Thy servant my husband is dead; and thou knowest that thy servant did fear the Lord: and the creditor is come to take unto him my two sons to be bondmen.

2 And Elisha said unto her, What shall I do for thee? tell me, what hast thou in the house? And she said, Thine handmaid hath not anything save a pot of oil.

3 Then he said, Go, borrow thee vessels abroad of all thy neighbors,

4 And when thou art come in, thou shalt shut the door and shalt pour out into all those vessels, and thou shalt set aside that which is full.

5 So she shut the door and poured out.

6 And it came to pass, when the vessels were full, that she said unto her son, Bring me yet a vessel. And he said unto her, There is not a vessel more. And the oil stayed.

7 Then she came and told the man of God. And he said, Go, sell the oil, and pay thy debt, and live thou and thy children of the rest.

THE first Book of Kings had an illustrious beginning in the glories of the kingdom of Israel when it was entirely under King David and in the beginning of the reign of Solomon; but the second book has a melancholy outlook in the desolation and division of the kingdom of Israel and of Judea. Then Elijah and Elisha, their prophets, instructed the princes and the people in all that would come to pass, the captivity of the ten tribes, the destruction of Jerusalem, and the good reigns of Josiah and of Hezekiah.

This book contains the mention of four women, but only in a perfunctory manner, more to exhibit the accomplishments of the prophet Elisha than his beneficiaries. He raises the dead, surpasses our Standard Oil Company in the production of that valuable article of commerce, cures one man of leprosy and cruelly fastens the disease on his servant for being guilty of a pardonable prevarication. Only one of the women mentioned has a name. One is the widow of a prophet, whom Elisha helps to pay off all her debts; for another he intercedes with the Lord to give her a son; another, is the little captive maid of the tribe of Israel; and the last a wicked queen, Athaliah, who sought to kill the heir apparent. She rivalled Jezebel in her evil propensities and suffered the same tragic death.

As the historian proceeds from book to book less is said of the mothers of the various tribes, unless some deed of darkness is called for, that the men would fain avoid, then some Jezebel is resurrected for that purpose. They are seldom required to rise to a higher moral altitude than the men of the tribe, and are sometimes permitted to fall below it.

2 Kings iv.

8 And it fell on a day, that Elisha passed to Shunem, where was a great woman; and she constrained him to eat bread.

9 And she said unto her husband, Behold now, I perceive that this is a holy man of God.

10 Let us make a little chamber on the wall.

11 And it fell on a day that, he came thither; and he turned into the chamber, and lay there.

12 And he said to Gehazi his servant, Call this Shunammite. And she came and stood before him. And he said, Thou shalt embrace a son. And she said, Nay, thou man of God, do not lie unto thine handmaid.

17 And the woman bare a son.

18 And when the child was grown, he went out to his father to the reapers.

19 And said, My head, my head! And he said to a lad, Carry him to his mother.

20 And when he had brought him to his mother, he sat on her knees till noon, and then died.

21 And she went up, and laid him on the bed of the man of God, and shut the door upon him, and went out.

24 And she saddled an ass, and said to her servant, Drive; slack not thy riding, except I bid thee.

25 So she went unto the man of God to Mount Carmel.

32 And when Elisha was come into the house, behold the child was dead.

33 He went in and shut the door and prayed unto the Lord.

34 And lay upon the child, and put his mouth upon his mouth, and his eyes upon his eyes, and his hands upon his hands; and he stretched himself upon the child; and the flesh of the child waxed warm.

35 Then he walked to and fro; and went up, and stretched upon him; and the child sneezed seven times, and opened his eyes.

36 And he called Gehazi, and said, Call this Shunammite. So he called her. And when she was come in unto him, he said, Take up thy son.

37 Then she fell at his feet, and bowed herself to the ground, and took up her son.

Elisha seems to have had the same power of working miracles which Elijah possessed. In his travels about the country he often passed the city of Shunem, where he heard of a great woman who was very hospitable and had a rich husband. She had often noticed the prophet passing by; and knowing that he was a godly man, and that he could be better entertained at her house than elsewhere, she proposed to her husband to invite him there. So they arranged an apartment for him in a quiet part of the house that he might have opportunities for worship and contemplation.

After spending much time under her roof, he naturally desired to make some recompense. So he asked her if there was anything that he could do for her at court, any favor which she desired of the king.

But she said "no," as she had all the blessings which she desired, ex-cept, as they had great wealth and no children to inherit it, she would like a son. She had probably heard of all that the Lord had done in that line for Sarah and Rebecca and the wives of Manoah and Elkanah; so she was not much surprised when the prophet sug-gested such a contingency; and she bare a son.

In due time, when the son was grown, he was taken suddenly ill and died. The mother supposed that, as by a miracle he was brought into life, the prophet might raise him from the dead. Accord-ingly, she harnessed her mule and hastened to the prophet, who promptly returned with her and restored him to life. She was a very discreet and judicious woman and her husband had always entrusted everything to her management. She was devout and conscientious and greatly enjoyed the godly conversation of the prophet. She was known in the city as a great and good woman. Though we find here and there among the women of the Bible some exceptionally evil minded, yet the wise and virtuous predominate, and, fortunately for the race, this is the case in the American Republic to-day.

2 Kings v.

1 Now Naaman, captain of the hosts of the king of Syria, was a great man with his master, and honorable, because by him the Lord had given deliverance unto Syria: he was also a mighty man of valor, but he was a leper.

2 And the Syrians had brought away cap-tive out of the land of Israel a little maid; and she waited on Naaman's wife.

3 And she said unto her mistress, Would my lord were with the prophet that is in Samaria! for he would recover him of his leprosy.

4 And one went in and told his lord, say-ing, Thus and thus said the maid that is of the land of Israel.

Naaman, a Syrian general and prime minister, was a great man in a great place. He was happy, too, in that he had been serviceable to his country and honored by his prince. But alas! he was a leper. It was generally supposed that this was an affliction for evil doing, but Naaman was an exceptionally perfect man.

A little maid from Israel had been carried captive into Syria and fortunately was taken into the family of the great general, as an at-tendant on his wife. While making the wife's toilet they no doubt chatted quite freely of what was going on in the outside world. So the little maid, sympathizing with her master in his affliction, told the

wife there was a prophet in Israel who could cure him of his leprosy.
Her earnestness roused him and his wife to make the experiment.
But after loading his white mules with many valuable gifts, and taking a great retinue of soldiers to dazzle the prophet with Syrian magnificence, the prophet did not deign to meet him, but sent word to him
to bathe in the river Jordan. Even a letter from the king did not
ensure a personal interview. So the general, with all his pomp, went
off in great wrath. "Are not," said he, "the rivers of Damascus,
Abana and Pharpar, greater than the Jordan? Cannot all the skill in
Syria accomplish as much as the prophet in Israel?" However, the
little maid urged him to try the river Jordan, as he was near that
point, so he did and was healed.

2 Kings viii.

Then spake Elisha unto the woman,
whose son he had restored to life, saying,
sojourn wheresoever thou canst for a famine shall come upon the land seven years.

2 And the woman arose, and did after
the saying of the man of God:

3 And it came to pass at the seven years'
end, that the woman returned out of the
land of the Philistines: and she went forth
to cry unto the king for her house and land.

4 And the king talked with Gehazi saying, Tell me, I pray thee, all the great
things that Elisha hath done.

5 And it came to pass, as he was telling
the king how he had restored a dead body
to life, that, behold, the woman cried to the
king for her house and land. And Gehazi
said, My lord, O king, this is the woman,
and this is her son, whom Elisha restored
to life.

6 And when the king asked the woman,
she told him. So the king appointed unto
her a certain officer, saying, Restore all that
was hers, and all the fruits of the field
since the day that she left the land, even
until now.

In due time her husband died; and there was a famine; and she
went for a season to the land of the Philistines; and when she returned she could not recover her possessions. Then Elisha be-
friended her and appealed to the king; and she was reinstated in her
own home.

Elisha was very democratic. He had his servant sleep in his
own chamber and consulted him in regard to many important matters. Gehazi never forgot his place but once, when he ran after the
great Syrian general to ask for the valuable presents which the
prophet had declined. Both Elijah and Elisha preferred to do their
missionary work among the common people, finding them more
teachable and superstitious. Especially is this true of woman at all
periods. In great revival seasons in our own day, one will always

see a dozen women on the anxious seat to one man, and the same at the communion table.

2 Kings xi.

And when Athaliah the mother of Ahaziah saw that her son was dead, she arose and destroyed all the seed royal.

2 But Jehosheba, sister of Ahaziah, took Joash the son of Ahaziah, and stole him from among the king's sons which were slain; and they hid him and his nurse.

3 And he was with her hid in the house of the Lord six years. And Athaliah did reign over the land.

12 And Jehoiada the priest brought forth the king's son, and put the crown upon him; and they made him king, and anointed him; and they clapped their hands, and said, God save the king.

13 And when Athaliah heard the noise of the guard and of the people, she came into the temple of the Lord.

14 And when she looked, behold, the king stood by a pillar; and she rent her clothes and cried, Treason, treason.

20 And they slew Athaliah with the sword beside the king's house.

21 Seven years old was Jehoash when he began to reign.

Never was royal blood more profusely shed, and never a meaner ambition than to destroy a reigning family in order to be the last occupant on the throne. The daughter of a king, the wife of a king, and the mother of a king, should have had some mercy on her family descendants. Personal ambition can never compensate for the loss of the love and companionship of kindred. Such characters as Athaliah are abnormal, their lives not worth recording.

2 Kings xxii.

11 And it came to pass, when the king had heard the words of the book of the law, that he rent his clothes.

12 And the king commanded Hilkiah the priest,

13 Go ye, inquire of the Lord for me, and for the people, and for all Judah, concerning the words of this book that is found: for great is the wrath of the Lord that is kindled against us, because our fathers have not hearkened unto the words of this book, to do according unto all that which is written concerning us.

14 So Hilkiah the priest, and the wise men went unto Huldah the prophetess, the wife of Shallum keeper of the wardrobe; (now she dwelt in Jerusalem in the college); and they communed with her.

15 Aid she said unto them, Thus saith the Lord God of Israel, Tell the man that sent you to me.

16 Thus saith the Lord, Behold, I will bring evil upon this place, and upon the inhabitants thereof, even all the words of the book which the king of Judah hath read:

17 Because they have forsaken me, and have burned incense unto other gods,

18 But to the king of Judah which sent you to inquire of the Lord, thus shall ye say to him,

19 Because thine heart was tender, and thou hast humbled thyself before the Lord, when thou heardest what I spake against this place,

20 Behold therefore, I will gather thee unto thy fathers, and thou shalt be gathered into thy grave in peace; and thine eyes shall not see all the evil which I will bring upon this place. And they brought the king word again.

The greatest character among the women thus far mentioned is Huldah the prophetess, residing in the college in Jerusalem. She was a statesman as well as a prophetess, understanding the true policy of government and the Jewish system of jurisprudence, able not only to advise the common people of their duties to Jehovah and their country, but to teach kings the sound basis for a kingdom. Her wisdom and insight were well known to Josiah the king; and when the wise men came to him with the "Book of the Law," to learn what was written therein, Josiah ordered them to take it to Huldah, as neither the wise men nor Josiah himself could interpret its contents.   It is fair to suppose that there was not a man at court who could read the book; hence the honor devolved upon Huldah. Even Shallum her husband was not consulted, as he occupied the humble office of keeper of the robes.

While Huldah was pondering great questions of State and Ecclesiastical Law, her husband was probably arranging the royal buttons and buckles of the household.   This is the first mention of a woman in a college.   She was doubtless a professor of jurisprudence, or of the languages.   She evidently had other gifts besides that of prophecy.

We should not have had such a struggle in our day to open the college doors had the clergy read of the dignity accorded to Huldah. People who talk the most of what the Bible teaches often know the least about its contents.   Some years ago, when we were trying to establish a woman's college, we asked a rich widow, worth millions, to contribute.   She said that she would ask her pastor what she ought to do about it.   He referred her to the Bible, saying that this book makes no mention of colleges for women.   To her great surprise, I referred her to 2 Kings xxii.   Both she and her pastor felt rather ashamed that they did not know what their Bible did teach. The widow gave $30,000 soon after to a Theological Seminary, being more interested in the education of boys and in the promulgation of church dogmas, creeds and superstitions, than in the education of the Mothers of the Race in the natural sciences.

Now, women had performed great deeds in Bible times. Miriam had helped to lead Israel out of Egypt.   Deborah judged them, and led the army against the enemy, and Huldah instructed them in their duties to the nation. Although Jeremiah and Zephaniah were

prophets at this time, yet the king chose Huldah as the oracle. She was one of the ladies of the court, and resided in the second rank of buildings from the royal palace. Marriage, in her case, does not appear to have been any obstacle in the way of individual freedom and dignity. She had evidently outgrown the curse of subjection pronounced in the Garden of Eden, as had many other of the Jewish women.

There is a great discrepancy between the character and the conduct of many of the women, and the designs of God as set forth in the Scriptures and enforced by the discipline of the Church to-day. Imagine the moral hardihood of the reverend gentlemen who should dare to reject such women as Deborah, Huldah and Vashti as delegates to a Methodist conference, and claim the approval of God for such an indignity.

In the four following books, from Kings to Esther, there is no mention of women. During that long, eventful period the men must have sprung, Minerva-like, from the brains of their fathers, fully armed and equipped for the battle of life. Having no infancy, there was no need of mothers. As two remarkable women flourished at the close of one period and at the dawn of the other, we shall make no record of the masculine dynasty which intervened, satisfied that Huldah and Vashti added new glory to their day and generation—one by her learning and the other by her disobedience; for "Resistance to tyrants is obedience to God." E. C. S.

THE BOOK OF ESTHER.

2 In those days when King Ahasuerus sat upon the throne in the palace at Shushan,

3 In the third year of his reign, he made a feast unto all his princes and his servants; the power of Persia and Media, the nobles and princes of the provinces being before him:

4 When he shewed the riches of his glorious kingdom and the honor of his excellent majesty many days.

5 And when these days were expired, the king made a feast unto all the people that were present in Shushan the palace, both unto great and small, seven days, in the court of the garden;

6 Where were white, green and blue hangings, fastened with cords of fine linen and purple to silver rings and pillars of marble: the beds were of gold and silver, upon a pavement of red, and blue, and white, and black marble.

7 And they gave them drink in vessels of gold, and royal wine in abundance.

9 Also Vashti the queen made a feast for the women in the royal house.

10 On the seventh day, when the heart of the king was merry with wine, he commanded:

11 To bring Vashti the queen with the crown royal, to shew the people and the princes her beauty: for she was fair to look on.

12 But the queen Vashti refused to come: therefore was the king very wroth.

13 Then the king said to the wise men,

15 What shall we do unto the queen Vashti according to the law?

16 And Memucan answered, Vashti the queen hath not done wrong to the king only, but also to all the people that are in the provinces of the king.

17 For this deed shall come abroad unto all women, so that they shall despise their husbands. The king Ahasuerus commanded Vashti the queen to be brought in before him, but she came not.

18 Likewise shall the ladies of Persia and Media say this day unto all the king's princes, which have heard of the deed of the queen.

19 If it please the king, let there go a royal command from him, and let it be written among the laws of the Persians and the Medes, That Vashti come no more before king Ahasuerus; and let the king give her royal estate unto another that is better than she.

20 And when the king's decree shall be published throughout his empire, all the wives shall give to their husband's honor, both to great and small.

21 And the saying pleased the king and the princes; and the king did accordingly to the word of Memucan:

22 For he sent letters into all the provinces, that every man should bear rule in his own house.

THE kingdom of Ahasuerus extended from India to Ethiopia, consisting of one hundred and twenty-seven provinces, an overgrown kingdom which in time sunk by its own weight. The king was fond of display and invited subjects from all his provinces to come by turns to behold his magnificent palaces and sumptuous entertainments.

He gave two great feasts in the beginning of his reign, one to the nobles and the princes, and one to the people, which lasted over a hundred days. The king had the feast for the men spread in the court under the trees. Vashti entertained her guests in the great hall of the palace. It was not the custom among the Persians for the sexes to eat promiscuously together, especially when the king and the princes were partaking freely of wine.

This feast ended in heaviness, not as Balshazzar's with a hand-writing on the wall, nor like that of Job's children with a wind from the wilderness, but by the folly of the king, with an unhappy falling out between the queen and himself, which ended the feast abruptly and sent the guests away silent and ashamed. He sent seven different messages to Vashti to put on her royal crown, which greatly enhanced her beauty, and come to show his guests the majesty of his queen. But to all the chamberlains alike she said, "Go tell the king I will not come; dignity and modesty alike forbid."

This vanity of a drunken man illustrates the truth of an old proverb, "When the wine is in, the wit is out." Josephus says that all the court heard his command; hence, while he was showing the glory of his court, he also showed that he had a wife who would do as she pleased.

Besides seven chamberlains he had seven learned counsellors whom he consulted on all the affairs of State. The day after the feast, when all were sober once more, they held a cabinet council to discuss a proper punishment for the rebellious queen. Memucan, Secretary of State, advised that she be divorced for her disobedience and ordered "to come no more before the king," for unless she was severely punished, he said, all the women of Medea and of Persia would despise the commands of their husbands.

We have some grand types of women presented for our admiration in the Bible. Deborah for her courage and military prowess; Huldah for her learning, prophetic insight and statesmanship, seated in the college in Jerusalem, where Josiah the king sent his cabinet ministers to consult her as to the policy of his government; Esther, who ruled as well as reigned, and Vashti, who scorned the Apostle's command, "Wives, obey your husbands." She refused the king's orders to grace with her presence his revelling court. Tennyson pays this tribute to her virtue and dignity:

"Oh, Vashti! noble Vashti!
Summoned forth, she kept her state,
And left the drunken king to brawl
In Shushan underneath his palms."

E. C. S.

The feast, with the preliminary exhibition of the king's magnificent palace and treasures, was not a social occasion in which the king and the queen participated under the same roof. The equal dignity of woman and of queen as companion of the king was not recognized. The men feasted together purely as a physical enjoyment. If there was any intellectual feature of the occasion it is not recorded. On the seventh day, when appetite was satiated and the heart of the king was merry with wine, as a further means of gratifying sensual tastes and exhibiting his power, the king bethought him of the beauty of the queen.

The command to the chamberlains was to bring Vashti. It was such an order as he might have sent to the jester, or to any other person whose sole duty was to do the king's bidding, and whose presence might add to the entertainment of his assemblage of men. It was not an invitation which anywise recognized the queen's condescension in honoring the company by her presence.

But Vashti refused to come at the king's command! An unprecedented act of both wife and queen. Probably Vashti had had previous knowledge of the condition of the king when his heart was merry with wine and when the physical man was under the effects of seven day's conviviality. She had a higher idea of womanly dignity than placing herself on exhibition as one of the king's possessions, which it pleased him to present to his assembled princes. Vashti is conspicuous as the first woman recorded whose self-respect and courage enabled her to act contrary to the will of her husband. She was the first "woman who dared."

This was the more marked because her husband was also king. So far as the record proves, woman had been obedient to the commands of the husband and the father, or, if seeking to avoid them, had sought indirect methods and diplomacy. It was the first exhibition of the individual sovereignty of woman on record. Excepting Deborah as judge, no example had been given of a woman who formed her own judgment and acted upon it. There had been no exhibition of a self-respecting womanhood which might stand for a higher type of social life than was customary among men.

Vashti was the prototype of the higher unfoldment of woman beyond her time. She stands for the point in human development when womanliness asserts itself and begins to revolt and to throw off the yoke of sensualism and of tyranny. Her revolt was not an overt act, or a criticism of the proceedings of the king. It was merely exercising her own judgment as to her own proceeding. She did not choose to be brought before the assembly of men as an exhibit. The growth of self-respect and of individual sovereignty in woman has been slow. The sequence of Vashti's refusal to obey the king suggests at least one of the reasons why the law has been made, as it has down to the present day, by men alone. Woman has not been consulted, as she is not consulted to-day about any law, even such as bears especially upon herself, but was and is expected to obey it.

The idea of maintaining the respect of women and of wives by worthiness and by nobility of character and of manner, had not been born in the man of that day. The husband was to be held an authority. His superiority was his power to command obedience.

"And when the king's decree which he shall make shall be published throughout all his empire, all the wives shall give to their husbands honour, both great and small."

King Ahasuerus was but a forerunner of the more modern lawmaker, who seeks the same end of male rulership, by making the wife and all property the possession of the husband. That every living soul has an inherent right to control its life and activities, and that

woman equally with man should enjoy this opportunity, had not
dawned upon the consciousness of the men of the times of Ahasuerus.

Vashti stands out a sublime representative of self-centred womanhood. Rising to the heights of self-consciousness and of self-respect, she takes her soul into her own keeping, and though her position both as wife and as queen are jeopardized, she is true to the Divine aspirations of her nature.   L. B. C.

Esther ii.

After these things, when the wrath of
king Ahasuerus was appeased, he remembered Vashti, and what she had done, and
what was decreed against her.

2 Then said his servants, Let there be
fair young virgins sought for the king:

3 And let him appoint officers in all the
provinces that they may gather together the
fair young virgins unto Shushan the palace,

4 And let the maiden which pleaseth the
king be queen instead of Vashti. And the
thing pleased the king; and he did so.

5 Now in Shushan the palace there was
a certain Jew, whose name was Mordecai.

7 And he brought up Hadassah, that is,
Esther, his uncle's daughter; for she had
neither father nor mother, and the maid
was fair and beautiful; whom Moredcai,
when her father and mother were dead,
took for his own daughter.

8 So it came to pass, when the king's
commandment was heard, and when many
maidens were gathered together, that Esther was brought also unto the king's
house.

11 And Mordecai walked every day before the court of the women's house, to
know how Esther did, and what should become of her.

17 And the king loved Esther above all
the women, and she obtained grace and
favour in his sight; so that he set the royal
crown upon her head, and made her queen
instead of Vashti.

18 Then the king made a great feast, even
Esther's feast; and he made a release to
the provinces, and gave gifts, according to
the state of the king.

Esther was a Jewess, one of the children of the captivity, an or-
phan whom Mordecai adopted as his own child. She was beautiful,
symmetrical in form, fair in face, and of rare intelligence. Her wisdom and virtue were her greatest gifts. "It is an advantage to a
diamond even to be well set." Mordecai was her cousin-german
and her guardian. It was said that he intended to marry her; but
when he saw what her prospects in life were, and what she might do
as a favorite of the king for his own promotion and the safety of his
people, he held his individual affection in abeyance for the benefit
of his race and the safety of the king; for he soon saw the dishonest,
intriguing character of Haman, whom he despised in his heart and
to whom he would not bow in passing, nor make any show of respect.

As he was a keeper of the door and sat at the king's gate, he had many opportunities to show his disrespect.

He discovered a plot against the king's life which he revealed to Esther, that, in due time, secured him promotion to the head of the king's cabinet. But in the meantime Haman had the ear of the king; and to revenge the indignities of Mordecai, he decided to slay all the Jews throughout all the provinces of the kingdom, and procured an edict to that effect from the king, and stamped with the king's signet ring the letters that he sent by post into all the provinces. The day was set for this terrible slaughter; and the Jews were fasting in sack-cloth and ashes.

The king loved Esther above all the women and had made her his queen. She was not known at court as a Jewess, but was supposed to be of Persian extraction. Mordecai had told her to say nothing on that subject. Ahasuerus placed the royal crown upon her head, and solemnized her coronation with a great feast, which Esther graced with her presence, at the request of the king. She profited by the example of Vashti, and saw the good policy of at least making a show of obedience in all things. Mordecai walked up and down past her door many times a day; and through a faithful messenger kept her informed of all that transpired, so she was aware of the plot Haman had laid against her people. So she made a banquet for the king and Haman, and told the king the effect of his royal edict and letters sent by post in all the provinces stamped with his ring. She told him of Mordecai's faithfulness in saving his life; that she and Mordecai were Jews, and that it was their people who were to be slain, young and old, women and children, without mercy; that all their possessions were to be confiscated to raise the money which Haman promised to put into the royal treasury, and that Haman had already built a gallows thirty feet high on which Mordecai was to be hanged.

Haman trembled in the presence of the king, who ordered him to be hanged on the gallows which he had prepared for Mordecai; and the latter was installed as the favorite of the king. The family and the followers of Haman were slain by the thousands, and the Jews were filled with gladness. The day appointed for their destruction was one of thanksgiving. They appointed a certain day in the last month of the year, just before the Passover, to be kept ever after as the feast of Purim, one of thanksgiving for their deliverance from the vengeance of Haman. Purim is a Persian word. It is not a holy day feast, but of human appointment. It is celebrated at the present time, and in the service the whole story is told. It is to be regretted that this feast often ends in gluttony.

One commentator says that the Talmud states that in the feast of Purim a man may drink until he knows not the difference between "cursed be Haman" and "blessed be Mordecai." If the Talmud means that he may drink the wine of good fellowship until all feelings of vengeance, hatred and malice are banished from the human soul, the sentiment is not so objectionable as at the first blush it appears. There is one thing in the Jewish service worse than this, and that is for each man to stand up in the synagogue every Sabbath morning and say: "I thank thee, O Lord, that I was not born a woman," as if that were the depth of human degradation. It is to be feared that the thanksgiving feast of the Purim has degenerated in many localities into the same kind of a gathering as the Irish wake.

In the history of Esther, those who believe in special Providence will see that in her coming to the throne multitudes of her people were saved from a cruel death, hence the disobedience of Vashti was providential. A faith "that all things are working together for good," "that good only is positive, evil negative," is most cheerful and sustaining to the believer. I have always regretted that the historian allowed Vashti to drop out of sight so suddenly. Perhaps she was doomed to some menial service, or to entire sequestration in her own apartments. E. C. S.

———

The record fails to state whether or not the king's judgment was modified in regard to Vashti's refusal to appear on exhibition when his wrath abated. But the decree had gone forth, and could not be altered; and Vashti banished, no further record of her fate appears.

The king's ministers at once set about providing a successor to Vashti.

The king in those days had the advantage of the search for fair young virgins, in that he could command the entire collection within his dominions. The only consideration was whether or not the maiden *"pleased"* him. There is no hint that the maiden was expected to signify her acceptance or rejection of the king's choice. She was no more to be consulted than if she had been an animal. Her position as queen was but an added distinction of her lord and master.

Esther, the orphaned and adopted daughter of Mordecai the Jew, was the favored maiden. She was "fair and beautiful." The truth of the historic record of the men of those days is indisputable. Down to the present the average man sums up his estimate of woman by her "looks." Is she fair to look upon is the criterion. Esther was destined to play an important part in the salvation of her people from the destructive purposes of Haman, who had been "set above all the princes who were with him." This young woman, who had been crowned by her royal master because she *"pleased"* him, was called upon by the peril of her people, whom Haman was seeking to destroy, to place her own life in jeopardy, by venturing to obtain audience with the king, without having been summoned into his presence.

When Esther received from Mordecai the assurance, "Think not with thyself that thou shalt escape in the king's house more than all the Jews," he asked, "Who knoweth, whether thou art come to the kingdom for such a time as this?" then this young woman rose to the extremity of the situation. She exercised a high degree of wisdom and courage, and bade them return Mordecai this answer:

Go gather together all the Jews that are present in Shushan, and fast ye for me, and neither eat nor drink three days, night or day; I also and my maidens will fast likewise; and so will I go in unto the king, which is not according to the law; and if I perish, I perish.— Vs. 15, 16.

She prepared herself thus by fasting to receive and to exercise the power of spirit. Her high purpose was only equalled by her unfaltering courage and entire self-abnegation. Vashti had exercised heroic courage in asserting womanly dignity and the inherent human right never recognized by kingship, to choose whether to please and to obey the king. Esther, so as to save her people from destruction, risked her life.

This King Ahasuerus, who, according to the record, was only a man of selfish purposes, delighting in power and given to the enjoyment of his passions, was the legal lord and master of two women, each distinguished by a nobility of character well worthy of the distinction of queen. Their royalty was of a higher order than that of sceptres and of crowns. While we rejoice in the higher manhood which the centuries have evolved, we are in this hour reminded of the dominating disposition of King Ahasuerus and the habits of those times. A distinguished man and a scholar in this closing nineteenth century claims that "the family is necessarily a despotism," and that man is the "ruler of the household."

Women as queenly, as noble and as self-sacrificing as was Esther, as self-respecting and as brave as was Vashti, are hampered in their creative office by the unjust statutes of men; but God is marching on; and it is the seed of woman which is to bruise the head of the serpent. It is not man's boasted superiority of intellect through which the eternally working Divine power will perfect the race, but the receptiveness and the love of woman.   L. B. C.

THE BOOK OF JOB.

There was a man in the land of Uz, whose name was Job; and that man was perfect and upright, and one that feared God.

2 And there were born unto him seven sons and three daughters.

3 His substance also was seven thousand sheep, and three thousand camels, and five hundred yoke of oxen, and five hundred she asses, and a very great household; so that this man was the greatest of all the men of the east.

4 And his sons feasted in their houses; and sent and called for their three sisters to eat with them.

6 Now there was a day when the sons of God came to present themselves before the Lord, and Satan came also.

7 And the Lord said unto Satan, Whence comest thou? Satan answered, From going to and fro in the earth.

8 And the Lord said unto Satan, Hast thou considered my servant Job, that there is none like him in the earth, a perfect and an upright man.

9 Then Satan answered, Doth Job fear God for nought?

10 Hast not thou made a hedge about him, and about his house, and about all that he hath on every side? thou hast blessed the work of his hands.

11 But put forth thine hand now, and touch all that he hath, and he will curse thee to thy face.

12 And the Lord said unto Satan, all that he hath is in thy power: only upon himself put not forth thine hand. So Satan went forth from the presence of the Lord.

14 And there came a messenger unto Job, and said, The oxen were ploughing, and the asses feeding beside them:

15 And the Sabeans fell upon them, and took them away; yea, they have slain the servants.

16 There came another, and said, fire is fallen from heaven, and hath burned up the sheep.

17 There came also another, and said, The Chaldeans fell upon the camels, and have carried them away.

18 There came also another, and said, Thy sons and thy daughters were eating and drinking.

19 And, behold there came a great wind and smote the four corners of the house, and it fell upon the young men, and they are dead.

20 Then Job arose, and rent his mantle, and shaved his head, and fell down upon the ground, and worshiped.

9 Then said his wife unto him, Dost thou still retain thine integrity? curse God and die.

10 But he said unto her, Thou speakest as one of the foolish women speaketh. What? shall we receive good at the hand of God, and shall we not receive evil?

11 Then came there unto him his brethren, and his sisters, and they that had been of his acquaintance before, and did eat bread with him in his house: and they comforted him over all the evil that the Lord had brought upon him: every man also gave him a piece of money, and every one an earring of gold.

12 So the Lord blessed the latter end of Job more than his beginning; for he had fourteen thousand sheep, and six thousand camels, and a thousand yoke of oxen, and a thousand she asses.

13 He had also seven sons and three daughters.

15 And in all the land were no women found so fair as the daughters of Job; and their father gave them inheritance among their brethren.

16 After this lived Job a hundred and forty years.

17 So Job died, being old and full of days.

THE Book of Job opens with an imaginary discussion between the Lord and Satan as to the true character of Job. Satan hates him because he is good, and envies him because he is a favorite of the Lord, who expresses unbounded faith in his steadfastness to religious principles. Satan replies that Job is all right in prosperity, when surrounded with every comfort; but stripped of his blessings, his faith in a superintending Providence would vanish like dew before the rising sun. The Lord said, "You may test Job. I give you permission to do your worst and to see if he will not remain as true in adversity as he is in prosperity."

The Book of Job is an epic poem, an allegory, to show the grand elements in human nature, enabling mortals to rise superior to all trials and temptations, to the humiliations of the spirit, and to prolonged suffering in the flesh. Though illustrated in the personality of a man, yet the principle applies equally to the wisdom and the virtue of woman. The elements of Job's goodness and greatness must have existed in his mother. But little is said of women in this book; and that little is by no means complimentary. Job's wife's name was Dinah; some commentators say that she was the daughter of Jacob. Satan uses her as the last and most subtle influence for the downfall of his victim. Between the two forces of good and of evil, the triumph of the spiritual nature over the temptations of the flesh, the god-like in the human, was thoroughly proven. Job is represented as a great man. He has wealth, inflexible integrity and a charming family life, seven sons and three daughters, immense herds of oxen, sheep, asses, camels, and servants without number.

The spirit of evil, to test his faithfulness, strips him of all his possessions. In one day Job's houses were destroyed, his lands made desolate, his cattle stolen and his children carried off in a whirlwind. Job was stunned by these calamities. He put on sackcloth, shaved his head, as was the custom, and calmly accepted the situation; and his faith in the goodness of God remained. Then the spirit of evil, to test him still further, afflicted him with a terrible disease, loathsome to endure and pitiful to behold. His three friends, Eliphaz, Bildad and Zophar, mocked him in his misery.

His last affliction was the disgust of his wife. She ridiculed his faith in God, and scoffed at his piety, as Michal did at David. She was spared to be his last tempter when all his comforts were taken away. She bantered him for his constancy, "Dost thou still maintain thy confidence in the God who has punished thee? Why dost thou be so obstinate in thy religion, which serves no good to thee? Why truckle to a God who, so far from rewarding thy services with marks of his favor, seems to take pleasure in making thee miserable and scourges thee without any provocation? Is this a God to be still loved and served? 'Curse God and die.'" She urges him to commit suicide. Better to die at once than to endure his life of lingering misery.

Deserted by wife, by friends, and, seemingly by God, too, Job's faith wavered not. The spirit of evil had done its worst. Man had proven his Divine origin, himself the incarnation of the great Spirit of Good; and now that Job had proved himself superior to all human calamities, he is restored to health; and all his earthly possessions are returned fourfold.

Nothing more is said of his first wife, but his ten children are restored. The names of his three daughters are significant, though not euphonious: Jemima, the day, because of Job's prosperity; Kezia, a spice, because he was healed, and Karen-Happuch, plenty restored. God adorned them with great beauty, no women being so fair as were the daughters of Job. In the Old Testament we often find women praised for their beauty; but in the New Testament we find no notice of physical charms, not even in the Virgin Mary herself. Job gave to his daughters an equal inheritance with his sons. It is pleasant to see that the brothers paid them marked attention, and always invited them to their dinners, and that his ten children were reproduced just as his flocks and his herds had been.

Much more sympathy has been expressed by women for the wife, than for Job. Poor woman, she had scraped lint, nursed him and waited on him to the point of nervous exhaustion—no wonder that she was resigned to see him pass to Abraham's bosom. Job lived one hundred and forty years. Some conjecture that he was seventy years old when his calamities came upon him, so that his age was doubled with his other blessings. Whether Dinah lived to cheer Job's declining years, or whether she was lured by Satan to his kingdom, does not appear; but he is supposed to have had a second wife, by the name of Sitis—the probable mother of the second brood.   E. C. S.

BOOKS OF PSALMS, PROVERBS, ECCLESIASTES

AND

THE SONG OF SOLOMON.

———

PSALMS.

Psalms xlv.

9 Kings' daughters were among thy honourable women: upon thy right hand did stand the queen in gold of Ophir.

10 Hearken, O daughter, and consider, and incline thine ear; forget also thine own people, and thy father's house;

11 So shall the King greatly desire thy beauty: for he is thy Lord; and worship thou him.

12 And the daughter of Tyre shall be there with a gift: even the rich among the people shall entreat thy favour.

13 The King's daughter is all glorious within: her clothing is of wrought gold.

14 She shall be brought unto the King in raiment of needlework: the virgins her companions that follow her shall be brought unto thee.

15 With gladness and rejoicing shall they be brought: they shall enter into the King's palace.

———

THIS book is supposed to have been written by David, the son of Jesse, called the sweet psalmist of Israel. He had a taste for the arts, a real genius for poetry and song. Many of the poems are beautiful in sentiment and celebrated as specimens of literature, as are some passages in Job; but the general tone is pessimistic. David's old age was full of repinings over the follies of his youth and of his middle age. The declining years of a well-spent life should be the most peaceful and happy. Then the lessons of experience are understood, and one knows how to bear its joys and sorrows with equal philosophy. Yet David in the twilight of his days seemed to dwell in the shadows of despair, in sackcloth and ashes, repenting for his own sins and bemoaning the evil tendency of men in general. There is a passing mention of the existence of women as imaginary beings in the Psalms, the Proverbs, and The

Song of Solomon, but not illustrated by any grand personalities or individual characters.

Psalms li.

To the chief Musician, A Psalm of David, when Nathan the prophet came unto him, after he had gone in to Bath-sheba.

1 Have mercy upon me, O God, according to thy loving-kindness: according unto the multitude of thy tender mercies blot out my transgressions.

2 Wash me thoroughly from mine iniquity, and cleanse me from my sin.

3 For I acknowledge my transgressions: and my sin is ever before me.

David's treatment of Uriah was the darkest passage in his life; and to those who love justice it is a satisfaction to know that his conscience troubled him for this act to the end of his days. We are not told whether Bath-sheba ever dropped a tear over the sad fate of Uriah, or suffered any upbraidings of conscience.

PROVERBS.

ix., 13 A foolish woman is clamorous: she is simple, and knoweth nothing.

xi., 16 A gracious woman retaineth honour: and strong men retain riches.

xiv. Every wise woman buildeth her house: but the foolish plucketh it down with her hands.

xvii., 25 A foolish son is a grief to his father and bitterness to her that bare him.

xix., 14 House and riches are the inheritance of fathers: and a prudent wife is from the Lord.

xxi., 9 It is better to dwell in a corner of the housetop, than with a brawling woman in a wide house.

xxi., 19 It is better to dwell in the wilderness, than with a contentious and an angry woman.

xxvii., 15 A continual dropping in a very rainy day and a contentious woman are alike.

xxx., 21 For three things the earth is disquieted, and for four which it cannot bear:

22 For a servant when he reigneth; and a fool when he is filled with meat;

23 For an odious woman when she is married; and a handmaid that is heir to her mistress.

xxxi., 10 Who can find a virtuous woman? for her price is far above rubies.

11 The heart of her husband doth safely trust in her.

12 She will do him good and not evil all the days of her life.

13 She seeketh wool, and flax, and worketh willingly with her hands.

16 She considereth a field, and buyeth it: with the fruit of her hands she planteth a vineyard.

20 She stretcheth out her hand to the poor.

21 She is not afraid of the snow; for all her household are clothed with scarlet.

22 She maketh herself coverings of tapestry; her clothing is silk and purple.

23 Her husband is known in the gates, when he sitteth among the elders of the land.

24 She maketh fine linen, and selleth it.

26 She openeth her mouth with wisdom; and in her tongue is the law of kindness.

28 Her children arise up, and call her blessed; her husband also, and he praiseth her.

29 Many daughters have done virtuously, but thou excellest them all.

30 Favour is deceitful, and beauty is vain; but a woman that feareth the Lord, shall be praised.

With these pen pictures of the foolish, contentious wife contrasted with the more gracious woman, surely every reader of common sense will try to follow the example of the latter. A complaining woman is worse than a leaky house, because with paint and putty you can stop the dropping; but how can one find the source of constant complaints?

Heretofore Biblical writers have given to us battles, laws, histories, songs; now we have in Solomon's writings a new style in short, epigrammatic sentences. The proverb was the most ancient way of teaching among the Greeks. The seven wise men of Greece each had his own motto on which he made himself famous. These were engraved on stone in public places. Thus the gist of an argument or a long discussion may be thrown into a proverb, in which the whole point will be easily seen and remembered.

Solomon's idea of a wise woman, a good mother, a prudent wife, a saving housekeeper and a successful merchant, will be found in the foregoing texts, which every woman who reads should have printed, framed and hung up at her family altar. As Solomon had a thousand women in his household, he had great opportunity for the study of the characteristics of the sex, though one would naturally suppose that wise women, even in his day, preferred a larger sphere of action than within his palace walls. Solomon's opinion of the sex in general is plainly expressed in the foregoing texts.

Solomon is supposed to have written his Song when he was young, Proverbs in middle life, and Ecclesiastes when he was old. He gave admirable rules for wisdom and virtue to all classes, to men, to women and to children, but failed to practise the lessons which he taught.

ECCLESIASTES.

This book, written in Solomon's old age, is by no means comforting or inspiring. Everything in life seems to have been disappointing to him. Wealth, position, learning, all earthly possessions and acquirements he declares alike to be "vanity of vanities and vexation of spirit." To one whose life has been useful to others and sweet to himself, it is quite impossible to accept these pessimistic pictures of human destiny.

Eccles. ii.

I said in mine heart, I will prove thee with mirth; therefore enjoy pleasure: and, behold, this also is vanity.

4 I made me great works; I builded me houses; I planted me vineyards:

5 I made me gardens and orchards.

7 I had great possessions above all that were in Jerusalem before me:

8 I gathered me also silver and gold and particular treasures: I gat me men singers and women singers, and musical instruments.

10 And whatsover mine eyes desired I kept not from them, I withheld not my heart from any joy.

13 Then I saw that wisdom excelleth folly, as far as light excelleth darkness.

14 The wise man's eyes are in his head; but the fool walketh in darkness: and I myself perceived also that one event happeneth to them all.

This constant depreciation of human dignity and power is very demoralizing in its influence on character. When we consider the struggles of the race from savagism to civilization, all the wonderful achievements, discoveries and inventions of man, we must feel more like bowing down to him as an incarnation of his Creator than deploring his follies like "a poor worm of the dust." The Episcopal service is most demoralizing in this view. Whole congregations of educated men and women, day after day, year after year, confessing themselves "miserable sinners," with no evident improvement from generation to generation. And this confession is made in a perfunctory manner, as if no disgrace attended that mental condition, and without hope or promise of a change from that unworthy attitude.

Eccles. vii.

26 And I find more bitter than death the woman, whose heart is snares and nets, and her hands as bands: whoso pleaseth God shall escape from her; but the sinner shall be taken by her.

28 One wise man among a thousand have

I found; but a woman among all those have I not found.

29 Lo, this only have I found, that God hath made man upright; but they have sought out many inventions.

Solomon must have had a sad experience in his relations with women. Such an opinion is a grave reflection on his own mother, who was so devoted to his success in the world. But for her ambition he would never have been crowned King of Israel. The commentators vouchsafe the opinion that there are more good women than men. It is very kind in some of the commentators to give us a word of praise now and then; but from the general tone of the learned fabulists, one would think that the Jezebels and the Jaels predominated. In fact, Solomon says that he has not found one wise woman in a thousand.

THE SONG OF SOLOMON.

The name of God does not appear in this Song, neither is the latter ever mentioned in the New Testament. This book has no special religious significance, being merely a love poem, an epithalamium, sung on nuptial occasions in praise of the bride and the groom. The proper place for this book is before either Proverbs or Ecclesiastes, as it was written in Solomon's youth, and is a more pardonable outburst for his early days than for his declining years. The Jewish doctors advised their young people not to read this book until they were thirty years old, when they were supposed to be more susceptible to spiritual beauties and virtues than to the mere attractions of face and of form.

The Church, as an excuse for retaining this book as a part of "Holy Scriptures," interprets the Song as expressive of Christ's love for the Church; but that is rather far-fetched, and unworthy the character of the ideal Jesus. The most rational view to take of the Song is, it was that of a luxurious king to the women of his seraglio.   E. C. S.

BOOKS OF ISAIAH AND DANIEL,
MICAH AND MALACHI.

ISAIAH.

THE closing books of the Old Testament make but little mention of women as illustrating individual characteristics. The ideal woman is used more as a standard of comparison for good and for evil, the good woman representing the elements of success in building up the family, the tribe, the nation, as a devout worshiper of the God of Israel; the wicked woman, the elements of destruction in the downfall of great cities and nations. As woman is chosen to represent the extremes of human conditions she has no special reason to complain.

The Prophets sum up the graces of the "daughters of men" in the following texts:

Isaiah iii.

16 Moreover the Lord saith, Because the daughters of Zion are haughty, and walk with stretched forth necks and wanton eyes, walking and mincing as they go, and making a tinkling with their feet:

18 In that day the Lord will take away the bravery of their tinkling ornaments about their feet, and their cauls, and their round tires like the moon,

19 The chains, and the bracelets, and the mufflers,

20 The bonnets, and the ornaments of the legs, and the headbands, and the tablets, and the earrings,

21 The rings, and nose jewels,

22 The changeable suits of apparel, and the mantles, and the wimples, and the crisping pins,

23 The glasses, and the fine linen, and the hoods, and the vails.

Before the sacred canon of the Old Testament was written there were Prophets who took the place of Bibles to the Church. It is said that God himself spake to the children of Israel from the top of Mount Sinai, but that it was so terrible they entreated the Lord ever after to speak to them through men. So ever after he did com-

municate with them through Prophets and Angels.   Isaiah was of
the royal family; he was nephew to King Uzziah.   The Prophet in
the above texts reproves and warns the daughters of Zion and tells
them of their faults.   He does not like their style of walking, which
from the description must have been much like the mincing gait of
some women to-day.

The Prophet expressly vouches God's authority for what he said
concerning their manners and elaborate ornamentation, lest they
should be offended with his criticisms.   If the Prophets could visit
our stores and see all the fashions there are to tempt the daughters
of to-day, they would declaim against our frivolities on the very
doorsteps, and in view of the Easter bonnets, at the entrance to our
churches.   The badges which our young women wear as members
of societies, pinned in rows on broad ribbons, the earrings, the ban-
gles, the big sleeves, the bonnets trimmed with osprey feathers,
answer to the crisping pins, the wimples, the nose jewels, the tablets,
the chains, the bracelets, the mufflers, the veils, the glasses and the
girdles of the daughters of Zion.   If the Prophets, instead of the
French milliners and dressmakers, could supervise the toilets of our
women, they would dress in far better taste.

DANIEL.

The name of this Prophet in Hebrew was "Darnil," which signifies "the judgment of God."   His Chaldean name was Bethshazzai.
He was of the tribe of Judah of the royal family.   Josephus calls him
one of the greatest of the Prophets.

Daniel v.

Belshazzar the king made a great feast
and commanded to bring the golden and
silver vessels which his father Nebuchadnezzar had taken out of the temple which
was in Jerusalem; that the king and his
princes, his wives and his concubines,
might drink therein.

3 Then they brought the golden vessels,
. . . and praised the gods of gold, and
of silver, of brass, of iron, of wood, and of
stone.

5 In the same hour came forth 'fingers
of a man's hand, and wrote over against
the candlestick upon the plaster of the
wall: and the king saw the part of the hand
that wrote.

6 Then the king's countenance was
changed, and his thoughts troubled him, so
that his knees smote one against another.

7 The king cried aloud to bring in the
astrologers, the Chaldeans, and the sooth--
sayers. And the king spoke, and said to

the wise men of Babylon, Whosoever shall read this writing, and shew me the interpretation thereof, shall be clothed with scarlet, and have a chain of gold about his neck, and shall be the third ruler in the kingdom.

8 Then came in all the king's wise men: but they could not read the writing, nor make known the interpretation thereof.

10 Now the queen came into the banquet house, and said, O king, live forever: let not thy thoughts trouble thee.

11 There is a man in thy kingdom in whom is the spirit of the holy gods; and in the days of thy father light and understanding and wisdom, like the wisdom of the gods, was found in him; whom Nebuchadnezzar thy father made master of the magicians, astrologers, Chaldeans and soothsayers; . . . now let Daniel be called, and he will shew the interpretation.

13 Then was Daniel brought in; and he said, I will read the writing unto the king.

25 And this is the writing that was written, MENE, MENE, TEKEL, UPHARSIN.

26 This is the interpretation of the thing: MENE; God hath numbered thy kingdom, and finished it.

27 TEKEL; Thou are weighed in the balance, and art found wanting.

28 PERES; Thy kingdom is divided, and given to the Medes and Persians.

29 Then commanded Belshazzar, and they clothed Daniel with scarlet, and put a chain of gold about his neck, and made a proclamation concerning him, that he should be the third ruler in the kingdom.

20 In that night was Belshazzar the king of the Chaldeans slain.

Historians say that Cyrus was at this time besieging the city and knew of this feast, and took this opportunity to make his attack and to slay the king.

In the midst of the consternation at the feast the queen entered to advise Belshazzar. It is supposed that this queen was the widow of the evil Merodach, and was that famous Nitocris whom Herodotus mentions as a woman of extraordinary prudence and wisdom. She was not present at the feast, as were the king's wives and concubines. It was not agreeable to her age and gravity to dissipate at night; but tidings of the consternation in the banquet hall were brought to her, so that she came and entreated him not to be discouraged by the incapacity of the wise men to solve the riddle; for there was a man in his kingdom who had more than once helped his father in emergencies and would no doubt advise him. She could not read the writing herself; but she said, let the Prophet Daniel be called. The account she gives of the respect Nebuchadnezzar had for him, for his insight into the deepest mysteries, and of his goodness and wisdom, moved the king to summon Daniel into his presence.

Daniel was now near ninety years of age, and for a long time had not been in court circles; but the queen dowager remembered him in the court of the king's father. She reminded her son of the high esteem in which he was held by his father. The interpretation which Daniel gave of these mystic characters was far from easing the king of his fears. Daniel being in years, and Belshazzar still young, he took greater liberty in dealing plainly with him than he had with his father. He read the warning as written on the wall:

"Thou hast been weighed in the balance and found wanting, and thy kingdom is divided and rent from thee."

Although the exposition of the handwriting was most discouraging, yet the king kept his promise, and put on Daniel the scarlet gown and the gold chain.

MICAH.

Micah ii.
9 The women of my people have ye cast out from their pleasant houses; from their children have ye taken away my glory forever.

Micah vii.
6 For the son dishonoureth the father, the daughter riseth up against her mother, the daughter in law against her mother in law.

Here the Israelites are rebuked for their cruel treatment of their own people, robbing widows and selling children into slavery. Family life as well as public affairs seems to have become unsettled. The contempt and the violation of the laws of domestic duties are a sad symptom of universal corruption.

MALACHI.

Malachi ii.
11 Judah hath profaned the holiness of the Lord which he loved, and hath married the daughter of a strange god.
14 Yet ye say, Wherefore? Because the Lord hath been witness between thee and the wife of thy youth, against whom thou

hast dealt treacherously: yet is she thy companion, and the wife of thy covenant.
15 That he might seek a godly seed. Therefore take heed to your spirit, and let none deal treacherously against the wife of his youth.

These Israelites were always violating the national law which forbade them to marry strange women. The corruption of the nation began, say the historians, with the intermarriage of the "sons of God" with the "daughters of men," meaning, I suppose, those of the tribes who had a different religion. "He that marries a heathen woman is as if he made himself son-in-law to an idol." They put away the wives of their own nation, and, as was the fashion at one time, married those of other nations. This spoiled the lives of the daughters of Israel. They were uncertain as to their social relations, family, right to their children, and support in their old age, as a paper of divorce could be given to them at any time. The denunciations of the Prophets had no great weight in matters where strong feeling and sound judgment conflicted.

Charming women, of the Hittites and of the Midianites, with their novel dress, manners and conversation, attracted the men of Israel. They could not resist the temptation. When the strongest man and the wisest one are alike led captive, there is no significance in calling woman—"the weaker sex."

Though few women appear in the closing tragedies of the Old Testament, yet the idiosyncrasies of the sex are constantly used to point a moral or to condemn a sin.   E. C. S.

THE KABBALAH.

THE Bible is an occult book, and a remarkable one. About all creeds and faiths this side of Pagandom go to it for their authority. Read in the light of occult teachings, it becomes something more than the old battle ground of controversy for warring religions. Occultism alone furnishes the key to this ancient treasury of wisdom. But to turn now to another point, it may be well to call the attention of the readers of The Woman's Bible to a few quotations from MacGregor Mathers' "Kabbalah Unveiled," which has been pronounced by competent authorities the work of a master hand. This work is a translation of Knorr Von Rosenroth's "Kabbalah Denudata."

The Kabbalah—the Hebrew esoteric doctrines—is a system of teachings with which only the very learned attempt to wrestle. It is claimed to have been handed down by oral tradition from angelic sources, through Adam, Noah, Abraham, Moses, the Seventy Elders, to David and to Solomon. No attempt was made to commit this sacred knowledge to writing, till, in the early centuries of the Christian era (authorities differ widely as to the date) the pupils of Rabbi Simeon ben Joachi put his teachings into writing; and this in later ages became known as the "Zohar," or "Book of Splendor." Around the name of this Rabbi Simeon ben Joachi, as one scholarly writer puts it, "cluster the mystery and the poetry of the religion of the Kabbalah as a gift of the Deity to mankind." The Zohar, which is only a part of the Kabbalah, is the great store-house of the esoteric teaching of the ancient Hebrews.

Returning to the quotations referred to above, MacGregor Mathers in his preface says: "I wish particularly to direct the reader's attention to the stress laid by the Kabbalah on the feminine aspects

106

of the Deity, and to the shameful way in which any allusion to these has been suppressed in the ordinary translations of the Bible, also to the Kabbalistical equality of male and female.

Referring to the Sephiroth (the ten Kabbalistical attributes of God), Mr. Mathers says:

"Among these Sephiroth, jointly and severally, we find the development of the persons and the attributes of God. Of these, *some are male and some are female*. Now, for some reason or other, best known to themselves, the translators of the Bible have carefully crowded out of existence and smothered up every reference to the fact that the Deity is both masculine and feminine. They have translated *a feminine plural by a masculine singular* in the case of the word Elohim. They have, however, left an inadvertent admission of their knowledge that it was plural in Genesis iv., 26: 'And Elohim said: Let US make man.'

"Again (v., 27), how could Adam be made in the image of the Elohim, male and female, unless the Elohim were male and female also? The word Elohim is a plural formed from the feminine singular ALH, *Eloh*, by adding IM to the word. But inasmuch as IM is usually the termination of the masculine plural, and is here added to a feminine noun, it gives to the word Elohim the sense of a female potency united to a masculine idea, and thereby capable of producing an offspring. Now we hear much of the Father and the Son, but we hear nothing of the Mother in the ordinary religions of the day. But in the Kabbalah we find that the Ancient of Days conforms himself simultaneously into the Father and the Mother, and thus begets the Son. Now this Mother is Elohim.

The writer then goes on to show that the Holy Spirit, usually represented as masculine, is in fact feminine. The first Sephira contained the other nine, and produced them in succession. The second is Chokmah (Wisdom), and is the active and evident Father to whom the Mother is united. The third is a feminine passive potency called Binah (Understanding), and is co-equal with Chokmah. Chokmah is powerless till the number three forms the triangle. Thus this Sephira completes and makes evident the supernal Trinity. It is also called AMA, Mother, the great productive Moth-

"Sophia"

er, who is eternally conjoined with the Father for the maintenance of the universe in order. Therefore is she the most evident form in whom we can know the Father, and therefore is she worthy of all honor. She is the supernal Mother, co-equal with Chokmah, and the great feminine form of God, the Elohim, in whose image man and woman were created, according to the teaching of the Kabbalah, *equal before God. Woman is equal with man, not inferior to him,* as it has been the persistent endeavor of so-called Christians to make her. Aima is the woman described in the Apocalypse (ch. 12)."

"This third Sephira is also sometimes called the Great Sea. To her are attributed the Divine names, ALAIM, Elohim, and IaHVeh ALHIM; and the angelic order, ARHLIM, the Thrones. She is the supernal Mother as distinguished from Malkuth, the inferior Mother, Bride and Queen. . . . In each of the three trinities or triads of the Sephiroth is a dual of opposite sexes, and a uniting intelligence which is the result. In this, the masculine and feminine potencies are regarded as the two scales of the balance, and the uniting Sephira as the beam which joins them."

In chapter viii. we read: "Chokmah is the Father, and Binah is the Mother, and therein are Chokmah (Wisdom) and Binah (Understanding), counterbalanced together in most perfect equality of Male and Female. And therefore are all things established in the equality of Male and Female; if it were not so, how could they subsist? . . . In their conformations are They found to be the perfections of all things—Father and Mother, Son and Daughter. These things have not been revealed save unto the Holy Superiors who have entered therein and departed therefrom, and have known the paths of the Most Holy God, so that they have not erred in them, either on the right hand or on the left."

In a note in regard to Chokmah and Binah the author says: "Chokmah is the second and Binah is the third of the Sephiroth. This section is a sufficient condemnation of all those who wish to make out that woman is inferior to man."

The Kabbalah also speaks of the separation of the sexes as the cause of evil, or as the author puts it in a note: "Where there is unbalanced force, there is the origin of evil." Further on it is written:

"And therefore is Aima (the Mother) known to be the consumma-
tion of all things; and She is signified to be the beginning and the
end. . . . And hence that which is not both Male and Female
together is called half a body. Now, no blessing can rest upon a
mutilated and defective being, but only upon a perfect place and
upon a perfect being, and not at all in an incomplete being. And a
semi-complete being cannot live forever, neither can it receive blessing forever."

The following is the author's comment upon the above: "This
section is another all-sufficient proof of the teachings maintained
throughout the Kabbalah, namely, that man and woman are from
the creation co-equal and co-existent, perfectly equal, one with the
other. This fact the translators of the Bible have been at great pains
to conceal by carefully suppressing every reference to the feminine
portion of the Deity, and by constantly translating feminine nouns
by masculine. And this is the work of so-called religious men!"

A learned Jewish Rabbi, with whom the writer is acquainted,
says: "Those who write on the Bible must be very careful when
they come to speak of the position of woman to make a clear
distinction between the Old and the New Testaments. In the Old
Testament, except in the second chapter of Genesis, woman occupies
a true and a dignified position in society and in the family. For example, take the position of Sarah, of the Prophetess Miriam, the sister of Moses, and Deborah the Prophetess. They all exemplify the
true position of woman in the Old Testament. While Paul, the
Apostle of the Gentiles, and the chief writer in the New Testament,
condemned woman to silence in the Church and to strict obedience
to her husband, making her thereby inferior to the man, the Old
Testament gave free scope to the development of the Holy Spirit in
woman. To intensify this teaching upon the position of woman, we
find even the voice of the Deity telling Abraham: 'Whatever Sarah
tells thee, thou shalt hearken unto her voice,' showing that woman in
her own home was the guiding power.' In regard to another point
this Rabbi says: 'The learned Jewish Rabbis of modern times do
not take the rib story literally. And this may be said of many of
the olden times.'"

The Kabbalah and its learned expositors may be said to be "the throbbing heart" of the Jewish religion, as was graphically said of the mystic teachings of another occult fraternity. And in view of the Kabbalah's antiquity, and the fact that it is the fountain head of the body of the Old Testament teachings, these quotations as to the real Kabbalistic teachings in regard to woman, or to the feminine aspects of the Deity, are of first-class importance in such a book as "The Woman's Bible." In Kabbalistic teachings "there is one Trinity which comprises all the Sephiroth, and it consists of the crown, the king and the queen. . . . It is the Trinity which created the world, or, in Kabbalistic language, the universe was born from the union of the crowned king and queen."

The rib story is veiled in the mystic language of symbolism. According to occult teachings, there was a time before man was differentiated into sexes—that is, when he was androgynous. Then the time came, millions of years ago, when the differentiation into sexes took place. And to this the rib story refers. There has been much ignorance and confusion in regard to the real nature of woman, indicating that she is possessed of a mystic nature and a power which will gradually be developed and better understood as the world becomes more enlightened. Woman has been branded as the author of evil in the world; and at the same time she has been exalted to the position of mother of the Saviour of the world. These two positions are as conflicting as the general ideas which have prevailed in regard to woman—the great enigma of the world.

Theological odium has laid its hand heavily upon her. "This odium," as a Rev. D. D. once said to the writer, "is a thing with more horns, more thorns, more quills and more snarls than almost any other sort of thing you have ever heard of. It has kindled as many fires of martyrdom; it has slipnoosed as many ropes for the necks of well-meaning men; it has built as many racks for the dislocation of human bones; it has forged as many thumb-screws; it has built as many dungeons; it has ostracised as many scholars and philosophers; it has set itself against light and pushed as hard to make the earth revolve the other way on its axis, as any other force of mischief of whatever name or kind."

And that is the fearful thing with which woman has had to contend. When she is free from it we may be assured that the dawn of a new day is not far off. And among the indications pointing that way is the fact that the Bible itself has been "under treatment" for some time. What is known as the "Higher Criticism" has done much to clear away the clouds of superstition which have enveloped it.

One of the latest works on this line is "The Polychrome Bible"—the word meaning the different colors in which the texts, the notes, the dates, the translations, etc., are printed for the sake of simplifying matters. Prof. Paul Haupt, of Johns Hopkins University, is at the head of this great work, ably assisted by a large corps of the best Biblical scholars in the world. It is not to be a revision of the accepted version, but a new translation in modern English. The translation is not to be literal except in the highest sense of the word, viz., "to render the sense of the original as faithfully as possible." There are to be explanatory notes, historical and archælogical illustrations of the text, paraphrases of difficult passages, etc. In short, everything possible is to be done to simplify and to make plain this ancient book. The contributors have instructions not to hesitate to state what they consider to be the truth, but with as little offence to the general reader as possible. This work has been pronounced the greatest literary undertaking of the century—a work which will prepare the way for the coming generation to give an entirely new consideration to the religious problem. It was begun in 1890, and will probably not be completed before 1900.

Another important work, small in actual size but big with significance, has just been issued in England under the title of "The Bible and the Child." It is not, as its name might imply, a book for children, but it is for the purpose of "showing the right way of presenting the Bible to the young in the light of the Higher Criticism." Its eight contributors are headed by Canon F. W. Farrar, of England, and includes a number of noted English divines. An English writer outside of the orthodox pale says: "It is one of the most extraordinary books published in the English language. It is small; but it is just the turning-scale to the side of common sense in matters religious. The Church has at last taken a step in the right direction.

We cannot expect it to set off at a gallop; but it is fairly ambling along on its comfortable palfrey."

The advance is all along the line; and we need not fear any retrograde movement to the past. Canon Farrar says that the manner in which the Higher Criticism has progressed "is exactly analogous to the way in which the truths of astronomy and of geology have triumphed over universal opposition. They were once anathematized as 'Infidel;' they are now accepted as axiomatic." When an official of the Church of England of the high standing of Canon Farrar comes out so boldly in the interest of free thought and free criticism on lines hitherto held to be too sacred for human reason to cross, it is one of the "signs of the times," and a most hopeful one of the future.

And now that we are coming to understand the Bible better than to worship it as an idol, it will gradually be lifted from the shadows and the superstitions of an age when, as a fetich, it was exalted above reason, and placed where a spiritually enlightened people can see it in its true light—a book in which many a bright jewel has been buried under some rubbish, perhaps, as well as under many symbolisms and mystic language—a book which is not above the application of reason and of common sense. And with these new lights on the Bible, it is gratifying to know at the same time that the stately Hebrew Kabbalah, hoary with antiquity, and the fountain source of the Old Testament, places woman on a perfect equality in the Godhead. For better authority than that one can hardly ask.

We are nearing the close of a remarkable century, the last half of which, and especially the last quarter, has been crowded with discoveries, some of them startling in their approximation to the inner, or occult world—a world in which woman has potent sway. The close of this century has long been pointed to by scholars, by writers and by Prophets, within the Church and out of it, as the close of the old dispensation and the opening of the new one. And in view of the rapid steps which we are taking in these latter years, we can almost feel the breath of the new cycle fan our cheeks as we watch the deepening hues of the breaking dawn.　　　　　F. E. B.

THE NEW TESTAMENT.

"Great is Truth, and mighty above all things."—*I Esdras, iv., 41.*

DOES the New Testament bring promises of new dignity and of larger liberties for woman? When thinking women make any criticisms on their degraded position in the Bible, Christians point to her exaltation in the New Testament, as if, under their religion, woman really does occupy a higher position than under the Jewish dispensation. While there are grand types of women presented under both religions, there is no difference in the general estimate of the sex. In fact, her inferior position is more clearly and emphatically set forth by the Apostles than by the Prophets and the Patriarchs. There are no such specific directions for woman's subordination in the Pentateuch as in the Epistles.

We are told that the whole sex was highly honored in Mary being the mother of Jesus. Surely a wise and virtuous son is more indebted to his mother than she is to him, and is honored only by reflecting her superior characteristics. Why the founders of the Christian religion did not improvise an earthly Father as well as an earthly Mother does not clearly appear. The questionable position of Joseph is unsatisfactory. As Mary belonged to the Jewish aristocracy, she should have had a husband of the same rank. If a Heavenly Father was necessary, why not a Heavenly Mother? If an earthly Mother was admirable, why not not an earthly Father? The Jewish idea that Jesus was born according to natural law is more rational than is the Christian record of the immaculate conception by the Holy Ghost, the third person of the Trinity. These Biblical mysteries and inconsistencies are a great strain on the credulity of the ordinary mind.　　　　　　　　E. C. S.

Jesus was the great leading Radical of his age. Everything that he was and said and did alienated and angered the Conservatives, those that represented and stood for the established order of what they believed to be the fixed and final revelation of God. Is it any wonder that they procured his death? They had no power to put him to death themselves, and so they stirred the suspicions of the Roman authorities.

We owe the conquest of Christianity to two things. First, to Paul. Christianity never would have been anything but a little Jewish sect if it had not been for Paul. And the other thing is— what? The conquest over death. It was the abounding belief of the disciples that Jesus was alive, their leader still, though in the invisible, which made them laugh in the face of death, which made them fearless in the presence of the lions in the arena, which made them seek for the honor and glory of martyrdom, and which gave them such conquest over all fear, all sorrow, all toil, as can come only to those who believe that this life is merely a training school, that death is nothing but a doorway and that it leads out into the eternal glories and grandeurs beyond.

I think that the doctrine of the Virgin birth as something higher, sweeter, nobler than ordinary motherhood, is a slur on all the natural motherhood of the world. I believe that millions of children have been as immaculately conceived, as purely born, as was the Nazarene. Why not? Out of this doctrine, and that which is akin to it, have sprung all the monasteries and the nunneries of the world, which have disgraced and distorted and demoralized manhood and womanhood for a thousand years. I place beside the false, monkish, unnatural claim of the Immaculate Conception my mother, who was as holy in her motherhood as was Mary herself.

Another suggestion. This thought of Jesus as the second person of an inconceivable trinity, a being neither of heaven nor earth, but between the two; a being having two natures and one will; a being who was ignorant as a man, and who suffered as a man, while he knew everything as God and could not suffer as God—this conception is part of a scheme of the universe which represents humanity as ruined and lost and hopeless, God as unjust, and man as looking only to a fearful judgment in the ages that are to be. I believe that thousands of people have lived since the time of Jesus as good, as tender, as loving, as true, as faithful, as he. There is no more mystery in the one case than in the other, for it is all mystery. Old Father Taylor, the famous Methodist Bethel preacher in Boston, was a Perfectionist, and when he was asked if he thought anybody had since lived who was as good as Jesus, he said: "Yes; millions of them." This is Methodist authority.

What made Jesus the power he was of his time? In the first place, there was an inexplicable charm about his personality which drew all the common people to him, as iron filings are drawn by a magnet. He loved the people, who instinctively felt it, and loved him. Then there was his intellectual power of speech. Most of the sayings of Jesus are not original in the sense that nobody else ever uttered any similar truths before. Confucius, six thousand years before Jesus, gave utterance to the Golden Rule. And then there was the pity, the sympathy, the tenderness of the man. And then he had trust in God—a trust in the simple Fatherhood of God, that never could be shaken. Jesus taught us, as no one else has ever done it, the humanness of God and the divineness of man, so that, standing there eighteen hundred years ago, he has naturally and infallibly attracted the eyes, the thought, the love, the reverence of the world.

When it is dark in the morning, and before the sun rises, there are high peaks that catch the far-off rays and begin to glow, while the rest of the world still lies in shadow. So there are mountainous men, not supernatural, but as natural as the mountains and the sun— mountainous men who catch the light before our common eyes on the plains and in the valleys can see it, who see and proclaim from their lofty heights far-off visions of truth and beauty that we as yet cannot discern. ANON.

THE BOOK OF MATTHEW.

CHAPTER I.

Matthew i.

16 And Jacob begat Joseph the husband of Mary, of whom was born Jesus, who is called Christ.

17 So all the generations from Abraham to David are fourteen generations; and from David until the carrying away into Babylon are fourteen generations; and from the carrying away into Babylon unto Christ are fourteen generations.

———

SAINT MATTHEW is supposed to be distinguished from the other Apostles by the frequency of his references to the Old Testament. He records more particulars of Jesus than the others do, far more of his birth, his sayings and his miracles.

There has been much difference of opinion among writers of both sacred and profane history as to the paternity of Jesus, and whether he was a real or an ideal character. If, as the Scriptures claim, he descended from heaven, begotten by the Holy Ghost, the incarnation of God himself, then there was nothing remarkable in his career, nor miraculous in the seeming wonders which he performed, being the soul and the centre of all the forces of the universe of matter and of mind. If he was an ideal character, like the gifted hero of some novel or tragedy, his great deeds and his wise sayings the result of the imagination of some skilful artist, then we may admire the sketch as a beautiful picture. But if Jesus was a man who was born, lived and died as do other men, a worthy example for imitation, he is deserving of our love and reverence, and by showing us the possibilities of human nature he is a constant inspiration, our hope and salvation; for the path, however rough, in which one man has walked, others may follow. As a God with infinite power he could have been no example to us; but with human limitations we may emulate his virtues and walk in his footsteps.

Some writers think that his mother was a wise, great and beautiful Jewish maiden, and his father a learned rabbi, who devoted much time and thought to his son's education. At a period when learning was confined to the few, it was a matter of surprise that as a mere boy he could read and write, and discuss the vital questions of the hour with doctors in the sacred temples. His great physical beauty, the wisdom of his replies to the puzzling questions of the Pharisees and the Sadducees, his sympathy with the poor and the needy, his ambition for all that is best in human development, and his indifference to worldly aggrandizement, altogether made him a marked man in his day and generation. For these reasons he was hated, reviled, persecuted, like the long line of martyrs who followed his teachings. He commands far more love and reverence as a true man with only human possibilities, than as a God, superior to all human frailties and temptations.

What were years of persecution, the solitude on the mountain, the agonies on the cross, with the power of a God to sustain him? But unaided and alone to triumph over all human weakness, trials and temptation, was victory not only for Jesus but for every human being made in his image.

Matthew ii.

1 Now when Jesus was born in Bethlehem of Judea in the days of Herod the king, behold, there came wise men from the east to Jerusalem,

2 Saying, Where is he that is born King of the Jews? for we have seen his star in the east, and are come to worship him.

3 When Herod the king had heard these things, he was troubled, and all Jerusalem with him.

4 And when he had gathered all the chief priests together, he demanded of them where Christ should be born.

5 And they said unto him, In Bethlehem of Judea:

8 And he sent them to Bethlehem, and said, Go and search diligently for the young child; and when ye have found him, bring me word.

9 And they departed; and lo, the star, which they saw in the east, went before them, till it came and stood over where the young child was.

11 And when they were come into the house, they saw the young child with Mary his mother, and fell down, and worshiped him: and when they had opened their treasures, they presented unto him gifts; gold, and frankincense, and myrrh.

12 And being warned of God in a dream that they should not return to Herod, they departed into their own country another way.

13 And the angel of the Lord appeareth to Joseph in a dream, saying, Arise, and take the young child and his mother, and flee into Egypt; for Herod will seek to destroy him.

14 And he arose, and departed into Egypt;

19 But when Herod was dead, behold, an angel of the Lord appeareth in a dream to Joseph

20 Saying, Arise, and take the young child and his mother, and go into the land of Israel.

These sages were supposed to be men of great learning belonging to a sect called Magians, who came from Arabia. There was a general feeling that the king of the Jews was yet to be born, and that they were soon to see the long expected and promised Messiah. Herod was greatly troubled by the tidings that a child had been born under remarkable circumstances. The star spoken of was supposed to be a luminous meteor the wise men had seen in their own country before they set out on their journey for Bethlehem, and which now guided them to the house where the young child was. Notwithstanding the common surroundings, the wise men recognizing something more than human in the child, fell down and worshiped him and presented unto him the most precious gifts which their country yielded. Some have supposed that the frankincense and the myrrh were intended as an acknowledgment of his deity, as the gold was of his royalty.

To defeat the subtle malice of Herod, who was determined to take the child's life, Joseph was warned in a dream to flee into Egypt with the child and his mother. The wise men did not return to Herod as commanded, but went at once to their own country.

Matthew ix.

18 Behold, there came a certain ruler, saying, My daughter is even now dead; but come and lay thy hand upon her, and she shall live.

19 And Jesus arose and followed him.

20 And behold, a woman, which was diseased twelve years, came behind him, and touched the hem of his garment:

21 For she said within herself, If I may but touch his garment, I shall be whole.

22 But Jesus turned him about, and when he saw her, he said, Daughter, be of good comfort: thy faith hath made thee whole. And the woman was made whole from that hour.

23 And when Jesus came into the ruler's house, * * *

24 He said, Give place: for the maid is not dead, but sleepeth. And they laughed him to scorn.

25 But when the people were put forth, he went in, and took her by the hand, and the maid arose.

Matthew xiv.

3 For Herod had laid hold on John, and put him in prison for Herodias' sake, his brother Philip's wife.

4 For John said unto him, It is not lawful for thee to have her.

5 And when he would have put him to death, he feared the multitude, because they counted him as a prophet.

6 But when Herod's birthday was kept, the daughter of Herodias danced before them, and pleased Herod.

7 Whereupon he promised to give her whatsoever she would ask.

8 And she, being before instructed of her mother, said, Give me here John Baptist's head in a charger.

9 And the king was sorry: nevertheless for the oath's sake he commanded it to be given her.

10 And he sent, and beheaded John in the prison.

11 And his head was brought in a charger, and given to the damsel: and she brought it to her mother.

12 And his disciples came, and took up the body, and buried it, and went and told Jesus.

Josephus says that Herodias was niece both to her former husband, Philip, and to Herod, with whom she at this time lived. Herod had divorced his own wife in order to take her; and her husband Philip was still living, as well as the daughter Salome, whom he had by her. No connection could be more contrary to the law of God than this. John, therefore, being a prophet and no courtier, plainly reproved Herod, and declared that it was not lawful for him to retain Herodias. This greatly offended Herod and Herodias, and they cast John into prison. Herodias waited her opportunity to wreak her malice on him, counting John's reproof an insult to her character as well as an interference with her ambition.

At length when Herod celebrated his birthday, entertaining his nobles with great magnificence, the daughter of Herodias danced before them all, with such exquisite grace as to delight the company, whereupon Herod promised her whatever she desired, though equal in value to half his kingdom. Salome consulted her mother, who urged her to demand the head of John the Baptist. By the influence of Herodias, Herod, contrary to his own conscience, was induced to put John to death, for he feared him as a righteous man.

It must have been a great trial to the daughter, who might have asked so many beautiful gifts and rare indulgences, to yield all to her wicked mother's revenge. But these deeds were speedily avenged. It is said that Salome had her head cut off by the ice breaking as she passed over it. Herod was shortly after engaged in a disastrous war on account of Herodias, and was expelled from his territories; and both died in exile, hated by everybody and hating one another.

E. C. S.

In regard to the charge against Herodias, which is current among theological scandal-mongers, there is not a moderately intelligent jury of Christendom (if composed half of men and half of women) which, after examining all the available evidence, would not render a verdict in her favor of "Not Guilty." The statement that she "paid the price of her own daughter's debasement and disgrace for the head of John the Baptist," is an assertion born wholly of the ecclesiastical, distorted imagination. Not even a hint, much less an iota of proof, to warrant such an assertion, is found anywhere in history —sacred or profane. While some anonymous writer of the early Christian centuries did put in circulation the charge that John the Baptist was put to death at the instigation of Herodias (without implicating her daughter's character, however), Josephus, on the contrary, explicitly declares that his death was wholly a political matter, with which the names of Herodias and her daughter are not even connected by rumor. Says Josephus: "When others came in crowds about him (John the Baptist), for they were greatly moved by hearing his words, Herod, who feared lest the great influence John had over the people might put it into his power and inclination to raise a rebellion (for they seemed ready to do anything he should advise), thought it best, by putting him to death, to prevent any mischief he might cause. . . . Accordingly he was sent a prisoner, *out of Herod's suspicious temper*, to Macherus, the castle I before mentioned, and was there put to death."

Now, the jury must remember that Josephus was born in Jerusalem about 38 A. D., that he was an educated man and in a position to know the facts in this case, owing both to his prominent position among the Jews and to his study of contemporaneous history. But that, on the other hand, the anonymous writers who bring Herodias' name into the transaction, are not traceable further back than the fourth century of our era, and that even they do not bring any charge against her character as a mother.   E. B. D.

Matthew xv.

21 Then Jesus departed into the coasts of Tyre and Sidon.

22 And, behold, a woman of Canaan cried unto him, saying, Have mercy on me, O Lord, thou son of David; my daughter is grievously vexed with a devil.

23 But he answered her not a word. And his disciples besought him to send her away.

24 But he answered and said, I am not sent but unto the lost sheep of the house of Israel.

25 Then came she and worshiped him, saying, Lord, help me.

26 But he said, It is not meet to take the children's food, and to cast it to dogs.

27 And she said, Truth, Lord: yet the dogs eat of the crumbs which fall from their master's table.

28 Then Jesus answered and said unto her, O woman, great is thy faith: be it unto thee even as thou wilt. And her daughter was made whole from that very hour.

Peter had a house in Capernaum; and his wife's mother lived

with them; and Jesus lodged with them when in that city. It is hoped that his presence brought out the best traits of the mother-in-law, so as to make her agreeable to Peter. As soon as Jesus rebuked the fever, she was able without delay to rise and to wait on Jesus and his disciples. These displays of the power of Christ in performing miracles, according to the text, are varied, in almost every conceivable way of beneficence; but he wrought no miracles of vengeance, even the destruction of the swine was doubtless intended in mercy and conducive to much good—so say the commentators. He not only healed the sick and cast out devils, but he made the blind to see and the dumb to speak.

The woman of Canaan proved herself quite equal in argument with Jesus; and though by her persistency she tired the patience of the disciples, she made her points with Jesus with remarkable clearness. His patience with women was a sore trial to the disciples, who were always disposed to nip their appeals in the bud. It was very ungracious in Jesus to speak of the Jews as dogs, saying, "It is not meet to take the children's food, and to cast it to dogs." Her reply, "Yet the dogs eat of the crumbs which fall from the master's table," was bright and appropriate. Jesus appreciated her tact and her perseverance, and granted her request; and her daughter, the text says, was healed.

We might doubt the truth of all these miracles did we not see so many wonderful things in our own day which we would have pronounced impossible years ago. The fact of human power developing in so many remarkable ways proves that Jesus's gift of performing miracles is attainable by those who, like him, live pure lives, and whose blood flows in the higher arches of the brain. If one man, at any period of the world's history, performed miracles, others equally gifted may do the same.

Matthew xx.

20 Then came to him the mother of Zebedee's children with her sons, worshiping him, and desiring a certain thing of him.

21 And he said unto her, What wilt thou? She saith unto him, Grant that these my two sons may sit, the one on thy right hand, and the other on the left, in thy kingdom.

Zebedee, the father of James and of John, was dead; and he was not so constant a follower of Christ as his wife; so she is mentioned as the mother of Zebedee's children, which saying has passed into a conundrum, "Who was the mother of Zebedee's children?" Scott in his commentaries gives her name as Salome. Whatever her name, she had great ambition for her sons, and asked that they might have the chief places of honor and authority in his kingdom. Her son James was the first of the Apostles who suffered martyrdom. John survived all the rest and is not supposed to have died a violent death.

A mother's ambition to lift her sons over her own head in education and position, planning extraordinary responsibilities for ordinary men, has proved a misfortune in many cases. Many a young man who would be a success as a carpenter would be a failure as the governor of a State. Mothers are quite apt to overestimate the genius of their children and push them into niches which they cannot fill.

Matthew xxii.

23 The same day came to him the Sadducees, which say that there is no resurrection and asked him,

24 Saying, Master, Moses said, If a man die, having no children, his brother shall marry his wife, and raise up seed unto his brother.

25 Now there were with us seven brethren: and the first, when he had married a wife, deceased, and, having no issue, left his wife unto his brother:

26 Likewise the second also, and the third, unto the seventh.

27 And last of all the woman died also.

28 Therefore in the resurrection, whose wife shall she be of the seven? for they all had her.

29 Jesus answered and said unto them, Ye do err, not knowing the Scriptures, nor the power of God.

30 For in the resurrection they neither marry, nor are given in marriage, but are as the angels of God in heaven.

Jesus reminded the Sadducees that marriage was intended only for the present world, to replenish the earth and to repair the ravages which death continually makes among its inhabitants; but as in the future state there was to be no death, so no marriage. There the body even would be made spiritual; and all the employments and the pleasures pure and angelic. The marriage relation seems to have been a tangled problem in all ages. Scientists tell us that both the masculine and feminine elements were united in one person in the beginning, and will probably be reunited again for eternity.

E. C. S.

CHAPTER II.

Matthew xxv.

1 Then shall the kingdom of heaven be likened unto ten virgins, which took their lamps, and went forth to meet the bridegroom.

2 And five of them were wise, and five were foolish.

3 They that were foolish took their lamps, and took no oil with them:

4 But the wise took oil in their vessels with their lamps.

5 While the bridegroom tarried, they all slumbered and slept.

6 And at midnight there was a cry made, Behold, the bridegroom cometh; go ye out to meet him.

7 Then all those virgins arose, and trimmed their lamps.

8 And the foolish said unto the wise, Give us of your oil; for our lamps are gone out.

9 But the wise answered, saying, Not so, lest there be not enough for us and you: but go ye rather to them that sell, and buy for yourselves.

10 And while they went to buy, the bridegroom came; and they that were ready went in with him to the marriage: and the door was shut.

11 Afterward came also the other virgins, saying, Lord, Lord, open to us.

12 But he answered and said, Verily I say unto you, I know you not.

IN this chapter we have the duty of self-development impressively and repeatedly urged in the form of parables, addressed alike to man and to woman. The sin of neglecting and of burying one's talents, capacities and powers, and the penalties which such a course involve, are here strikingly portrayed.

This parable is found among the Jewish records substantially the same as in our own Scriptures. Their weddings were generally celebrated at night; yet they usually began at the rising of the evening star; but in this case there was a more than ordinary delay. Adam Clarke in his commentaries explains this parable as referring chiefly to spiritual gifts and the religious life. He makes the Lord of Hosts the bridegroom, the judgment day the wedding feast, the foolish virgins the sinners whose hearts were cold and dead, devoid of all spiritual graces, and unfit to enter the kingdom of heaven. The wise virgins were the saints who were ready for translation, or for the bridal procession. They followed to the wedding feast; and when the chosen had entered *"the door was shut."*

This strikes us as a strained interpretation of a very simple parable, which, considered in connection with the other parables, seems to apply much more closely to this life than to that which is to come, to the intellectual and the moral nature, and to the whole round of human duties. It fairly describes the two classes which help to make up society in general. The one who, like the foolish virgins, have never learned the first important duty of cultivating their own individual powers, using the talents given to them, and keeping their own lamps trimmed and burning. The idea of being a helpmeet to somebody else has been so sedulously drilled into most women that an individual life, aim, purpose and ambition are never taken into consideration. They oftimes do so much in other directions that they neglect the most vital duties to themselves.

We may find in this simple parable a lesson for the cultivation of courage and of self-reliance. These virgins are summoned to the discharge of an important duty at midnight, alone, in darkness, and in solitude. No chivalrous gentleman is there to run for oil and to trim their lamps. They must depend on themselves, unsupported, and pay the penalty of their own improvidence and unwisdom. Perhaps in that bridal procession might have been seen fathers, brothers, friends, for whose service and amusement the foolish virgins had wasted many precious hours, when they should have been trimming their own lamps and keeping oil in their vessels.

And now, with music, banners, lanterns, torches, guns and rockets fired at intervals, come the bride and the groom, with their attendants and friends numbering thousands, brilliant in jewels, gold and silver, magnificently mounted on richly caparisoned horses —for nothing can be more brilliant than were those nuptial solemnities of Eastern nations. As this spectacle, grand beyond description, sweeps by, imagine the foolish virgins pushed aside, in the shadow of some tall edifice, with dark, empty lamps in their hands, unnoticed and unknown. And while the castle walls resound with music and merriment, and the lights from every window stream out far into the darkness, no kind friends gather round them to sympathize in their humiliation, nor to cheer their loneliness. It matters little that women may be ignorant, dependent, unprepared for trial and for temptation. Alone they must meet the terrible emergencies of life, to be sustained and protected amid danger and death by their own courage, skill and self-reliance, or perish.

Woman's devotion to the comfort, the education, the success of men in general, and to their plans and projects, is in a great measure due to her self-abnegation and self-sacrifice having been so long and so sweetly lauded by poets, philosophers and priests as the acme of human goodness and glory.

Now, to my mind, there is nothing commendable in the action of young women who go about begging funds to educate young men for the ministry, while they and the majority of their sex are too poor to educate themselves, and if able, are still denied admittance into some of the leading institutions of learning throughout our land. It is not commendable for women to get up fairs and donation parties for churches in which the gifted of their sex may neither pray, preach, share in the offices and honors, nor have a voice in the business affairs, creeds and discipline, and from whose altars come forth Biblical interpretations in favor of woman's subjection.

It is not commendable for the women of this Republic to expend much enthusiasm on political parties as now organized, nor in national celebrations, for they have as yet no lot or part in the great experiment of self-government.

In their ignorance, women sacrifice themselves to educate the men of their households, and to make of themselves ladders by which their husbands, brothers and sons climb up into the kingdom of knowledge, while they themselves are shut out from all intellectual companionship, even with those they love best; such are indeed like the foolish virgins. They have not kept their own lamps trimmed and burning; they have no oil in their vessels, no resources in themselves; they bring no light to their households nor to the circle in which they move; and when the bridegroom cometh, when the philosopher, the scientist, the saint, the scholar, the great and the learned, all come together to celebrate the marriage feast of science and religion, the foolish virgins, though present, are practically shut out; for what know they of the grand themes which inspire each tongue and kindle every thought? Even the brothers and the sons whom they have educated, now rise to heights which they cannot reach, span distances which they cannot comprehend.

The solitude of ignorance, oh, who can measure its misery!

The wise virgins are they who keep their lamps trimmed, who burn oil in their vessels for their own use, who have improved every advantage for their education, secured a healthy, happy, complete development, and entered all the profitable avenues of labor, for self-support, so that when the opportunities and the responsibilities of life come, they may be fitted fully to enjoy the one and ably to discharge the other.

These are the women who to-day are close upon the heels of man in the whole realm of thought, in art, in science, in literature and in government. With telescopic vision they explore the starry firmament, and bring back the history of the planetary world. With chart and compass they pilot ships across the mighty deep, and with skilful fingers send electric messages around the world. In galleries of art, the grandeur of nature and the greatness of humanity are immortalized by them on canvas, and by their inspired touch, dull blocks of marble are transformed into angels of light. In music they speak again the language of Mendelssohn, of Beethoven, of Chopin, of Schumann, and are worthy interpreters of their great souls. The poetry and the novels of the century are theirs; they, too, have touched the keynote of reform in religion, in politics and in social life. They fill the editors' and the professors' chairs, plead at the bar of justice, walk the wards of the hospital, and speak from the pulpit and the platform.

Such is the widespread preparation for the marriage feast of science and religion; such is the type of womanhood which the bridegroom of an enlightened public sentiment welcomes to-day; and such is the triumph of the wise virgins over the folly, the ignorance and the degradation of the past as in grand procession they enter the temple of knowledge, and *the door is no longer shut.*

Matthew xxvi.

6 Now when Jesus was in Bethany, in the house of Simon the leper,

7 There came unto him a woman having an alabaster box of very precious ointment, and poured it on his head.

8 But when his disciples saw it, they said, To what purpose is this waste?

9 For this ointment might have been sold for much, and given to the poor.

10 When Jesus understood it, he said unto them, Why trouble ye the woman?

11 For ye have the poor always with you; but me ye have not always.

12 For in that she hath poured this ointment on my body, she did it for my burial.

13 Verily, I say unto you, wheresoever this gospel shall be preached, there shall also this be told for a memorial of her.

Matthew xxvii.

19 When Pilate was set down on the judgment seat, his wife sent unto him, saying, Have thou nothing to do with that just man: for I have suffered many things this day in a dream, because of him.

24 When Pilate saw that he could prevail nothing, but that rather a tumult was made, he took water, and washed his hands before the multitude, saying, I am innocent of the blood of this just person: see ye to it.

25 Then answered all the people, and said, His blood be on us, and on our children.

55 And many women were there beholding afar off, which followed Jesus from Galilee, ministering unto him;

56 Among which was Mary Magdalene, and Mary, the mother of James and Joses, and the mother of Zebedee's children.

61 And there was Mary Magdalene, and the other Mary, sitting over against the sepulchre.

It is a common opinion among Christians that the persecutions of the Jews in all periods and latitudes is a punishment on them for their crucifixion of Jesus, and that this defiant acceptance of the responsibility is being justly fulfilled.

Matthew xxviii.

1 In the end of the Sabbath, as it began to dawn came Mary Magdalene and the other Mary to see the sepulchre.

2 And, behold, there was a great earthquake: for the angel of the Lord descended from heaven, and came and rolled back the stone from the door, and sat upon it.

3 His countenance was like lightning, and his raiment white as snow:

4 And for fear of him the keepers did shake, and became as dead men.

5 And the angel answered and said unto the women, Fear not ye; for I know that ye seek Jesus, which was crucified.

7 Go quickly and tell his disciples that he is risen from the dead; and behold, he goeth before you into Galilee; there shall ye see him.

8 And they departed quickly from the sepulchre with great joy.

9 And as they went to tell his disciples, behold, Jesus met them, saying, All hail. And they came and held him by the feet, and worshiped him.

10 Then said Jesus unto them, Be not afraid: tell my brethren that they go into Galilee, and there shall they see me.

Among the witnesses of the crucifixion, this melancholy and untimely scene, there were some women who had followed Jesus from Galilee and had waited on him, supplying his wants from their substance. Affection and anxious concern induced them to be present, and probably they stand afar off, fearing the outrages of the multitude.   Words cannot express the mixed emotions of true gratitude, reverence, sorrow and compassion which must have agitated their souls on this occasion.   We find from John, who was also present, that Mary the mother of Jesus was a spectator of this distressing scene.

When Jesus was brought before Pilate, he was greatly troubled as to what judgment he should give, and his hesitation was increased by a warning from his wife, to have no part in the death of that righteous man; for she had terrifying dreams respecting him, which made her conclude that his death would be avenged by some unseen power.   E. C. S.

THE BOOK OF MARK.

Mark iii.

31 There came then his brethren and his mother, and, standing without, sent unto him,

32 And the multitude sat about him, and said unto him, Behold, thy mother and thy brethren seek for thee.

33 And he answered them, saying, Who is my mother, or my brethren?

34 And he looked round about and said. Behold my mother and my brethren!

35 For whosoever shall do the will of God, the same is my brother, and my sister. and mother.

MANY of the same texts found in the Book of Matthew are repeated by the other Evangelists. It appears from the text that the earnestness of Jesus in teaching the people, made some of his friends, who did not believe in his mission, anxious. Even his mother feared to have him teach doctrines in opposition to the public sentiment of his day. His words of seeming disrespect to her, simply meant to imply that he had an important work to do, that his duties to humanity were more to him than the ties of natural affection.

Many of the ancient writers criticise Mary severely, for trying to exercise control over Jesus, assuming rightful authority over him. Theophylact taxes her with vainglory; Tertullian accuses her of ambition; St. Chrysostom of impiety and of disbelief; Whitby says it is plain that this is a protest against the idolatrous worship of Mary. She was generally admitted to be a woman of good character and worthy of all praise; but whatever she was, it ill becomes those who believe that she was the mother of God to criticise her as they would an ordinary mortal.

Mark x.

2 And the Pharisees came to him, and asked him, Is it lawful for a man to put away his wife? tempting him.

3 And he answered and said unto them, What did Moses command you?

4 And they said, Moses suffered to write a bill of divorcement, and to put her away.

5 And Jesus answered and said unto them, For the hardness of your heart he wrote you this precept.

6 But from the beginning of the creation God made them male and female.

7 For this cause shall a man leave his father and mother, and cleave to his wife;

8 And they twain shall be one flesh:

9 What therefore God hath joined together, let not man put asunder.

The question of marriage was a constant theme for discussion in the days of Moses and of Jesus, as in our own times. The Pharisees are still asking questions, not that they care for an answer on the highest plane of morality, but to entrap some one as opposed to the authorities of their times. Life with Jesus was too short and his mission too stern to parley with pettifoggers; so he gives to them a clear cut, unmistakable definition as to what marriage is: "Whoever puts away his wife save for the cause of unchastity, which violates the marriage covenant, commits adultery." Hence, under the Christian dispensation we must judge husband and wife by the same code of morals.

If this rule of the perfect equality of the sexes were observed in all social relations the marriage problem might be easily solved. But with one code of morals for man and another for woman, we are involved in all manner of complications. In England, for example, a woman may marry her husband's brother; but a man may not marry his wife's sister. They have had "a deceased wife's sister's bill" before Parliament for generations. Ever and anon they take it up, look at it with their opera glasses, air their grandfather's old platitudes over it, give a sickly smile at some well-worn witticism, or drop a tear at a pathetic whine from some bishop, then lay the bill reverently back in its sacred pigeon-hole for a period of rest.

The discussion in the United States is now in the form of a homogeneous divorce law in all the States of the Union, but this is not in woman's interest. What Canada was to the Southern slaves under the old régime, a State with liberal divorce laws is to fugitive wives. If a dozen learned judges should get together, as is proposed, to revise the divorce laws, they would make them more stringent in liberal States instead of more lax in conservative States. When such a commission is decided upon, one-half of the members should be women, as they have an equal interest in the marriage and divorce laws; and common justice demands that they should have an equal voice in their reconstruction. I do not think a homogeneous law desirable; though I should like to see New York and South Carolina liberalized, I should not like to see South Dakota and Indiana more conservative.

Mark xii.

41 And Jesus sat over against the treasury, and beheld how the people cast money into the treasury; and many that were rich cast in much.

42 And there came a certain poor widow, and she thew in two mites, which make a farthing.

43 And he called unto him his disciples, and saith unto them, Verily I say unto you, That this poor widow hath cast more in than all they which have cast into the treasury:

44 For all *they* did cast in of their abundance; but she of her want did cast in all that she had, *even* all her living.

The widow's gift no doubt might have represented more generosity than all beside, for the large donations of the rich were only a part of their superfluities, and bore a small proportion to the abundance which they still had, but she gave in reality of her necessities. The small contribution was of no special use in the treasury of the Church, but as an act of self-sacrifice it was of more real value in estimating character. Jesus with his intuition saw the motives of the giver, as well as the act.

This woman, belonging to an impoverished class, was trained to self-abnegation; but when women learn the higher duty of self-development, they will not so readily expend all their forces in serving others. Paul says that a husband who does not provide for his own household is worse than an infidel. So a woman, who spends all her time in churches, with priests, in charities, neglects to cultivate her own natural gifts, to make the most of herself as an individual in the scale of being, a responsible soul whose place no other can fill, is worse than an infidel. "Self-development is a higher duty than self-sacrifice," should be woman's motto henceforward.

E. C. S.

THE BOOK OF LUKE.

Luke i.

5 There was in the days of Herod, the king of Judea, a certain priest named Zacharias, and his wife was of the daughters of Aaron, and her name was Elizabeth.

6 And they were both righteous before God, walking in all the commandments and ordinances of the Lord blameless.

7 And they had no child; and they both were now well stricken in years.

8 And it came to pass, that, while he executed the priest's office before God—his lot was to burn incense when he went into the temple of the Lord.

11 And there appeared unto him an angel standing on the right side of the altar of incense.

12 And when Zacharias saw him, he was troubled, and fear fell upon him.

13 But the angel said unto him, Fear not, Zacharias: for thy prayer is heard; and thy wife Elisabeth shall bear thee a son, and thou shalt call his name John.

14 And thou shalt have joy and gladness; and many shall rejoice at his birth.

15 For he shall be great in the sight of the Lord, and shall drink neither wine nor strong drink; and he shall be filled with the Holy Ghost.

LUKE was the companion of the Apostle Paul in all of his labors during many years. He also wrote the Acts of the Apostles. He was a Syrian, and became acquainted with the Christians at Antioch. He is called by Paul "the beloved physician."

Luke opens his book with the parentage and the birth of John. His father, Zacharias, was a priest, and his mother, Elizabeth, was also descended from Aaron. They were exemplary persons. They habitually walked in an upright course of obedience to all the commandments. They had no children, but in answer to their prayers a son was at last given to them, whose name was John, which signifies "grace, or favor of the Lord."

While Zacharias ministered at the altar, an angel appeared to him to tell him of the advent of his son. The vision was so startling that Zacharias was struck dumb for a season. The same angel appeared soon after to Mary, the mother of Jesus, with glad tidings of her motherhood. She and Elizabeth met often during that joyful period, and talked over the promised blessings. John was born about six months before Jesus, and is sometimes called his fore-runner. Elizabeth and Mary were cousins on the mother's side.

Soon after the angel appeared to Mary she went in haste to the home of Zacharias, and saluted Elizabeth, who said, "Blessed art thou among women; and how comes this honor to me, that the mother of my Lord should cross my threshold?" Mary replied, "My soul doth magnify the Lord that he hath thus honored his hand-maiden. Henceforth all generations shall call me blessed."

When Elizabeth's son was born, the neighbors, cousins and aunts all assembled and at once volunteered their opinions as to the boy's name, and all insisted that he should be named "Zacharias," after his father. But Elizabeth said, "No; his name is John, as the angel said." As none of the family had ever been called by that name, they appealed by signs to the father (who was still dumb); but he promptly wrote on the table, "His name is John."

Luke ii.

36 And there was one Anna, a prophet-ess.

37 And she was a widow of about four-score and four years, which departed not from the temple, but served God with fast-ings and prayers night and day.

Anna having lost her husband in the prime of her life, remained a widow to her death. She resided near the temple that she might attend all its sacred ordinances. Having no other engagements to occupy her attention, she spent her whole time in the service of God, and joined frequent fastings with her constant prayers for herself and her people. She was employed day and night in those religious exercises, so says the text; but Scott allows the poor widow, now over eighty years of age, some hours for rest at night (more merci-ful than the Evangelist). She came into the temple just as Simon held the child in his arms, and she also returned thanks to God for the coming of the promised Saviour, and that her eyes had beheld him.

41 Now his parents went to Jerusalem every year at the feast of the passover.

42 And when he was twelve years old, they went up to Jerusalem after the custom of the feast.

43 And when they had fulfilled the days, as they returned, the child Jesus tarried be-hind in Jerusalem: and Joseph and his mother knew not of it.

44 But they, supposing him to have been

in the company, went a day's journey: and they sought him among their kinsfolk and acquaintance.

45 And when they found him not, they turned back again to Jerusalem, seeking him.

46 And it came to pass, that after three days they found him in the temple, sitting in the midst of the doctors, both hearing them, and asking them questions.

47 And all that heard him were astonished at his understanding and answers.

48 And when they saw him, his mother said unto him, Son, why hast thou thus dealt with us? Behold, thy father and I have sought thee sorrowing.

49 And he said unto them, How is it that ye sought me? wist ye not that I must be about my Father's business?

50 And they understood not the saying which he spake unto them.

51 And he went with them to Nazareth, and was subject unto them: but his mother kept all these sayings in her heart.

These texts contain all that is said of the childhood and the youth of Jesus, though we should have expected fuller information on so extraordinary a subject. Joseph and Mary went up to the feast of the passover every year, and it was the custom to take children of that age with them. They journeyed in a great company for mutual security, and thus in starting they overlooked the boy, supposing that he was with the other children. But when the families separated for the night they could not find him, so they journeyed back to Jerusalem and found him in a court of the temple, listening to, and asking questions of the doctors, who were surprised at his intelligence.

It is often said that he was *disputing* with the doctors, which the commentators say gives a wrong impression; he was modestly asking questions. Neither Mary nor Joseph remembered nor fully understood what the angel had told them concerning the mission of their child; neither did they comprehend the answer of Jesus. However, he went back with them to Nazareth, and was subject to them in all things, working at the carpenter's trade until he entered on his mission. It was a great mistake that some argel had not made clear to Mary the important character and mission of her son, that she might not have been a seeming hindrance on so many occasions, and made it necessary for Jesus to rebuke her so often, and thus subject herself to criticism for his seeming disrespect.

Luke xiii.

11 And, behold, there was a woman which had a spirit of infirmity eighteen years, and was bowed together, and could in no wise lift up herself.

12 And when Jesus saw her, he called her to him, and said unto her, Woman, thou art loosed from thine infirmity.

13 And he laid his hands on her: and im-

mediately she was made straight, and glorified God.

14 And the ruler of the synagogue answered with indignation, because that Jesus had healed on the Sabbath day, and said unto the people, There are six days in which men ought to work: in them therefore come and be healed, but not on the Sabbath day.

15 The Lord then answered him, and said, Thou hypocrite, doth not each one of you on the Sabbath loose his ox or his ass from the stall, and lead him away to watering?

16 And ought not this woman, being a daughter of Abraham, whom Satan hath bound, lo, these eighteen years, be loosed from this bond on the Sabbath day?

17 And when he had said these things, all his adversaries were ashamed: and all the people rejoiced for all the glorious things that were done by him.

Jesus was teaching in one of the synagogues on the Sabbath day, and saw the distress of this woman who attended worship; he called her to him, and, by the laying on of his hands and by prayer, immediately restored her; and being made straight, she glorified God before all for this unexpected deliverance. The ruler of the synagogue, who hated the doctrines of Jesus and envied the honor, tried to veil his enmity with pretence of singular piety, telling the people that they should come for healing other days and not on the holy rest of the Sabbath, as if the woman had come there on purpose for a cure, or as if a word and a touch attended with so beneficent an effect could break the Sabbath. Jesus' rebuke of the malice and hypocrisy of the man was fully justified.

The Sabbath-day-Pharisees are not all dead yet. While more rational people are striving to open libraries, art galleries and concert halls on Sundays, a class of religious bigots are endeavoring to close up on that day, all places of entertainment for the people. The large class of citizens shut up in factories, in mercantile establishments, in offices, and in shops all the week, should have the liberty to enjoy themselves in all rational amusements on Sunday. All healthy sports in the open air, music in parks, popular lectures in all the school buildings, should be encouraged and protected by law for their benefit.

Luke xviii.

2 There was in a city a judge, which feared not God, neither regarded man:

3 And there was a widow in that city; and she came unto him, saying, Avenge me of mine adversary.

4 And he would not for a while: but afterward he said within himself, Though I fear not God, neither regard man;

5 Yet because this widow troubleth me. I will avenge her, lest by her continual coming she weary me.

6 And the Lord said, Hear what the unjust judge saith.

7 And shall not God avenge his own elect, which cry day and night unto him, though he bear long with them?

The lesson taught in this parable is perseverance. Everything can be accomplished by continued effort. Saints hope to acquire all spiritual graces through prayers; philanthropists to carry out their reform measures through constant discussion; politicians their public measures by continued party combat and repeated acts of legislation. Through forty years of conflict we abolished slavery. Through fifty years of conflict we have partially emancipated woman from the bondage of the old common law of England, and crowned her with the rights of full citizenship in four States in the American Republic.

The condition of the woman in this parable, bowed to the earth with all her disabilities, well represents the degraded condition of the sex under every form of government and of religion the world over; but, unlike her, women still, in many latitudes, make their appeals in vain at cathedral altars and in the halls of legislation.

E. C. S.

———

The sentiment concerning the equality of male and female, which Paul avowed to the Galatians, is perfectly in accord with what "Luke" reports of Jesus' own custom. It will be remembered that the chief adherents of Paul accepted only this report (and this only partly) as worthy of credit; and therein we find the statement that many female ministers had accompanied Jesus and the male ministers, as they wandered (in Salvation Army fashion) "throughout every city and village preaching." It is true that we now find a qualifying passage in reference to the female ministers, namely, "which ministered unto him of their substance" (Luke, ch. 8, v. 3). But this is, plainly, one of those numerous marginal comments, made at late date (when all the original manuscripts had disappeared), by men who had, doubtless, lost knowledge of women's original equality in the ministry; for Ignatius of Antioch, one of the earliest Christian writers, expressly affirms that the deacons were "not ministers of meats and drinks, but ministers of the Church of God."

Although this is well known, our modern theologians seem to have been unable to avoid jumping to the conclusion that, whenever *women* are mentioned in the ministry, it must be only as ministers of their substance, either as a kind of commissaries, or, at most, as kindergarten officials. It is manifestly true that the early Church was immensely indebted to the benefactions of rich widows and virgin heiresses for the means of sustaining life in its fellowship. Thecla, Paula, Eustochium, Marcella, Melanie, Susanna, are but a few of the women of wealth who gave both themselves and their large fortunes to the establishment of the ethics of Jesus. Yet Paula's greatest work (from men's standpoint of great works) is rarely mentioned in Christendom, and it is significant of the degradation which women suffered at the hands of the Church that the time came when Churchmen could not believe that she had performed it, even with Jerome's acknowledgment confronting them, and consequently erased the word "sister" accompanying the name Paula, substituting therefor the word "brother!"

Paula founded and endowed monasteries, won to the Christian cause allegiance from one of the noblest families of Greece and Rome, and originated within the monasteries the occupation of copying manuscripts, to which civilization is indebted for the preservation of much precious literature; but her most important service to the Church was her co-labor with Jerome in the great task of translating the Jewish scriptures from the original Hebrew into Latin. It was Paula who suggested and inspired the undertaking, furnishing the expensive works of reference, without which it would have been impossible, and being herself a woman of fine intellect, highly trained, and an excellent Hebrew scholar, revised and corrected Jerome's work; then, finally, assisted by her brilliant daughter, Eustochium, performed the enormous task of copying it accurately for circulation. It was the least that Jerome could do to dedicate the completed work to those able coadjutors, and it is an amazing thing to find Churchmen still eulogizing Jerome as "author of the Vulgate," without the slightest reference to the fact that, but for Paula's help, the Vulgate would not have come into existence. But until men and women return to more natural relations, until women cast off their false subserviency, thereby helping men to get rid of their unnatural arrogance, nothing different from the injustice Christendom has shown Paula can be looked for.   E. B. D.

THE BOOK OF JOHN.

And the third day there was a marriage in Cana of Galilee; and the mother of Jesus was there:

2 And both Jesus was called, and his disciples, to the marriage.

3 And when they wanted wine, the mother of Jesus saith unto him, They have no wine.

4 Jesus saith unto her, Woman, what have I to do with thee? mine hour is not yet come.

5 His mother saith unto the servants, Whatsoever he saith unto you, do it.

7 Jesus saith unto them, Fill the water-pots with water. And they filled them up to the brim.

8 And he saith unto them, Draw out now. and bear unto the governor of the feast. And they bare it.

9 When the ruler of the feast had tasted the water that was made wine, he called the bridegroom.

10 And saith unto him, Every man at the beginning doth set forth good wine; and when men have well drunk, then that which is worse: but thou hast kept the good wine until now.

JOHN was distinguished among the Apostles for his many virtues, and was specially honored as the bosom friend of Jesus.

He is supposed to have lived in the neighborhood of Judea until the time approached for the predicted destruction of Jerusalem; then he went to Asia and resided some years in Ephesus, was banished to the Island of Patmos by the Emperor Domitian, and returned to Asia after the death of that Emperor. He lived to be a hundred years of age, and died a natural death, being the only Apostle who escaped martyrdom. John alone records the resurrection of Lazarus, and many things not mentioned in the other Gospels.

Probably Mary was related to one of the parties to the marriage, for she appears to have given directions as one of the family. As Joseph is not mentioned either on this occasion or afterwards, we may suppose that he died before Jesus entered into his public ministry. There was no disrespect intended in the word "woman" with which Jesus addressed his mother, as the greatest princesses were accosted even by their servants in the same manner among the ancients. Jesus merely intended to suggest that no one could command when he should perform miracles, as they would in any ordinary event subject to human discretion.

The Jews always kept a great number of water-pots filled with water in their houses for the ceremonial washing prescribed by law. Commentators differ as to how much these pots contained, but it is estimated that the six contained a hogshead. The ruler of the feast was generally a Levite or a priest; and he expressed his surprise that they should have kept the best wine until the last.

John iv.

5 Then cometh he to a city of Samaria, which is called Sychar.

6 Now Jacob's well was there. Jesus therefore, being wearied with his journey, sat thus on the well: and it was about the sixth hour.

7 There cometh a woman of Samaria to draw water: Jesus saith unto her, Give me to drink.

8 (For his disciples were gone away unto the city to buy meat.)

9 Then saith the woman of Samaria unto him, How is it that thou, being a Jew, askest drink of me, which am a woman of Samaria? for the Jews have no dealings with the Samaritans.

10 Jesus answered and said unto her, If thou knewest the gift of God, and who it is that saith to thee, Give me to drink; thou wouldest have asked of him, and he would have given thee living water.

27 And upon this came his disciples, and marvelled that he talked with the woman. yet no man said, What seekest thou? or, Why talkest thou with her?

As the Samaritans were not generally disposed to receive the Jews into their houses, Jesus did not try to enter, but sat down by Jacob's well, and sent his disciples into the town to buy some necessary provisions. The prejudices against each other were so inveterate that they never asked for a favor, hence the woman was surprised when Jesus spoke to her. They might buy of each other, but never borrow nor receive a favor or gift, nor manifest friendship in any way.

But Christ, despising all such prejudices that had no foundation either in equity or in the law of God, asked drink of the Samaritan woman. He did not notice the woman's narrow prejudices, but directed her attention to matters of greater importance. He told her though she should refuse him the small favor for which he asked because he was a Jew, yet he was ready to confer far greater benefits on her, though a Samaritan. The living water to which Jesus referred, the woman did not understand.

16 Jesus saith unto her, Go, call thy husband, and come hither.

17 The woman answered and said, I have no husband. Jesus said unto her, Thou hast well said, I have no husband:

18 For thou hast had five husbands: and he whom thou now hast is not thy husband: in that saidst thou truly.

19 The woman saith unto him, Sir, I perceive that thou art a prophet.

28 The woman then left her waterpot, and went her way into the city, and saith to the men.

29 Come, see a man, which told me all things that ever I did: is not this the Christ?

39 And many of the Samaritans of that city believed on him for the saying of the woman, which testified, He told me all that ever I did.

40 So when the Samaritans were come unto him, they besought him that he would tarry with them: and he abode there two days.

41 And many more believed because of his own word.

The woman could not understand Jesus' words because she had no conviction of sin nor desire for a purer, better life; and as soon as possible she changed the subject of the conversation from her private life to the subjects of controversy between the Jews and the Samaritans.

John viii.

2 And early in the morning he came again into the temple, and all the people came unto him: and he sat down, and taught them.

3 And the Scribes and Pharisees brought unto him a woman taken in adultery; and when they had set her in the midst,

4 They say unto him, Master, this woman was taken in adultery,

5 Now Moses in the law commanded us, that such should be stoned: but what sayest thou?

6 This they said, tempting him, that they might have to accuse him. But Jesus stooped down, and with his finger wrote on the ground, as though he heard them not.

7 So when they continued asking him, he

lifted up himself, and said unto them, He that is without sin among you, let him first cast a stone at her.

8 And again he stooped down, and wrote on the ground.

9 And they which heard it, being convicted by their own conscience, went out one by one, beginning at the eldest, even unto the last: and Jesus was left alone, and the woman standing in the midst.

10 He said unto her, Woman, where are those thine accusers? hath no man condemned thee?

11 She said, No man, Lord. And Jesus said unto her, Neither do I condemn thee: go, and sin no more.

The Scribes and the Pharisees concocted a plan to draw Jesus into a snare. They concluded from many of his doctrines that he deemed himself authorized to alter or to abrogate the commands of Moses; therefore they desired his opinion as to the fitting punishment for an adulteress. If he had ordered them to execute her, they would doubtless have accused him to the Romans of assuming a judicial authority, independent of their government; had he directed them to set her at liberty, they would have represented him to the people as an enemy to the law, and a patron of the most infamous characters; and had he referred them to the Roman authority, they would have accused him to the multitude as a betrayer of their liberties.

John ix.
And as Jesus passed by, he saw a man which was blind from *his* birth.

2 And his disciples asked him, saying, Master, who did sin, this man, or his parents, that he was born blind?

3 Jesus answered, Neither hath this man sinned, nor his parents: but that the works of God should be made manifest in him.

A prevalent idea of the Jews was that, in accord with the ten commandments, the sins of the parents were visited upon the children. This is recognized as absolute law to-day; but it by no means follows that all afflictions are the result of sin. The blindness may have resulted from a combination of circumstances beyond the control of the parents. The statement does not disprove the law of transmission, but simply shows that defects are not always the result of sin.

John xi.
Now a certain man was sick, named Lazarus, of Bethany, the town of Mary and her sister Martha.

3 Therefore his sisters sent unto him, saying, Lord, behold, he whom thou lovest is sick.

5 Now Jesus loved Martha, and her sister, and Lazarus.

6 When he had heard therefore that he was sick, he abode two days still in the same place where he was.

17 When Jesus came, he found that he had lain in the grave four days already.

20 Martha, as soon as she heard that Jesus was coming, went and met him: but Mary sat still in the house.

21 Then said Martha unto Jesus, Lord, if thou hadst been here, my brother had not died.

22 But I know, that even now, whatsoever thou wilt ask of God, God will give it thee.

23 Jesus saith unto her, Thy brother shall rise again.

24 Martha saith unto him, I know that he shall rise again in the resurrection at the last day.

25 Jesus said unto her, I am the resurrection and the life:

28 And she went her way, and called Mary her sister, saying, The Master is come, and calleth for thee.

29 As soon as she heard that, she arose quickly, and came unto him.

32 When Mary was come where Jesus was, and saw him, she fell down at his feet, saying unto him, Lord, if thou hadst been here, my brother had not died.

35 Jesus wept.

36 Then said the Jews, Behold how he loved him!

41 Then they took away the stone from the place where the dead was laid.

43 And Jesus cried with a loud voice, Lazarus, come forth.

44 And he that was dead came forth.

It appears that Jesus was a frequent visitor at the home of Mary, Martha and Lazarus, and felt a strong friendship for them. They lived in Bethany, two miles from Jerusalem. Many Jews came out from the city to express their sympathy. Martha did not fully un-

derstand Jesus; she considered him as a prophet who wrought
miracles by faith and prayer in the same manner as the ancient
prophets.

The grief of Mary, the tears of the Jews, and his own warm
friendship for the sisters, affected Jesus himself to tears and groans.
In appealing to Divine power, Jesus wished to show the unbelieving
Jews that his miracles were performed by influence from above and
not by the spirit of evil, to which source they attributed his wonderful works.   Many who were said to witness this miracle did not believe.

After this Jesus again rested at the home of Mary, where she
washed his feet and wiped them with the hair of her head, and then
anointed him with costly spices from an alabaster box.   He then
went up to Jerusalem to attend the passover.

John xx.

The first day of the week cometh Mary
Magdalene early, when it was yet dark, unto the sepulchre, and seeth the stone taken
away from the sepulchre.

2 Then she runneth, and cometh to Simon Peter, and to the other disciple, whom
Jesus loved, and saith unto them, They
have taken away the Lord out of the sepulchre, and we know not where they have
laid him.

3 Peter therefore went forth, and that
other disciple, and came to the sepulchre.

4 So they ran both together: and the
other disciple did outrun Peter, and came
first to the sepulchre.

5 And he stooping down and looking in,
saw the linen clothes lying; yet went he
not in.

6 Then cometh Simon Peter following
him, and went into the sepulchre, and
seeth the linen clothes lie.

7 And the napkin, that was about his
head, not lying with the linen clothes, but
wrapped together in a place by itself.

8 Then went in also that other disciple,
which came first to the sepulchre, and he
saw, and believed.

9 For as yet they knew not the Scripture, that he must rise again from the
dead.

10 Then the disciples went away again
unto their own home.

11 But Mary stood without at the sepulchre weeping: and as she wept, she stooped
down, and looked into the sepulchre.

12 And seeth two angels in white sitting,
the one at the head, and the other at the
feet, where the body of Jesus had lain.

13 And they say unto her, Woman, why
weepest thou? She saith unto them, Because they have taken away my Lord, and
I know not where they have laid him.

14 And when she had thus said, she
turned herself back, and saw Jesus standing, and knew not that it was Jesus.

15 Jesus saith unto her, Woman, why
weepest thou? whom seekest thou? She,
supposing him to be the gardener, saith
unto him, Sir, if thou hast borne him
hence, tell me where thou hast laid him,
and I will take him away.

16 Jesus saith unto her, Mary. She
turned herself, and saith unto him, Rabboni, which is to say, Master.

17 Jesus saith unto her, Touch me not;
for I am not yet ascended to my Father:
but go to my brethren, and say unto them,
I ascend unto my Father, and your Father,
and to my God, and your God.

18 Mary Magdalene came and told the
disciples that she had seen the Lord, and
that he had spoken these things unto her.

Mary appears to have arrived at the sepulchre before any of the other women, and conversed with Jesus. Though the disciples, in visiting the tomb, saw nothing but cast-off clothes, yet Mary sees and talks with angels and with Jesus. As usual, the woman is always most ready to believe miracles and fables, however extravagant and though beyond all human comprehension. Several women purposed to be at the tomb at sunrise to embalm the body.

The men who visited the tomb saw no visions; but all the women saw Jesus and the angels, though the men, who went to the tomb twice, saw nothing. Mary arrived at the tomb before light, and waited for the other women; but seeing some one approaching, she supposed he was the person employed by Joseph to take care of the garden, so asked him what had been done to him. Though speaking to a supposed stranger, she did not mention any name. Jesus then called her by name; and his voice and his address made him known to her. Filled with joy and with amazement, she called him "Rabboni," which signifies, "teacher." Jesus said unto her, "Touch me not."

This finishes the consideration of the four Gospels—the direct recorded words of Jesus upon the question of purity; and all further references should harmonize, in spirit, with his teachings, and should be so interpreted, without regard to contrary assertions by learned but unwise commentators. E. C. S.

Is it not astonishing that so little is in the New Testament concerning the mother of Christ? My own opinion is that she was an excellent woman, and the wife of Joseph, and that Joseph was the actual father of Christ. I think there can be no reasonable doubt that such was the opinion of the authors of the original Gospels. Upon any other hypothesis it is impossible to account for their having given the genealogy of Joseph to prove that Christ was of the blood of David. The idea that he was the Son of God, or in any way miraculously produced, was an afterthought, and is hardly entitled now to serious consideration. The Gospels were written so long after the death of Christ that very little was known of him, and substantially nothing of his parents. How is it that not one word is said about the death of Mary, not one word about the death of Joseph? How did it happen that Christ did not visit his mother after his resurrection? The first time he speaks to his mother is when he was twelve years old. His mother having told him that she and his father had been seeking him, he replied: "How is it that ye sought me? Wist ye not that I must be about my father's business?" The second time was at the marriage feast in Cana, when he said to her: "Woman, what have I to do with thee?" And the third time was at the cross, when "Jesus, seeing his mother standing by the disciple whom he loved, said to her: 'Woman, behold thy son;' and to the disciple: 'Behold thy mother.'" And this is all.

The best thing about the Catholic Church is the deification of Mary; and yet this is denounced by Protestantism as idolatry. There is something in the human heart that prompts man to tell his faults more freely to the mother than to the father. The cruelty of Jehovah is softened by the mercy of Mary.

Is it not strange that none of the disciples of Christ said anything about their parents—that we know absolutely nothing of them? Is there any evidence that they showed any particular respect even for the mother of Christ? Mary Magdalene is, in many respects, the tenderest and most loving character in the New Testatment. According to the account, her love for Christ knew no abatement, no change—true even in the hopeless shadow of the cross. Neither did it die with his death. She waited at the sepulchre; she hastened in the early morning to his tomb; and yet the only comfort Christ gave to this true and loving soul lies in these strangely cold and heartless words: "Touch me not."   ANON.

THE BOOK OF ACTS.

Acts v.

But a certain man named Ananias, with Sapphira his wife, sold a possession.

2 And kept back a part of the price, and brought a certain part, and laid it at the apostles' feet.

3 But Peter said, Ananias, why hath Satan filled thine heart to lie to the Holy Ghost, and to keep back part of the price of the land?

4 While it remained, was it not thine own? and after it was sold, was it not in thine own power? why hast thou conceived this thing in thine heart? Thou hast not lied unto men, but unto God.

5 And Ananias hearing the words fell down, and gave up the ghost: and great fear came on all them that heard these things.

6 And the young men arose and carried him out, and buried him.

7 And it was about the space of three hours after, when his wife not knowing what was done, came in.

8 And Peter answered her, Tell me whether ye sold the land for so much? And she said, Yea, for so much.

9 Then Peter said unto her, How is it that ye have agreed together to tempt the Spirit of the Lord? Behold, the feet of them which have buried thy husband are at the door, and shall carry thee out.

10 Then she fell down straightway at his feet, and yielded up the ghost.

THIS book is supposed to have been written by Luke about thirty years after the death of Jesus, as an appendix to the Evangelists. It contains brief mention of a few women of varied characters and fortunes. We have the usual number afflicted with religious mysteries, with the gift of prophecy, and some possessed of the devil, who promptly comes forth at the commands of Jesus and of his Apostles.

The case of Ananias and Sapphira was very peculiar. This example was made, not of avowed enemies, but avowed friends. Many expositors say that Ananias had made a vow to give his estate for the support of the Christian cause, and that sacrilege was the crime for which he was punished. He had, from corrupt motives, attempted to impose upon the Apostles in pretending to give all that he had to the church, while withholding a good share for himself. He had evidently instructed his wife to substantiate his assertions.

145

Obedience of one responsible being to another may ofttimes prove dangerous, even if the command comes from a husband.

Acts ix.

36 Now there was at Joppa a certain disciple named Tabitha, which by interpretation is called Dorcas: this woman was full of good works and alms-deeds.

37 And it came to pass in those days, that she was sick and died.

38 And as Lydda was nigh to Joppa, and the disciples had heard that Peter was there, they sent unto him two men, desiring him to come to them.

39 Then Peter arose and went with them,

and they brought him into the upper chamber: and all the widows stood weeping, and shewing the garments which Dorcas made.

40 But Peter put them all forth, and kneeled down, and prayed; and turning him to the body said, Tabitha, rise. And she opened her eyes: and when she saw Peter, she sat up.

41 And when he had called the saints and widows, he presented her alive.

Tabitha was called by this name among the Jews; but she was known to the Greeks as Dorcas. She was considered an ornament to her Christian profession; for she so abounded in good works and alms-deeds that her whole life was devoted to the wants and the needs of the poor. She not only gave away her substance, but she employed her time and her skill in laboring constantly for the poor and the unfortunate. Her death was looked upon as a public calamity. This is the first instance of any Apostle performing a miracle of this kind. There was no witness to this miracle. What men teach in their high places, such women as Dorcas illustrate in their lives.

Acts xii.

12 And he came into the house of Mary the mother of John, whose surname was Mark, where many were gathered together praying.

13 And as Peter knocked at the gate, a damsel came to hearken, named Rhoda.

14 And when she knew Peter's voice, she opened not the gate for gladness, but ran in, and told how Peter stood before the gate.

15 And they said unto her, Thou art mad. But she constantly affirmed that it was even so. Then they said, It is an angel.

16 But Peter continued knocking: and when they had opened the door, and saw him, they were astonished.

17 But he declared unto them how the Lord had brought him out of the prison. And he said, Go shew these things unto James, and to the brethren.

Herod the king, at this time, killed James, the brother of John, and cast Peter into prison, and intended to destroy the other Apostles as soon as he could entrap them. Peter, it is said, escaped from prison by the miraculous interposition of an angel, who led him to the gate of one Mary, the sister of Barnabas, where Christians often assembled for religious worship. Although they often prayed for

Peter's deliverance, they could not believe Rhoda when she said that Peter stood knocking at the gate.

Acts xvi.

14 And a certain woman named Lydia, a seller of purple, of the city of Thyatira, which worshiped God, heard us; whose heart the Lord opened unto the things which were spoken of Paul.

15 And when she was baptized, and her household, she besought us, saying, If ye have judged me to be faithful to the Lord, come into my house, and abide there.

16 And it came to pass, as we went to prayer, a certain damsel possessed with a spirit of divination met us, which brought her masters much gain by soothsaying:

17 The same followed Paul and us, and cried, saying, These men are the servants of the most high God.

18 And this did she many days. But Paul said to the spirit, I command thee in the name of Jesus Christ to come out of her. And he came out the same hour.

19 And when her masters saw that the hope of their gains was gone, they caught Paul and Silas,

20 And brought them to the magistrates, saying, these men, being Jews, do exceedingly trouble our city.

22 And the multitude rose up against them; and the magistrates rent off their clothes, and commanded to beat them.

23 And when they had laid many stripes upon them, they cast them into prison, charging the jailer to keep them safely.

Lydia, a native Thyatiran, who at this time resided at Philippi, was a merchant who trafficked in purple clothes, which were held in great estimation.   She was a Gentile, but was proselyted to the Jewish religion, believed in the teachings of Paul and was baptized with her household.   She was a person in affluent circumstances; and being of a generous disposition, was very hospitable.   As the Apostles were poorly accommodated elsewhere, she entertained them in her own house.

The Apostles and their friends on their way to the oratory, where they went to worship, were met by a female slave who was possessed with a spirit of divination and uttered ambiguous predictions.   She had acquired great reputation as an oracle or fortune-teller and for making wonderful discoveries.   By this practice she brought her masters considerable gain and was very valuable to them.   When Paul cast out the evil spirit and restored the maiden to her normal condition of body and mind, her master was full of wrath, as she was no longer of any value to him; and he accused Paul before the magistrates.   The people were all stirred with indignation; so they stripped Paul and Silas, scourged them severely; and, without trial, the magistrates threw them into prison.

Acts xviii.

After these things Paul departed from Athens, and came to Corinth;

2 And found a certain Jew named Aquila, born in Pontus, lately come from Italy, with his wife Priscilla, (because that Claudius had commanded all Jews to depart from Rome,)

3 And because he was of the same craft, he abode with them, and wrought: (for by their occupation they were tentmakers).

18 And Paul after this tarried there yet a good while, and then took his leave of the brethren, and sailed thence into Syria, and with him Priscilla and Aquila;

24 And a certain Jew named Apollos, born at Alexandria, an eloquent man, and mighty in the Scriptures, came to Ephesus.

25 This man was instructed in the way of the Lord; and being fervent in the spirit, he spake and taught diligently the things of the Lord, knowing only the baptism of John.

26 And he began to speak boldly in the synagogue: whom when Aquila and Priscilla had heard, they took him and expounded the way of God more perfectly.

It was an excellent custom of those days for educated people to be also instructed in some mechanical trade. This served them as an amusement in prosperity, and was a certain resource in case other prospects failed. Thus Paul was now prepared to support himself in an emergency. He was frequently compelled to work with his hands to provide for his own necessities.

Apollos was a native of Alexandria, in Egypt, a ready and graceful speaker, with a thorough knowledge of the Scriptures. Coming to Ephesus, he boldly preached in the synagogue in the presence of Aquila and of Priscilla; and they seeing his ability, zeal and piety, said nothing to his disadvantage, though they perceived that his views of the Christian doctrines were very imperfect. So they sought his acquaintance and instructed him more fully in the gospel of Jesus. He, with great humility, received their instructions, for he had never been much among Christians; and no one knew when or by whom he was baptized.

Acts xxi.

8 And the next day we that were of Paul's company departed, and came unto Cesarea, and we entered into the house of Philip the evangelist, which was one of the seven; and abode with him.

9 And the same man had four daughters, virgins, which did prophesy.

Philip, one of the seven deacons in Cesarea, was also an Evangelist, and had the peculiar honor of having four daughters, all endowed with the gift of prophecy; and perhaps they gave intimations to Paul of his approaching trials. With Philip's four daughters, all endowed with the spirit of prophecy, and Priscilla as a teacher of great principles to the orators of her time, and one of Paul's chosen travelling companions, women are quite highly honored in the Book of Acts, if we except the tragedy of the unfortunate wife who obeyed her husband.

Acts xxiv.

24 And after certain days, when Felix came with his wife Drusilla, which was a Jewess, he sent for Paul, and heard him concerning the faith in Christ.

25 And as he reasoned of righteousness, temperance, and judgment to come, Felix trembled, and answered, Go thy way for this time; when I have a convenient season, I will call for thee.

Drusilla was a daughter of that Herod who beheaded James, the brother of John, and sister to King Agrippa. She was married to the king of the Emerines, Azizas; but she left her husband and went to live with Felix. He and Drusilla were curious to hear more authentic accounts of Jesus and his doctrines. They do not seem to have been much impressed with the purity of his teachings. Their curiosity did not arise from a love of the truth, nor from a desire for a higher, better life, but was a mere curiosity, for which it is probable that Felix was responsible, as Drusilla doubtless asked her husband at home all she desired to know. E. C. S.

———

The Rev. Dr. Edwin Hatch expresses the latest decision of historical theology concerning Paul, in frankly confessing: "His life at Rome and *all the rest of his history* are enveloped in mists from which no single gleam of certain light emerges. . . . The place and occasion of his death are not less uncertain than are the facts of his later life. . . . The chronology of the rest of his life is as uncertain as the date of his death. We have no means of knowing when he was born, or how long he lived, or at what date the several events of his life took place." Exactly the same may be said of Peter. The strongest probability is that Paul and Peter were two obscure men who lived in the latter part of the first, or beginning of the second century, neither of whom could have seen the first century Jesus. It can easily be shown that the Christian Church admit-

ted women into her regularly ordained ministry during the first two
hundred years of Christianity. Whether Bishop Doane is ignorant
of this fact, or whether he is merely presuming upon women's ignorance thereof, it is impossible to say. But one thing is clear, and that
is, that the time has arrived when all women should be informed of
the true status of their sex in the ministry of the primitive Church.

The first important truth for them to learn concerning the question is that there is a missing link of some five hundred years between the close of that body of literature known to us as the "Old
Testament" and the compilation of that collection of letters, nar-
ratives, etc., now presented to us as the "New Testament." Girls
of Christian families are commonly inoculated in their ignorant, and
therefore helplessly credulous youth, with unquestioning belief that
the New Testament was written in the first century of our era, by
disciples who were contemporary with Jesus, and that Peter and
Paul were first century Christians, the former of whom had personally known and followed Jesus, while the latter was a convert from
Judaism after Jesus' death, never having seen the teacher himself.

Yet he is, indeed, a very ignorant ecclesiastic who to-day is not
perfectly well aware that the above belief is pure theory, resting on
nothing more stable than vague conjecture, irresponsible tradition,
and slowly evolving fable. Among scholarly Christian theologians
no questions are now more unsettled than are the queries: Who
wrote the Gospels? In which of the first three centuries did they
assume their present shape? And at what time did Peter and Paul
live and quarrel with each other concerning Christian polity?

As for the passages now found in the New Testament epistles of
Paul, concerning women's non-equality with men and duty of subjection, there is no room to doubt that they are bare-faced for-
geries, interpolated by unscrupulous bishops, during the early
period in which a combined and determined effort was made to re-
duce women to silent submission, not only in the Church, but also in
the home and in the State. A most laudably intended attempt to
excuse Paul for the inexcusable passages attributed to his authorship has been made by a clergyman, who, accepting them as genuine
Pauline utterances, endeavors to show that they were meant to apply

only to Greek female converts, natives of Corinth, and that the command to cover the head and to keep silent in public was warranted, both because veiling the head and face was a Grecian custom, and because the women of Corinth were of notoriously bad character. In support of this theory our modern apologist quotes the testimony of numerous writers of antiquity who denounced Corinthian profligacy. But, setting aside the fact that the men of Corinth must always have been, at least, as bad as the women, and that a sorry case would be made out for Paul, if it were on the score of morals that he ordered Greek women to subject themselves to such men, there are yet two serious impediments in the way of this theory. In the first place, that wealthy and luxurious Corinth to which the writers quoted refer, was no longer in existence in Paul's time; 146 B. C. it was conquered by the Romans, who killed the men, carried the women and children into slavery, and levelled the dwellings to the ground. For a whole century the site of the once famous city remained a desolate waste, but about 46 B. C. it was colonized by some Roman immigrants, and a Romanized city, with Roman customs, it was when Paul knew it. Now, not only did the Roman women go unveiled, mingling freely in all public places with men (a fact which Paul, as citizen of a Roman province must have known), but Paul specially commends the Greek woman, Phebe, whom he endorses as minister of the Church in the Greek city, Cenchrea (a seaport within a few miles of Corinth), and in Acts, chapter 17, we are explicitly told that the Greek converts made by Paul, in Greece, were "chief women," "honorable women."

This is sufficient refutation of the argument of the clergyman who strives to clear the character of Paul at the expense of the character of the women of Corinth.　　　　　E. B. D.

EPISTLE TO THE ROMANS.

Romans xvi.

I commend unto you Phebe our sister, which is a servant of the church which is at Cenchrea:

2 That ye receive her in the Lord, as becometh saints, and that ye assist her in whatsoever business she hath need of you; for she hath been a succourer of many, and of myself also.

3 Greet Priscilla and Aquila, my helpers in Christ Jesus:

4 Who have for my life laid down their own necks: unto whom not only I give thanks, but also all the churches of the Gentiles.

6 Greet Mary, who bestowed much labor on us.

12 Salute Tryphena and Tryphosa, who labour in the Lord. Salute the beloved Persis, which laboured much in the Lord.

13 Salute Rufus, chosen in the Lord, and his mother and mine.

15 Salute Philologus, and Julia, Nereus and his sister, and Olympas, and all the saints which are with them.

CENCHREA was the seaport of Corinth, where a separate church was founded. Phebe was a deaconess, and was probably employed in visiting the sick and in teaching the women in the doctrines of the Church. She appears to have been a woman in good circumstances, and probably had more than ordinary intelligence and education. Even Paul acknowledged himself under great obligations to her. Aquila and Priscilla had risked their lives in protecting the Apostles at Corinth and Ephesus. So Paul sent his affectionate salutations and good wishes to all the women who had helped to build up the churches and spread the Gospel of Christianity.

In good works men have always found a reserved force in the women of their generation. Paul seems to have been specially mindful of all who had received and hospitably entertained him. The men of our times have been equally thankful to women for serving them, for hospitable entertainment, generous donations to the priesthood, lifting church debts, etc., and are equally ready to remand them to their "divinely appointed sphere," whenever women claim an equal voice in church creeds and discipline. Then the Marys, the Phebes, and the Priscillas are ordered to keep silence and to discuss all questions with their husbands at home, taking it for granted that all men are logical and wise. E. C. S.

Martin Luther had good cause to declare: "There is something in the office of a bishop which is dreadfully demoralizing. Even good men change their natures at consecration; Satan enters into them, as he entered into Judas, as soon as they have taken the sop." But to return to the primitive Church, a famous Apostle of that simple era was Priscilla, a Jewess, who was one of the theological instructors of Apollos (the fellow-minister, or fellow-servant, to whom Paul refers in his first letter to the Corinthians). There is strong reason to believe that the Apostle Priscilla, in co-operation with her husband, the Apostle Aquila, performed the important task of founding the Church of Rome: for Paul, writing to the Christians, admits that he himself has not yet visited that city; there is no proof whatever that Peter ever went to Rome at all (but, on the contrary, much proof that he wished to confine Christianity to Jewish converts); and yet Paul, hailing Priscilla by the current term which specially active Apostles and bishops used in addressing other specially active workers in the Apostolate, "Helper in Christ Jesus," eulogizes her as one known, gratefully, by "all the churches of the Gentiles," and recognizes a Church of Rome as established in Priscilla's own house (see Paul's letter to the Romans, chapter 16). It is highly probable that that was the tiny acorn from which has grown the present great oak—the Roman Catholic Church, which would profit much by more remembrance and imitation of the modest and undogmatic women who helped to give it being and who nursed it through its infancy.

The inability of modern men to comprehend the position of women in the primitive Church, is strikingly shown in Chalmers' commentary on the fact that Paul used exactly the same title in addressing Priscilla that he uses in greeting Urbane. Although conceding that Priscilla had shared the work of an Apostle in teaching Apollos "the way of God more perfectly," and, although he knows nothing whatever of Urbane's work, yet Chalmers unhesitatingly concludes that Urbane's help to Paul *must* have been in things spiritual, but that Priscilla's *must* have been in regard to things temporal only: and, as Aquila and Priscilla were an inseparable couple, poor Aquila, too, is relegated to Priscilla's assumedly inferior position! There is not, however, the slightest reason for such a conclusion by Chalmers. It is manifestly due to the modern prejudice which renders the Paul-worshipping male Protestants incapable of comprehending that "Our Great Apostle," Paul, was not a great Apostle at all, in those days, but a simple, self-sent tent-maker with a vigorous spirit, who gladly shared the "Apostolic dignity" with all the good women he could rally to his assistance. Chalmers conjectures that if Priscilla really did help Paul, it must have been as "a teacher of women and children," even while the fact stares him in the face that she was a recognized teacher of the man whom Paul specially and emphatically pronounces his own equal. (Compare Acts, chap. 18, v. 26, with 1st Cor., chap. 3.)

To one who uses unbiassed common sense in regard to the New Testament records, there can be no question of women's activity and prominence in the early ministry. Paul not only virtually pronounces Priscilla a fellow-Apostle and fellow-bishop (Romans, chap. 16, verses 3-5), but specially commends Phebe, a Greek woman, as a minister (diakonos), which, as we have seen, may be legitimately interpreted either presbyter, bishop, or Apostle. That it was well understood, throughout the whole Church, that women had shared the labors of the Apostles, is evidenced by Chrysostom's specific eulogy thereupon. Phebe was the bishop of the Church in Cenchrea, and that she was both a powerful and useful overseer in the episcopate, Paul testifies in affirming that she had not only been a helper to him, but to many others also. (Romans, chap. 16, verses 1-2.) Addressing that first Church of Rome (which was in the house of Priscilla and Aquila before Paul, or Peter, or the barely-mentioned Linus, are heard of in Rome), Paul indicates the equality of male and female Apostles by mentioning in one and the same category Priscilla and Aquila, Andronicus and Junia, Mary, "who bestowed much labor among you," Amphis, Urbane, Tryphena and Tryphosa, Persis. Julia, Rufus and Hermas.   E. B. D.

EPISTLES TO THE CORINTHIANS.

1 Corinthians vii.

2 Let every man have his own wife, and let every woman have her own husband.

3 Let the husband render unto the wife due benevolence: and likewise also the wife unto the husband.

10 And unto the married I command, yet not I, but the Lord, Let not the wife depart from her husband:

11 But if she depart, let her remain unmarried, or be reconciled to her husband, and let not the husband put away his wife.

12 But to the rest speak I, not the Lord: If any brother hath a wife that believeth not: and she be pleased to dwell with him, let him not put her away.

13 And the woman which hath a husband that believeth not, and if he be pleased to dwell with her, let her not leave him.

14 For the unbelieving husband is sanctified by the wife, and the unbelieving wife is sanctified by the husband: else were your children unclean: but now are they holy.

16 For what knowest thou, O wife, whether thou shalt save thy husband? or how knowest thou, O man, whether thou shalt save thy wife?

THE people appear to have been specially anxious to know what the Christian idea was in regard to the question of marriage. The Pythagoreans taught that marriage is unfavorable to high intellectual development. On the other hand, the Pharisees taught that it is sinful for a man to live unmarried beyond his twentieth year. The Apostles allowed that in many cases it might be wise for a man to live unmarried, as he could be more useful to others, provided that he were able to live with that entire chastity which the single life required.

The Apostle says that Christians should not marry unbelievers, but if either should change his or her opinions after, he would not advise separation, as they might sanctify each other. Scott thinks that the children are no more holy with one unbelieving parent, than when both are unbelieving; and he has not much faith in their sanctifying each other, except in a real change of faith. A union with an unbeliever would occasion grief and trouble, yet that ought patiently to be endured, for God might make use of the unbelieving wife or husband as an instrument in converting the other by affectionate and conscientious behavior; as this might not be the case, there is no reason to oppose the dissolution of the marriage.

There are no restrictions in the Scriptures on divorced persons marrying again, though many improvised by human laws are spoken of as in the Bible.   E. C. S.

———

In this chapter Paul laments that all men are not bachelors like himself; and in the second verse of that chapter he gives the only reason for which he was willing that men and women should marry. He advised all the unmarried and all widows to remain as he was. Paul sums up the whole matter, however, by telling those who have wives or husbands to stay with them—as necessary evils only to be tolerated; but sincerely regrets that anybody was ever married, and finally says that, "they that have wives should be as though they had none;" because, in his opinion, "he that is unmarried careth for the things that belong to the Lord, how he may please the Lord; but he that is married careth for the things that are of the world, how he please his wife."

"There is this difference, also," he tells us, "between a wife and a virgin. The unmarried woman careth for the things of the Lord, that she may be holy both in body and spirit; but she that is married careth for the things of the world, how she may please her husband." Of course, it is contended that these things have tended to the elevation of woman. The idea that it is better to love the Lord than to love your wife or husband is infinitely absurd. Nobody ever did love the Lord—nobody can—until he becomes acquainted with him.

· Saint Paul also tells us that "man is the image and glory of God; but woman is the glory of man." And, for the purpose of sustaining this position, he says: "For the man is not of the woman, but the woman of the man; neither was the man created for the woman, but the woman for the man." Of course we can all see that man could have gotten along well enough without woman. And yet this is called "inspired!" and this Apostle Paul is supposed to have known more than all the people now upon the earth. No wonder Paul at last was constrained to say: "We are fools for Christ's sake."

ANON.

---

1 Corinthians xi.

3 But I would have you know, that the head of every man is Christ; and the head of the woman is the man; and the head of Christ is God.

4 Every man praying or prophesying, having his head covered, dishonoureth his head.

5 But every woman that prayeth or prophesieth with her head uncovered dishonoureth her head.

7 For a man indeed ought not to cover his head, forasmuch as he is the image and glory of God: but the woman is the glory of the man.

8 For the man is not of the woman; but the woman of the man.

9 Neither was the man created for the woman; but the woman for the man.

10 For this cause ought the woman to have power on her head because of the angels.

11 Nevertheless neither is the man without the woman, neither the woman without the man, in the Lord.

13 Judge in yourselves: is it comely that a woman pray unto God uncovered?

14 Doth not even nature itself teach you, that, if a man have long hair, it is a shame unto him?

15 But if a woman have long hair, it is a glory to her: for her hair is given her for a covering.

According to the custom of those days a veil on the head was a token of respect to superiors; hence for a woman to lay aside her veil was to affect authority over the man. The shaving of the head was a disgraceful punishment inflicted on women of bad repute; it not only deprived them of a great beauty, but also of the badge of virtue and honor.

Though these directions appear to be very frivolous, even for those times, they are much more so for our stage of civilization. Yet the same customs prevail in our day and are enforced by the Church, as of vital consequence; their non-observance so irreligious that it would exclude a woman from the church. It is not a mere social fashion that allows men to sit in church with their heads uncovered and women with theirs covered, but a requirement of canon law of vital significance, showing the superiority, the authority, the headship of man, and the humility and the subservience of woman. The aristocracy in social life requires the same badge of respect of all female servants. In Europe they uniformly wear caps, and in many families in America, though under protest after learning its significance.

It is certainly high time that educated women in a Republic should rebel against a custom based on the supposition of their heaven-ordained subjection. Jesus is always represented as having long, curling hair, and so is the Trinity. Imagine a painting of these Gods all with clipped hair. Flowing robes and beautiful hair add greatly to the beauty and dignity of their pictures.   E. C. S.

———

The injunctions of St. Paul have had such a decided influence in fixing the legal status of women, that it is worth our while to consider their source. In dealing with this question we must never forget that the majority of the writings of the New Testament were not really written or published by those whose names they bear. Ancient writers considered it quite permissible for a man to put out letters under the name of another, and thus to bring his own ideas before the world under the protection of an honored sponsor. It is not usually claimed that St. Paul was the originator of the great religious movement called Christianity; but there is a strong belief that he was Divinely inspired. His inward persuasions, and especially his visions, appeared as a gift or endowment which had the force of inspiration; therefore, his mandates concerning women have a strong hold upon the popular mind; and when opponents to the equality of the sexes are put to bay, they glibly quote his injunctions.

We congratulate ourselves that we may shift some of these Biblical arguments that have such a sinister effect from their firm foundation. He who claims to give a message must satisfy us that he has himself received such a message. The origin of the command that women should cover their heads is found in an old Jewish or Hebrew legend which appears in literature for the first time in Genesis vi. There we are told that the sons of God, that is, the angels, took to wives the daughters of men, and begat the giants and the heroes who were instrumental in bringing about the flood. The Rabbins held that the way in which the angels got possession of women was by laying hold of their hair; they accordingly warned women to cover their heads in public so that the angels might not get possession of them.

Paul merely repeats this warning, which he must often have heard at the feet of Gamaliel, who was at that time prince or president of the Sanhedrim, telling women to have a power (that is, protection) on their heads because of the angels: "For this cause ought the woman to have power on her head because of the angels." Thus the command had its origin in an absurd old myth. This legend will be found fully treated in a German pamphlet, "Die Paulinische Angolologie und Daemonologie." Otto Everling, Gottingen, 1883.

If the command to keep silence in the churches has no higher origin than that to keep covered in public, should so much weight be given it, or should it be so often quoted as having Divine sanction?   L. S.

---

1 Corinthians xiv.

34 Let your women keep silence in the churches: for it is not permitted unto them to speak; but they are commanded to be under obedience, as also saith the law.

35 And if they will learn anything, let them ask their husbands at home: for it is a shame for woman to speak in the church.

The church at Corinth was peculiarly given to diversion and to disputation; and women were apt to join in and to ask many troublesome questions; hence they were advised to consult their husbands at home. The Apostle took it for granted that all men were wise enough to give to women the necessary information on all subjects. Others, again, advise wives never to discuss knotty points with their husbands; for if they should chance to differ from each other, that fact might give rise to much domestic infelicity. There is such a wide difference of opinion on this point among wise men, that perhaps it would be as safe to leave women to be guided by their own unassisted common sense.   E. C. S.

EPISTLES TO THE EPHESIANS AND PHILLIPPIANS.

Ephesians v.

22 Wives, submit yourselves unto your own husbands, as unto the Lord.

23 For the husband is the head of the wife, even as Christ is the head of the church.

24 Therefore as the church is subject unto Christ, so let the wives be to their own husbands in every thing.

25 Husbands, love your wives, even as Christ also loved the church, and gave himself for it;

28 So ought men to love their wives as their own bodies. He that loveth his wife loveth himself.

31 For this cause shall a man leave his father and mother, and shall be joined unto his wife, and they two shall be one flesh.

33 Nevertheless, let every one of you in particular so love his wife even as himself: and the wife see that she reverence her husband.

IF every man were as pure and as self-sacrificing as Jesus is said to have been in his relations to the Church, respect, honor and obedience from the wife might be more easily rendered. Let every man love his wife (not wives) points to monogamic marriage. It is quite natural for women to love and to honor good men, and to return a full measure of love on husbands who bestow much kindness and attention on them; but it is not easy to love those who treat us spitefully in any relation, except as mothers; their love triumphs over all shortcomings and disappointments. Occasionally conjugal love combines that of the mother. Then the kindness and the forbearance of a wife may surpass all understanding.

Phillippians iv.

2 I beseech Euodias, and beseech Syntyche, that they be of the same mind in the Lord.

3 And I entreat thee also, true yokefel-low, help those women which laboured with me in the Gospel, with Clement also, and with other my fellow-laborers, whose names are in the book of life.

There were women of note at Phillippi who disagreed and caused divisions in the Church. The Apostle therefore entreated them to make mutual concessions for the welfare of the Church. The yokefellow referred to was supposed by some to have been the husband of one of the women, while others think that he was some eminent minister. But such mention by the Apostle must have been highly appreciated by any man or woman for whom it was intended.

E. C. S.

EPISTLES TO TIMOTHY.

CHAPTER I.

THE Apostle Paul, though older than Timothy, had travelled much with him, and was at one time imprisoned with him in Rome. Paul had converted Timothy to the faith and watched over him as a father. He often speaks of him as my son, and was peculiarly beloved by him. When Paul was driven from Ephesus he wrote this epistle to Timothy for his direction.

It is perhaps not fair to judge Paul by the strict letter of the word. We are not well informed of the habits of women in his time in regard to personal adornment. What Paul means by "modest apparel" (supposing the translation to be correct), we may not precisely understand. Paul speaks especially of "braided hair." In his time Paul evidently considered as of account the extreme susceptibility of his sex to the effect of the garb and adornment of women.

The Apostles all appeared to be much exercised by the ornaments and the braided hair of the women. While they insisted that women should wear long hair, they objected to having it braided lest the beautiful coils should be too attractive to men. But women had other reasons for braiding their hair beside attracting men. A compact braid was much more comfortable than individual hairs free to be blown about with every breeze.

It appears very trifling for men, commissioned to do so great a work on earth, to give so much thought to the toilets of women. Ordering the men to have their heads shaved and hair cropped, while the women were to have their locks hanging around their shoulders, looks as if they feared that the sexes were not distinguishable and that they must finish Nature's work.   Woman's braids and ornaments had a deeper significance than the Apostles seem to have understood.   Her necessities compelled her to look to man for support and protection, hence her efforts to make herself attractive are not prompted by feminine vanity, but the economic conditions of civilization.   E. C. S.

———

The injunction that women should adorn themselves through good works was sensible.   The Apostle did not imply that this adornment was not already possessed by women.   Neither did he testify that the generations of men, of Prophets and of Apostles had been objects of the good works and all the ministrations of self-abnegation, which are required only of the mothers of men.   Comparatively few women, who have fulfilled the special function which man assigns to them as their chief duty in life, lack the adornment of good works.   In addition to these good works of motherhood in the family, woman has ministered to the necessities and the comfort of the sick, the feeble and the poor, through the centuries.

Could Paul have looked down to the nineteenth century with clairvoyant vision and beheld the good works of a Lucretia Mott, a Florence Nightingale, a Dorothea Dix and Clara Barton, not to mention a host of faithful mothers, he might, perhaps, have been less anxious about the apparel and the manners of his converts. Could he have foreseen a Margaret Fuller, a Maria Mitchell, or an Emma Willard, possibly he might have suspected that sex does not determine the capacity of the individual.   Or, could he have had a vision of the public school system of this Republic, and witnessed the fact that a large proportion of the teachers are women, it is possible that he might have hesitated to utter so tyrannical an edict: "But I permit not a woman to teach."

Had the Apostle enjoined upon women to do good works without envy or jealousy, it would have had the weight and the wisdom of a Divine command. But that, from the earliest record of human events, woman should have been condemned and punished for trying to get knowledge, and forbidden to impart what she has learned, is the most unaccountable peculiarity of masculine wisdom. After cherishing and nursing helpless infancy, the most necessary qualification of motherhood is that of teaching. If it is contrary to the perfect operation of human development that woman should teach, the infinite and all wise directing power of the universe has blundered. It cannot be admitted that Paul was inspired by infinite wisdom in this utterance. This was evidently the unilluminated utterance of Paul, the man, biassed by prejudice. But, it may be claimed that this edict referred especially to teaching in religious assemblies. It is strikingly inconsistent that Paul, who had proclaimed the broadest definition of human souls, "There is neither Jew nor Greek, bond nor free, male or female, but ye are one in Christ Jesus," as the Christian idea, should have commanded the subjection of woman, and silence as essential to her proper sphere in the Church.

It is not a decade since a manifesto was issued by a religious convention bewailing the fact that woman is not only seeking to control her property, but claiming the right of the wife to control her person! This seems to be as great an offence to ecclesiasticism in this hour and this land of boasted freedom, as it was to Paul in Judea nineteen centuries ago. But the "new man," as well as the "new woman," is here. He is inspired by the Divine truth that woman is to contribute to the redemption of the race by free and enlightened motherhood. He is proving his fitness to be her companion by achieving the greatest of all victories—victory over himself. The new humanity is to be born of this higher manhood and emancipated womanhood. Then it will be possible for motherhood to "continue in sanctification."

The doctrine of woman the origin of sin, and her subjection in consequence, planted in the early Christian Church by Paul, has been a poisonous stream in Church and in State. It has debased marriage and made both canon and civil law a monstrous oppression to wo-

man.   M. Renan sums up concisely a mighty truth in the following
words: "The writings of Paul have been a danger and a hidden rock
—the causes of the principal defects of Christian theology."   His
teachings about woman are no longer a hidden rock, however,
for, in the light of science, it is disclosed to all truth seeking minds.
How much satisfaction it would have been to the mothers adown
the centuries, had there been a testimony by Mary and Elizabeth recording their experiences of motherhood.   Not a statement by them,
nor one about them, except what man wrote.

Under church law, woman's property, time and services were all
at the husband's disposal.   Woman was not rescued from slavery by
the Reformation.   Luther's ninety-five theses, nailed upon the
church door in Wittenberg, did not assert woman's natural or religious equality with man.   It was a maxim of his that "no gown
worse becomes a woman, than that she should be wise."   A curious
old black letter volume, published in London in 1632, declares that
"the reason why women have no control in parliament, why they
make no laws, consent to none, abrogate none, is their original sin."
The trial of Mrs. Anne Hutchinson, in the seventeenth century, was
chiefly for the sin of having taught men.

To-day, in free America, a wife cannot collect damages for injury to her person by a municipality.   Legally her husband owns
her person; and he alone can collect damages if the wife is injured
by any defect or mishap for which the administration of the municipality is responsible.   This was tested in the Court of Appeals
in New York in 1890.   The judges decided that "the time and the
services of the wife belong to the husband, and if she has received
wages from him it was a gift."   Thus the spirit and the intent of the
church law to make the wife a servant of the husband, subject to and
controlled by him, and engrafted in common law, is a part of statute
law operative in these United States to-day.   Blackstone admits the
outgrowth of common law from canon law, in saying: "Whoever
wishes to gain insight into that great institution, common law, can do
so most efficiently by studying canon law in regard to married women."

Jesus is not recorded as having uttered any similar claim that woman should be subject to man, or that in teaching she would be a usurper. The dominion of woman over man or of man over woman makes no part of the sayings of the Nazarene. He spoke to the individual soul, not recognizing sex as a quality of spiritual life, or as determining the sphere of action of either man or woman.

Stevens, in his "Pauline Theology," says: "Paul has been read as if he had written in the nineteenth century, or, more commonly, as if he had written in the fifth or seventeenth, as if his writings had no peculiarities arising from his own time, education and mental constitution." Down these nineteen centuries in a portion of the Christian Church the contempt for woman which Paul projected into Christianity has been perpetuated. The Protestant Evangelical Church still refuses to place her on an equality with man.

Although Paul said: "Neither is the man without the woman nor the woman without the man in the Lord," he taught also that the male alone is in the image of God. "For a man ought not to have his head veiled forasmuch as he is the image of God; but the woman is the glory of man." Thus he carried the spirit of the Talmud, "aggravated and re-enforced," into Christianity, represented by the following appointed daily prayer for pious Jews: "Blessed art thou, O Lord, that thou hast not made me a Gentile, an idiot nor a woman." Paul exhibits fairness in giving reasons for his peremptory mandate. "For Adam was first formed, then Eve," he says. This appears to be a weak statement for the higher position of man. If male man is first in station and authority, is superior because of priority of formation, what is his relation to "whales and every living creature that moveth which the waters bring forth, and every winged fowl after his kind," which were formed before him?

And again, "Adam was not beguiled, but, the woman being beguiled, hath fallen into transgression." There was then already existing the beguiling agency. The transgression of Eve was in listening to this existing source of error, which, in the allegory, is styled "the most subtle beast of the field which the Lord God hath made." Woman did not bring this subtle agency into activity. She was not therefore the author of sin, as has been charged. She was tempted by her desire for the knowledge which would enable her to distinguish between good and evil. According to this story, woman led the race out of the ignorance of innocence into the truth. Calvin, the commentator, says: "Adam did not fall into error, but was overcome by the allurements of his wife." It is singular that the man, who was "first formed," and therefore superior, and to whom only God has committed the office of teaching, not only was not susceptible to the temptation to acquire knowledge, but should have been the weak creature who was "overcome by the allurements of his wife."

But the story of the fall and all cognate myths and parables are far older and more universal than the ordinary reader of the Bible supposes them to be. The Bible itself in its Hebrew form is a comparatively recent compilation and adaptation of mysteries, the chief scenes of which were sculptured on temple walls and written or painted on papyri, ages before the time of Moses. History tells us, moreover, that the Book of Genesis, as it now stands, is the work not even of Moses, but of Ezra or Esdras, who lived at the time of the captivity, between five hundred and six hundred years before our era, and that he recovered it and other writings by the process of intuitional memory. "My heart," he says, "uttered understanding, and wisdom grew in my breast; for the spirit strengthened my memory."

With regard to the particular myth of the fall, the walls of ancient Thebes, Elphantine, Edfou and Karnak bear evidence that long before Moses taught, and certainly ages before Esdras wrote, its acts and symbols were embodied in the religious ceremonials of the people, of whom, according to Manetho, Moses was himself a priest. And the whole history of the fall of man is, says Sharpe, in a work on Egypt, "of Egyptian origin. The temptation of the woman by the serpent, the man by the woman, the sacred tree of knowledge, the cherubs guarding with flaming swords the door of the garden, the warfare declared between the woman and the serpent, may all be seen upon the Egyptian sculptured monuments."

This symbology signifies a deeper meaning than a material garden, a material apple, a tree and a snake. It is the relation of the soul or feminine part of man, "his living mother," to the physical and external man of sense. The temptation of woman brought the soul into the limitations of matter, of the physical. The soul derives its life from spirit, the eternal substance, God. Knowledge, through intellect alone, is of the limitation of flesh and sense. Intuition, the feminine part of reason, is the higher light. If the soul, the feminine part of man, is turned toward God, humanity is saved from the dissipations and the perversions of sensuality. Humanity is not alone dual in the two forms, male and female, but every soul is dual. The more perfect the balance in the individual of masculine and feminine, the more perfect the man or the woman. The masculine represents force, the feminine love. "Force without love can but work evil until it is spent."

Paul evidently was not learned in Egyptian lore. He did not recognize the esoteric meaning of the parable of the fall. To him it was a literal fact, apparently, and Eve was to be to all womankind the transmitter of a "curse" in maternity. We know that down to the very recent date of the introduction of anesthetics the idea prevailed that travail pains are the result of, and punishment for, the transgression of Mother Eve. It was claimed that it was wrong to attempt to remove "the curse" from woman, by mitigating her suffering in that hour of peril and of agony.

Whatever Paul may mean, it is a fact that the women of our aboriginal tribes, whose living was natural and healthful, who were not enervated by civilized customs, were not subject to the sufferings of civilized women. And it has been proven by the civilized woman that a strict observance of hygienic conditions of dress, of diet, and the mode of life, reduces the pangs of parturition. Painless child-bearing is a physiological problem; and "the curse" has never borne upon the woman whose life had been in strict accord with the laws of life. Science has come to the rescue of humanity, in the recognition of the truth, that the advancement as well as the conservation of the race is through the female. The great Apostle left no evidence that he apprehended this fact. His audacity was sublime; but it was the audacity of ignorance.

No more stupendous demonstration of the power of thought can be imagined, than is illustrated in the customs of the Church for centuries, when in the general canons were found that "No woman may approach the altar," "A woman may not baptize without extreme necessity," "Woman may not receive the eucharist under a black veil." Under canon 81 she was forbidden to write in her own name to lay Christians, but only in the name of her husband; and women were not to receive letters of friendship from any one addressed to themselves. Canon law, framed by the priesthood, compiled as early as the ninth century, has come down in effect to the nineteenth, making woman subordinate in civil law. Under canon law, wives were deprived of the control of both person and property. Canon law created marriage a sacrament "to be performed at the church door," in order to make it a source of revenue to the Church. Marriage, however, was reckoned too sinful "to be allowed for many years to take place within the sacred building consecrated to God, and deemed too holy to permit the entrance of a woman within its sacred walls at certain periods of her life."   L. B. C.

CHAPTER II.

1 Timothy iii.

2 A bishop then must be blameless, the husband of one wife, vigilant, sober, of good behavior, given to hospitality, apt to teach;

3 Not given to wine, no striker, not greedy of filthy lucre; but patient, not a brawler, not covetous;

4 One that ruleth well in his own house, having his children in subjection with all gravity:

5 (For if a man know not how to rule his own house, how shall he take care of the church of God?)

8 Likewise must the deacons be grave, not double-tongued, not given to much wine, not greedy of filthy lucre.

11 Even so must their wives be grave, not slanderers, sober, faithful in all things.

12 Let the deacons be the husbands of one wife, ruling their children and their own houses well.

IN this chapter the advice of the Apostle in regard to the overseer or bishop is unexceptionable. The first injunction that relates to woman is, that the bishop must be the husband of one wife. Under the present ideas of Christendom, the inference naturally is that the bishop was enjoined to be the husband of but one wife. If, as appears probable, this was an injunction in favor of monogamy, it was a true and progressive idea established with the foundation of the Christian Church.

Deacons also are instructed to be the husbands of one wife. "Women in like manner must be grave, not slanderers, temperate, faithful in all things." It is not clear whether this is spoken for the direction of women in general in the Church, or for the wives of deacons. The advice, however, is equally good for either class. The word "sober" in the old version is rendered "temperate" in the new one. Whether women in those days were liable to take too much wine does not appear. But nowhere in the Old or the New Testaments is there an account of drunkenness by women.

The directions for the conduct of the bishop are explicit. He is to be "gentle, not contentious," which sets aside much that distinguishes the masculine nature. In fact, with the exception of the qualification "apt to teach," before forbidden, the entire list of the necessary qualities of a bishop is that of womanly characteristics. Temperate, sober-minded (*i. e.*, not given to trifling speech), orderly, given to hospitality, no brawler, no striker (this supposedly refers to pugilistic tendencies), but gentle, not contentious. Every qualification is essentially womanly.

1 Timothy v.

3 Honour widows that are widows indeed.

4 But if any widow have children or nephews, let them learn first to shew piety at home, and to requite their parents: for that is good and acceptable before God.

5 Now she that is a widow indeed, and desolate, trusteth in God,

6 But she that liveth in pleasure is dead while she liveth.

8 But if any provide not for his own, and specially for those of his own house, he hath denied the faith, and is worse than an Infidel.

9 Let not a widow be taken into the number under threescore years, having been the wife of one man.

10 Well reported of for her good works; if she have brought up children, if she have lodged strangers, if she have washed the saints' feet, if she have relieved the afflicted, if she have diligently followed every good work.

11 But the younger widows refuse: for when they have begun to wax wanton against Christ, they will marry;

12 Having damnation, because they have cast off their first faith.

13 And withal they learn *to be* idle, wandering about from house to house; and not only idle, but tattlers also, and busybodies, speaking things which they ought not.

14 I will therefore that the younger women marry, bear children, guide the house, give none occasion to the adversary to speak reproachfully.

15 For some are already turned aside after Satan.

16 If any man or woman that believeth have widows, let them relieve them, and let not the church be charged; that it may relieve them that are widows indeed.

No one can be desolate who has a purpose and a sphere of action, with ability to work. Paul's widow, who was a widow indeed, "continueth in supplication and prayers night and day." What an existence! Desolate indeed. Exercising but one faculty of the soul—that of supplication! Women of this period cannot be too thankful, that the numerous opportunities for educational and philanthropic work are open to them in addition to the opportunities to win subsistence in the various avocations of life.

The widow who was to be enrolled, to be provided for by the Church, must be three score years old, having been the wife of one man. Whether this is a repudiation of second marriages, or refers to polyandry, is not apparent. This obligation of the early Church to provide for women who had fulfilled the duties of motherhood, ministered to the afflicted, washed the saints' feet, and diligently followed every good work, is a recognition of a right principle, and which should be made a part of social organization.

But he directs that younger women be refused. Paul thought that women could not be loyal followers of Christ and "desire to marry." Therefore he desires them all to marry, to bear children and to rule the family. Another inconsistency of Paul. Having stated as expressly the teaching of the spirit that the doctrine forbidding to marry was of devils, he here again claims that when the younger widows desire to marry they have waxed wanton against Christ. There is even by Paul one place in which woman is to be the head. If she may not teach, she may provide for the physical comfort of her husband and family.

The Apostle accuses women of learning to be idle, going about from house to house, of being tattlers and busybodies—these young widows, or unmarried women. What a spectacle the thousands of bread-winning young and unmarried women of to-day, would be to Paul if he could come here! And these young women have no time to go from house to house, or even to fulfill social obligations. And the students in our colleges and universities, Paul would not find them tattlers or busybodies. What could the unmarried women of Paul's time do? They had no absorbing mental pursuit or physical occupation. Perhaps they could not read; and there was little for them to study. Lacking mental furnishing to noble ends, they must of necessity deal with trivial matters. What could a woman do who had no home to care for, no business to attend to, perhaps nothing to read (if she could read), no social organizations in which she had a place and part except the religious assemblies in which she was to be "in quietness," "in silence"?

They were not worthy of condemnation if they were going from house to house and tattling. The unmarried woman will not lack opportunity for the dignity of self-support and the ministrations of philanthropy in the new dispensation. Womanhood and its high possibilities of mind and of heart are worthy attainments, even though not crowned with self-elected motherhood. Whether married or unmarried, the highest duty of every living soul, woman or man, is to seek truth and righteousness; and the liberty which is of the spirit of truth does not admit of the bondage of husband and wife, the one to the other.   Freedom to seek soul development is paramount to all other demands.

2 Timothy i.

2 To Timothy, my dearly beloved son: grace, mercy, and peace, from God the Father and Christ Jesus our Lord.
5 When I call to remembrance the un-

feigned faith that is in thee, which dwelt first in thy grand-mother Lois, and thy mother Eunice; and I am persuaded that in thee also.

Timothy, whom Paul calls his true child in faith, and whom he placed as overseer, or bishop of the first church at Ephesus, as all commentators agree, was the child of mixed parentage, his father being a Greek and his mother a Jewess.   It is supposed that his father died in Timothy's childhood, as no mention is made of him. Timothy, then, was educated religiously by the teaching and the example of his mother and his grandmother.   Paul expresses with fervent emotion his remembrance of his "beloved child," and of the unfeigned faith which is in him, and, "which dwelt first in thy grandmother Lois and thy mother Eunice."

After having instructed Timothy to exercise all the gentle virtues which are feminine and womanly, the Apostle in this acknowledgment that he was the child of a devout mother and grandmother, discloses a fact which places in no favorable light his strenuous opposition to woman's equality in the Church.   This mother and grandmother under whose teaching Timothy had become qualified to receive the important office of bishop, and whose faithfulness so endeared him to the Apostle, were required to keep silence in the Church equally with all other women whose evidence of faith were not so conclusive.   There was no distinction.   The ban was placed upon woman solely on the ground of sex.

The Church has only in this nineteenth century partially amended this record, by establishing the order of deaconesses for women who devote themselves to good works and to religious teaching. While in the liberal denominations the pulpit is accessible to woman, it is only in very recent years that in any evangelistic denomination it has been permissible for woman to "teach."   The priesthood are as unwilling to-day as was Paul in the first century, that women shall be placed on an equality in offices of distinction. Perhaps this disposition comes of a dim, not fully evolved consciousness that, "when the present evolution of woman is complete, a new world will result; for woman is destined to rule the world. She is the centre and the fountain of its life," which the new man has recently announced from his pulpit.

There is no prerogative more tenaciously held by the common man than that of rulership. There is no greater opposition to woman's equality in the State than there is in the Church, and this notwithstanding the fact that the Church and the pulpit are largely sustained by women. The Church is spiritually and actually a womanly institution, and this is recognized by the unvarying expression, "Mother Church." Yet man monopolizes all offices of distinction and of leadership, and receives the salaries for material support. As the inevitable result, spiritual life has become so languid as to be ineffectual, and an effort is being persistently pushed by a portion of the Evangelical Church, a portion, too, which most strenuously keeps its women silent, to fortify the Church by the power of civil government.

There is no suggestion in the teaching of Jesus, as recorded, of compelling individuals, authorities, or powers, to acknowledge God. The religion of Jesus is a voluntary acceptance of truth. "God is a spirit, and they who worship him must worship in spirit and in truth." There can be no compulsory life of the spirit, quickened by the source of life, light and love. The masculine idea of compelling a formal acknowledgment of God by the State is entirely unchristian.

Until the feminine is recognized in the Divine Being, and justice is established in the Church by the complete equality of woman with man, the Church cannot be thoroughly Christian. "Honor thy father and thy mother" is the commandment. The human race cannot be brought to its highest state until motherhood is equally honored with fatherhood in human institutions. L. B. C.

EPISTLES OF PETER AND JOHN.

1 Peter iii.

1 Likewise, ye wives, be in subjection to your own husbands; that, if any obey not the word, they also may without the word be won by the conversation of the wives;

3 Whose adorning, let it not be that outward adorning of plaiting the hair, and of wearing of gold, or of putting on of apparel;

7 Likewise, ye husbands, dwell with them according to knowledge, giving honour unto the wife, as unto the weaker vessel.

WOMAN'S influence is most clearly set forth by all the Apostles in meek submission to their husbands and to all the Church ordinances and discipline. A reverent silence, a respectful observance of rules and authorities was their power. They could not aid in spreading the gospel and in converting their husbands to the true faith by teaching, by personal attraction, by braided hair or ornaments. The normal beauty of a sanctified heart would be manifested by a meek and quiet spirit, valuable in the sight of God as well as their husbands, and do far more to fix their affections and to secure their esteem than the studied decoration of fashionable apparel. Woman's love of satins, of velvets, of laces, and of jewels, has its corresponding expression in man's love of wealth, of position, and his ambition for personal and family aggrandizement.

There is much talk of the poor and the needy, especially during political campaigns. In the autumn of 1896, when the workingman's interests formed the warp and woof of every speech, three thousand children stood in the streets of New York City, for whom there was no room in the schoolhouses and no play-grounds; and yet thousands of dollars were spent in buying votes. Large, well-ventilated homes for those who do the work of the world, plenty of schoolhouses and play-grounds for the children of the poor, would be much more beneficial to the race than expensive monuments to dead men, and large appropriations from the public treasury for holidays and convivial occasions to honor men in high places.

The Apostles having given such specific directions as to the toilets of women, their hair, ornaments, manners and position, in the Church, the State and the home, one is curious to know what kind of honor is intended for this complete subordination. Man is her head, her teacher, her guardian and her Saviour. What Christ is to him, that is he to the weaker vessel. It is fair to infer that what he has done in the past he will continue to do in the future. Unless she rebels outright, he will make her a slave, a subject, the mere reflection of another human will. E. C. S.

---

2 John i.
1 The elder unto the elect lady and her children,
5 And now I beseech thee, lady, not as though I wrote a new commandment unto thee, but that which we had from the beginning, that we love one another.

6 And this is love, that we walk after his commandments.
12 Having many things to write unto you, I would not write with paper and ink; but I trust to come unto you, and speak face to face, that our joy may be full.

Some critics conjecture that the Church at Jerusalem is meant by the "elect lady," and the one at Ephesus by her elect sister. Others suppose that an eminent and honorable Christian woman was intended by the "elect lady," and that some other Christian woman, well known in the Church, was intended by her elect sister. The aged Apostle wrote this short letter to this lady, who was a person of rank, hence he did not scruple to give to her the title of honor. He assured her children of his deep interest in their welfare. The word *lady* was always used in addressing, or speaking of one who was an acknowledged superior. In their travels about the country the Apostles especially enjoyed the hospitality of families of rank. Though democratic in their principles, they were susceptible to the attractions of wealth and of culture. E. C. S.

REVELATION.

CHAPTER I.

JOHN MORLEY once said to the priests: "We shall not attack you, we shall explain you." The Book of Revelation, properly Re-Veilings, cannot even be approximately explained without some knowledge of astrology. It is a purely esoteric work, largely referring to woman, her intuition, her spiritual powers, and all she represents. Even the name of its putative author, John, is identical in meaning with "dove," the emblem of the Holy Ghost, the female principle of the Divinity.

This book came down from old Egyptian "mystery" times, and was one of the profoundly "sacred" and profoundly "secret" books of the great temple of Luxor, the words "sacred" and "secret" possessing the same meaning during the mysteries. All knowledge was anciently concealed in the mysteries; letters, numbers, astrology (until the sixteenth century identical with astronomy), alchemy, the parent of chemistry, these, and all other sciences were hidden from the common people. Even to all initiates the most important part of the mysteries was not revealed.

It is not then strange that such a profoundly mystic book as Re-Veilings should be so little understood by the Christian Church as to have been many times rejected from the sacred canon. It did not appear in the Syriac Testament as late as 1562. Neither did Luther, the great reformer of the sixteenth century, nor his co-worker, Erasmus, respect it, Luther declaring that for his part he would as soon it had not been written; Calvin, also, had small regard for it. The first collection of the New Testament canon, decided upon by the Council of Laodicea (A. D. 364), omitted the entire book from its list of sacred works; Jerome said that some Greek churches would not receive it. The celebrated Vatican codex in the papal library, the oldest uncial or Biblical manuscript in existence, does not contain Revelation. The canon of the New Testament was fixed as it now is by Pope Innocent I., A. D. 405, with the Book of Revelation still in dispute.

Its mystic character has been vaguely surmised by the later Church, which, while claiming to be the exponent of spiritual things, has yet taught the grossest materialism, and from no part of the Bible more fully than from Revelation. It asserts a literal coming of Christ in the literal clouds of heaven, riding a literal horse, while Gabriel (angel of the moon), with a literal trumpet sounds the blast of earth's destruction. A literal devil is to be bound for a thousand years, during which time the saints are to dwell on earth, "every man to have a farm," as I once heard a devout Methodist declare. "But there will not be land enough for that," objected a brother. "O, well, the earth is now two-thirds water, and that will be dried up," was the reply. To such straits have Christians been driven in their efforts to comprehend this book.

But during the centuries a few students have not failed to apprehend its character; the Abbé Constant (Eliphas Levi), declaring it to be one of the masterpieces of occult science. While for even a partial comprehension of Re-Veilings, some knowledge of astrology is required, it is no less true that the whole Bible from Genesis to Revelation demands a knowledge of astrology, of letters, and of numbers, with their interchangeable values as they were understood by those who wrote it, "a book written by initiates for initiates." Sir William Drummond proved that all names of places in the holy land of the Hebrews were astronomical.

Not only were Hebrew feasts and seasons based upon that science, but many Christian ones, as Easter and Christmas are due to the same cause. The festival of St. John the Baptist takes place at the time of the sun's lowest southern declination, December 22. In like manner the festival of St. John the Evangelist occurs at midsummer day, when the sun reaches its highest northern declination. All those church periods are purely astronomical or astrological in character. The "Alpha" and "Omega" of Revelation contain profound evolutionary truths, significative of spirit and of matter, or God unmanifested and manifested.

The famous seven churches of Asia, to whom this book was largely addressed, were all astrological and based upon the seven planets of the ancients. Of these seven churches that of Ephesus stood first. On the shores of Ægean Sea, it was famous for its magnificent temple to the moon-goddess Artemis, or Diana. This temple was one of the seven wonders of the ancient world, nations vieing with each other in their gifts to add to its splendor. The moon being the emblem or "angel" of Ephesus, the cry of the multitude when Paul spake there, "Great is Diana of the Ephesians!" was an astrological recognition of the power of the moon over human affairs. It is to be noted that none of the seven churches of Asia received the writings of Paul. In the astrology of Chaldea, as in that of Asia Minor, the moon was first among the planets. It must be remembered that the numbers seven and twelve, so frequently mentioned in Re-Veilings, are of great occult significance in relation to the earth.

The angel of the church of Smyrna, to whom the second letter was addressed, was the sun, "the only sun" dying and rising each day; that of Pergamos, the beneficent Jupiter, who became the supreme god of the Greek world. The angel of Thyatira, the lovely and loving Venus, by some deemed the most occult of the planets, sustained her old-time character for lasciviousness in her connection with that church. The fiery, warlike Mars, angel of the church of Sardis, called "the Great King," and Saturn, the angel of the church of Philadelphia, are astrologically known as malefic planets. Saturn identified with Satan, matter and time, is for occult reasons looked

upon as the great malefic. The angel of the church of Lao
Mercury or Hermes, the ambiguous planet, is, next to Venus, the
most occult of all the planets; it is, masculine or feminine, the patron
of learning or of thieves, as it is aspected. Most profound secrets
connected with the spiritual interests of the race during the middle
portion of the fifth round are hidden in the letter to the angel of the
church of Laodicea.   M. J. G.

———

This book is styled the Apocalypse or Revelation, and is supposed to have been written by John, called the Divine, on the Island
of Patmos, in the Ægean Sea, whither he was banished. Professor
Goldwin Smith, in a recent work entitled "Guesses at the Riddle of
Existence," thinks that we have but little reliable information as to
the writers of either the Old or the New Testaments. In this case
the style is so different from that of John, that the same Apostle
could not have written both books. Whoever wrote The Revelation
was evidently the victim of a terrible and extravagant imagination
and of visions which make the blood curdle.

Revelation ii.

18 And unto the angel of the church in Thyatira write:

19 I know thy works, and charity, and service, and faith, and thy patience.

20 Notwithstanding I have a few things against thee, because thou sufferest that woman Jezebel, which calleth herself a prophet, to teach and to seduce my servants.

21 And I gave her space to repent; and she repented not.

22 Behold, I will cast her into great tribulation.

23 And I will kill her children and all the churches shall know that I am he which searcheth the hearts; and I will give unto every one of you according to your works.

The town of Thyatira lay to the southeast of Pergamos. The
epistle to the church was sent by John, with some commendations;
but it was said that there was a worm at the root of its prosperity,
which would destroy the whole unless it were removed. It is not
agreed whether the expression Jezebel, is to be understood literally
or figuratively. From the reading of some manuscripts it has been
thought, that the wife of the presiding minister was intended, that
she had obtained great influence in the affairs of the church and

made a bad use of it; that she pretended to have prophetic gifts, and under that sanction propagated abominable principles.

The figurative meaning, however, seems more suited to the style and the manner of this book; and in this sense it denotes a company of persons, of the spirit and character of Jezebel, within the church under one principal deceiver.   Jezebel, a Zidonian and a zealous idolater, being married to the King of Israel (Ahab) contrary to the Divine law, used all her influence to draw the Israelites from the worship of Jehovah into idolatry.   Satan and woman are the chief characters in all the frightful visions; and the sacred period of maternity is made to illustrate some of the most terrible upheavals in national life, as between the old dragon and the mother of the race.   Whatever this book was intended to illustrate, its pictures are painfully vivid.   E. C. S.

CHAPTER II.

THE constellation Draco, the Great Serpent, was at one time ruler of the night, being formerly at the very centre of the heavens and so large that it was called the Great Dragon. Its body spread over seven signs of the Zodiac, which were called its seven heads. So great a space did it occupy, that, in mystic language, it "drew a third part of the stars from heaven and cast them to the earth." Thuban, in its tail, was formerly the pole-star, or "judge of the earth." It approached much nearer the true pole than Cynosura, the present pole-star, which is one and a half degrees distant and will never approach nearer than twelve minutes, while Thuban was only ten minutes distant.

At an early day serpents were much respected; they were thought to have more "pneuma" or spirit than any other living thing and were termed "fiery." For this cause high initiates were called "naga," or serpents of wisdom; and a living serpent was always carried in the celebration of the mysteries. During the brilliant eighteenth and nineteenth Egyptian dynasties, Draco was a great god; but when this constellation lost its place in the heavens,

181

and Thuban ceased to be the guiding sidereal Divinity, it shared
the fate of all the fallen gods. "The gods of our fathers are our
devils," says an Arabic proverb. When Re-Veilings was written,
Draco had become a fallen angel representing evil spirituality. By
precessional motion the foot of Hercules rests upon its head, and we
find it depicted as of the most material color, red.

Colors and jewels are parts of astrology; and ancient cities, as
Ectabana, were built and colored after the planets. The New Jerusalem of Re-Veilings is purely an astrological city, not to be understood without a knowledge of mystic numbers, letters, jewels and
colors. So, also, the four and twenty elders of Re-Veilings are
twenty-four stars of the Chaldean Zodiac, "counsellors" or "judges,"
which rose and set with it. Astrology was brought into great prominence by the visit of the magi, the zodiacal constellation Virgo, the
"woman with a child," ruling Palestine, in which country Bethlehem
is situated. The great astronomer and astrologer, Ptolemy, judged
the character of countries from the signs ruling them, as to this day
is done by astrologers.

The woman attacked by the great red dragon, Cassiopea, was
known as Nim-Makh, the Mighty Lady. For many centuries, at
intervals of about three hundred years, a brilliant star suddenly appeared in this constellation, remaining visible a few months, then
as suddenly disappearing. In mystic phraseology this star was a
child. It was seen A. D. 945, A. D. 1264, and was noted by Tycho
Brahe and other astronomers in 1562, when it suddenly became so
brilliant that it could be seen at midday, gradually assuming the appearance of a great conflagration, then as gradually fading away.
Since thus caught up to the throne of God, this star-child has not
again appeared, although watched for by astronomers during the
past few years. The Greeks, who borrowed so much from the
Egyptians, created from this book the story of Andromeda and the
monster sent by Neptune to destroy her, while Madame Blavatsky
says that St. John's dragon is Neptune, a symbol of Atlantaen magi.

The crown of twelve stars upon the head of the apocalyptic
woman are the twelve constellations of the Zodiac. Clothed with
the sun, woman here represents the Divinity of the feminine, its

spirituality as opposed to the materiality of the masculine; for in Egypt the sun, as giver of life, was regarded as feminine, while the moon, shining by reflected light, was looked upon as masculine. With her feet upon the moon, woman, corresponding to and representing the soul, portrays the ultimate triumph of spiritual things over material things—over the body, which man, or the male principle, corresponds to and represents.

"There was war in heaven." The wonderful progress and freedom of woman, as woman, within the last half century, despite the false interpretation of the Bible by the Church and by masculine power, is the result of this great battle; and all attempts to destroy her will be futile. Her day and hour have arrived; the dragon of physical power over her, the supremacy of material things in the world, as depicted by the male principle, are yielding to the spiritual, represented by woman. The eagle, true bird of the sun and emblem of our own great country, gives his wings to her aid; and the whole earth comes to help her against her destroyer.

And thus must Re-Veilings be left with much truth untouched, yet with the hope that what has been written will somewhat help to a comprehension of this greatly misunderstood yet profoundly "sacred" and "secret" book, whose true reading is of such vast importance to the human race.   M. J. G.

———

Here is a little well intended respect for woman as representing the Church. In this vision she appears clothed with the sun, and the moon under her feet, which denotes her superiority, says the commentator, to her reflected feebler light of the Mosaic dispensation. The crown of twelve stars on her head represents her honorable maintenance of the doctrines of the Church. Just as the woman was watched by the dragon, and her children devoured, so was the Church watched and persecuted by the emissaries of the Papal hierachy. The seven heads of the dragon represent the seven hills on which Rome is built; the ten horns, ten kingdoms into which the Western empire was divided. The tail of the dragon drawing a third part of the stars represent the power of the Romans, who had conquered one-third part of the earth.

Revelation xvii.

3 So he carried me away in the spirit into the wilderness; and I saw a woman sit upon a scarlet colored beast, full of names of blasphemy, having seven heads and ten horns.

4 And the woman was arrayed in purple and scarlet color, and decked with gold and precious stones and pearls, having a golden cup in her hand.

5 And upon her forehead was a name written, Mystery, Babylon the Great.

18 And the woman which thou sawest is that great city, which reigneth over the kings of the earth.

The woman draped in scarlet, seated on a beast, was the emblem of the Church of Rome. The beast represents the temporal power by which it has been supported. These colors have always distinguished the popes and the cardinals, as well as the Roman emperors and senators. The horses and the mules were covered with scarlet cloth to answer the description, and the woman was decked in the brightest colors, in gold and jewels. No one can describe the pomp, splendor and magnificonce of the Church of Rome. The cup in the woman's hand contained potions to intoxicate her victims. It was the custom at that time for public women to have their names on their foreheads, and as they represented the abominations of social life, they were often named after cities. The writers of the Bible are prone to make woman the standard for all kinds of abominations; and even motherhood, which should be held most sacred, is used to illustrate the most revolting crimes. What picture can be more horrible than the mother, in her hour of mortal agony, watched by the dragon with his seven heads and ten horns!

Why so many different revising committees of bishops and clergymen should have retained this book as holy and inspiring to the ordinary reader, is a mystery. It does not seem possible that the Divine John could have painted these dark pictures of the struggles of humanity with the Spirit of Evil. Verily, we need an expurgated edition of the Old and the New Testaments before they are fit to be placed in the hands of our youth to be read in the public schools and in theological seminaries, especially if we wish to inspire our children with proper love and respect for the Mothers of the Race.   E. C. S.

APPENDIX.

" Ignorance is the mother of devotion."—*Jeremy Taylor*.

THE following letters and comments are in answer to the questions:

1. Have the teachings of the Bible advanced or retarded the emancipation of women?

2. Have they dignified or degraded the Mothers of the Race?

DEAR MRS. STANTON:—I believe, as you said in your birthday address, that "women ought to demand that the Canon law, the Mosaic code, the Scriptures, prayer-books and liturgies be purged of all invidious distinctions of sex, of all false teaching as to woman's origin, character and destiny." I believe that the Bible needs explanation and comment on many statements therein which tend to degrade woman. Christ taught the equality of the sexes, and Paul said: There is neither male nor female; ye are all one in Christ Jesus." Hence I welcome "The Woman's Bible" as a needed commentary in regard to woman's position.

PHEBE A. HANAFORD.

If the suggestions and teachings of the various books of our Bible, concerning women, are compared with the times in which severally they probably were written, in general they are certainly in advance of most contemporary opinion. The hurtful blunder of later eras has been the setting up of early, cruder standards touching the relations of men and of women, as moulding influences and guides to broader civilizations. They cannot be authoritative.

I believe that the Bible's Golden Rule has been the real substratum of all religions, *when fairly applied from their own point of view.* But the broader and more discriminating applications of the rule theoretically both to men and to women in every relation of life have made, and necessarily must have made, most of the earlier practical regulations and teachings, beneficent perhaps in their day, pernicious in ours when regarded as still authoritative. Interpreted by its fundamental principles, in the light of its time—not in the fast increasing light of ours, which, as I understand it, is your searchlight and that of your collaborators—I have very little quarrel with the Bible. But neither have I much quarrel with Buddhism, with Paganism in general, or with any serious religious cult, tested in the same way.

Turn on the light and so change the point of view. But criticism of ancient creeds, literatures or morals, to be entirely fair and just, must be comparative criticism. To be broadly comparative it must virtually include contemporary and intermediate as well as existing creeds, literatures or morals. Very sincerely yours,

ANTOINETTE BROWN BLACKWELL.

———

Like the shield which was gold on one side and silver on the other, the Bible has two sides or aspects. As travellers approaching the shield from opposite directions quarrelled over its nature because each saw only that side which he had approached, people have differed in their view of the Bible and its influence upon mankind because only one aspect has been visible to them.

Acceptance of the Bible literally tends to retard the development of both man and woman, and consequently the establishment of their highest and best relation to each other, a relation upon which depends their usefulness to the community. Both the law of Moses and the teachings of Paul, thus considered, belittle woman more than they exalt her. While words of praise and promises of future place and power are not altogether lacking, this is the impression left upon the mind of the reader who is not able to pass around to the other side and gain another view.

Exoterically considered, the Bible offers less of the ethical and the spiritual than of the physical possibilities of woman as the complement to man; but esoterically considered, it is found to exact the spiritual possibilities above the rest—above even the like possibilities of the man. The Bible has been, and will continue to be, a stumbling-block in the way of development of inherent resources, consequently of the truest civilization, in proportion to the strength of its exoteric aspect with the people. It will cease to be a stumbling block and become a powerful impetus in the desired direction instead, when its inner meaning becomes revelator, companion and friend.

In the literal rendering of the Bible, woman appears first and above all as man's subordinate; but this inner meaning shows her first and above all as the individual equal with him, and afterward his complement, or what she is able to be for him. Portrayed as the mother of the Saviour of the world, one woman is exalted above all women when only physical motherhood is seen; and the consequence has been that one woman has been worshiped and the sex has been crucified. This one woman has been lifted above her place; and all women have fallen correspondingly below it.

Not till "the light that lighteth every man that cometh into the world" shall pierce with its rays the darkness of the sensuous nature, will woman's spiritual motherhood for the race, be discerned as the way of its redemption from that darkness and its consequences. As that light is uncovered in individual souls the inner meaning of the Bible will appear, woman's nature as the individual and her true relativity to man be seen. Then the mistakes which have been ignorantly made will be rectified, because both sides of the shield will be seen. Men and women will clasp hands as comrades with a common destiny; religion and science will each reveal their destiny and prove that truth which the Bible even exotericaily declares that "the woman is the glory of the man."

URSUI A N. GESTEFELD.

It is requested that I shall answer two questions:

1. Has the Bible advanced or retarded woman's emancipation?
2. Has it elevated or degraded the Mothers of the Race?

If by "emancipation" is meant the social, legal and political position of women, and if by the "Bible" the authorized version of the Old Testament, it would be difficult to prove that the opponents of that emancipation have not derived their narrow views from many passages in the Bible. This, however, applies only to the exoteric interpretation, the weak points of which have been so mercilessly exposed in Part I. of "The Woman's Bible."

The Divine wisdom whose occult truths form the basis of Judaism, of Christianity and of all other religions, has nothing to do with the subjection of sex: and to be fair we must confess that there are many texts in the exoteric version which proclaim the equality of woman, notably the first chapter of Genesis. I believe that H. P. Blavatsky was right when she said of the Bible: "It is a grand volume, a masterpiece composed of clever, ingenious fables, containing great verities; but it reveals the latter only to those who, like the Initiates, have a key to its inner meaning; a tale sublime in its morality and didactics truly—still a tale and an allegory; a repertory of invented personages in its older Jewish portions, and of dark sayings and parables in its later additions, and thus quite misleading to any one ignorant of its esotericism."

This being the case, the discussion which "The Woman's Bible" raises is to my judgment somewhat futile. It is said that from Genesis to Revelation the Bible degrades woman. Does it not, as it stands, equally in many passages degrade the conception of the Supreme Being? Many noble and Divine truths have been utterly degraded by the coarse fallacies of men. All this is so sure to be made clear in the near future that I am doubtful of the wisdom of laying too much stress on passages whose meaning is entirely mis-understood by the vast majority of Christians.

Slowly we see a light breaking. When the dawn comes we shall have a revision of the Bible on very different lines from any yet attempted. In the meantime may we not ask, Is there any curse or crime which has not appealed to the Bible for support? Polygamy, capital punishment, slavery and war have all done so. Why not the subjection of women? Let us hold fast that which is good in the Bible and the rest will modify itself in the future, as it has done in the past, to the needs of humanity and the advance of knowledge.

London, England.   URSULA BRIGHT.

———

MRS. ELIZABETH CADY STANTON:—Dear Madam: I have received your letter and the specimen of "The Woman's Bible" which you have sent me. I have not had time to examine it minutely; but I have been aware of your purpose from the beginning. I am afraid that I cannot say anything which you will wish to print; for I look upon the Bible very differently from what you do.

I have no superstitious reverence for it, but hold it in high regard as a valuable collection of very old literature well representing the thought and the life of a great, earnest people at different periods of their career. As such, it is full of precious lessons of wisdom and of sweet and beautiful poetry. I certainly could not endorse Mr. White's statement; for I have very recently in public lectures spoken of the great value of this collection as one of the best educators of the common people in Christendom generally, and especially in Scotland and the United States. I should say the same, so far as my knowledge extends, of the Koran and other so-called sacred books.

That the *superstitious worship* of the Bible as a direct revelation from God, and the practice of using what is merely the history of human life as authority for human action now, or as prophecy, has produced or strengthened great evils in the world I readily admit, and I welcome all the thorough and searching criticism which can be applied to the Bible, but nothing is gained by exaggeration. There are noble examples of woman in the Old Testament of the heroic type, as in the New Testament of the tender and loving one.

The whole subject of the relations of the sexes is a deep and difficult one; and the ages have been struggling with it. That woman is handicapped by peculiarities of physical structure seems evident; and according to the character of the age these are more or less unfavorable. Civilization in many instances has emphasized and increased them to her great disadvantage; but it is only by making her limitations her powers that the balance can be restored, and in an age of more intellectual and spiritual superiority this will come to pass. I read this in the development of woman's life in education, in industry and in self-support.

I have tried to express my views frankly, although I cannot fully illustrate them in a brief letter, which is all I have time for at present. Your own active mind will follow out whatever there is of value in my thought.   Yours very respectfully,

Jamaica Plain, Mass.   EDNAH D. CHENEY.

———

The Bible—both the books of the Old Testament and of the New, express the views in regard to woman which prevailed when those books were written. The conception in regard to woman was that she was naturally man's inferior, that her position should be one of subordination, that she should have no will of her own, except as it was in accord with that of her father, husband, or master.

The enlightened portions of the world have gradually been outgrowing these ideas. This progress has constantly been opposed by the influence of Bible teachings on the subject. The influence of the Bible against the elevation of woman, like its influence in favor of slavery, has been great because of the infallibility and the Divine authority with which the teachings of the Bible have been invested. If the Bible had, like other books, been judged by its actual merits, in the light of reason and common sense, its teachings about woman would have had no authoritative weight; but when millions have for centuries been brought up to believe that the Bible is an inspired and infallible revelation from God, its influence has been mischievous in a thousand ways.

A collection of books which teaches, as from God, that man was made first for the glory of God, and woman for man simply; that woman was first to sin, and therefore should be in submission to man; that motherhood implies moral impurity and requires a sin offering (twice as much in the case of a female as a male child), must have continued to keep woman in a degraded condition just in proportion as such ideas have been believed to be true and inspired by God.

The advancement of woman throughout Christendom has been going on only where these doctrines have been outgrown or modified through the influence of science, of skepticism, and of liberal thought generally. That the Bible does teach that woman's position should be one of subordination and submission to man, and that through her first came sin into the world, is indisputable; and I do not see how such teachings, believed to be direct from God, can be accepted without retarding woman's progress. Mr. Lecky and others have shown historically that these Oriental conceptions have distinctly degraded woman wherever they have prevailed.

What we should naturally expect to have resulted from these conceptions is shown by experience actually to have been the result of such teachings, enforced by the authority of Moses and of St. Paul.

The idea of woman's equality with man in all natural rights and opportunities finds no support in the Bible. The doctrine that there is neither male nor female, neither bond nor free, in Christ Jesus, had no practical application to social conditions. It left the slave in chains, and the woman in fetters. Where the old theological dogmas respecting woman are the least impaired, woman's condition is the least hopeful. Where the authority of reason is in the ascendant, or where it is superseding the authority of book revelations, of creeds and of churches, woman's position is the most ad-

vanced, her rights are the most completely recognized, her opportunities for progress the most fully allowed, and her character the
most fully developed.   SARAH A. UNDERWOOD.

—————

A solution, in accordance with the fundamental laws of ethics,
of the woman question, which is a part of the great social question,
can be arrived at only by a transformation of the social order of
things, made in conformity with the principle of equal liberty and
equal justice to each and every one.

As a necessary proposition to let this principle be universally
recognized, we must designate the philosophical view of the world,
based upon scientific Materialism, which former, penetrated by the
conviction that the natural doctrine of evolution also retains its
validity with regard to the mental, vital principles of humanity, believes in the social, political and ethical evolution of human society,
from which progressive evolution the equal claim to all social relations of the female and the male halves of humanity are inseparable.

As the firmest enemy of modern ethics based upon scientific
knowledge of natural laws, there stands the Christian religion, the
outspring of the Jewish one, which former, resting upon the principle of the necessary subordination of woman to man, in consequence thereof energetically combats the attempts for equal rights
to both sexes, and, as far as lies in its power, ever will and must combat the same.

To the influence of the Christian Church upon social conditions
we must in the first instance ascribe that, notwithstanding all advances of culture, the mental development of the female sex has
been systematically kept back through all these tens of centuries.
And not only for the reason that the Christian religion considers
woman as a creature inferior to man, owing to the legendary eating
of the apple by Eve ("Satan," says St. Augustine, "considered the
man to be less credulous and approachable"), but also—and possibly foremost of all—for the reason that the Christian Church knows
very well that in woman, intellectually undeveloped, and therefore

easy to be led, and ready to lend a willing ear to priestly promptings, it possesses its most powerful ally, and knows that it would lose that powerful support as soon as women, by a thorough mental training, by an elevating education adapted to their condition of mind and of fortune, would be taken away from clerical influences.

As a contrast to the lying statement, which falsifies the historical facts, that the Christian religion has raised the condition of woman, the Christian Church offers to woman nothing but serfdom. And it is the first duty of those women who combat for right and liberty to unite in the fight against religious obscurity, against the powers of darkness and the suppression resting on the Church, that revolution of the mind for which the most elevated thinkers of all time have suffered and fought, and to whose deeds alone we owe all advances in the mental freeing of humanity and all accomplishments of the awakening consciousness of justice.

Vienna, Austria.   IRMA VON TROLL-BOROSTYANI.

My DEAR MRS. STANTON:—I thank you very much for the book which I have received and shall consider with interest. I respond at once and heartily to the inquiry with which you have honored me.

I consider the Bible the most wonderful record of the evolution of spiritual life which our race possesses. The sympathetic justice displayed by the Christ when he said, "Let him that is without sin cast the first stone," will be the inspiration of the future for man and for woman alike.

With cordial remembrance of the past and hope for the future, I am   Sincerely yours,

Hastings, London, England.   ELIZABETH BLACKWELL.

Since it is accepted that the status of woman is the gauge of civilization, this is the burning question which now presents itself to Christendom. If the Bible had elevated woman to her present status, it would seem that the fact could be demonstrated beyond question; yet to-day the whole Christian world is on the defensive, trying to prove the validity of this claim. Despite the opposition of Bible teaching, woman has secured the right to education, to speak and to print her thoughts; therefore her answer to these questions will decide the fate of Christian civilization.

In Genesis the Bible strikes the key-note of woman's inferiority and subjection; and the note rings true through every accepted and rejected book which has ever constituted the Bible. In the face of this fact, the supreme effort of the Christian Church has been to inculcate the idea that Christianity alone has elevated woman, and that all other religions have degraded and enslaved her. It has feared nothing so much as to face the truth.

Women have but to read the Bible and the history of Christianity in conjunction with the sacred books and the histories of other religions to discover the falsity of this claim, and that the Bible cannot stand the light of truth. The Bible estimate of woman is summed up in the words of the president of a leading theological seminary when he exclaimed to his students, "My Bible commands the subjection of women forever."

In an address to the graduating class of a woman's college in England, Mr. Gladstone, in awarding the diplomas, said: "Young women, you who belong to the favored half of the human race, enormous changes have taken place in your positions as members of society. It is almost terrible to look back upon the state of women sixty years ago, upon the manner in which they were viewed by the law, and the scanty provision made for their welfare, and the gross injustice, the flagrant injustice, the shameful injustice, to which in certain particulars they were subjected. Great changes are taking place, and greater are impending." For centuries England has been the light of the Christian world; yet what an indictment is this against Christian England by the greatest living defender of the Bible and the Christian religion.

This one statement of Mr. Gladstone at once refutes the claim that the Bible has elevated woman, and confirms the idea of the president of the theological seminary. Add to these declarations the true condition of women to-day, and the testimony that the Bible bears against itself, and the falsity of the claim that it has elevated woman is at once established. If Mr. Gladstone acknowledges the "gross, flagrant and shameful injustice" to woman sixty years ago in Christian England, what can be said of woman's condition six hundred, or sixteen hundred years ago, when the Bible held the greatest sway over the human mind and Christianity was at the zenith of its power, when it was denied that woman has a soul, when she was bought and sold as the cattle of the field, robbed of her name, her children, her property, and "elevated" (?) on the gibbet of infamy, and on the high altar of lust by the decree of the Christian priesthood?

If it can be proven that during the last thousand years the Christian clergy, with the Bible in their hands, have pointed out or attempted to remove one single cruelty or wrong which women have suffered, *now* is the opportune time to furnish such proof. Now, to-day, when woman herself is rising in her mental majesty, and when her wrongs are being righted, Christianity is dead in the strongest brains and the most heroic hearts of Europe and of America; and *now*, when the myth and the miracle of Bible teaching have lost their hold on the minds of people, this is the very age when the position of woman is more exalted than it has ever been since Chrisianity began.

If even the claim that the Bible has elevated woman to her present status were true, when the light is turned on to the social, domestic and religious life of the Christian world, this achievement reflects no credit on Bible teaching. After nineteen hundred years no woman's thought has ever been incorporated into the ecclesiastical or civil code of any Christian land.

Monogamic marriage is the strongest institution of the Christian system; yet all the men of the Old Testament were polygamists; and Christ and Paul, the central figures of the New Testament, were celibates and condemned marriage by both precept and example. In Christian lands monogamy is strictly demanded of women; but bigamy, trigamy, and polygamy are in reality practised by men as one of the methods of elevating women. Largely, the majority of men have one legal wife; but assisted by a small per cent. of youths and of bachelors, Christendom maintains an army of several millions of courtesans. Thousands of wretched women are yearly driven to graves in the potter's field, while manhood is degraded by deception, by drunkenness and by disease; and the blood of the innocents cries out against a system which thus "elevates" woman.

The Bible says that "a tree is known by its fruit;" yet this tree is carefully pruned, watered, and tended as the "Tree of life" whose fruit, in the words of Archdeacon Farrar, "alone elevates woman, and shrouds as with a halo of sacred innocence the tender years of the child." The Bible records that God created woman by a method. different from that employed in bringing into life any other creature, then cursed her for seeking knowledge; yet God declares in the Bible: "My people are destroyed for lack of knowledge." "Because thou hast rejected knowledge I will reject thee." "Add to your faith virtue, and to virtue knowledge," and knowledge is the savior of the human race.

Ever since Eve was cursed for seeking knowledge, the priest with the Bible in his hands has pronounced her the most unnatural, untrustworthy and dangerous creation of God. She has been given away as a sheep at the marriage altar, classed with the ox and the ass, cursed in maternity, required to receive purification at the hands of the priest for the crime of child-bearing, her body enslaved, and robbed of her name and of her property.

The ownership of the wife established and perpetuated through Bible teaching is responsible for the domestic pandemonium and the carnival of wife murder which reigns throughout Christendom. In the United States alone, in the eighteen hundred and ninety-seventh year of the Christian era, 3,482 wives, many with unborn children in their bodies, have been murdered in cold blood by their husbands; yet the Christian clergy from their pulpits reprove women for not bearing more children, in the face of the fact that millions of the children who have been born by Christian women are homeless tramps, degraded drunkards, victims of disease, inmates of insane asylums or prisons, condemned to the scaffold, or bond slaves to priests or to plutocrats who revel in wealth at the expense of women whom it is claimed that the Bible has "emancipated and elevated."

"Behold, I was shapen in iniquity, and in sin did my mother conceive me." This declaration of the Bible puts the brand of infamy upon every woman who ever bore a child; and this, it is claimed, elevates the Mothers of the Race. The wife who places her destiny in the keeping of the father of her children bestows upon him the wealth of her affection, who is to bear the blood and the name of her husband to conquests yet undreamed of, and to generations yet unborn, is by Divine decree made a fountain of iniquity. Would not men and women rather pluck their tongues out by the roots than brand with infamy the mothers who went down into the valley and the shadow of death to give birth to them?

Place the Bible Trinity of "Father, Son and Holy Ghost" beside the Homeric trinity, "Father, Mother and Child," and prove that the Bible has elevated woman. The Homeric conception of woman towers like the Norway pine above the noxious growth of the Mosaic ideal. Compare the men and the women of the Bible with the stately figures culled from the temple of Pagan antiquity. Zipporah denouncing Moses as a "bloody husband," Abraham sending Hagar and his child into the desert and pocketing twice over the gains from his wife's prostitution; Lot and his daughters; Judah and his daughter-in-law, Onan; Yamar, the Levite, and his concubine; David and Bath-sheba; Solomon in the sewer of sensualism; Rahab, Aholibah, Mary of Bethlehem, and Mary Magdala.

Place these by the side of the man and the woman, Hector and Andromache, of the "Iliad," who called upon the immortal gods to bless their child of love; the virgin Isis with her son Horus; the Vedic virgin Indrance, the mother of the savior-god, Indra; Devaki and her Divine child, Chrishna; Hipparchia, Pandora, Protogenia, Cornelia, Plotina, and a host of the noble and virtuous of Pagan history. Prove by comparing these with the position of woman in Christendom that woman owes all that she is to the Bible.

Compare Ruth of the Bible with the magnificent Pagan, Penelope, who refused the hands of kings, was as true to her love as the star is to the pole, who, after years of waiting, clasped the old wanderer in rags to her heart, her husband, her long-lost Ulysses; yet this Pagan woman lived ten centuries before the laws of Moses and of Christ were promulgated. While there are millions of Penelopes in Christendom, there are other millions of women, after centuries of Bible teaching, who lie outside the pale of motherhood, and even outside of the pale of swine-hood. Under Bible teaching the scarlet woman is "anathema, marantha," while the scarlet man holds high place in the Sanctuary and the State.

The by-paths of ecclesiastical history are fetid with the records of crimes against women; and "the half has never been told." And what of the history which Christianity is making to-day? Answer, ye victims of domestic warfare who crowd the divorce courts of Bible lands. Answer, ye wretched offspring of involuntary motherhood. Answer, ye five hundred thousand outcast women of Christian America, who should have been five hundred thousand blessings, bearing humanity in your unvitiated blood down the streams of time. Answer, ye mental dwarfs and moral monstrosities, and tell what the Holy Bible has done for you.

While these answers echo through the stately cathedrals of Bible lands, if the priest, with the Holy Bible in his hands, can show just cause why woman should not look to reason and to science rather than to Scripture for deliverance, "let him speak *now*, or forever after hold his peace."

When Reason reigns and Science lights the way, a countless host of women will move in majesty down the coming centuries. A voice will cry, "Who are these?" and the answer will ring out: "These are the mothers of the coming race, who have locked the door of the Temple of Faith and thrown the key away; 'these are they which came out of great tribulation and have washed their robes and made them white in the' fountain of knowledge."

JOSEPHINE K. HENRY.

―――――

MY DEAR MRS. STANTON:—To say that "the Bible for two thousand years has been the greatest block in the way of civilization" is misleading. Until the Protestant reformation, the Bible was hidden from the common people by the hierarchs of the Roman Catholic Church; and it is only about three centuries that it has been read in the vernacular.

I cannot agree with you that "the Bible degrades women from Genesis to Revelation." The Bible, which is a collection of ancient literature, historic, prophetic, poetic and epistolary, is valuable as showing the status of woman at the time when the books were written. And the advice, or the commands, to women given by Paul in the Epistles, against which there has been so much railing, when studied in the light of the higher criticism, with the aid of cotemporary history and Greek scholarship, show Paul to have been in advance of the religious teachers of his time.

All these commands that have offended us in the past appear in his Epistles to the churches in cities of Greece, where marriage was bitter slavery to women. Paul was aiming to uplift marriage to the level of the great Christian idea, as he uttered it, in Gal. iii., 28: "There is neither Jew nor Greek, there is neither bond nor free, there is neither male nor female; for ye are all one in Christ Jesus." Christianity is simply the universal fatherhood of God, and the universal brotherhood of man. And Paul was declaring this in the utterance which I have quoted. All the unjust distinctions of race and of caste, all the oppressions of slavery and the degradations of woman were effaced by the two cardinal doctrines of pristine Christianity; and Paul seems to have lived up to his teaching.

I cannot say that "Christianity has been the foe of woman." The study of the evolution of woman does not show this. My later studies have changed many of my earlier crude notions concerning the development of woman. She has developed slowly, and so has man; and the history of the past shows that every activity of man which has advanced him has been shared by her.

There is so wide a belief among orthodox people, nowadays, in what Professor Briggs calls "the errancy of the Bible," that I doubt if you will be attacked, no matter how startling may be your heresies in Part II. Nobody cares much about heresy in these days; and my desire to withhold my name from your work, as an endorser,

comes from my utter ignorance of it, and from my belief that I
should disagree with you, judging from your letter before me.

Yours very truly,

M. A. LIVERMORE.

———

MY DEAR MRS. STANTON:—You have sent to me the following
questions: "Have the teachings of the Bible advanced or retarded
the emancipation of women? Have they dignified or degraded the
Mothers of the Race?"

In reply I would say, that as a matter of fact, the nations which
treat women with the most consideration are all Christian nations;
the countries in which women have open to them all the opportunities for education which men possess are Christian countries; co-
education originated in Christian colleges; the professions and the
trades are closed to us in all except Christian lands; and woman's
ballot is unknown except where the Gospel of Christ has mellowed
the hearts of men until they became willing to do women justice.
Wherever we find an institution for the care and the comfort of the
defective or the dependent classes, that institution was founded by
men and women who were Christians by heredity and by training.

No such woman as Mrs. Elizabeth Cady Stanton, with her heart
aflame against all forms of injustice and of cruelty, with her intellect illumed and her tongue quickened into eloquence, has ever
been produced in a country where the Bible was not incorporated
into the thoughts and the affections of the people and had not been
so during many generations.

I think that men have read their own selfish theories into the
Book, that theologians have not in the past sufficiently recognized
the progressive quality of its revelation, nor adequately discrimin-
ated between its records as history and its principles of ethics and
of religion, nor have they until recently perceived that it is not in
any sense a scientific treatise; but I believe that the Bible comes to
us from God, and that it is a sufficient rule of faith and of practice.
I believe that it is no accident which has placed this Book at the

parting of the ways between a good life and a bad one, and enshrined it at the centre of the holiest scenes which the heart can know, placing it in the pastor's hand at the wedding and at the grave, on the father's knee at family prayer, in the trembling fingers of the sick, and at the pillow of the dying, making it the hope of the penitent and the power of God unto salvation of those who sin.

To me the Bible is the dear and sacred home book which makes a hallowed motherhood possible because it raises woman up, and with her lifts toward heaven the world. This is the faith taught to me by those whom I have most revered and cherished; it has produced the finest characters which I have ever known; by it I propose to live; and holding to the truth which it brings to us, I expect to pass from this world to one even more full of beauty and of hope.

Believe me, honored co-worker for the enfranchisement of women,

Yours with sisterly regard,

FRANCES E. WILLARD.

Among the letters in reply to the interrogatories propounded are two, noticeable because they are in such a striking contrast to that of Mrs. Josephine K. Henry, which immediately precedes them. Their first marked characteristic is their total lack of facts which are sufficient to sustain the conclusions therein stated. Conceding for the purpose of this discussion the truth of Mrs. Livermore's assertions contained in the first paragraph of her letter, she fails absolutely to show that the Holy Scriptures have been of any benefit, or have rendered any aid, to woman in her efforts to obtain her rights in either the social, the business, or the political world; and unless she is able to present stronger or more cogent reasons to justify that conclusion than any which are therein specified, I shall be compelled to adhere to my present conviction, which is, that this book always has been, and is at present, one of the greatest obstacles in the way of the emancipation and the advancement of the sex.

In regard to the letter of the distinguished President of the Wo-

man's Christian Temperance Union, her position is entirely inde-
fensible and completely lacking in logical conclusions. Her leading
proposition is in substance that to the extent that the Christian religion has prevailed there has been a corresponding improvement in
the condition of women; and the conclusion which she draws from
that premise is that this religion has been the cause of this advancement. Before I admit the truth of this conclusion I must first inquire whether or not the premise upon which it is based is true; and
judging from the fact that the condition of women is most degraded
in those countries where Church and State are in closest affiliation,
as in Spain, in Italy, in Russia and in Ireland, and most advanced in
nations where the power of ecclesiasticism is markedly on the wane,
the inference is obvious that the Bible and the religion based upon it
have retarded rather than promoted the progress of woman.

But, granting that her premise is true, her conclusion by no
means follows from it. She desires her reader to infer that the existence of Christianity in certain countries is responsible for the high
degree of civilization which there obtains, and that the improved
condition of women in those countries is owing entirely to the influence of that religion therein. This is what the logicians would
call a *non sequitur*, which means a conclusion which does not follow
from the premises stated.

It is now a well-settled principle recognized by all writers upon
the science of logic, that the co-existence of two facts does not necessarily imply that one is the cause of the other; and, as is often the
case, they may have no relation to each other, and each may exist
independently of the other. Many illustrations of this fallacy might
be presented were it necessary to do so; but I will refer to only one
of them. I have heard it asserted that more murders and other
crimes are committed in Christian countries than in any others.
Whether this be true or false, I am not prepared to state; but if it
were proven to be a fact, could one justly contend that the influence
of the Bible is in favor of the commission of crime? Indeed, there
would be more reason for so thinking than there is for the opinion
which she holds, as numerous passages may be found in that volume
which clearly justify both crime and vice.

The truth of the matter is, as Mrs. Stanton, Mrs. Henry, and other contributors to "The Woman's Bible" have clearly proven, that whatever progress woman has made in any department of effort she has accomplished independently of, and in opposition to, the so-called inspired and infallible "Word of God," and that this book has been of more injury to her than has any other which has ever been written in the history of the world.   E. M.

"Have the teachings of the Bible advanced or retarded the emancipation of women?"

"Have they dignified or degraded the Mothers of the Race?"

There are always two sides to every question. It sometimes happens that the Christian, the historian, the clergyman, and the devotee, in their enthusiasm, are long on assertion and short on proof. Turning the light on the past and present, the writer of this comment asserts "as a matter of fact that the nations which treat women with the most consideration are all" civilized nations. If the condition of woman is highest in Christian civilization, the question arises, Is it Christianity or civilization which has accorded to women the "most consideration"? Christianity means belief in the tenets laid down in a book called the Bible, claimed to be the Word of God. Civilization means the state of being refined in manners from the grossness of savage life, and improved in arts and in learning. If civilization is due entirely to the teachings of the Bible, then, as claimed, woman owes to Christianity all the "consideration" which she receives.

We claim that woman's advancement is due to civilization, and that the Bible has been a bar to her progress. It is true that "woman receives most consideration in Christian nations;" but this is due to the mental evolution of humanity, stimulated by climate and by soil, and the intercommunication of ideas through modern invention. All the Christian nations are in the north temperate zone, whose climate and soil are better adapted to the development of the race than any other portions of the earth. Christianity took its rise in thirty degrees north latitude. Mohammedanism took its rise in the torrid zone; and as it made its way north it advanced in education, in art, in science, and in invention, until the civilization of Moslem Spain far surpassed that of Christian Europe, and as it retreated before the Christian sword from the fertile valleys of Spain into the arid plains of Arabia it retrograded, after giving to the world some of the greatest scientific truths and inventions.

The women of the United States receive "more consideration" and are being emancipated more rapidly than are the women of Europe; yet, in Europe, Christianity holds iron sway, while in America the people are free to accept or to reject its teachings; and in the United States, out of a population of seventy millions, but twenty-two millions have accepted it; and a large percentage of these are children, who have not arrived at the years of discretion, and foreigners from Christian Europe. The consideration extended to woman does not depend upon the teachings of the Bible, but upon the mental and material advancement of the men of a nation. Now if it can be proven that Bible teaching has inspired men to explore and to subdue new lands, to give to the world inventions, to build ships, railroads and telegraphs, to open mines, to construct foundries and factories, and to amass knowledge and wealth, then the Bible has been woman's best friend; for she receives most consideration where men have liberty of thought and of action, have prospered materially, builded homes, and have bank accounts.

The women in the slums of Christian London and New York receive no more consideration than the women in the slums of Hong Kong or Bombay. If the nations which give the most consideration to women do so because of their Christianity, then it logically follows that the more intensely Christian a class or an individual may be, the greater consideration will be shown to their women. The most intensely Christian people in Christendom are negroes; yet it is an incontrovertible fact that negro women receive less consideration, and are more wronged and abused, than any class on the earth. The women of the middle and upper classes in Bible lands receive consideration just in proportion to the amount of intelligence and worldly goods possessed by their male relatives, while the pauper classes are abused, subjected, and degraded in proportion to the ignorance and the poverty of the men of their class.

The Church is the channel through which Bible influence flows. Has the Church ever issued an edict that woman must be equal with man before the canon or the civil law, that her thoughts should be incorporated in creed or code, that she should own her own body and property in marriage, or have a legal claim to her children born in wedlock, which Christianity claims is a "sacrament" and one of the "holy mysteries"? Has the Church ever demanded that woman be educated beyond the Bible (and that interpreted for her) and the cook book, or given a chance in all the callings of life to earn an honest living? Is not the Church to-day a masculine hierarchy, with a female constituency, which holds woman in Bible lands in silence and in subjection?

No institution in modern civilization is so tyrannical and so unjust to woman as is the Christian Church. It demands everything from her and gives her nothing in return. The history of the Church does not contain a single suggestion for the equality of woman with man. Yet it is claimed that women owe their advancement to the Bible. It would be quite as true to say that they owe their improved condition to the almanac or to the vernal equinox. Under Bible influence woman has been burned as a witch, sold in the shambles, reduced to a drudge and a pauper, and silenced and subjected before her ecclesiastical and marital law-givers. "She was first in the transgression, therefore keep her in subjection." These words of Paul have filled our whole civilization with a deadly virus, yet how strange is it that the average Christian woman holds the name of Paul above all others, and is oblivious to the fact that he has brought deeper shame, subjection, servitude and sorrow to woman than has any other human being in history.

The nations under Bible influence are the only drunken nations on the earth. The W. C. T. U. will certainly not claim that drunkenness elevates woman; indeed, its great work for our sex is a splendid protest against this idea. Throughout Christendom millions of wretched women wait in suspense and in terror for the return of drunken husbands, while in heathendom a drunkard's wife cannot be found unless a heathen husband is being Christianized by Christian whiskey. The Chinese women have their feet compressed, but, unlike Christian women, they do not need their feet to give broom drills or skirt dances for the "benefit of their church." The child-wives of India need to be rescued and protected, but no more than many adult wives in Bible lands need protection from drunken and brutal husbands. The heathen wife seeks death on her husband's funeral pyre, but the Christian wife is often sent to death by a bullet in her brain, or a knife in her heart.

It is said that "woman's ballot is unknown except where the Gospel of Christ has mellowed the hearts of men until they became willing to do women justice." Justice through the ballot has been accorded only to the women of Wyoming, Colorado, Idaho, Utah, and far away New Zealand. In these States the people are honest, industrious and law-abiding; but the "influence of the Gospel of Christ," according to religious statistics, is so small it would take a search-warrant to find it, while Utah is full of Mormons and New Zealand is a convict dumping ground for Christian nations. Is this the extent of justice to women after the "influence of the Gospel of Christ has mellowed the hearts of men" for nineteen hundred years?

The fact is that woman has been elevated in spite of Bible influence. Every effort that woman has made to secure education has been challenged by popes, bishops, priests, moderators, conferences and college presidents, yet against all these protests she has battered down the doors of Christian colleges and is now studying the Bible of Science in conjunction with the Bible of the Christian religion. With increasing knowledge woman is founding her faith on reason and demonstrated truth, instead of taking it second-hand from priest, parson or presbyter.

Remove from Bible lands the busy brains and hands which have guided the plow and the locomotive, driven the machinery of the mine, the foundry, the factory, the home, the mental and the physical labor which have brought material prosperity, broadened the mind, subdued the brutal instincts, and humanized the race—remove all these and leave but the Bible and its influence, and where, let me ask, would woman be to-day? Where, indeed, would man be? A crouching and cowering slave to the Bible doctrine of the Divine right of kings, living as the brutes of the field, as he did when Bible Christianity was at the zenith of its power. Wherever in Christian lands man has been a slave, woman has been the slave of a slave.

Imagine the condition of woman if to-day should be removed from Christian civilization the school, the steam engine, the smoke-stack and the printing press, and leave but the Scriptures, the steeple and the parson. Would Elizabeth Cady Stantons, Mary A. Liver-mores and Frances E. Willards be the products of this strictly Christian civilization?

Christianity has instilled into woman the canting falsehood that the women of all other religions are degraded and immoral. Through tyranny and falsehood alone is Christianity able to hold woman in subjection. To tell her the truth would rend the temple of faith in twain and strike terror to the heart of the priest at the altar. Nothing but the truth will set woman free. She should know that Christian England captures the Hindoo girl to act as a harlot to the British soldier, and that a Christian chaplain is commanded to see that she performs her duty. She should know that in Christian Austria the maiden must partake of the Holy Eucharist before she will be granted a license as a prostitute. She should know that Christian Europe and America trade upon the bodies, the hearts and the hopes of millions of wretched women, victims of ignorance and of poverty, and that the centres of Christian civilization are seething cauldrons of immorality, dissipation and disease, which spread ruin and despair in the shadow of the loftiest cathedrals and palatial Christian temples.

These things are too shocking for pure Christian women to know, so they expend their prayers and pelf on the "poor heathen" who have never heard that Adam ate an apple, or that the whale swallowed Jonah. Christianity feeds and fattens on the sentiment and the credulity of women. It slanders the women of India, of China and of Japan that it may rob the woman of Europe and of America. Dr. Simmons, of the National Hospital at Yokohama, who has lived in the Orient for thirty-five years, says:

"The family in Japan is the cornerstone of the nation. The

father and the mother are regarded with reverence. Politeness and self-restraint are instilled into children, and an uncivil word is rarely heard. The Japanese are truthful and honest. The wife has equal influence with the husband; while divorce is rarely heard of in Oriental lands; and laws are more stringent protecting the chastity of women."

O that women could learn the truth! The laws of the Orient are against trafficking in young girls, but Christian England, which has an iron hand on the throat of India and a sword thrust into her heart, carries on a lively trade in native and foreign women, to be the prey of the Christian soldier, who makes way for the Christian missionary. Here, in Christian America, marriageable young women are trotted off to church, the theatre or the ball, and practically set up for sale in the market of holy matrimony; and the Christian minister, for a consideration, seals the "Divine mystery." The Church would indignantly deny that it is a marriage mart, but denial does not throttle the truth.

Truth makes her way slowly but surely, because the eternities are hers. Mrs. Elizabeth Cady Stanton, the greatest liberator of our time, has, with magnificent courage, pressed into humanity's Thermopylæ, and turned the light on the superstitions which have visited cruelties and wrongs on woman, and this, too, under a system which claims to extend "great consideration" to the Mothers of the Race. O women of Christendom! will ye not seek the truth? Leave the priestly mendicants who demand your devotion and your dollars, leave to their religion the heathen women on the banks of the Yangtse-Kiang and the Ganges, and turn your eyes to millions of your enslaved, toiling, struggling sisters in Christendom whom it is claimed the Bible has elevated; and remember that these are the victims upon whom the "glad feet" of the Gospel have been trampling for two thousand years.

Versailles, Ky.   JOSEPHINE K. HENRY.

The Christian theory of the sacredness of the Bible has been at the cost of the world's civilization. Whether we regard the work as custodian of the profoundest secrets of the "ancient mysteries," a spiritual book trebly veiled, or as the physical and religious history of the world in its most material forms, its interpretation by the Church, by the State, and by society has ever been prejudicial to the best interests of humanity. Science, art, inventions, reforms of existing wrongs, all, all have been opposed upon its authority. That even the most enlightened nations are not yet out of barbarism is due to the teachings of the Bible.

From "Thou shalt not make any graven image, or any likeness of anything in heaven above, the earth beneath, or the waters under the earth," down to "A woman shall not speak in church, but shall ask her husband at home," the tendency of the Bible has been to crush out aspiration, to deaden human faculties, and to humiliate mankind. From Adam's plaint, "The woman gave me and I did eat," down to Christ's "Woman, what have I to do with thee?" the tendency of the Bible has been degradation of the divinest half of humanity—woman. Even the Christian Church itself is not based upon Christ as a savior, but upon its own teachings that woman brought sin into the world, a theory in direct contradiction, not alone to the mysteries, but to spiritual truth. But our present quest is not what the mystic or the spiritual character of the Bible may be; we are investigating its influence upon woman under Judaism and Christianity, and pronounce it evil.

MATILDA JOSLYN GAGE.

There is nothing tending to show that the women spoken of in the Bible were superior to the ones we know. There are to-day millions of women making coats for their sons; hundreds of thousands of women, true, not simply to innocent people falsely accused, but to criminals. Many a loving heart is as true to the gallows as Mary was to the cross. There are hundreds of thousands of women accepting poverty and want and dishonor for the love they bear un-

worthy men; hundreds and thousands—hundreds and thousands—
working day and night, with strained eyes and tired hands, for husbands and children—clothed in rags, housed in huts and hovels,
hoping day after day for the Angel of Death. There are thousands
of women in Christian England working in iron, laboring in the
fields and toiling in the mines. There are hundreds and thousands
in Europe, everywhere, doing the work of men—deformed by toil,
and who would become simply wild and ferocious beasts, except
for the love they bear for home and child.

We need not go back four thousand years for heroines. The
world is filled with them to-day. They do not belong to any nation,
nor any religion, nor exclusively to any race. Wherever woman is
found, they are found. There are no women portrayed in the Bible
who equal thousands and thousands of known to-day. The women of the Bible fall almost infinitely below, not simply those in
real life, but the creations of the imagination found in the world of
fiction. They will not compare with the women born of Shake-
speare's brain. You will find none like Isabella, in whose spotless
life, love and reason blended into perfect truth; nor Juliet, within
whose heart, passion and purity met like white and red within the
bosom of a rose; nor Cordelia, who chose to suffer loss rather than
show her wealth of love with those who gilded dross with golden
words in hope of gain; nor Miranda, who told her love as freely as
a flower gives its blossom to the kisses of the sun; nor Imogene, who
asked, "What is it to be false?" nor Hermione, who bore with perfect faith and hope the cross of shame, and who at last forgave with
all her heart; nor Desdemona, her innocence so perfect and her love
so pure that she was incapable of suspecting that another could suspect, and sought with dying words to hide her lover's crime.

If we wish to find what the Bible thinks of woman, all that is
necessary to do is to read it. We shall find that everywhere she is
spoken of simply as property—as belonging absolutely to the man.
We shall find that, whenever a man got tired of his wife, all he had
to do was to give her a writing of divorcement, and that then the
mother of his children became a houseless and homeless wanderer.
We shall find that men were allowed to have as many wives as they

could get, either by courtship, purchase, or conquest. The Jew-ish people in the olden time were, in many respects, like their bar-barian neighbors. ANON.

———

The Bible, viewed by men as the infallible "Word of God," and translated and explained for ages *by men only*, tends to the subjec-tion and degradation of woman. Historical facts to prove this are abundant. In the dark days of "witchcraft"—through centuries—alleged witches were arrested, tried in ecclesiastical courts, tortured and hung or burned at the stake by men under priestly direction, and the great majority of the victims were women. Eve's alleged transgression, and the Bible edict in the days of the reputed Witch of Endor, "Thou shalt not suffer a witch to live," being the warrant and Divine authority for this awful slaughter of women.

In the days of chattel-slavery in our country, the slave-laws, *framed by men only*, degraded woman by making her the defenseless victim of her slave-master's passions, and then inflicting a cruel stab, reaching the heart of motherhood, by laws which made her children follow the condition of the mother, as slaves; never that of the father, as free women or men. The clergy became slaveholders and defenders of slavery without loss of priestly position or influence, and quoted "Cursed be Canaan" as their justification.

The Lord gave the Word, great was the company of those that published it.—Old version of the Bible, 68th Psalm.

The Lord giveth the Word, and great is the multitude of women who publish it.—Revised version of the Bible, 68th Psalm.

Here is "a reform" *not* "against Nature," nor the facts of history, but is true to the Mother of the Race, to her knowledge of "the Word," to her desire to promulgate it, to her actual participation in declaring and proclaiming it. And true to a present and continu-ous inspiration and influx of the Spirit, it is *giveth*, and not "gave," in the past. And this one recognition of *woman as preacher and Apostle* forbids the assertion that woman is degraded from Genesis to Revelation.

The light of a more generous religious thought, a growth out of the old beliefs, impelled the learned "Committee on Revision" to speak the truth in regard to the religious character and work of women, and they have *exalted* her where before she was "degraded."

This revision is also prophetic of *this era*, for never were women doing so excellently *the world's work*, or, like Tryphena and Tryphosa, prophesying the light still to come.

CATHARINE A. F. STEBBINS.

———

The general principles of righteousness and justice laid down in the Bible have elevated the race in general, the mothers included, and have aided in securing reforms for women, as well as for other classes. But the specific texts of Saint Paul enjoining subjection upon women have undoubtedly been a hindrance.

ALICE STONE BLACKWELL.

———

1. In my opinion the teachings of the Bible have advanced woman's emancipation.

Look at the freedom of the Jewish women of the Old Testament —of Miriam, Deborah, Abigail, Ruth and Esther. In comparison, where were the Gentile women who knew not God?

2. The teachings of the Bible, particularly the New Testament, have dignified the Mothers of the Race. Christ was very severe to the men who were sinners, he called them Scribes and Pharisees and hypocrites, and pronounced, "Woe be unto you." He even whipped the money changers out of the temple. But no rebuke to woman ever fell from his lips save the gentle one to Martha, that she cared too much for her home and her nice housekeeping. Christ's mission meant the elevation of womanhood. Compare Christian countries with the heathen countries, and see how Christianity elevates and heathenism degrades womanhood.

I have studied the questions in the Indian Territory in our own

United States. Under the influence of the Christian missionaries the Indian woman is an important factor in Church and State. Where the Gospel of Christ is not preached the women are slaves to the men. In their long tramps they do not even walk beside their husbands, but follow behind like dogs. I am aware that small ministers still preach foolishness, defining "woman's sphere," but the real Biblical Christianity elevates womanhood.

SARAH M. PERKINS.

MY DEAR MRS. STANTON:—I regard the Bible as I do the other so-called sacred books of the world. They were all produced in savage times, and, of course, contain many things that shock our sense of justice. In the days of darkness women were regarded and treated as slaves. They were allowed no voice in public affairs. Neither man nor woman were civilized, and the gods were like their worshipers. It gives me pleasure to know that women are beginning to think and are becoming dissatisfied with the religion of barbarians.

I congratulate you on what you have already accomplished and for the work you are now doing. Sincerely yours,

EVA A. INGERSOLL.

In reading some of these letters and comments I have been deeply impressed with the difficulty of substituting reason for superstition in minds once perverted by a false faith. Women have been taught by their religious guardians that the Bible, unlike all other books, was written under the special inspiration of the Great Ruling Intelligence of the Universe. Not conversant with works on science and higher criticism, which point out its fabulous pretensions, they cling to it with an unreasoning tenacity, like a savage to his fetich. Though it is full of contradictions, absurdities and impossibilities, and bears the strongest evidence in every line of its human origin, and in moral sentiment is below many of the best books of our own day, they blindly worship it as the Word of God.

When you point out what in plain English it tells us God did say to his people in regard to woman, and there is no escape from its degrading teaching as to her position, then they shelter themselves under false translations, interpretations and symbolic meanings. It does not occur to them that men learned in the languages have revised the book many times, but made no change in woman's position. Though familiar with "the designs of God," trained in Biblical research and higher criticism, interpreters of signs and symbols and Egyptian hieroglyphics, learned astronomers and astrologers, yet they cannot twist out of the Old or New Testaments a message of justice, liberty or equality from God to the women of the nineteenth century!

The real difficulty in woman's case is that the whole foundation of the Christian religion rests on her temptation and man's fall, hence the necessity of a Redeemer and a plan of salvation. As the chief cause of this dire calamity, woman's degradation and subordination were made a necessity. If, however, we accept the Darwinian theory, that the race has been a gradual growth from the lower to a higher form of life, and that the story of the fall is a myth, we can exonerate the snake, emancipate the woman, and reconstruct a more rational religion for the nineteenth century, and thus escape all the perplexities of the Jewish mythology as of no more importance than those of the Greek, Persian and Egyptian.

ELIZABETH CADY STANTON.

"THE WOMAN'S BIBLE" REPUDIATED.

At the twenty-eighth annual convention of the National-American Woman Suffrage Association, held in Washington, D. C., in January, 1896, the following, was reported by the Committee on Resolutions:

"That this Association is non-sectarian, being composed of persons of all shades of religious opinion, and that it has no official connection with the so-called 'Woman's Bible,' or any theological publication."

Charlotte Perkins Stetson moved to amend by striking out everything after the word "opinion."

Anna R. Simmons moved, as an amendment to the amendment, to omit the words "the so-called Woman's Bible, or."

This was followed by a long and animated discussion, in which the following persons participated:

Frances A. Williamson, Helen Morris Lewis, Annie L. Diggs, Carrie Chapman Catt, Rachel Foster Avery, Henry B. Blackwell, Laura M. Johns, Elizabeth U. Yates, Katie R. Addison, Alice Stone Blackwell and Rev. Anna Howard Shaw, speaking for the resolution; and Charlotte Perkins Stetson, Mary Bentley Thomas, J. B. Merwin, Clara B. Colby, Harriette A. Keyser, Lavina A. Hatch, Lillie Devereux Blake, Caroline Hallowell Miller, Victoria Conkling Whitney, Althea B. Stryker, and Cornelia H. Cary speaking against it.

The President, Susan B. Anthony, left the chair and spoke with much earnestness against the adoption of the resolution as follows:

"The one distinct feature of our Association has been the right of individual opinion for every member. We have been beset at every step with the cry that somebody was injuring the cause by the expression of some sentiments that differed with those held by the majority of mankind. The religious persecution of the ages has been done under what was claimed to be the command of God. I distrust those people who know so well what God wants them to do to their fellows, because it always coincides with their own desires. All the way along the history of our movement there has been this same contest on account of religious theories. Forty years ago one of our noblest men said to me: 'You would better never hold another convention than let Ernestine L. Rose stand on your platform,' because that talented and eloquent Polish woman, who ever stood for justice and freedom, did not believe in the plenary inspiration of the Bible. Did we banish Mrs. Rose? No, indeed! Every new generation of converts threshes over the same old straw. Twenty-five years ago a prominent woman, who stood on our platform for the first time, wanted us to pass a resolution that we were not free lovers; and I was not more shocked than I am to-day at this attempt. The question is whether you will sit in judgment on one who has questioned the Divine inspiration of certain passages in the Bible derogatory to women. If she had written approvingly of these passages, you would not have brought in this resolution because you thought the cause might be injured among the liberals in religion. In other words, if she had written your views, you would not have considered a resolution necessary. To pass this one is to set back the hands on the dial of reform. It is the reviving of the old time censorship, which I hoped we had outgrown.

"What you should do is to say to outsiders that a Christian has neither more nor less rights in our Association than an atheist. When our platform becomes too narrow for people of all creeds and of no creeds, I myself shall not stand upon it. Many things have been said and done by our orthodox friends that I have felt to be extremely harmful to our cause; but I should no more consent to a resolution denouncing them than I shall consent to this. Who is to draw the line? Who can tell now whether Mrs. Stanton's commentaries may not prove a great help to woman's emancipation from old superstitions that have barred her way? Lucretia Mott at first thought Mrs. Stanton had injured the cause of all woman's other rights by insisting upon the demand for suffrage, but she had sense enough not to bring in a resolution against it. In 1860, when Mrs. Stanton made a speech before the New York Legislature in favor of a bill making drunkenness a cause for divorce, there was a general cry among the friends that she had killed the woman's cause. I shall be pained beyond expression if the delegates here are so narrow and illiberal as to adopt this resolution. You would better not begin resolving against individual action or you will find no limit. This year it is Mrs. Stanton; next year it may be me or one of yourselves who will be the victim.

"Are you going to cater to the whims and prejudices of people who have no intelligent knowledge of what they condemn? If we do not inspire in woman a broad and catholic spirit, they will fail, when enfranchised, to constitute that power for better government which we have always claimed for them. You would better educate ten women into the practice of liberal principles than to organize ten thousand on a platform of intolerance and bigotry. I pray you, vote for religious liberty, without censorship or inquisition. This resolution, adopted, will be a vote of censure upon a woman who is without a peer in intellectual and statesmanlike ability; one who has stood for half a century the acknowledged leader of progressive thought and demand in regard to all matters pertaining to the absolute freedom of women."

The Resolution was then adopted by a vote of 53 to 41.

"The Truth shall make you free."—*John viii., 32.*

THE END.

GREAT BOOKS IN PHILOSOPHY PAPERBACK SERIES

ESTHETICS

❑ Aristotle—*The Poetics*
❑ Aristotle—*Treatise on Rhetoric*

ETHICS

❑ Aristotle—*The Nicomachean Ethics*
❑ Marcus Aurelius—*Meditations*
❑ Jeremy Bentham—*The Principles of Morals and Legislation*
❑ John Dewey—*Human Nature and Conduct*
❑ John Dewey—*The Moral Writings of John Dewey, Revised Edition*
❑ Epictetus—*Enchiridion*
❑ David Hume—*An Enquiry Concerning the Principles of Morals*
❑ Immanuel Kant—*Fundamental Principles of the Metaphysic of Morals*
❑ John Stuart Mill—*Utilitarianism*
❑ George Edward Moore—*Principia Ethica*
❑ Friedrich Nietzsche—*Beyond Good and Evil*
❑ Plato—*Protagoras, Philebus, and Gorgias*
❑ Bertrand Russell—*Bertrand Russell On Ethics, Sex, and Marriage*
❑ Arthur Schopenhauer—*The Wisdom of Life* and *Counsels and Maxims*
❑ Adam Smith—*The Theory of Moral Sentiments*
❑ Benedict de Spinoza—*Ethics* and *The Improvement of the Understanding*

LOGIC

❑ George Boole—*The Laws of Thought*

METAPHYSICS/EPISTEMOLOGY

❑ Aristotle—*De Anima*
❑ Aristotle—*The Metaphysics*
❑ Francis Bacon—*Essays*
❑ George Berkeley—*Three Dialogues Between Hylas and Philonous*
❑ W. K. Clifford—*The Ethics of Belief and Other Essays*
❑ René Descartes—*Discourse on Method* and *The Meditations*
❑ John Dewey—*How We Think*
❑ John Dewey—*The Influence of Darwin on Philosophy and Other Essays*
❑ Epicurus—*The Essential Epicurus: Letters, Principal Doctrines, Vatican Sayings, and Fragments*
❑ Sidney Hook—*The Quest for Being*
❑ David Hume—*An Enquiry Concerning Human Understanding*
❑ David Hume—*A Treatise on Human Nature*
❑ William James—*The Meaning of Truth*
❑ William James—*Pragmatism*
❑ Immanuel Kant—*The Critique of Judgment*
❑ Immanuel Kant—*Critique of Practical Reason*
❑ Immanuel Kant—*Critique of Pure Reason*
❑ Gottfried Wilhelm Leibniz—*Discourse on Metaphysics* and *The Monadology*
❑ John Locke—*An Essay Concerning Human Understanding*
❑ George Herbert Mead—*The Philosophy of the Present*

- ❑ Charles S. Peirce—*The Essential Writings*
- ❑ Plato—*The Euthyphro, Apology, Crito,* and *Phaedo*
- ❑ Plato—*Lysis, Phaedrus, and Symposium*
- ❑ Bertrand Russell—*The Problems of Philosophy*
- ❑ George Santayana—*The Life of Reason*
- ❑ Sextus Empiricus—*Outlines of Pyrrhonism*
- ❑ Ludwig Wittgenstein—*Wittgenstein's Lectures: Cambridge, 1932–1935*

PHILOSOPHY OF RELIGION

- ❑ Jeremy Bentham—*The Influence of Natural Religion on the Temporal Happiness of Mankind*
- ❑ Marcus Tullius Cicero—*The Nature of the Gods* and *On Divination*
- ❑ Ludwig Feuerbach—*The Essence of Christianity*
- ❑ Paul Henri Thiry, Baron d'Holbach—*Good Sense*
- ❑ David Hume—*Dialogues Concerning Natural Religion*
- ❑ William James—*The Varieties of Religious Experience*
- ❑ John Locke—*A Letter Concerning Toleration*
- ❑ Lucretius—*On the Nature of Things*
- ❑ John Stuart Mill—*Three Essays on Religion*
- ❑ Friedrich Nietzsche—*The Antichrist*
- ❑ Thomas Paine—*The Age of Reason*
- ❑ Bertrand Russell—*Bertrand Russell On God and Religion*

SOCIAL AND POLITICAL PHILOSOPHY

- ❑ Aristotle—*The Politics*
- ❑ Mikhail Bakunin—*The Basic Bakunin: Writings, 1869–1871*
- ❑ Edmund Burke—*Reflections on the Revolution in France*
- ❑ John Dewey—*Freedom and Culture*
- ❑ John Dewey—*Individualism Old and New*
- ❑ John Dewey—*Liberalism and Social Action*
- ❑ G. W. F. Hegel—*The Philosophy of History*
- ❑ G. W. F. Hegel—*Philosophy of Right*
- ❑ Thomas Hobbes—*The Leviathan*
- ❑ Sidney Hook—*Paradoxes of Freedom*
- ❑ Sidney Hook—*Reason, Social Myths, and Democracy*
- ❑ John Locke—*The Second Treatise on Civil Government*
- ❑ Niccolo Machiavelli—*The Prince*
- ❑ Karl Marx (with Friedrich Engels)—*The Economic and Philosophic Manuscripts of 1844* and *The Communist Manifesto*
- ❑ Karl Marx (with Friedrich Engels)—*The German Ideology,* including *Theses on Feuerbach* and *Introduction to the Critique of Political Economy*
- ❑ Karl Marx—*The Poverty of Philosophy*
- ❑ John Stuart Mill—*Considerations on Representative Government*
- ❑ John Stuart Mill—*On Liberty*
- ❑ John Stuart Mill—*On Socialism*
- ❑ John Stuart Mill—*The Subjection of Women*
- ❑ Montesquieu, Charles de Secondat—*The Spirit of Laws*
- ❑ Friedrich Nietzsche—*Thus Spake Zarathustra*

- ❑ Thomas Paine—*Common Sense*
- ❑ Thomas Paine—*Rights of Man*
- ❑ Plato—*Laws*
- ❑ Plato—*The Republic*
- ❑ Jean-Jacques Rousseau—*Émile*
- ❑ Jean-Jacques Rousseau—*The Social Contract*
- ❑ Mary Wollstonecraft—*A Vindication of the Rights of Men*
- ❑ Mary Wollstonecraft—*A Vindication of the Rights of Women*

GREAT MINDS PAPERBACK SERIES

ART

- ❑ Leonardo da Vinci—*A Treatise on Painting*

ECONOMICS

- ❑ Charlotte Perkins Gilman—*Women and Economics: A Study of the Economic Relation between Women and Men*
- ❑ John Maynard Keynes—*The General Theory of Employment, Interest, and Money*
- ❑ John Maynard Keynes—*A Tract on Monetary Reform*
- ❑ Thomas R. Malthus—*An Essay on the Principle of Population*
- ❑ Alfred Marshall—*Money, Credit, and Commerce*
- ❑ Alfred Marshall—*Principles of Economics*
- ❑ Karl Marx—*Theories of Surplus Value*
- ❑ John Stuart Mill—*Principles of Political Economy*
- ❑ David Ricardo—*Principles of Political Economy and Taxation*
- ❑ Adam Smith—*Wealth of Nations*
- ❑ Thorstein Veblen—*Theory of the Leisure Class*

HISTORY

- ❑ Edward Gibbon—*On Christianity*
- ❑ Alexander Hamilton, John Jay, and James Madison—*The Federalist*
- ❑ Herodotus—*The History*
- ❑ Charles Mackay—*Extraordinary Popular Delusions and the Madness of Crowds*
- ❑ Thucydides—*History of the Peloponnesian War*

LAW

- ❑ John Austin—*The Province of Jurisprudence Determined*

LITERATURE

- ❑ Jonathan Swift—*A Modest Proposal and Other Satires*
- ❑ H. G. Wells—*The Conquest of Time*

PSYCHOLOGY

❏ Sigmund Freud—*Totem and Taboo*

RELIGION/FREETHOUGHT

❏ Desiderius Erasmus—*The Praise of Folly*
❏ Thomas Henry Huxley—*Agnosticism and Christianity and Other Essays*
❏ Ernest Renan—*The Life of Jesus*
❏ Upton Sinclair—*The Profits of Religion*
❏ Elizabeth Cady Stanton—*The Woman's Bible*
❏ Voltaire—*A Treatise on Toleration and Other Essays*
❏ Andrew D. White—*A History of the Warfare of Science with Theology in Christendom*

SCIENCE

❏ Jacob Bronowski—*The Identity of Man*
❏ Nicolaus Copernicus—*On the Revolutions of Heavenly Spheres*
❏ Marie Curie—*Radioactive Substances*
❏ Charles Darwin—*The Autobiography of Charles Darwin*
❏ Charles Darwin—*The Descent of Man*
❏ Charles Darwin—*The Origin of Species*
❏ Charles Darwin—*The Voyage of the* Beagle
❏ René Descartes—*Treatise of Man*
❏ Albert Einstein—*Relativity*
❏ Michael Faraday—*The Forces of Matter*
❏ Galileo Galilei—*Dialogues Concerning Two New Sciences*
❏ Ernst Haeckel—*The Riddle of the Universe*
❏ William Harvey—*On the Motion of the Heart and Blood in Animals*
❏ Werner Heisenberg—*Physics and Philosophy*
❏ Julian Huxley—*Evolutionary Humanism*
❏ Thomas H. Huxley—*Evolution and Ethics and Science and Morals*
❏ Edward Jenner—*Vaccination against Smallpox*
❏ Johannes Kepler—*Epitome of Copernican Astronomy and Harmonies of the World*
❏ James Clerk Maxwell—*Matter and Motion*
❏ Isaac Newton—*Opticks, Or Treatise of the Reflections, Inflections, and Colours of Light*
❏ Isaac Newton—*The Principia*
❏ Louis Pasteur and Joseph Lister—*Germ Theory and Its Application to Medicine and On the Antiseptic Principle of the Practice of Surgery*
❏ William Thomson (Lord Kelvin) and Peter Guthrie Tait—*The Elements of Natural Philosophy*
❏ Alfred Russel Wallace—*Island Life*

SOCIOLOGY

❏ Emile Durkheim—*Ethics and the Sociology of Morals*